Americans in China

Americans in China

Encounters with the People's Republic

TERRY LAUTZ

OXFORD

UNIVERSITY PRESS

Oxford University Press is a department of the University of Oxford. It furthers
the University's objective of excellence in research, scholarship, and education
by publishing worldwide. Oxford is a registered trade mark of Oxford University
Press in the UK and certain other countries.

Published in the United States of America by Oxford University Press
198 Madison Avenue, New York, NY 10016, United States of America.

© Oxford University Press 2022

CIP data is on file at the Library of Congress

ISBN 978-0-19-751283-8

DOI: 10.1093/oso/9780197512838.001.0001

1 3 5 7 9 8 6 4 2

Printed by Sheridan Books, Inc., United States of America

In memory of Douglas P. Murray
Friend, mentor, and advocate for understanding
between the United States and China

Contents

Preface and Acknowledgments

In July 1960, I sailed across the Pacific Ocean from San Francisco to Taiwan with my parents and sister. After a calm and pleasant voyage, with a stop along the way in Japan, we disembarked at the port of Keelung on a hot, steamy day and drove for an hour to the capital city of Taipei where we would live for the next two years. I was nearly fourteen and it was my first encounter with anything Chinese.

The United States had diplomatic relations and a defense treaty with the Republic of China (ROC) on Taiwan, and my father, an Ordnance Corps Army officer, was assigned to the US Military Assistance Advisory Group (MAAG). Chiang Kai-shek, who had lost the civil war to the Communists a decade earlier, made speeches about recovering the mainland, but no one seemed to take his words seriously. While still under martial law, the island nation, some ninety miles off the Chinese mainland, was a poor, sleepy, peaceful backwater in those days.

That experience in Taiwan, where I attended Taipei American School, made me wonder about the People's Republic of China (PRC), a land shrouded in mystery that we could only see from a hillside on the Hong Kong side of its border. It made me curious enough to pursue Chinese studies as an undergraduate at Harvard, one of the few US schools offering that option in those days. "That's very interesting," my mother said when I announced my major, "but what are you going to do with it?" She was asking a serious question because there were so few China-related jobs. I simply trusted that something would work out.

Yet it was only after college, after serving in Vietnam with the US Army, that my curiosity became more purposeful. The people of South Vietnam feared communism—many of them had escaped from the North—but their government's alliance with the United States undermined their claims to in-dependence and nationalism. Reading Bernard Fall's books about Ho Chi Minh's defeat of the French in 1954 made it painfully clear that the United States, perceived as another colonial power, was repeating the same fatal mistakes. The tragic result of our leaders' ignorance of Vietnam, a war fought as a proxy against China, was a wake-up call for me. Understanding our fraught history in Asia had become more than an abstract intellectual exercise.

My timing was fortunate. During my graduate school days at Stanford, US-China relations began to improve with the advent of ping-pong diplomacy and President Nixon's historic trip to the People's Republic. I returned to Taiwan—the mainland was still off-limits—for Chinese language study and research on a Fulbright-Hays Scholarship. After receiving a PhD in history, I landed a job in New York with the Asia Society's China Council, a national public education program, led by Robert Oxnam, that connected with American scholars, journalists, businesspeople, and community leaders to provide balanced information on the PRC. Public interest was strong, but there was still a dearth of knowledge; we had yet, for instance, to realize the extent of devastation during the Cultural Revolution.

My first trip to mainland China, in December 1978, coincided with a major shift in the geopolitical landscape. I was escorting a small group of Americans, members of the National Committee on US-China Relations, on a three-week tour of several cities, starting in the north and ending in the south. On our final day, during a visit to the Huadong Commune on the outskirts of Guangzhou, I tuned in to Voice of America on my shortwave radio and listened to President Carter announcing that the PRC and the United States would establish full diplomatic relations. Our Chinese hosts were thrilled by the news and considerable toasting and drinking followed. Normalization, as it was called, ushered in a hopeful new era in Sino-American relations.

Now that the People's Republic was opening up to Americans, I accepted an offer from the Yale-China Association, directed by John Starr, to represent its programs in Hong Kong and China. My wife Ellen and I arrived with our two young sons, Bryan and Colin, at New Asia College at the Chinese University of Hong Kong (CUHK) in the summer of 1981, our home base for the next three years. Everyone was concerned about Hong Kong's transition from British control to Chinese sovereignty, scheduled for 1997, but with the Sino-British Joint Declaration signed in December 1984, Beijing reassured the world that it would be a smooth process. The city, while not a full-fledged democracy, had a strong legal and judicial system, freedom of speech, and freedom of the press—rights that were absent on the other side of the border. Under a policy of "one country, two systems," Beijing would assume responsibility for foreign affairs and defense, but Hong Kong could maintain its own way of life as a special autonomous region for at least fifty years after the handover in 1997.

In addition to teaching and managing various projects at CUHK, I was responsible for overseeing Yale-China's programs with Xiangya Medical School in Changsha and with Huazhong University and Wuhan University in Wuhan, relationships that had been restored after a thirty-year absence. On one occasion, some of the young Americans teaching English in Wuhan were accused of being spies. I quickly went there to meet with our Chinese colleagues, who soon put an end to the harassment. It was a distressing experience for the Yale-China teaching fellows and was a potent reminder that suspicion of the United States still ran deep. It also drove home the fact that the success of any American venture depended on having supportive Chinese partners.

In 1984, my family and I moved from Hong Kong to New York, where I joined the staff of the Henry Luce Foundation. Founded by Henry R. Luce, publisher of *Time* and *Life* magazines, who was born to missionary parents in China, it was chaired by his son Henry Luce III and led by Robert Armstrong. The foundation's Asia program supported the creation of resources—language teaching, library materials, fellowships, faculty positions, policy studies, cooperative research, and cultural and scholarly exchange—to increase America's capacity for understanding East and Southeast Asia. Much of my work centered on building cultural and scholarly ties between the United States and China. In addition to trips to the PRC, my travels also took me to Cambodia, Laos, Indonesia, the Philippines, Taiwan, Thailand, Singapore, Vietnam, Japan, South Korea, and North Korea.

Of these journeys, the most unforgettable was a trip in the spring of 1989 to review some of the Luce Foundation's grants. I flew from Hong Kong to Beijing on May 29 and after checking in to my hotel took a taxi to Tiananmen Square where thousands of students had been protesting against the Chinese government for weeks. Red banners with university names were stretched above their tents and, after finishing evening meals, they were lounging about playing cards, writing in their diaries, talking with passers-by. A few of them asked me, "What do the people of America think about what we are doing?" "Are you allowed to have protests in America?" "Do you think we can succeed?"

Loudspeakers broadcast a steady stream of statements from the protest leaders, interspersed with music, including a new democracy song from Hong Kong. Food, drink, and popsicle vendors were doing a brisk business.

I wrote in my journal, "Here and there are piles of discarded jackets and clothing for cooler weather, donated by the citizens of Beijing. There is a good deal of litter and occasional piles of garbage, but for the most part it looks like organized disorder. Visitors are taking photos of themselves in front of the tents and banners. The students seem terribly idealistic, committed, determined, and cheerful."

Late that night, a thirty-foot "Goddess of Democracy" built by students at the Central Academy of Arts was brought to the square on four flat carts and plastered together on top of a wooden platform. After it was unveiled early the next morning, directly facing Mao's giant portrait on the entrance to the Forbidden City, thousands of people flocked to Tiananmen to have a look. "You have your Statue of Liberty in America," a man said to me, "and now we have ours here in China." The government labeled it "an insult to socialism" and demanded that it be taken down. With a sense of foreboding, I left Beijing for a flight to Tokyo and Los Angeles on the morning of Saturday, June 3. That night, the non-violent protest movement was suppressed with brutal military force and the statue was toppled and destroyed.

I was disturbed, perplexed, and concerned about the future. Had young Chinese been misled into believing that American-style democracy could be accepted by a communist regime? What principles would guide US-China relations after the Tiananmen debacle, which China's leaders blamed on the "black hand" of the United States? Were we destined to live through never-ending cycles of suspicion and distrust, or would it someday prove possible for Chinese and American interests and values to converge? The relationship between the United States and China has waxed and waned in the years since, but questions like these persist, questions that have led me to write this book.

———

I have long been interested in Americans whose firsthand encounters have informed and shaped our understanding of China, a number of whom have helped to make this book possible. First and foremost, I owe a great debt to those whose stories are told in the following chapters for allowing me to interview and quote them: Jerome Cohen, Joan Cohen, John Kamm, Melinda Liu, Elizabeth Perry, Stapleton Roy, and Shirley Young. It has been a privilege to write about each of them. (Other figures in the book have passed from the scene, and I was unable to meet with C. N. Yang.)

David McBride, my editor at Oxford University Press, first urged me to consider this project, and he and his team have expertly guided me through the publication process. I am also grateful to Mary Child, an independent editor of China studies, for her thoughtful advice and for gently but firmly pushing me to make my prose clear and strong. Sincere thanks friends who have read and commented on drafts of various chapters, including Mary Brown Bullock, Richard Bush, John Holden, Sophie Richardson, Douglas Spelman, and I am grateful to Jan Berris and David M. Lampton for reviewing the full manuscript.

Special appreciation is due to Molly Linhorst and Amanda Mikesell for their excellent research assistance, and to Anni Feng and Lingyu Fu for helping with translations and other parts of the book. I also express my appreciation to my students at Syracuse University who helped me think through some of these biographies at an early stage of the project: Johanna Arnott, Gwendolyn Burke, Corey Driscoll, Dasha Foley, Michael Kosuth, Tanushri Majumdar, Liam McMonagle, Nicholas Miller, Lilibeth Wolfe, and Brianna Yates.

It is a great pleasure to acknowledge the generosity of many friends and colleagues who have shared their China experiences and offered advice through emails, phone calls, interviews, and conversations: William Alford, Halsey Beemer, Carroll Bogert, Mary Lou Carpenter, Lo-Yi Chan, Millie Chan, Frank Ching, Maryruth Coleman, Carl Crook, Elizabeth Economy, Bill Engst, Fred Engst, Jaime FlorCruz, Gao Yanli, Tom Gold, Lee Hamilton, Beverley Hooper, Nicholas Howson, Virginia Kamsky, Ambrose Y. C. King, Helena Kolenda, Mary Kay Magistad, Alfreda Murck, Christian Murck, Douglas Paal, Lynn Pascoe, Charles E. Perry, Steve Orlins, Nicholas Platt, Joshua Rosenzweig, Marni Rosner, Bill Russo, Rudy Schlais, Deborah Seiselmyer, David Shambaugh, Mark Sheldon, Robert Snow, Anne Keatley Solomon, Jane Su, Oscar Tang, Matt Tsien, Ezra Vogel, Genevieve Young, and Kenneth Young. My sincere thanks to Marni Rosner for giving me audio files of Neil Burton's extensive conversations with Joan Hinton and Sid Engst.

I am grateful to Bloomsbury Academic for permission to quote from my chapter "Unstoppable Force Meets Immovable Object: Normalizing US-China Relations," in *United States Relations with China and Iran*, Osamah F. Khalil, ed. (Bloomsbury Academic, 2019).

I also want to recognize the assistance of librarians and archivists at the following institutions: Andover Harvard Theological Library; Cornell University Archives; the Chinese University of Hong Kong (C. N. Yang Archives); Houghton Library and Pusey Library at Harvard University;

Hoover Institution Archives at Stanford University; University of Michigan's Bentley Historical Library; George Washington University Archives; and Syracuse University Library.

Lastly, I offer my deepest gratitude and love to Ellen Stromberg Lautz, who has encouraged and sustained me at every step of the way.

A Chronology of US-China Relations[1]

1849–69   Chinese laborers are recruited to work in gold mines and to construct the transcontinental railroad in America's West.

1872–81   The Chinese Educational Mission sends 120 Chinese young men to New England to study Western science and engineering.

1882   The US Congress passes the Chinese Exclusion Act, which severely limits Chinese immigration to the United States.

1900   Eight nations, including the United States, suppress the antiforeign Boxer Rebellion. The United States uses some of the indemnity money for fellowships to educate Chinese in the United States.

1911–12   Sun Yat-sen establishes the Nationalist (Kuomintang) Party after the collapse of the Qing dynasty and founds the Republic of China.

1916–22   The New Culture Movement attacks Confucianism and traditional society as the source of China's weakness.

1919   The May Fourth Movement, sparked by the treatment of China in the Treaty of Versailles, marks the birth of modern Chinese nationalism.

1921   The Chinese Communist Party is established in Shanghai.

1925   Chiang Kai-shek succeeds the late Sun Yat-sen as leader of the Nationalist government. Chiang agrees to become a Christian when he marries US-educated Soong Mei-ling in 1927.

1928   China is unified under a single government led by the Nationalists.

1930s   The high-tide of American missionary efforts to provide medical training, relief work, and Western-style liberal arts education in China.

1931   Pearl Buck's *The Good Earth*, a sympathetic novel about the lives of Chinese peasants, is a major bestseller in the United States.

1941–45 During World War II, the United States allies with Chiang Kai-shek's Nationalists and cooperates with Mao Zedong's Communists against Japan. US support is limited to air power.

1943 The 1882 Exclusion Act is repealed, but restrictions on Chinese and Asian immigration to the United States remain in place until the Immigration Reform Act of 1965.

1945 Japan surrenders after atomic bombs are dropped on Hiroshima and Nagasaki.

1945–49 During the Chinese Civil War between the Nationalists and Communists, the United States gives military and economic aid to the Nationalists despite concerns about widespread corruption and incompetence.

1949 Founding of the People's Republic of China (PRC), led by Mao Zedong, chairman of the Chinese Communist Party (CCP). The Truman administration is charged with the "loss of China." Some ten thousand Chinese students and professionals who are not US citizens are stranded in the United States.

Chiang Kai-shek's Nationalist government retreats to the island of Taiwan (Formosa). Beijing claims Taiwan as part of China, but the United States continues to recognize the Republic of China (ROC) as China's legitimate government.

1950–53 The United States and PRC are the primary combatants during the Korean War, which ends in a stalemate and a divided Korean peninsula. Twenty-one captured American soldiers decide to go to China instead of returning to the United States, and thousands of Chinese POWs go to Taiwan.

American missionaries and businessmen are forced to leave China; only a small number of Westerners are allowed to stay.

1950–71 US containment policy prohibits any trade or travel between the two countries. The United States successfully opposes the PRC's admission to the United Nations.

1954–55 The First Taiwan Strait Crisis over PRC attacks on islands along China's mainland held by the Nationalists. The United States and Taiwan agree to a Mutual Defense Treaty.

1955–70 US–PRC ambassadorial talks in Geneva and Warsaw, a series of 136 meetings, in the absence of diplomatic relations.

1957 A group of forty-one young Americans visit the PRC for six weeks, despite a US State Department ban on travel to Red China.

1958 The People's Liberation Army bombards offshore islands controlled by Nationalist forces during the Second Taiwan Strait Crisis.

1958 Mao launches the Great Leap Forward to rapidly industrialize the PRC's agrarian economy.

1959–61 An estimated thirty million people die during the Great Chinese Famine.

1964 The PRC successfully tests a nuclear bomb.

1966 The National Committee on US-China Relations is established to promote discussion about reconsidering Washington's containment policy.

The Committee on Scholarly Communication with the PRC (CSCPRC) is founded to sponsor short-term academic exchanges, mainly in the sciences.

1966–76 The Great Proletarian Cultural Revolution, Mao's bid to reassert his control over the CCP, leads to massive social, economic, and political turmoil and bloodshed.

1971 American ping-pong players visit China, the first sign of a thaw between Beijing and Washington. National Security Adviser Henry Kissinger secretly visits Beijing to lay the groundwork for President Nixon's trip to China. The PRC is admitted to the United Nations and the ROC (Taiwan) is forced to withdraw.

1972 President Richard Nixon meets Mao and Zhou Enlai and signs the Shanghai Communiqué acknowledging that Taiwan and China agree there is only one China.

1976 Death of Mao Zedong and arrest of the Gang of Four, who are blamed for the Cultural Revolution.

1977 The National Association of Chinese Americans (NACA) advocates for diplomatic relations between Washington and Beijing.

1978 Deng Xiaoping launches the era of Reform and Opening to modernize China. Wei Jingsheng posts a manifesto on Democracy Wall in Beijing calling democracy "the fifth modernization."

1979 Washington establishes full diplomatic relations with Beijing and breaks diplomatic relations with the ROC on Taiwan. Deng Xiaoping visits the United States for talks with President Carter. The US Congress passes the Taiwan Relations Act to maintain unofficial relations with Taiwan.

1980 The United States and China sign a trade agreement. Business, scholarly and cultural exchanges expand, and American news organizations establish bureaus in Beijing.
China joins the International Monetary Fund and the World Bank.

1982 The Reagan administration signs a third joint communiqué with the PRC, stating that the United States "intends to reduce gradually the sales of arms to Taiwan."

1983–84 Deng Xiaoping announces the "one country, two systems" policy to reassure the people of Hong Kong and Taiwan that they will retain considerable autonomy after reunification with the PRC.

1983–84 The CCP promotes a campaign against "spiritual pollution" to limit Western influence.

1987 The Anti-Bourgeois Liberalization Campaign demonstrates renewed conservative Chinese concern over imported Western values.
Martial law is lifted and Taiwan becomes a constitutional democracy.

1989 Pro-democracy protests take place in Beijing's Tiananmen Square and other cities in China. The People's Liberation Army brutally ends the movement on June 4. The Bush administration imposes economic and military sanctions in response.
The Committee of 100 is established in New York City to advance US-China Relations and to advocate for the rights of Chinese Americans.

1990 President H. W. Bush signs an executive order allowing as many as forty thousand Chinese students to stay in the United States. Dissident Fang Lizhi is allowed to leave for the United States after taking refuge in the US embassy for a year.

1992 Deng Xiaoping's "Southern Tour" of China signals the resumption of economic reforms that had been paused after the 1989 Tiananmen crisis.

1993 The United States claims that the Chinese ship *Yinhe* is carrying chemical weapon materials to Iran. The ship is boarded and no evidence is found.

1994 President Clinton's administration ends its policy linking Most Favored Nation (MFN) status for China with its progress on human rights.

1995–96 Taiwan's President Lee Teng-hui visits Cornell University despite PRC protests. During the Third Taiwan Strait Crisis, Beijing fires missiles into Taiwan's territorial waters to warn the ROC government against independence. The United States deploys two carrier battle groups to the western Pacific in response.

1997–98 Presidents Jiang Zemin and Bill Clinton hold meetings in Washington and Beijing, the first summits since 1989.

1997 The British colony of Hong Kong is returned to Chinese sovereignty. Beijing promises that Hong Kong can retain its own system for fifty years.

1999 Taiwanese American scientist Wen Ho Lee is accused of giving classified information to the PRC, but the case against him is not proved.

A US plane bombs China's embassy in Belgrade, Kosovo, killing three Chinese citizens. Refusing to believe it was an accident, Chinese citizens take to the streets to demonstrate in major cities.

The Portuguese colony of Macao is returned to Chinese sovereignty.

2001 A US spy plane and PRC fighter jet collide over the South China Sea. The Chinese pilot is killed and the US crew is held for ten days on Hainan Island.

The PRC is admitted to the World Trade Organization (WTO) with US backing, which provides a major boost to its economy.

2003 President George W. Bush warns Taiwan President Chen Shui-bian against seeking independence.

2008 President Bush attends the Beijing Summer Olympics despite protests over repression in Tibet.

2010 China surpasses Japan as the world's second-largest economy. Dissident Liu Xiaobo receives the Nobel Peace Prize but cannot accept in person because he is in prison in China.

2011 The United States announces a "pivot" to Asia to counter China's growing power.

2012–13 Xi Jinping is elected general secretary of the CCP and president of the PRC. He consolidates his power and warns against the dangers of Western values.

President Obama and Xi Jinping meet at the Sunnylands estate in California to discuss climate change, cybersecurity, US arms sales to Taiwan, North Korea's nuclear program, and other issues.

2015 The United States warns China against building military outposts on islands in the South China Sea.

2017 President Trump hosts Xi Jinping in Florida for discussions on North Korea and trade in April. Trump makes a state visit to China.

2018 The Trump administration imposes substantial tariffs on China for the alleged theft of intellectual property and other unfair trade practices. China responds with its own tariffs on US goods.

2019 Uyghur Muslims are detained in mass internment camps in Xinjiang.

The US Congress passes the Hong Kong Human Rights and Democracy Act, which mandates an annual review of Hong Kong's autonomy to justify its special trading status with the United States.

2020 Coronavirus disease (COVID-19) erupts in Wuhan, disrupting global trade and travel and initiating a downward spiral in US-China relations.

China passes a National Security Law to crack down on pro-democracy protests in Hong Kong. President Trump signs an executive order ending Hong Kong's preferential trade status.

The United States withdraws the Peace Corps from China and shuts down the PRC consulate in Houston based on charges of spying. China closes the US consulate in Chengdu in retaliation. Both countries impose restrictions on journalists.

Secretary of State Mike Pompeo declares that the era of engagement with the Chinese Communist Party is over. Fears of a new Cold War between the United States and China increase.

Introduction

A Tale of Two Chinas

In the summer of 1957, the Chinese government invited a group of young Americans who were attending a World Youth Festival in Moscow to visit the People's Republic of China (PRC). The US State Department sternly warned them against accepting. If they did so, their passports—stamped "not valid for travel to those portions of China, Korea, and Viet-Nam under Communist control"—would be revoked, fines could be imposed, and they might be liable to prosecution. (No such restrictions applied to the Soviet Union, which established diplomatic relations with the United States in 1933.) President Eisenhower called the potential trip "ill-advised." If they made the journey, said Under Secretary of State Christian Herter, they would be "willing tools" of the Chinese Communists.[1]

Several decided against going to the PRC, but forty-one, most of them students, were willing to defy the US government. The Chinese embassy issued visas on separate pieces of paper so their passports would have no evidence of their having been in Red China. The *New York Times* reported that "a brass band blared and a thousand flower-bearing Russians waved" as the exuberant group set off on the Trans-Siberian Express from Moscow Yaroslavsky station.[2]

A wildly enthusiastic crowd of young Chinese greeted the delegation when they arrived one week later at the Peking Railway Station on August 23. "As soon as they stepped on the forbidden land," wrote a Reuters correspondent, "they were surrounded by hand-shaking, clapping, back-slapping Chinese who pressed flowers into their hands." The cheering redoubled when one of the Americans unfurled a large Stars and Stripes flag which the Russians had made for the Youth Festival. The Chinese began singing "John Brown's Body" and everyone joined in chanting "Long Live World Peace." From their hotel a short while later, the Americans issued a statement that they regarded the visit as "an important step toward free interchange between China and the United States." They wanted not only to learn about contemporary China but also hoped to "give the Chinese people some understanding our own

Chinese students welcoming an American youth group arriving from Moscow
at the Peking Railway Station, August 1957.
Keystone-France/Gamma-Keystone via Getty Images.

country."[3] The official *People's Daily* carried a front-page story celebrating
their visit.

As guests of the All-China Federation for Democratic Youth, which covered all expenses for the trip, the group toured eight cities over a period of
six weeks. During their visit to Changchun, an industrial city in the northeast, they demonstrated basketball, jitterbugging, and truck driving. They
attended the October 1 National Day parade in Beijing and met with Premier
and Foreign Minister Zhou Enlai who agreed with the visitors that achieving
world peace and improved US-China relations would depend on not only the
efforts of professional diplomats but also direct communication between citizens of the two countries.[4]

Because the US government prevented American news organizations
from sending their own journalists to cover the story, the Associated Press,
United Press International, and NBC enlisted members of the delegation as
special correspondents.[5] NBC gave a movie camera to Robert C. Cohen, who
had studied film at UCLA, asking him to document their visits to schools,

hospitals, factories, and a Peking Opera performance. "China may be changing, but it is still a land of great contrasts," narrated Cohen in the film he made after the trip. He was impressed by the PRC's progress in eliminating epidemics and diseases, but tuberculosis was still widespread. The construction of locomotives, bridges, and ships showed China's rapid industrialization, but the use of "primitive" manual labor instead of machines was commonplace. The country was largely self-sufficient, but Russian technicians worked at some sites. The government paid for and controlled university education, but between eight and ten students were "crammed" into small dormitory rooms. There were a small number of Chinese Christians, but foreign missionaries were banned.[6]

Most of the stories that generated headlines back in the United States, however, did not depict everyday Chinese life; instead they were blunt reminders that the two nations remained Cold War foes. On one occasion, several members of the group were taken to a prison in Beijing where they spoke with John Downey and Richard Fecteau, CIA agents whose plane was shot down on Chinese territory in 1952. In Shanghai, others met with Hugh Redmond, an American businessman serving a life sentence, also accused of working for the CIA, as well as two US Catholic priests, Joseph McCormick and John Wagner, who were being held as prisoners. A more upbeat conversation was arranged with Morris Wills (whose story is told in Chapter 2), a US Korean War veteran who chose to live in China and was studying Chinese language and literature at Peking University.[7]

In retrospect, the unprecedented 1957 trip was not, as the young Americans had hoped, "an important step toward free interchange between China and the United States." Fourteen members of the group who flew back to Moscow said they were glad they had made the trip, but were told by a US Embassy official that they had violated US regulations, and their passports would be stamped as good only for the return trip to the United States.[8] Needless to say there was no reciprocal invitation for Chinese students to visit the United States. The gulf between the two nations simply was too wide and deep, and the unexpected encounter was soon forgotten, leaving barely a trace in the annals of Sino-American history.

What a world of difference fourteen years later when an American ping-pong team received a sudden invitation to visit China in April 1971. This time, the

US government, which had ended its ban on travel to Communist China one month earlier, welcomed Beijing's initiative. The US athletes, who were competing in the World Table Tennis Championship in Nagoya, Japan, flew to Hong Kong and crossed the PRC border from there. In contrast to the 1957 trip, professional journalists representing NBC, the Associated Press, and *Life* magazine were allowed to accompany them. This time, the American public treated the sports delegation as celebrities, and Chinese and Americans alike were captivated by the antics of Glenn Cowan, a long-haired hippie who wore a floppy yellow hat. (Various publications mistakenly reported they were the first group of Americans to enter China since the Communist takeover in 1949.)

The ping-pong delegation represented a sensational unofficial opening that permitted the two governments to sidestep divisive policy issues. Nine players, four officials, and two family members toured Guangzhou, Shanghai, and Beijing; their visit to the Great Wall was featured on the cover of *Time* with a banner "Yanks in Peking" and the headline "China: A Whole New Game." Exhibition matches were played under the slogan "Friendship First and Competition Second," which was fortunate because the Chinese players were the best in the world. China's ambivalence about the United States was nonetheless in evidence: a sign in one stadium read "Welcome to the American Team" while another said, "Down with Yankee Oppressors and Their Running Dogs." Zhou Enlai received the Americans at the Great Hall of the People, along with table tennis teams from several other countries, and congratulated them on opening "a new chapter in the relations of the American and Chinese people." On the same day, President Nixon announced that the United States was lifting its twenty-year-old trade embargo on Communist China.

Twelve months later, China's ping-pong team arrived in the United States for a tour of eight cities, cosponsored by the US Table Tennis Association and the National Committee on United States-China Relations, both private organizations. Cultural differences sometimes puzzled the Chinese players, and politics occasionally intervened. During their initial match in Cobo Hall in Detroit, an anti-communist group dropped white paper parachutes with dead mice from a balcony onto the arena below. Small pro-Taiwan groups showed up at other venues shouting, "Down with the Communists" and "The Republic of China is Free China." Nixon received the Chinese team in a Rose Garden reception at the White House, but they refused to tour the Kennedy Center for the Performing Arts because both the ROC (Republic of China)

American ping-pong players on Great Wall, April 1971.
STAFF/AFP via Getty Images.

and PRC flags were displayed there.[9] But on the whole, Jan Berris, a National Committee staff member who traveled with the team, remembers the large crowds of people at the matches as being enormously curious and expressing "a huge amount of warmth and friendliness" toward the Chinese.

Despite a few disruptions, the 1971–72 exchange of table tennis teams was deemed a major success, in stark contrast to the unauthorized 1957 tour that had barely registered on America's consciousness. Ping-pong diplomacy signaled that the United States and China were ready to reevaluate their adversarial relationship. President Nixon said there would be winners and losers in the matches, but "the big winner will be the friendship between the people of the United States and the people of the People's Republic of China."[10] The interchange of individual Americans and Chinese had paved the way for a much bigger game.

Misunderstanding China

Neither in 1957 nor in 1971 did the Americans who visited China have any idea of what to expect. Most knew little beyond popular stereotypes of the day: the diabolical Dr. Fu Manchu, the clever detective Charlie Chan, the peasants of Pearl Buck's *The Good Earth*, and the adventures of comic strip characters in Milton Caniff's *Terry and the Pirates*. Chinese Americans, few in number and concentrated mainly in San Francisco and New York Chinatowns, were the subject of curiosity, suspicion, and disdain. China was mysterious and captivating, fearful and foreboding. A jumble of contradictory images oscillated between admiration and contempt, brilliantly documented in Harold Isaacs' book *Scratches on Our Minds* and Irv Drasnin's film *Misunderstanding China*.[11]

Beyond such clichés, there was a more serious, equally persistent, liberal dream for China, rooted in the Christian missionary movement, which had given birth to the belief that the United States had an obligation to share its version of prosperity with the rest of the world. During the late nineteenth and early twentieth centuries, China was by far the most exciting and compelling destination for American missionaries, including a sizable number of single women who had few opportunities for professional employment beyond teaching and nursing. They went not only to share the Gospel but also to build schools and hospitals and to provide social services and relief work as expressions of their faith. During sabbaticals back home, they visited churches and college campuses where they showed lantern slides and talked about China's great need for help. They embodied the idea that the United States had a moral responsibility to aid China in becoming a progressive society in its own image. This well-meaning, paternalistic vision, which assumed the superiority of Western values, gave rise to a relationship that was unusually emotional and sentimental.

The lure of China as a potentially vast market for business was another aspect of America's ambition to remake the Middle Kingdom. The application of Western-style management and advertising was the key to success for companies like British American Tobacco, the Singer Sewing Machine Company, and John D. Rockefeller's Standard Oil Company, under the slogan "Oil for the Lamps of China." Other firms pioneered modern business practices for newspapers, banking, and insurance. Like the missionaries—who never converted more than a very small percentage of the Chinese population—total US trade and investment in China was modest. Nevertheless, the free enterprise model left its mark and added to the idea of China's becoming "just like us."

With the advent of Communist rule in 1949, the American dream for China was extinguished—at least for the time being. Prior to the Communist revolution, missionaries and businessmen tried to persuade the Chinese that Christianity and capitalism offered the path to a strong, prosperous, just society. Rejecting these interlopers as agents of "cultural imperialism," the Communists preached a radical faith that cast the West in general and the United States in particular as the enemy. The Chinese Communist Party blamed outsiders for a "century of humiliation."

As historian Jonathan Spence has written, China had "regained the right, precious to all great nations, of defining her own values and dreaming her own dreams without alien interference. China's leaders could now formulate their own definition of man, restructure their own society, pursue their own foreign policy goals."[12] Except for a handful of Western sympathizers and thousands of Russian advisers, anyone who did not hold a Chinese passport either chose to leave the PRC or was forced to do so.[13] A number of foreigners, notably Catholic nuns and priests, were imprisoned. China was no longer a feeble victim that looked to other countries for deliverance, but a unified nation with a singular purpose.

The American public responded to the so-called "loss of China" with a mixture of anger, confusion, and regret when the long-standing ambition to save a poor, benighted China disappeared with the sudden collapse of the Nationalist (Kuomintang) government, followed by the Communist victory. Yet, had it not been for the Korean War, the United States most likely would have recognized Beijing as representing the mainland's legitimate government. Instead, three years of bloody combat between American and Chinese troops on the Korean peninsula confirmed the two countries as mortal enemies. The US government refused to accept the PRC's existence, clinging to the myth that the Republic of China on the island of Taiwan—with a population of eight million as compared with the mainland's 550 million in 1950—represented the entire country. For two decades, Americans and Chinese had nothing more than stereotypes and official propaganda to shape their opinions, and attitudes on both sides were reduced to one-dimensional stereotypes.

China's Mandate for Modernization

Modern China was founded on the premise that fundamental change was essential to revive the nation's fortunes. Reform during the Qing dynasty was a case of too little and too late, and the Nationalist government under Chiang Kai-shek made progress but was stymied by regional warlords and undermined by war with Japan. The Communists rose to power based on military prowess and popular support for a sweeping mandate to transform politics, society, and the economy.

China's revolutionary origins sprang from the early twentieth century New Culture Movement, which called for a sharp break with the ideas and institutions of the past. For the Chinese people to rise again, the nation would need to discard the moribund traditions of Confucianism and accept radical ideas such as individualism and equal rights, including women's rights. These disruptive views would coincide with the birth of Chinese nationalism when students took to the streets during the May Fourth Movement, responding to the injustices of the Versailles Peace Treaty. Inspired by the triumph of Russia's October Revolution, a small group of intellectuals founded the Chinese Communist Party (CCP) in Shanghai in 1921. Marx's vision of a classless society when combined with Lenin's analysis of colonialism and imperialism seemed to be the answer to China's afflictions.

Throughout seven decades of constant, often violent experimentation, the PRC has struggled to balance pragmatism and idealism, old and new, native and foreign.

The Chinese Communists first drew upon Mao Zedong's ideology of self-reliance and his supreme belief that human behavior could be transformed to support the goals of the state. Added to this vision after 1949 was the wholesale adoption of the Soviet Union's institutions, from education and law to industry and the military. Identical to the USSR, the economy was centrally controlled and Party members were embedded at every level of society to enforce the government's policies.

When these first two wellsprings reached their limits—after the Sino-Soviet split and the death of Mao—China looked to the capitalist West, and especially to the United States, for investment, trade, technology, and training in order to accelerate its scientific and economic development. Yet the PRC's leadership was, and continues to be, ambivalent about the United States, just as the United States has been unsure about China. Like two powerful magnetic fields with electrical currents that either attract or repel, the relationship has sharply alternated between partnership and opposition.

Learning to Live with "New" China

The human perspective is too often overlooked in discussions and debates about grand strategy or policy disputes between China and the United States over trade, technology, human rights, Taiwan, Hong Kong, the South China Sea, and other matters. Yet it is individual Chinese and Americans—including Americans of Chinese descent—who have breathed life into the Sino-American relationship. Their personal interactions are the flesh and blood that animate the skeleton of state-to-state relations.

While scores of Americans have China stories worth telling—and just as many Chinese have significant US stories—the thirteen dramatis personae selected for this book illuminate critical phases and facets of US relations with the PRC. They include a missionary-turned-politician, soldiers, scientists, a farmer, a lawyer, an art historian, a diplomat, a scholar, a businesswoman, a human rights defender, and a journalist. Like the Indian fable of the blind men and the elephant, each of them has touched a different part of China and has reached different conclusions about its reality.

The inspiration for my study comes from Jonathan Spence, professor emeritus at Yale, who has done so much to explain Chinese history and culture to Western audiences. Early in his career, he wrote a series of short biographies entitled *To Change China: Western Advisers in China, 1620–1960*. From Jesuit missionaries and British physicians to Russian revolutionaries and American military generals, Spence showed how outsiders brought technical skills and knowledge to China in the fields of religion, astronomy, medicine, politics, education, and more. The conundrum for the Chinese was how to assimilate Western scientific knowledge and techniques without endangering the core values of their civilization, a question that resonates loudly even today.

Most of Spence's protagonists inhabited the Middle Kingdom during a period of prolonged internal decline, external aggression, and profound disagreement over how to recover China's lost glory. His foreign actors made significant contributions, but their stories added up to a cautionary tale; more often than not they were absorbed and defeated, overwhelmed by forces beyond their control. In almost every case, China altered their lives more than they were able to change China. The characters in Spence's book speak to us still, he wrote, "about the ambiguities of superiority, and about that indefinable realm where altruism and exploitation meet."[14]

Americans in China: Encounters with the People's Republic picks up where Spence left off and poses similar questions: How did foreigners respond to Communist China's drive for wealth, power, and respect? What were the new rules of engagement and what roles could outsiders play as adversaries and friends, emissaries and educators, mediators and advocates, interpreters and reporters? In what ways did the Western ambition to change China persist? To what extent were these women and men changed by China? And what lessons we can draw from their experiences?

What follows is neither strictly chronological—some stories overlap in their coverage of key events—nor intended as a comprehensive account. It ranges across four periods of relations between the United States and China: hostility and mutual isolation (1949–1971); discovery and engagement (1971–1989); disillusion and accommodation (1989–2001); and cooperation, competition, and a return to hostility (2001–present).

Spence's *To Change China* covered four hundred years of history, while my timeframe is much shorter. His characters were European, Russian, Canadian, and American—all of them White males—while my actors are Americans, including five women, three Chinese Americans, and one African American. Some were involved with China due to accidents of birth, while others were attracted out of a sense of curiosity and adventure. Some were ideological, defending a particular belief, while others were more dispassionate and objective. They were present at the creation of a new US-China relationship, testing personal assumptions, ideas, and values as they pushed up against moral, ethical, and political boundaries. In one way or another, each of them was a trailblazer charting a unique path.

From Estrangement to Rapprochement

Part One of this book focuses on the American response to the Chinese revolution during a prolonged period of military, economic, and ideological confrontation with the United States. In a world divided between socialism and capitalism, democracy and communism, the United States government opposed the PRC's legitimacy. Washington pejoratively referred to "Red China," refusing to acknowledge the People's Republic by its official name. Chinese Communists were disparaged as "Commies" or "Chicoms." An earlier image of a "Yellow peril" was revived in the form of mindless hordes of Red Chinese brainwashed by their totalitarian leaders. Mao's victory was not "liberation" (*jiefang*), but a "takeover." Taiwan, previously known as Formosa, represented Free China, and the Nationalist government dismissed the Communists as "bandits" who had led a rebellion against their authority. Framed in terms of isolation and containment, US-China relations were reduced to a Manichaean system of darkness and light. Threatened by US hostility, the PRC retaliated by spreading its revolutionary ideology to other parts of the world. No longer a helpless giant in need of rescuing, China exported its own version of change, imbued with a fervent anti-imperialist, anti-capitalist message.

Americans in China opens with the life of Walter Judd, a former China missionary who served in Congress for twenty years. He actively sought to save the Chinese from communism, believing that Mao's regime had been imposed against the will of the Chinese people. Judd presented his opposition as a moral choice between liberty and oppression, and was certain that the CCP eventually would collapse if only Washington would stay the course and isolate the mainland. "The crux of the matter," wrote Judd, "is this: if China is free, she can and will move rapidly toward greater democracy and better government."[15]

In spite of such hostility, a handful of US citizens were determined to make up their own minds about China. In Chapter 2 we meet Clarence Adams and Morris Wills, two US prisoners of war in in Korea, who shocked the American public when they voluntarily went to China with nineteen other soldiers instead of repatriating to the United States. Adams, an African American, was fleeing racism and Wills was escaping a dead-end future. What accounted for their decision to reject Cold War orthodoxy and accept the PRC's version of truth?

Chapter 3 introduces two other Americans, Joan Hinton, a nuclear physicist, and her husband, Sid Engst, a dairy farmer, who arrived in the Communist-held northwest in the late 1940s. Participating in the radical reform of society in the countryside, they were won over to communism not so much by the rhetoric of political campaigns as by what they saw with their own eyes. Even after the PRC abandoned Mao's failed policies in favor of free market reforms, Hinton and Engst held fast to the Chairman's radical egalitarian vision.

When US-China relations thawed during the early 1970s, it was imperative for Beijing and Washington to construct a government-to-government framework that would enable both sides to pursue their goals. Chapters 4 and 5 describe a two-pronged approach, one informal and the other official. In the first instance, Beijing courted C. N. Yang, a prominent Chinese American scientist who was instrumental in forming connections between the two countries and effective in convincing Chinese in the United States to put aside the rancorous politics of the past for the sake of reconciliation with the motherland. For Yang, assisting the PRC through science and education was the best way to overcome the humiliation of the past. Being Chinese was less a matter of nationality than an intense feeling of patriotism that transcended time, place, and politics.

On the official side, J. Stapleton Roy, a US Foreign Service Officer and son of China missionaries, played a key role in the secret negotiations that led to full diplomatic relations with Beijing in 1979, opening the door to an era of robust engagement. Richard Nixon and Henry Kissinger had accomplished an historic breakthrough seven years earlier, but the relationship remained hostage to Washington's continued recognition of the Republic of China. The turning point came when the United States "de-recognized" Taiwan, which coincided with Deng Xiaoping's opening to the West. The problem of Taiwan was never fully resolved, however, and it remains a dangerous flashpoint more than four decades later.

Engaging with China

Part Two deals with a period of rapidly expanding interaction between the United States and the People's Republic after normalization of diplomatic relations. C. N. Yang, Stapleton Roy, and many others had laid the groundwork for an explosion of tourism, trade, investment, and scholarly and cultural exchange between the two nations. Now that US citizens could live, work, and study in China, there came a rebirth of the expectation that intense collaboration would lead in the direction of democracy, or at least humane governance. It was an exhilarating time fueled by the notion that China once again wanted to emulate the United States, just as it had during the first half of the twentieth century. China was a new frontier ripe for exploration and America's zeal for discovery now expanded far beyond the original Christian missionary project.

When Jerome and Joan Cohen, presented in Chapter 6, gave up a secure existence for the uncertainties of living and working in the PRC, their decision captured the same spirit of adventure and ambition that attracted earlier Americans to the Middle Kingdom. He taught and practiced corporate law, a point of entry for revising China's entire legal system, and she lectured on modern Western art, a source of inspiration for the post-Mao generation of Chinese artists. Both fields were testing grounds for freedom of expression. After returning to the United States, Jerome fostered two-way legal training programs and advocated for the rights of Chinese dissidents, while Joan introduced contemporary Chinese art and culture to Western audiences.

Elizabeth Perry, the subject of Chapter 7, was among the first young American scholars who were able to conduct research and fieldwork in the PRC and became a life-long advocate for unfettered academic exchange. She arrived at Nanjing University with an idealized image of Maoism as a promising alternative model for social and political change, but was dismayed to learn about the injustices of the Cultural Revolution, a revelation that led her to investigate the historical roots of protest and rebellion in China. Her fresh thinking about the origins of the Communist revolution contradicted the conventional Marxist narrative and raised questions deemed too sensitive for Chinese scholars to ask for themselves in public.

The massive expansion of China's economy in the 1990s made long-time dreams of a vast China market an actual possibility for US business. In Chapter 8, Shirley Young's story is a case study of a Chinese American who played a pivotal role in negotiating a highly successful joint venture in Shanghai for General Motors, partly due to her family background. With experience in advertising and marketing, she had an open mind about the PRC's ambitions for developing its own automotive industry. At the same time, her concern for mutual understanding led her to advocate for Chinese American rights and to promote cultural exchange between China and the United States.

Human rights—a highly contentious area where the PRC has resisted fundamental change—became the focus of John Kamm's life, told in Chapter 9, after the 1989 Tiananmen uprising, when he jettisoned a profitable business career and decided to use his considerable skills as a salesman to negotiate for the release or reduced sentences of Chinese political prisoners. Building on an extensive understanding of Chinese and American political and cultural differences—but without prior experience as a human rights activist—he set up a non-profit organization based on a philosophy of dialogue and negotiation.

Journalist Melinda Liu, the subject of the final chapter, has reported on China for more than four decades, shaping American opinion and perceptions in the process. She has tracked the China story across repeated cycles, from the progressive era of Deng Xiaoping's reforms to the Tiananmen crackdown and from the more relaxed period of the 2008 Olympics to Xi Jinping's restrictions on political liberties. In the face of the Communist Party's efforts to control the message, Liu has constantly contended with the tradeoffs between getting the news and defending freedom of the press.

Sino-American relations is a tale of two Chinas, one alien and forbidden, the other accessible and appealing, one closed and the other open. The young Americans who journeyed from Moscow to Beijing in 1957 did so in defiance of the US government, and their quixotic mission to improve understanding between the United States and China was fruitless. By contrast, the American table tennis players of 1971 were innocent harbingers of "a new chapter in the relations of the American and Chinese people," as Zhou Enlai told them. The two trips, in the context of altered geo-politics, reflected the United States' uncertainty about whether to accept or reject Communist China.

With the exception of Walter Judd, the women and men who figure in this book were determined to get beyond the divisive politics of the Cold War so they could discover and define the "real" China for themselves. All of them were remarkably courageous, dedicated, and persistent. Their distinctive stories hold up a mirror to US society, helping to explain how our two countries have arrived at the present moment and suggesting where we might travel from here.

PART I
FROM COLD WAR
TO RECONCILIATION

1

Walter Judd

Cold War Crusader

Walter Judd, one of the most influential and passionate voices on China policy during the Cold War, served in the US House of Representatives for twenty years from 1942 to 1962. He was an unlikely member of Congress. Trained as a physician and surgeon, he had spent nearly ten years as a medical missionary in two regions of China prior to the Communist triumph. Had it not been for the Second World War, he would not have run for public office, and if Mao Zedong had not taken power, he might have gone back to China to practice medicine.

Judd was best known for his unyielding hostility to communism, which he called "a disease of human behavior." In politics, as in medicine, his approach was "to find out the things that are not basically sound and work to cure or remove them."[1] He believed that combating communism was like treating cancer; the sickness would spread if no action was taken. Judd resolved to save China—and the rest of the world—from such a scourge. To him, this meant that Red China must be isolated and contained. It should not be recognized as a legitimate government; trade and travel should not be permitted; and United Nations membership, held by the Republic of China on Taiwan, should not be granted. Together with other anti-communist stalwarts, Judd successfully made the case for US opposition to the PRC for two decades.

While Judd was an especially ardent, vocal, and effective adversary of China, he was also a well-respected legislator. Lee Hamilton, a former long-time member of the House of Representatives from Indiana who chaired the House Committee on Foreign Affairs, remembers him as a formidable presence in the Congress. "Before the Vietnam War in the 1960s," said Hamilton, "the members of the House just didn't take that much interest in foreign policy. Congressmen looked upon their job as representing their districts, and most of them had a very limited view of the role of the Congress in foreign policy. Judd was highly thought of as a person who did his homework and who spoke intelligently on foreign policy issues. He was not in the

Chicago Tribune Midwest isolationist tradition, and he was looked on as a progressive voice."[2]

Indeed, the missionary-turned-politician marched to his own drummer and did not vote in lockstep with his fellow Republicans. He voiced strong support for the Marshall Plan, NATO, and the United Nations, and was open-minded and forward looking on immigration reform. He advocated for foreign aid and was enthusiastic about President Kennedy's Peace Corps. Judd was also prescient about Asia's future importance: "If America gets into another war," he cautioned as early as 1945, "almost certainly it will be through Asia."[3] Prolonged conflicts to halt the spread of communism in Korea and Vietnam proved him correct.

Yet Judd's antipathy toward Mao's regime was absolute. His certainty about the democratic nature of the Chinese people combined with his devotion to the Nationalists on Taiwan were principles that influenced the direction of US China policy for much of the Cold War. His ideas, which once seemed obsolete, are remarkably current in an increasingly hostile environment where the wisdom of US cooperation with the PRC is doubted.

Medical Missionary to China

Walter Henry Judd was smart, determined, and single-minded. He grew up in Rising City, Nebraska, a farming community of five hundred people on a railway line south of the Platte River. (The town was named for two brothers with the surname Rising.) Born September 25, 1898, he was the sixth of seven children and grew up in a house with no electricity. His father, Horace, owned the local lumberyard, and his mother, Mary Elizabeth Greenslit, a New Englander, taught music and was his Sunday School teacher.

At the age of seventeen, Judd resolved to become a foreign missionary, inspired by a biography of David Livingstone, the famous nineteenth-century Scottish evangelist and African explorer. China loomed large in Judd's imagination because it was there that "the need was greatest and the workers were fewest." China, moreover, "is going to be the key to Asia," reasoned Judd, and "would have enormous impact upon the world and upon my own country." But rather than preaching or teaching, he decided on medicine as a profession. It was a choice colored by family tragedies; his younger brother had died after hitting his head on a rock and two other siblings perished from typhus when they were teenagers.[4]

Judd worked his way through college at the University of Nebraska in Lincoln, fifty miles from Rising City, and toward the end of the First World War, left to serve in the US Army in Kentucky for one year. He graduated Phi Beta Kappa in 1920 and received his medical degree from Nebraska's medical school in Omaha three years later. During college, Judd, who played the trumpet, attended a meeting of a Student Volunteer Movement (SVM) band, thinking it was a musical group. He quickly learned that the purpose of the SVM—which had chapters called "bands" on campuses throughout the country—was to recruit young men and women to spread the Christian Gospel in foreign lands. Through the SVM—much like the secular Peace Corps established in the 1960s—tens of thousands of young idealists were inspired to become missionaries, convinced that the American way of life should be shared with the rest of the world. After finishing medical school, Judd spent two years visiting colleges and universities in the United States as an SVM traveling secretary.[5]

Walter Judd was five feet nine inches tall, rail thin, wore glasses, and was not athletic, having injured his knee in a backyard football game. When he was eighteen, his face was badly burned and scarred, the result of excessive x-rays a doctor had prescribed to clear up a serious case of acne. (Radiation therapy was used for a variety of ailments in the early twentieth century, before its dangers were fully understood.) The damage was ugly and permanent. On looking in the mirror, "I wanted to crawl into the ground," he later told a journalist. Understandably self-conscious, he stopped asking girls for dates. "Finally," Judd recalled, "I took myself in hand and said: 'You'll have this face for the rest of your life. You've got to live with it or go into hiding. And you aren't going to go into hiding.'" His appearance did not improve with age. Starting in his thirties, basal cell carcinomas regularly appeared on his face. In subsequent years, cancerous growths were removed from his upper lip, lower lip, and under his chin. But the affliction toughened his resolve. "A person can either quit or he can stand up and face life," said Judd.[6]

Yet if anyone was put off by Judd's physical appearance, they were attracted to his energy and zeal. By all accounts he was a riveting speaker, widely known for his oratorical skills. He was unusually single-minded, strong-willed, and self-possessed. "He is one of the most mentally alert young men I think I have ever met. He has a perfectly marvelous brain," wrote a Miss Cashing when she heard Judd speak in Boston, after he had become a missionary. A colleague wrote, "Judd has a photographic mind, a tenacious memory and a very eloquent tongue. He sees clearly, remembers accurately and recalls graphically any experience . . . . He lives intensely each moment. He assumes that he is right and he knows the reasons why. He is likely to reveal impatience with those whose observation is less keen or judgment is less quick and sure . . . . His own ideals are very high indeed and in utmost sincerity he tries to live up to them."[7] In his earnestness and strong sense of conviction, the young man from Nebraska embodied the self-confident, self-assured spirit of the US heartland.

In 1925, at the age of twenty-seven, Walter Judd sailed by steamship from Seattle to China under the auspices of the Congregational Church, the denomination in which he had been raised. The collapse of the Qing dynasty in 1911 had ushered in a prolonged period of chaotic politics and internal warfare. It was also a time of virulent nationalism directed against the Western powers and Japan, nations that had special privileges and occupied various territories in China. By the time Judd arrived, Chiang Kai-shek, who he would later champion as the country's best hope for the future, was a rising military man who had recently succeeded Sun Yat-sen as the leader of the Nationalist Party.

Unlike earlier generations of missionaries who went directly into the field, Judd spent his first year at Nanjing University—one of thirteen Protestant Christian colleges—where he studied Chinese language, history, and culture. He also taught English at a local YMCA and worked in a medical clinic. It marked the beginning of a life-long attachment. He admired the people for their solid optimism and friendly good cheer; they were constantly singing at work. Yet he also found them fearfully superstitious, "caught up in demon worship," extremely poor, hungry, and filthy.[8] While there was a kernel of truth to such generalizations, missionaries often dramatized China's conditions to appeal to the emotions and the pocketbooks of churchgoers back home.

After the preparatory year in Nanjing, Judd was assigned to a mission station at Shaowu, a city in the mountainous interior of the southeastern province of Fujian. Getting there required a ten-day, 190-mile boat trip up the Min River from the coastal city of Fuzhou. No highway or train service existed. Staffed by fifteen foreign missionaries and 125 Chinese workers, the Shaowu area, about the size of Massachusetts, boasted a church, two hospitals, boarding schools for girls and boys, and an experimental farm.[9]

Edward Bliss, a New England doctor who had been in Shaowu since 1892, was thrilled to welcome Judd as his colleague, and Judd believed Dr. Bliss was "one of finest, most benevolent, loving men who ever lived." Yet he criticized the older generation of missionaries like Bliss for seeking to remake China in their own image, seeing themselves as "benevolent benefactors" instructing the "humble, backward, inferior recipients." The Chinese should not be treated as ignorant heathens awaiting enlightenment from the superior West, insisted Judd, who had come to realize that the struggling nation would have to determine its own path. The modern missionary should "not say or believe that all of our ideas and customs are right and all theirs are wrong," wrote Judd in a letter to the Congregational board. "Unless we are willing to meet the Chinese on this basis of building on their best and allowing them to develop their own church organizations and forms of worship as they are led to God, we might almost as well pack up and go home."[10]

Too many Protestant missionaries, complained Judd, literally walled themselves off from the Chinese in comfortable brick compounds where they constructed little replicas of America. Was it any wonder, he asked, that the Chinese resented these outsiders who sought to "sow superiority complexes, special privileges, patronizing philanthropy, foreign concessions, gunboats, foreign flags on missions and Chinese churches, etc.?" He noted that Catholic priests, who worked in rural areas and were not burdened by families, were more effective in integrating themselves into the local society.[11]

There was, however, good reason for missionaries to be concerned for their safety. The Shaowu hospital was overrun several times by hostile forces of one kind or another, and marauding bandits and soldiers regularly kidnapped foreigners and held them for ransom. In 1927, troops allied with Chiang Kai-shek's Northern Expedition entered the town and threatened to execute Judd. He was spared only when one of his former patients convinced the soldiers that he was a US citizen and not British, who were considered the worst of the Western imperialists.

Judd first encountered the recently established Chinese Communists after they set up a base in the remote border region of Jiangxi Province, next door to Fujian. They adopted a radical, violent form of revolutionary class warfare, targeting landlords as class enemies and missionaries as imperialist spies. An estimated twenty-five missionaries were held by Communist groups in southeastern China in 1930.[12] Rarely were they murdered since they were worth more alive than dead.

The Communists periodically showed up in the Shaowu area. "I had them as patients," recalled Judd. "And they were working primarily for the well-being of the people. The Communists, yes. At the beginning . . . I was impressed by them; these guys were good and they worked hard and they didn't extort from the people." They were "the first military outfit I ever saw that never had a case of venereal disease." One well-educated young man told Judd that capitalism and the right to own property lead to selfishness, greed, classes, and war. Marxism, on the other hand, would produce "concern for the masses, a good society and everyone well-taken-care-of." Judd admitted that this sounded reasonable, but objected that it was "against human nature," and concluded that the Communists were "unscrupulous" and devoid of morality. "They don't believe there's a God, and therefore whatever served their Communist ends is moral. There isn't any such thing as right or wrong."[13]

In 1928, Judd accompanied Edward Bliss, who was seriously ill, possibly with encephalitis, back to the United States.[14] Upon his return to Shaowu the following year, he was the only foreigner working at the hospital for the next thirteen months. Judd took his evening meals with a Mrs. Yao, a generous Christian woman who had twelve children, and he would sit and practice his Chinese with her younger boys after dinner. He was determined not to give up on China, but after suffering repeated bouts of malaria—his weight was down to about 112 pounds and his hair had fallen out—he left for Japan in May 1931 to recover his strength for a few months before sailing to America.[15] Unable to go back to Fujian because of his health, he gave recruitment speeches for the Student Volunteers, fell in love, and got married, all in the space of two years.

Marriage and Missionary Life

Miriam Louise Barber was well prepared for life as a foreign missionary. She was born in India, a middle child and only daughter, where her parents served with the YMCA in Calcutta (now called Kolkata). After graduating from Mount Holyoke College, she worked at the SVM's headquarters in New York City, organizing conferences and editing their *Far Horizons* magazine. She then taught English at the Christian Kodaikanal School in South India for two years, before returning to the SVM and studying for a master's degree at Columbia Teachers College. Her daughter Mary Lou describes her as "bright, warm, and humble, a bridge builder between people," as compared with her father who was "direct and blunt."[16]

Miriam and Walter first crossed paths when he spoke to students at Mount Holyoke, before he first went to China, and they met again in 1931 when he gave a rousing keynote address at an SVM conference in Buffalo, New York.

When she was twenty-seven and he was thirty-three, they were married in Montclair, New Jersey, where her parents lived, in 1932. After two years in Rochester, Minnesota, where Walter had a surgery fellowship at the Mayo Clinic, they sailed for China from San Francisco in September 1934 on the *President Hoover* with nine-month-old Mary Lou.

Married life in China was not altogether what Miriam expected. Walter's love for her was undeniable, but she came to realize that his total devotion to his work would always come first. After arriving in Beijing (then called Beiping), he soon left to become superintendent of a 125-bed mission hospital in Fenzhou (now known as Fenyang) in Shanxi Province, while she stayed behind to study Chinese at the Union Language School. Except for a two-week Christmas visit, she did not see her husband for seven months.

She nevertheless was enthusiastic about living in Beijing. One highlight was a luncheon for alumnae of American women's colleges with Soong Mei-ling—Madame Chiang Kai-shek—a graduate of Wellesley College. "She is a charming person to meet," wrote Miriam. "Slight, or perhaps slender is a better word, she speaks English without any accent and in a lovely toned voice." Miriam was happy to learn that Soong and her husband were Christians and was encouraged to hear about the central government's New Life Movement, a mass campaign to promote morality, combat corruption, and improve public health.[17]

Miriam and Mary Lou joined Walter in Fenzhou, a two-day train ride from Beijing, in the summer of 1935. Shanxi, which had a dry, malaria-free climate, was a poor region with a history of xenophobia, where thousands of Chinese Christians and scores of Western missionaries had been killed in the Boxer Uprising of 1900. Historian Donald Gillin describes Shanxi's inhabitants as shrewd, diligent, persistent, frugal, and conservative. Yan Xishan, the warlord governor who had controlled the province since 1911, encouraged social and economic development and supported both Chinese and Western medicine.[18]

In addition to the hospital and a nurses' training school, the Fenzhou Congregational mission ran a kindergarten, primary school, men's and women's Bible schools, and a coed middle school. The Judds lived in a spacious house inside the city walls. For the sake of his family's safety, Walter had come to accept the comfortable "little America" compounds that he had railed against when he was a single missionary in Shaowu. On what would have been a modest salary in the United States, they were able to afford three servants: an amah to care for their child, a cook, and a gardener. Their flower and vegetable gardens were watered from wells every day. Spring winds carried finely powdered yellow dust that covered the floors of their rooms.[19]

Miriam wrote privately about her frustrations with the Chinese, who were "always courteous but aloof, evasive . . . . They will not tell you what they think, or what you want to know, but only what would flatter you, or sound nice." She thought this was partly because Chinese women lived so simply with few possessions, while she had a huge house with servants, "hundreds of books, toys, piano, Victrola."[20] The gap between their way of life and hers was too wide to easily overcome.

Chinese Communists and Japanese Invaders

Walter Judd did not expect to see Chinese Communists as far north as Shanxi, but in the fall of 1934 the Red Army—which later formed the People's Liberation Army—escaped from the Nationalist government's encirclement campaign in the south and retreated some 3,700 miles to the northwest, a feat later glorified as the Long March. The survivors set up their new base in Yan'an in Shaanxi, the province to the west of where the Judds were stationed. In February 1936, thirty-four thousand Red Army troops crossed the frozen Yellow River into southwestern Shanxi, where impoverished farmers welcomed them. As the Communists approached Fenzhou, however, thousands of residents fled, and the Judds escaped to another city, just thirty hours after Miriam had given birth to their second child, Carolyn. After ensuring his family's well-being, Walter returned to his hospital. Without artillery, the Communists were unable to breach Fenzhou's high walls and the crisis ended.

Judd's letters from this period say very little about the Chinese Communists, who operated mainly in rural areas. He did call them "at all odds the most experienced and toughest body of fighting men in the world today." The conduct of the CCP's Eighth Route Army, wrote Donald Gillin, was "a welcome relief from the rapacity and brutality of other armies fighting in Shansi [Shanxi]. Communist soldiers always paid in full for whatever they needed, never molested women and treated the peasants like allies."[21]

When the Communists suspended their violent anti-foreign and anti-Christian policies in late 1936, after Chiang Kai-shek agreed to a united front to fight the Japanese, some Congregational missionaries expressed admiration for their reform work in the countryside and applauded their suppression of banditry, opium smoking, and prostitution. They viewed the Communists "as fellow workers and fellow human beings, who were also on a crusade to save the Chinese masses from poverty and oppression." Fox Butterfield writes that the independent-minded Judd was skeptical. He was confident that Chiang Kai-shek had the Communists "licked," and believed "the Chinese masses have rejected" their program.[22]

The Communists were troubling, but a much greater, more immediate threat came from the Japanese military, which occupied Fenzhou in February 1938. Several months earlier, Miriam, four months pregnant with her third child, had left for the United States with her two daughters, traveling by way of Hong Kong, to stay with her parents in New Jersey. Walter, who was not imprisoned by the Japanese since the United States and Japan were not yet at war, stayed on to care for patients and manage the hospital. It would be nearly eleven months before he saw his family again. In a twenty-one-page letter to the Congregational mission board in Boston, he agonized over his decision to return to the United States. "I have given three and a half of the best years of my life, to the exclusion of every other interest," including his own family, to reorganize the hospital and put it on a sound financial footing. Even so, he concluded that he could do more good by returning to the United States to sound the alarm about Japanese military aggression in China.[23]

Exchanging Medicine for Politics

After the Judds settled in Minneapolis with their daughters, Walter not only practiced medicine but also gave numerous of speeches pleading for the United States to stop trading with Japan. He explained that the continued sale of oil, scrap iron and steel, trucks, aviation fuel, and other goods to the Japanese only aided their war against China. He told audiences that he had amputated the gangrenous leg of a wounded Chinese officer in Fenzhou and had removed a piece of shrapnel which was stamped with the word "Erie," which he realized was from Erie, Pennsylvania. "I carried it around in my pocket for three or four years, so I wouldn't forget."[24] During Madame Chiang's visit to the United States in 1943, he wrote to her that "it was not only senseless, it was wholly un-Christian and even criminal for American churches to be helping by their silence in the sending of scrap iron for the Japanese to shoot into the bodies of Chinese, and then to be raising money to send missionaries to take the scrap iron out."[25]

Miriam and Walter Judd with their daughters (from left to right) Carolyn, Eleanor, and Mary Lou in New Jersey, 1940.
Courtesy Mary Lou Judd Carpenter.

The US government protested Japan's "unprovoked and utterly cruel attack on China" but continued to allow Japan "unlimited access to our markets and materials," charged Judd. "We are the unofficial but indispensable partners in Japan's guilt."[26] He gave speeches to anyone who would listen—at Rotary and Kiwanis clubs, American Legion posts, chambers of commerce, trade unions, universities, and churches. In April 1939, he was invited to testify before the House Foreign Affairs Committee and the Senate Foreign Relations Committee in Washington. For her part, Miriam led a nationwide boycott of stockings made from silk imported from Japan, adopting the slogan, "American Women's Legs Can Defeat Japanese Arms."

Dispirited by the lack of response to his message, Judd gave up and focused on his medical practice. A majority of Americans had no stomach for war and, in any event, were more concerned about Hitler's aggression in Europe than Japan's bellicosity in Asia. Nevertheless, the Roosevelt administration finally limited exports of aviation fuel, steel, and scrap iron to Japan in June 1940, hoping to force its withdrawal from north China. When the Japanese invaded Indochina (Vietnam, Cambodia, and Laos) in July 1941, the United States placed an embargo on all exports to Japan, including shipments of heavy oil, which was essential to the Japanese navy.

After speaking at the Mayflower Congregational Church in Minneapolis on Sunday, December 7, 1941, Judd was driving to see a patient in the hospital when he heard reports on the radio about Japan's surprise attack on Pearl Harbor. "I remember pulling up at the side of the street, and listening to it, and thinking it was so totally unnecessary, and we'd brought it on ourselves." He concluded that the United States should learn never again to "build up our enemies at the expense of our friends."[27] (Similar misgivings about having created a "monster" through engagement with the PRC have been expressed by some American critics today.) He did not realize, as Franklin Roosevelt had feared, that US economic sanctions would lead Japan's high command to conclude that their country's survival depended on going to war with the United States. The effort to deter aggression may have sparked it.

Running for public office was not Judd's life-long ambition, but after Pearl Harbor, his Asia expertise seemed valuable. "My being in Congress was a fluke," he said later in life. "Some people have got a goal to get into politics and it eats them away. I felt it was my duty to share my experience and the dangers I saw to my own country."[28] Well known as a forceful and compelling public speaker, he was persuaded to run for Minnesota's 5th Congressional District in Minneapolis/St. Paul and was elected as a Republican. Miriam had no love for politics, but campaigned with her husband, editing and typing his speeches, and, after he was in office, sometimes filling in for him on a biweekly radio broadcast when he was overseas. She respected his dedication and passion but lamented his inability to listen and despaired over his constant absences from home while she was left to raise their three children. When he was campaigning for Eisenhower in 1952, she wrote tongue-in-cheek to her parents, "Walter still lives here, I think, as I see his shirts in the wash each week."[29]

In Judd's maiden speech on the floor of the House in February 1943, he analyzed the war in the Pacific "exactly as a doctor studies the body of a patient at the autopsy table . . . trying to see why and where we went astray." The chief reason for the war with Japan, he said, "has been because we have tended to project our own ideas and our own reactions over into the minds of people who have not had our background and who, therefore, naturally, do not have many of our ideas and our reactions."

To understand the enemy, Japan, he proceeded to make three observations. First, the Japanese are "a people of small stature," and for this reason "have had a terrific inferiority complex." Second, the Japanese are "a singularly unimaginative, uncreative people. They are efficient, determined, disciplined, capable, and as resolute as any people in the world," but their lack of innovation is "the result of centuries of regimentation." Third, because Japan constantly has been subject to typhoons, earthquakes, and volcanic eruptions, their people have become "the most moody, self-pitying, and morbidly introspective people in the world." They suffer from "a true persecution psychosis . . . . Now, when you take a nation with such a psychological background and suddenly liberate it from its inferiority complex, you have a situation that is loaded with dynamite."[30] The speech was well received— his simplistic, racist stereotypes went unchallenged in the fervor of total war—and he and Miriam were invited for lunch with Franklin and Eleanor Roosevelt at the White House, an unusual honor for a freshman member of Congress.[31]

Judd failed to mention the US government's incarceration of 120,000 Japanese citizens and non-citizens living in states west of the Mississippi because they were deemed a security threat. To his credit, however, he spoke forcefully against colonialism and imperialism, and denounced the 1924 US Immigration Act, which excluded "Orientals" from US citizenship based solely on race. Non-Caucasians, he said, had been "automatically and inescapably branded as inferior, forever condemned to a level below us—officially stigmatized . . . . We are reaping today in bloodshed what we sowed then in arrogance."[32]

As for the Chinese, the 1882 Exclusion Act, the 1892 Geary Act, and other legislation strictly limited their immigration into the United States, although students and teachers, diplomats, business owners, and temporary visitors were permitted to enter. Judd and others urged abolishing these restrictions, as well as laws that denied Chinese the right to become US citizens unless they were born in the United States. Racial discrimination was a humiliating insult to an ally fighting with the United States against Japan, said Judd. Treating China as an equal "is not starry-eyed idealism or sentimental generosity." It was essential to win China's wholehearted cooperation. He reassured his Congressional colleagues that the proposed bill "does not remove our immigration barriers." Under the existing quota system, based on the percentage of those of Chinese origin living in the United States in 1920, only 105 Chinese would be permitted to immigrate annually. Such a small number would pose no threat to American workers. The legislation, however, "would remove that stigma of biological inferiority . . . . The chief thing is the principle of being treated as equals."[33] With President Roosevelt's strong backing, Congress repealed the discriminatory laws—and the United States also gave up its extraterritorial rights in China—in December 1943.

During the Cold War, when lines were drawn between the Communist bloc and the anti-communist Free World, Judd treated US immigration policy as a humanitarian issue as well as an instrument of public diplomacy. He headed Aid Refugee Chinese Intellectuals (ARCI), an ostensibly private organization founded in New York in 1951, whose purpose was to assist with the resettlement of Chinese teachers, professors, scientists, and others who had fled Communist China, many of whom had been trained in the United States. State Department funding helped some refugees in Hong Kong to relocate to Taiwan and Southeast Asia, and Congress granted non-quota visas for others to enter the United States under the Refugee Relief Act of 1953. As Meredith Oyen writes, the ostensible purpose was to prove to Chinese and other Asians that Americans were not racist. Allowing scientists and technicians to immigrate also had the practical benefit of bringing their talents to the United States and keeping them out of Communists hands.[34]

"The Truth About China"

Judd's obsession with Japanese aggression and his fixation on communism were two sides of the same coin. In both instances, he believed there was a moral imperative for the United States to defend the Chinese from brutal forms of authoritarianism that also posed an imminent threat to the security of the United States. Communism, thought Judd, was the more dangerous of the two evils because it posed an existential threat to China's age-old culture.

After returning from a trip to China in the spring of 1945—flying from India over the Himalayan mountains to get there and back—Judd delivered a speech to Congress asking "What is the Truth About China?" According to *Time* magazine, which quoted him at length, "Of all Americans occupying elective office, the man who knows most about the Far East is almost certainly Congressman Walter H. Judd (Republican) of Minnesota."[35]

Judd acknowledged the inflation, graft, corruption, profiteering, black market activities, and censorship under the Nationalist government, but excused these failings as understandable in a country fighting a prolonged, exhausting war. "If America were to go through half of what China has gone through, for half so long, and come through in no worse condition internally, I should be astonished and proud." Speaking nearly five years before Mao Zedong seized power, Judd warned that the Chinese Communists were not the democratic "agrarian reformers" that some thought them to be; their movement was an armed rebellion against Chiang Kai-shek's legitimate government. He acknowledged the "absolute devotion" of the Communist military and the CCP's "brilliantly skillful propaganda and organization of the peasants. But it is at the price of rigid regimentation and the loss of basic freedoms." He claimed to have seen for himself, during his years as a missionary, the Communists' "utterly ruthless purges and slaughterings of anyone who crossed their will."

The United States, said Judd, needed to "cut out this irresponsible, unbalanced criticism" of Nationalist China and to "stop trying to force the Chinese to do what we think is best." Chiang's army needed more material assistance, more political assistance, and more spiritual assistance, although Judd did not favor sending US troops to fight in the mounting civil war. The Nationalists "can and will fight on valiantly and with increasing effectiveness if we will make it clear to them that this is a war for their freedom, too. That will save a good many American [military] divisions and billions of dollars. If we fail to do so," he continued, using blatantly biased language that was not uncommon at the time, "we will have two-thirds of the people in the world who are colored against the one-third who are white.... Are the Chinese, the most numerous and incomparably the strongest of the colored peoples, to stay on the side of the democracies, or are they to be driven in despair to the other side?"[36]

Judd was increasingly convinced that "the primary allegiance of the Chinese Communists is to Russia, that their purpose is to make Russia overwhelmingly the strongest power in Asia as well as in Europe." Not everyone agreed that communism was an ideology imposed by ruthless dictators who took their orders from Moscow. A lengthy *Washington Post* editorial, published in November 1947, criticized "the persistent advocacy of Representative Judd of Minnesota" for further US aid to the Nationalist government. He "has a profound respect for the Chinese people born of actual experience.... But both the love of the Chinese and the loathing of the Communists seem to have robbed him of perspective. In China, the Communist threat is not a phenomenon of Soviet expansionism." The Communists, moreover, have thrived "far more on Chiang's ineptitude than on Soviet help." China's civil war, in short, was far more national than international, wrote the *Post*. Judd's position that US aid to Western Europe should be contingent on aid to China was misguided.[37]

Judd rejected his critics. As Mao's troops gained ground in 1948, he contended on a radio program that the failure of the Nationalist government "would have the gravest consequence for Asia, for Europe, and for the United States. It would bring the vast resources and manpower of China under the control of a ruthlessly efficient Communist government, subservient to the Soviet Union. Asia would be taken under the Soviet wing almost at will . . . . The crux of the matter is this: If China is free, she can and will move rapidly toward greater democracy and better government."[38] Of course, Judd was wrong about a united communist movement directed from Moscow. Yet his belief that a "free" China would choose greater democracy would persist and shape US policy for decades to come.

When the Truman administration decided that the Nationalist government was a lost cause and a Communist victory was inevitable, members of the Republican Party seized on the issue to attack the Democrats. Senator William Knowland (R-CA), Senator H. Alexander Smith (R-NJ), and Representative Walter Judd (R-MN)—whose influence grew after he joined the House Committee on Foreign Affairs in 1947—were among the fiercest, most persistent voices in the "Who Lost China?" campaign. They leveled charges that the Democrats' actions—Roosevelt's concessions to the Soviet Union at the Yalta Conference to ensure the Russians would enter the war against Japan, George Marshall's mission to arrange for the Communists and Nationalists to share power, and delays in providing military aid to the Nationalists—were ignorant as best and treasonous at worst.

Judd joined a chorus of voices blaming US Foreign Service officers for undermining Chiang Kai-shek. There are "traitorous elements within our own government," he insisted in a letter to a constituent. "Please be assured that I shall continue to do everything in my power to ferret out these elements whose primary loyalty is to a foreign power."[39] Judd, however, did not subscribe to the extremism of Senator Joseph McCarthy or Robert Welch, founder of the John Birch Society. McCarthyism was a passing phenomenon, he thought, and Welch had gone too far in calling President Eisenhower "a dedicated, conscious agent of the Communist conspiracy." "Such actions help the Communist enemy, rather than hurt him," said Judd. "If we become like the Communists in trying to defeat them, then they have already won."[40]

Judd was closely identified with the China Lobby, a loose-knit group of like-minded Americans "united in their concern for the fate of China and the Chinese people," as he put it. They knew that "the conquest of China by either the Japanese or the Communists would prove a great disaster to our own country and to the whole world."[41] One of the group's most prominent voices was Henry R. Luce—the influential publisher of *Time* and *Life* and son of Presbyterian missionaries to China—who greatly admired Chiang Kai-shek and featured him on his magazine covers multiple times. Judd and Luce were genuinely concerned about China's future; others were political opportunists who seized on the issue to denounce the Truman administration and equated opposition to Chiang with disloyalty to the United States.[42]

Judd's advocacy was not limited to the halls of Congress. In 1946, he allied himself with the American China Policy Association (ACPA), a group that published pamphlets and issued press releases to rally support for "Free China." Based in New York and managed by Alfred Kohlberg, a wealthy textile merchant, the ACPA constituted "the backbone of the China Lobby," according to historian Joyce Mao.[43]

Containing a Worldwide Conspiracy

US diplomatic recognition of the new Beijing government was widely considered inevitable after the CCP assumed power in 1949, even with the division of the world into opposing ideological camps. That aspiration proved impossible after China's People's Volunteer Army entered the Korean War in October 1950. The horrendous loss of life during the three-year conflict defined the United States and China as mortal enemies, and Soviet military support for the Chinese forces seemed to prove beyond any shadow of a doubt that communism was a global peril directed from the Kremlin. Opposition to Red China was no longer a partisan issue for the US government; it was an article of faith for Republicans and Democrats alike. Communism should not be mistaken as an economic system or a political philosophy, said Judd. It was a worldwide conspiracy with conquest of the United States as its ultimate goal. "Communists are *not* nationalists," he insisted. "They are world revolutionists."[44]

Judd was obsessed with keeping Beijing out of the United Nations, where China's seat in the General Assembly and on the Security Council continued to be held by the Republic of China on Taiwan. Using a mixture of emotion and logic, he marshaled moral, legal, and political arguments against any compromise whatsoever. Beijing was guilty of aggression in Korea, Tibet, and Indochina, as well as the repression, enslavement, and religious persecution of its own people. Rewarding such a government would make a mockery of the United Nations, a body dedicated to human freedom and human rights. Accepting Communist China in the UN, he wrote to former President Truman, "would weaken the security of ourselves and the free world by giving legitimacy, respectability, and increased prestige and power to cruel enemies of our country."

Abandoning "one-fifth of all human beings on this planet to Communist enslavement" was unacceptable, wrote Judd for *U.S. News & World Report.* Such a course would be "not only morally wrong—it would be shortsighted and foolish." It would be "a betrayal that neither God nor man nor history could ever forgive."[45] Awarding the UN seat to Beijing would, moreover, represent a betrayal of the Nationalist government on Taiwan, a loyal ally and friend of the United States. Red China was a total dictatorship, not a "People's Republic." It was not qualified to be accepted by the society of civilized nations. It was not a law-abiding legal government. Just as Judd had advocated for a US boycott of Japanese products during the Second World War, he now backed a complete trade embargo against the new Chinese state.

Judd was especially active in the Committee of One Million Against the Admission of Communist China to the United Nations, a private organization established in 1953. Twenty-four Senators and ninety-seven Representatives from both parties were among the one million who signed a petition to oppose any concessions to Beijing. (Even before the Committee was formed, Congress had passed four resolutions opposing the PRC's admission to the United Nations.) For two decades, the Committee, based in New York and led by Marvin Liebman, railed against the evils of Red China. Judd maintained that the organization was "more responsible for the fact that most of Asia is still free than any other single factor .... I am sure that there is nothing that I have done in all my years of service as a missionary or in public life that has done as much for the good of my country as the original sponsorship of this organization."[46]

As historian Nancy Tucker has shown, President Eisenhower, who regularly consulted with Judd, was privately in favor of the PRC joining the UN, but "dreaded the possibility that China's admission would escalate demands at home that the United States withdraw" from the United Nations. The domestic political risks simply were too high to change course, and Judd's intransigence prevailed.[47]

Taking a Second Look at Recognition

Not long after the Korean War, Harvard professor Edwin Reischauer, a son of missionaries to Japan, who would serve as US ambassador to Japan during the Kennedy administration, made the case for taking "a second look at the whole question of recognizing Communist China." The hope that Chiang Kai-shek's forces could reconquer China from Formosa, as Taiwan was then known, was, in his opinion, "a mere will-o'-the-wisp, not a reasonable possibility on which we can safely stake our hopes for the future." Instead of isolating China, said Reischauer, "it is to our advantage to have as many responsible Chinese government officials as possible out in the free world participating in every possible international conference or committee."

US diplomatic recognition would not mean approval of any sort; it would simply be a "formal adjustment to a reality," argued Reischauer. Those who defend non-recognition come "dangerously close to willful self-deception." He dismissed as misguided the notion that US recognition would strengthen the Communist hold on China, although he agreed that it might "undermine the will to resist communism in other parts of Asia." But "even non-Communist Asians for the most part regard Mao's triumph as a matter of Chinese choice rather than external aggression."

It was true that China's admission to the United Nations would give the Communists "greater voting strength in this important international body," but only one veto was all that was needed to block a resolution in the Security Council. He acknowledged that the United States should stand by Formosa [Taiwan]; if China was admitted, the Republic of China should be admitted as a new country. Reischauer must have known that suggesting such a compromise was disingenuous since both the PRC and ROC rejected the concept: much as monotheistic religions believe in only one god, the concept of two Chinas was blasphemous.

Possibly his most compelling argument for recognition and admission to the United Nations was the hope that China "can be induced to break off its close and exclusive co-operation with Russia; rather than pushing the Chinese into the arms of the Russians, the United States should take advantage of China's longstanding fear of foreign domination and find ways to drive a wedge between the two communist powers." Opening up communication between the United States and China had the potential to "sow some seeds of discord" between "the proud Chinese and domineering Russians."[48] This line of reasoning foreshadowed the Sino-Soviet split a few years later, as well as Richard Nixon's logic for rapprochement with the PRC in the early 1970s.

Judd scorned all such rationales for reconciling with Beijing, which in any event had little support in Congress or from the US public. Granting recognition to China's Communist regime was "unnecessary, inadvisable and morally wrong," he said. There was no possible benefit and many dangers. Accepting the PRC "would dishearten those courageous spirits who are resisting Communism in Japan, Korea, the Philippine Islands and other countries of Southeast Asia. It would still further reduce the confidence of peoples everywhere in the maturity and dependability of American foreign policy."[49] The theory that Asian nations would fall to communism one after another in the absence of US assistance would become known as the domino theory, one of the primary justifications for Washington's ill-advised intervention in Vietnam.

Unyielding Cold Warrior

The high point of Walter Judd's political career was the keynote address he delivered at the Republican National Convention in Chicago on July 25, 1960. In an old-fashioned stem-winder of a speech he did not mention China—perhaps fearing he was too closely identified with the issue—but did defend his Cold War ideology. "The Communists," he proclaimed, "don't believe the same things we do about man and about the universe, and that means about God." The *New York Times* gave him a favorable review: "This slender, 61-year-old former surgeon speaks with a rush of nervous energy when under pressure. At other times he is quiet, almost clinical. Among his greatest assets is a reputation for absolute integrity."[50] He was touted as a possible vice-presidential running mate for Richard Nixon, who lost to John Kennedy that November. After Minnesota's Twin Cities were redistricted two years later, Judd was voted out of Congress, having served for ten terms.

Neither President Kennedy, who was leery of being soft on communism, nor President Johnson, who presided over the escalation of US military involvement in Vietnam, was able to reconsider US policy on China. Public opinion, however, began to favor some form of reconciliation, despite a steady stream of negative news reports on the chaos of Mao's Cultural Revolution. Chiang Kai-shek's calls to recover control of the mainland rang hollow, the PRC clearly was no longer an ally of the Soviet Union, and growing disillusion with the Vietnam War all raised serious doubts about US foreign policy in Asia. Much to Judd's dismay, the longstanding bipartisan consensus opposing Red China began to crumble.

In 1966, Columbia University professor Doak Barnett testified before the Senate Foreign Relations Committee, chaired by William Fulbright, that Washington's goal on China should be "containment without isolation." No longer laboring under the shadow of McCarthyism, Barnett and others established the National Committee on United States-China Relations to foster informed debate.[51] In 1967, Richard Nixon, running for the presidency a second time, wrote that the United States "could not afford to have China forever outside the family of nations, there to nurture its fantasies, cherish its hates, and threaten its neighbors."[52] The tide was turning, and on October 25, 1971, the United Nations adopted a resolution to expel Taiwan and to recognize the People's Republic of China as the only legitimate representative of China. The Committee of One Million, which had worked for eighteen years against this day, quietly closed its doors and re-organized as the Committee for a Free China.

Nixon, who was elected president in 1968, held impeccable anti-communist credentials—he had visited Taiwan six times—and Judd respected his intelligence and knowledge of foreign affairs. It therefore came as a shock when Nixon announced that he would go to Beijing in February 1972. Miriam Judd wrote that her husband was "almost wild" about Nixon's meeting with Mao. Walter "cannot see one good thing coming out of it all, only disaster, and his anguish and hopelessness are hard to live with." So far as Judd was concerned, "Mao's regime represents nobody but itself: a self-selected, self-imposed, self-perpetuating clique—a total dictatorship that announces its determination to destroy the Chinese culture. We should be proper and correct in our relations with the PRC—it is there. But we don't need to bow down before tyrants or effervesce about them or pretend they aren't what undeniably they are."[53]

For Judd, President Carter's decision to establish full diplomatic relations with the PRC and break with Taiwan in 1979 (see Chapter 5) was a nothing less than betrayal. "To de-recognize, without cause and without any provocation, and in violation of our pledged word, our loyal ally, the Republic of

China on Taiwan, which had stood with us and fought on our side—this is one of the most unworthy actions in history."[54]

Judd stayed faithful to Taiwan for the rest of his days. During a 1986 visit to Taipei marking the hundredth anniversary of Chiang Kai-shek's birth, he eulogized the Generalissimo, who had died eleven years earlier, as a man of vision, quiet courage, steadfast patience and strength, and a calm faith. Judd had met Chiang in Chongqing, China's wartime capital, saw him in Nanjing in 1947, and visited him and Madame Chiang in Taiwan on a few occasions during the 1950s and 1960s. "I supported the Nationalist regime as by all odds better for the Chinese people than Communist or Japanese control—and, clearly, better for the United States; [Nationalist] China was still a loyal ally and friend of ours in peace as in war."[55]

In contrast to Mao's attacks on the "feudal past," Taiwan was working to preserve traditional Chinese values and culture. "They've demonstrated for the whole world to see what the Chinese people can and will do *if free*." Largely ignoring the political repression of the Nationalists, Judd boasted about Taiwan's "remarkable progress in land reform, housing, health, highways, education, village industries, manufacturing, prosperity, freedom of travel, residence, choice of jobs, plus increasing political freedom and increasing freedom of speech and of the press."[56] In fact, after decades of martial law, the island became a democracy during the presidency of Chiang Ching-kuo, Chiang Kai-shek's eldest son, in the late 1980s.

Deng Xiaoping's bloody crackdown on the Tiananmen Square protesters in 1989 was evidence to Judd that communism had failed. China's leaders have "exposed themselves until even the blindest can see that they are barbarians; they're not true Chinese," he told an audience in Washington, DC. "Tyrants have almost always looked invincible until the last five minutes and then all of a sudden they fell apart."[57] It was, of course, wishful thinking. Determined to avoid the fate of regimes in the Soviet Union and Eastern Europe in the 1990s, the Chinese Communist Party engaged in successive reforms that allowed the regime to adapt, survive, and prosper, much to the dismay of its opponents.

Full of Contradictions

"I didn't like being in politics. I never did," Judd confessed late in his life. "I'm a scientist by training and I like to deal with exact things."[58] Politics, of

Walter Judd with Chiang Kai-shek and Soong Mei-ling (Madame Chiang) in Taipei, Taiwan, 1953.
Walter Henry Judd Papers, Hoover Institution Archives.

course, is not an exact science, but that did not deter him from categorizing communism as a disease that must be eradicated. His moral absolutism was rooted in the conviction that the Chinese would never choose an oppressive alien creed of their own free will.

Judd was a pragmatic idealist who cautioned against wishful thinking, but his mind was full of contradictions. Curiously, his dogmatism went hand-in-hand with considerable open-mindedness. "Sometimes I think our intolerable arrogance regarding other peoples is surpassed only by our incredible ignorance of them," he once said. "We tend to judge China, not in terms of China's own past but in terms of the West.... All through history people have been trying to force the Chinese to do this or that. No one has yet succeeded for long."[59]

He opposed colonialism and imperialism and decried the narrowness and paternalism of Western missionaries, but was determined to save the

Chinese from communism. He was an internationalist who supported the United Nations, but insisted that the PRC was not qualified for membership. He spoke out against racism and advocated for immigration reform, but condemned the Chinese Communists as outcasts. He preached democracy, but excused Chiang Kai-shek's authoritarian rule. He recognized the limits of anyone's ability to change China, but persisted in believing the United States could influence the course of events.

When Ronald Reagan, a long-time friend of Taiwan, awarded Judd the prestigious Presidential Medal of Freedom in a White House ceremony in 1981, he introduced him as "a doctor who ministered to the world's need for freedom and liberty." "Freedom," said Judd in response, "has been central to the efforts I made as a missionary in China, and as a political missionary in the House of Representatives and, in these last 19 years, as what might perhaps be called 'missionary-at-large,' especially to the colleges and high schools of our country, working with the youth to help develop a deeper understanding of what freedom makes possible."[60]

Stubborn, passionate, determined, and uncompromising, Judd refused to soften his hardline stance toward the PRC, even as the course of events turned against him. He was rendered a political dinosaur, an anachronistic ideologue both out of favor and out of touch, dismissed as a relic who persisted in defending a lost cause. To the end of his life—he died of cancer in 1994—he was unwilling to cast aside his Cold War armor. He was fatalistic about the fact that history had passed him by, insisting "there won't be any real solution to problems in the Pacific until the Chinese people are free again. That doesn't suggest any invasion of the mainland, or use of force from without. It does mean that we should not help build up the tyrants on the mainland. The Chinese will ultimately pull them down, I am confident, if only we don't help build them up. We don't have to take hostile action; we can just wait—as the Oriental does. He has patience; we don't. We demand a quick solution—and it can't be achieved that rapidly. We must do better at this."[61]

Judd's prejudice and obstinacy are easy to dismiss, yet his core concerns about the repressive nature of communism have renewed currency today. Indeed, debate in the United States about an unexpectedly powerful China finds Judd's explicit fear at its core: Was the United States wrong to actively assist a future competitor some consider an enemy? The other side of the argument is that engagement bought forty years of peace, contributed to a better life for more than 20 percent of the world's population, and planted the seeds for positive change in the PRC.

The next chapter presents a little-known aspect of the Korean War that stands as a counterpoint to Walter Judd's intense hostility to the PRC. Despite the fact that communism was well understood as a dire threat to US interests and values, a small number of American soldiers who fought in Korea choose to live in the People's Republic rather than returning home to the United States when the war was over. They exercised their freedom of choice in a way that almost no one could imagine.

2

Clarence Adams and Morris Wills

Searching for Utopia

Twenty-one US prisoners of war (POWs) chose to live in China instead of returning home at the end of the Korean War, a token number compared with the 4,300 American prisoners who went back to the United States. It was enough, however, for the Communist Chinese government to make a propaganda statement about the superiority of their socialist system.[1]

The twenty-one were ordinary Americans, not much different from other GIs who fought in Korea. All of them were enlisted men and their average age was twenty-three. Only one was a draftee, and two had served in the Pacific during the Second World War. None was wealthy or advantaged. Three were married. Sixteen were Protestants, four were Roman Catholics, and one was Greek Orthodox. Eighteen were White and three were Black.[2]

Their decision to refuse repatriation underscored the confusing, unpopular nature of the conflict—fought mainly between China and the United States—which ended in a stalemate on Korea's 38th Parallel, exactly where it had started three years earlier, with the peninsula divided between a communist north and anti-communist south. Unlike previous US wars, there was no clear-cut victory. Yet the idea that *any* American soldier would turn his back on his country in favor of the enemy was baffling to the public. Why would these men leave their families for a repressive, tyrannical regime like Red China?

Before going to China, the POWs, as well as one British marine, were brought by trucks to the Demilitarized Zone in Panmunjom where an armistice agreement had been signed. Singing songs and waving banners, they participated in a press conference where they affirmed their decision: "Our greatest concern is to fight for peace and freedom, not only for ourselves but for the American people and people of the world," they proclaimed. When peace and freedom were achieved in the United States, they would return to their homes. For now, according to China's official *People's Daily*, it was "out of the question" for them to go back "because of McCarthyism, lynchings, and ethnic persecution." The non-repatriates had decided to reject racism and imperialism, said the article: "Washington's psychological warfare program has met with another fatal blow."[3]

Clarence Adams and Morris Wills were among this group of men who were branded as "turncoats" by the US press, the only two who subsequently wrote books about their experiences. They were neither radicals nor revolutionaries. Angry and disheartened by the war, curious and hopeful about China, they were inadvertently caught up in a fierce ideological contest to demonstrate the ascendancy of one way of life over the other.

The odyssey of these two soldiers foreshadowed the 1960s when some Americans, disaffected by social injustice and political discord in the United States, imagined the Chinese had succeeded in creating a people's paradise free of racism and other ills. Their experience was a frequently repeated syndrome in foreigners' encounters with China: initial infatuation, full of wonder and adulation, followed by disillusion and disenchantment.

A Tale of Two "Turncoats"

Clarence Adams and Morris Wills were strikingly different, not only because one was Black and from the south and the other was White and from the north. Adams was an exuberant personality who loved dancing, singing, drinking, and sports. He took risks and was quick to anger. Wills, by contrast, was careful, cautious, and introspective. He was the studious, taciturn outsider who found solace in reading books and became a librarian later in life. What both men shared was a hope for a better life and a hunger for social justice born of despair over their fate as prisoners.

Clarence Cecil Adams grew up in the segregated city of Memphis, Tennessee during the 1930s. His nickname was Skippy because he was such a happy, active kid, although he never knew his father, and his mother, by his account, showed little interest in him. He wore hand-me-down clothes and attended a school for African American children who "mostly played in streets because we did not have access to parks or swimming pools." In those days, he remembered, "black teachers taught only black students, black doctors treated exclusively black patients, and black mailmen delivered mail only to blacks." They were allowed to shop on Main Street but could not eat anywhere or use restrooms reserved for Whites. "That's the kind of society

I grew up in. It was shameful and unforgivable, especially when you consider we were all Americans."[4]

Adams learned to survive by his wits from an early age. He was short in stature, but quick and tough. "I was a hustler, which meant I always knew where and how to make a buck." In winter, he would steal coal through holes in a fence around the Chickasaw Coal Yard. In church, he would pocket pennies meant for the collection plate and buy candy instead. At the start of his final year in high school in 1947, he wounded a boy in a knife fight. In another incident earlier that same day, he had been with a group of friends by the railroad tracks, where they beat up a White man who kept asking them where they could find him a Black woman. When the police came looking for Adams, he panicked, ran out the back door, and enlisted in the Army at the nearest recruiting station.[5]

Adams spent a year with an African American military unit in Korea—before the war broke out—where he learned to eat kimchi and drink rice wine, and another year in Japan where he enjoyed boxing on the local army post team, had a Japanese girlfriend, and won money playing poker and shooting craps. He was at Fort Lewis, Washington, on the verge of being discharged, when the North Koreans invaded South Korea in June 1950. His enlistment was extended for twelve months and Adams was shipped back to Korea where he was assigned to an all-Black artillery battalion, first as an ammo bearer and then as a gunner. President Harry Truman had ordered the end of a segregated US military in 1948, but it was not until after the Korean War, in 1954, that Black units were disbanded.

"Initially, I believed we were there to help the Korean people, that we were freeing them from North Korean Communists so they could enjoy the fruits of democracy," wrote Adams. His doubts grew as he witnessed long lines of refugees and saw "young kids and old women lying dead alongside the roads." Aside from the horrors of war, he was disillusioned by discrimination in the army and believed that his Black regiment had been sacrificed to save White soldiers. "I could not understand how white America expected us to fight hard overseas when we were treated so badly at home. How could we really believe we were fighting for our country?"

Adams was captured on November 30, 1950, a few days after the Chinese People's Volunteer Army entered the war. In sub-zero temperatures, with frostbitten feet and an infected right leg, he barely survived a forced march to a camp near the Yalu River on the border between Korea and China. Conditions there were appalling, with no hot meals, no beds, no blankets, and no medicine, remembered Adams. Food was limited to corn, beans, or sorghum. Their wooden huts were so small that the men's legs would stretch over each other while they slept. Prisoners started to die from untreated wounds, malnutrition, and disease. "You could not walk anywhere without stepping in feces."[6]

———

Morris Robert Wills, who was captured about six months after Adams, had an equally harrowing experience as a prisoner in Korea. Born in 1933, Wills was the third of five children growing up on a farm in the Adirondack Mountains southwest of Lake George. His mother died from cancer when he was twelve years old, and he was not close to his father. He had no strong religious convictions or political beliefs, very little money, no girlfriend, and had never traveled far from home. A teenager with few prospects other than working on the family farm, he dropped out of high school and joined the US Army in 1950.

Wills "didn't have the faintest idea" where Korea was when the army shipped him there in January 1951. He went into combat soon after arriving, was seriously wounded, and spent a month in a Swedish Red Cross hospital near the port city of Pusan. On recovering, he was sent back to the front lines as a machine gunner. A few months later, his platoon was in a pitched battle for control of a hill; after fighting for three days he was captured by Chinese troops on May 18.[7]

Wills was marched northward, climbing peak after peak, with American, Australian, British, Dutch, Filipino, and Turkish prisoners, members of the United Nations (UN) Command who were fighting against the Chinese and North Koreans. They slept under trees during the day and moved at night under the cover of darkness to avoid bombing and strafing by US planes. Their Chinese guards were not violent or cruel—Wills called them "indifferent" and "disciplined"—but there was very little to eat, everyone was infested with lice, and many came down with dysentery. After a few weeks, "it was common to wake up and find the man next to you dead," wrote Wills. No one had the strength to attempt an escape; some men simply gave up trying to live.

Weeks after being captured, Wills arrived at a POW camp controlled by the Chinese close to the Yalu River. "There was not a person among us whose ribs you couldn't count." Yet there was a sense of relief at reaching the end of their grueling journey, and it seemed there was nothing more to worry about; they could just wait for the war to end. No one expected the conflict to drag on for two more years.

Wills and nine other men slept on the floor of a twelve-foot-square room with mud walls; later they were able to build bunk beds. Their food improved, and the Chinese provided them with padded blue-cotton uniforms as cold weather set in. Marijuana was growing wild all around the camp, and many prisoners smoked it until stopped by the guards. They were allowed to organize sports teams, and Wills enjoyed playing volleyball. Although the hope of being rescued grew more distant as time wore on, "the fear that you were going to be shot or that you wouldn't make it through was also more remote."[8]

In the camps, their captors subjected the POWs to political education, lecturing them about the Russian revolution and how foreigners had mistreated the Chinese. A number of the instructors spoke fluent English, since they had studied at Christian-run high schools and colleges in China. "They told us that the U.S. was an imperialist country and wanted to dominate the world and that the Korean War was only part of a master plan. They taught that we were all ordinary workers and that we had been deceived into fighting for the capitalists." Never having heard of Marxism and knowing almost nothing about communism, Wills found himself unprepared to counter arguments about poverty, unemployment, racism, and crime in the United States. Eventually, the Chinese gave up on the mass indoctrination lectures—which most of the Americans did not take seriously—in favor of voluntary study groups and libraries where prisoners were free to drop by and read approved books and magazines.

Choosing China

The POWs were divided into two groups: progressives, who were sympathetic to communism, and reactionaries, who were opposed. Some 80 percent were not classified one way or the other. Officers were moved to a camp separate from enlisted men, and African Americans, who numbered 120, were segregated from several thousand Whites after racial incidents broke out between them. The progressives wrote articles, signed peace petitions, and made propaganda recordings for the Chinese. In exchange, they were rewarded with better living conditions, food, and medical treatment. Adams and Wills sided with the progressives, whom the reactionaries scorned as informers and traitors.

Wills was dismayed that the United States had the power to win the war but refused to do so. President Truman had relieved General Douglas MacArthur of his command after he advocated taking the war across the border into China. The United States, moreover, had the atomic bomb but would not even threaten to use it. Disgusted, lonely, and depressed as the war dragged on, Wills was vulnerable to the blandishments of Chinese propaganda. Reading about China and talking with his captors gradually won him over to their point of view. "Before I was a prisoner, I thought China was a terrible tyranny where innocent people were shot and killed and put into prison." What Wills now discovered was completely different. Communism "seemed like a very orderly, systematic way of organizing society; no one was very rich, and no one was very poor. Everyone shared equally, more or less."[9]

After two years in captivity, Wills felt abandoned by the army, which he believed had left him to rot. "It didn't look like I'd ever get out of there. Not any of us." This was because negotiations between China and the United States over the fate of the prisoners had become a political test of strength that prolonged the war by eighteen months, doubling the time that many men spent in the camps. One POW from Georgia wrote to his girlfriend back home, "I wonder if they are going to wait until all we boys go crazy or die of old age before they finally end this thing."[10]

The core problem was that thousands of captured Chinese troops—many of whom were former Nationalist army soldiers conscripted by the Communists during and after the civil war—had no desire to return to China. The PRC demanded the repatriation of all their prisoners being held by United Nations Command, which the United States refused to do. As Charles S. Young explains, the Truman administration seized on the issue, realizing that *voluntary* repatriation "would be a humiliating political defeat for the enemy and demonstrate American commitment to individual rights and dignity."[11] Voluntary repatriation meant that individual POWs on both sides could decide whether or not to return to their home countries.

By the war's end, 7,109 Chinese had returned to the PRC where, as David Chang has documented, they faced "lifetime stigma and persecution." Twice as many, 14,342, went to Taiwan, where some were lauded as "anti-Communist heroes" and 97.4 percent "volunteered" to join the Nationalist military. It was a striking defeat for the PRC, although not all of the men made the decision to refuse repatriation of their own free will; many had been terrorized, even branded with tattoos, by fellow prisoners in camps on Koje and Cheju islands off the South Korean coast.[12]

During the protracted negotiations, Chinese cadres encouraged their UN prisoners to write letters home, sign petitions, and make public statements appealing for peace and praising the treatment they were receiving. The most damaging propaganda, however, was the charge that the United States had engaged in germ warfare. Thirty-eight out of 224 captured US Air Force fliers made forced confessions. In their statements, which they later recanted, they admitted to dropping canisters with infected insects and diseased microbes from their planes. When some of the pilots spoke about their alleged crimes at the POW camps, Adams and Wills weren't sure what to think. If it was true that the United States had used biological weapons, it was one more reason to doubt the US government's claim that it was fighting a just and moral war.[13]

Initially, the Chinese Communists hoped the progressive prisoners would return to their home countries and become a revolutionary vanguard advocating for socialism. When it became clear that significant numbers of Chinese and Korean prisoners would refuse repatriation, the Communists switched gears and decided to recruit Americans to defect to the PRC. Those who expressed an interest were promised an education and jobs, and were told they could marry, although they also were warned that China was poor, backward, and had different customs from the United States.

The selection process was not random. The overriding question was whether those who wished to go to China were sincere and could be trusted; three men were rejected as being unreliable. To ensure that their decisions had not been made under duress, the United Nations and Chinese authorities agreed that anyone who opted for non-repatriation would spend ninety days in a neutral zone monitored by the Indian Army. Some American mothers asked to meet with their sons during this period, but the Department of Defense denied their requests. Clarence Adams's mother, Gladys "Toosie" Adams, traveled from Memphis to Chicago to record a radio message, pleading with him to return home, but it is unlikely he heard it. During this waiting period, two of the Americans, Edward Dickenson and Claude Batchelor, who was married to a Japanese woman, changed their minds and asked to return to the United States. They were tried in a US military court, imprisoned, and released after serving sentences of three and a half years.[14]

Various reasons were offered to explain why the twenty-one men "renounced their own country and disappeared behind Red China's bamboo curtain," as one journalist put it. According to an article in *U.S. News & World*

Report, "a majority of those Americans refusing to come home appear to have earned the contempt or hatred of their fellow prisoners" because they had sided with the enemy. Once an informer "crosses the line and betrays others, he becomes the puppet of his captors," said one former prisoner. "Rats" and "stool pigeons" went to China out of fear that they would be tried for treason. The author of the piece admitted that "others probably were genuinely convinced that the Reds offered them a brighter future." Another story described the defectors as "lonely, bitter men who felt betrayed by fellow Americans. They were in a mood to swallow the Communist line . . . . They were unable to acquire the self-discipline needed to resist despair in prison camps [and] all of them appeared sullen and shifty-eyed."[15]

Journalist Virginia Pasley went around the United States to the hometowns of the GIs who stayed behind, including those of Adams and Wills, to conduct interviews with their families and friends. She concluded the men were "vulnerable" and "pitifully ill-equipped to withstand the psychological warfare the Reds waged against them."[16] A US Army commission confirmed that US soldiers were unprepared to resist Chinese propaganda; they had very little understanding of communism or why they were fighting in Korea. Neither did the American public grasp what thousands of men who languished in prison camps had been through. When the war ended, most veterans were not welcomed home as heroes but were regarded with distrust.

Long known as the "Forgotten War," it was not until 1995 that the Korean War Veterans Memorial was dedicated in Washington, DC. For the Chinese, however, the war is remembered as a major victory over US imperialism. The *New York Times* reported that the seventieth anniversary of China's entry into the war was celebrated in October 2020 "with a barrage of commemorative events, exhibitions, television documentaries and feature films." At a time of severe tensions between the United States and China, all of this conveyed a single message: "The Chinese people have stood up to the United States before and, regardless of the costs, they will again."[17]

The Power of Thought Reform

Brainwashing was by far the most popular explanation for the defection of American soldiers and the confessions of US pilots in Korea. It was Edward Hunter, a newspaper man who served with the OSS (forerunner of the CIA) during World War II, who popularized the term. According to his theory, the Communists had developed the ability to manipulate thinking and alter minds through subtle but ruthless indoctrination techniques. The POWs, in other words, had not acted of their own free will, but had been seduced by an insidious, unnatural force which threatened the entire non-communist world.

"Brainwashing is not done with electrodes stuck to your head; you are not turned into a robot obeying the orders of a Chinese master," Wills wrote. "What we call 'brainwashing' is a long, horrible process by which a man slowly, step by step, idea by idea, becomes totally convinced, as I was, that the Chinese Communists have unlocked the secret to man's happiness and that the United States is run by rich bankers, McCarthy types and 'imperialist aggressors.'"[18] Richard Condon's 1959 book *The Manchurian Candidate*, which was made into a major movie, tapped into these fears. The main character, a Korean War veteran, is brainwashed while being held as a prisoner and becomes the victim of a communist conspiracy after returning to the United States.

What Americans called brainwashing, the Chinese referred to as thought reform (*xixiang gaizao*). It was "the greatest campaign in human history to reshape the minds of men," according to Harriet C. Mills, an American scholar who was the daughter of Presbyterian missionaries in China. She received a Fulbright scholarship to study Chinese literature in Beijing in 1947, but was prevented from leaving the PRC at the start of the Korean War, was arrested in July 1951, accused of being a spy, and spent over four years in a prison for counter-revolutionaries. "No other Communist or authoritarian state, not even the Soviet Union, has ever equaled the scope and intensity of the Chinese Communist effort," Mills wrote for the *Atlantic Monthly* after her release. She explained that every office, factory, shop, school, commune, and military or residential unit in China is organized into a small study group. These groups meet regularly to persuade people to reject old ideas and accept the new ones mandated by the Communist Party. Everyone must participate and express an opinion—even political prisoners. Correct thinking is achieved through public criticism and self-criticism meetings, also known as struggle sessions. Either you conform to the Party line, or you are ostracized and treated as an outcast.[19]

Morris Wills—whose book *Turncoat: An American's 12 Years in Communist China* was published at the height of the Vietnam War—described the struggle sessions as "the glue that binds Communist China together" and compared the process to a religious conversion experience: you write your autobiography to confess past sins and realize that you must repent. "Once it's over, you feel better. A sense of exhilaration comes over you. You walk out feeling you have cleansed yourself." One learns "to put collective interests before your own self, absolutely and totally."[20]

Pursuing the Chinese Dream

At a celebration the night before leaving the neutral zone in Korea, the non-repatriates and their Chinese handlers all got very drunk. The next morning, dressed in Western-style suits and hats, they were photographed as they boarded a special train traveling northward to the border. Wills remembered it was "very dark, very gray, very cold" when they crossed the Yalu River at four o'clock in the morning on February 24, 1954. Upon reaching the Chinese city of Dandong, they were welcomed with a sumptuous banquet.[21]

The former prisoners were featured in the PRC's media as "peace fighters." Then, under the watchful care of the Red Cross Society of China, they were sent to the industrial city of Taiyuan in Shanxi Province, two hundred miles southwest of Beijing, out of the sight of foreign diplomats and journalists. "It was as though we had entered the U.S. at New York and been sent to a city in Wyoming," recalled Wills. His only connection with the outside world was listening to Voice of America on a short-wave radio. Adams was more positive than Wills: "Most of the Chinese in Taiyuan were very friendly. They had seen a lot of Russians, so they were accustomed to foreigners."[22]

An invitation to tour Beijing was a welcome break from their relative isolation, and they attended May Day celebrations where they sat with dignitaries in the review stands to watch a parade passing through Tiananmen Square. When they returned to Taiyuan, Rufus Douglas, from Texon, Texas, died from a heart condition. The Chinese insisted on arranging a Christian funeral for him.

For six months, the Americans were taught a Marxist version of Chinese history and were subjected to an intense program of ideological purification, even though they had already gone through political training during their time in the POW camps. To Wills, it seemed like a form of punishment because the additional indoctrination implied that his loyalty was in question.

The POWs presented something of a conundrum for their hosts since they did not fit easily into any established ideological categories. They were neither "foreign friends" nor enemies, revolutionaries nor counter-revolutionaries, peasants nor landlords, workers nor capitalists. They had no particular role to play in the ongoing mass campaigns deemed essential for overthrowing the old "feudal" system in order to achieve a classless, egalitarian society. The soldiers who had fought for the US imperialists had been valuable for propaganda purposes, but Wills came to believe that "once we reached China, we became a liability, a problem. We'd been used and were being gradually discarded."[23]

In the fall of 1954, nine of the former soldiers, including Adams and Wills, were selected to study Chinese language, history, and politics at People's University in Beijing. They were treated well, but lived and studied separately from other students, aside from a few from the Soviet Union and Czechoslovakia. Small-group and self-criticism meetings continued, and the Chinese who befriended them were usually official "minders" who would report on their activities. Dating Chinese women was discouraged, but some of the Americans spent time with women who wanted to marry a foreigner to escape China or consorted with prostitutes. A few had White Russian girlfriends, descendants of a stateless diaspora who found refuge in China after the Bolshevik revolution.[24]

The eleven POWs who did not qualify for a university education were assigned work as tractor technicians at a state farm in Henan Province or at a paper mill in Shandong. Three of those on the farm were the first to leave China, by way of Hong Kong, in 1955, and Chinese authorities did not stand in their way. Lewis Griggs, from the small town of Neches in the red clay hills of East Texas, had been a stretcher bearer in a medical company in Korea. Otho Bell was a country boy from Mississippi who married a few months before shipping out to Korea and had never seen his daughter, born just before he was captured. He told a *New York Times* reporter that he was led to China by "a great dream," but the dream had gone wrong. William Cowart of Dalton, Georgia, who was captured three weeks into the Korean War, said communism was worse than Hitler: "Hitler destroyed the body, communism destroys the soul."[25]

A US court dismissed desertion charges against the three men because the army no longer had legal jurisdiction over them; they had been dishonorably discharged after their names were dropped from the rolls by the Secretary of Defense in January 1954. Learning that they would not be punished upon return to the States, two more POWs left China in 1956 and another two in 1957. One of them, David Hawkins from Oklahoma City, was a truck driver in Wuhan who married a Russian woman who had grown up in China. Thirteen of the original twenty-one now remained.

By 1956, Wills had good command of the Chinese language and was the only American given the privilege of studying literature at the top-ranked Peking University. His first year was the best. At six-feet two-inches, he was welcomed by the university's basketball team, played center, and became a star. There were no more self-criticism sessions and much freer contact between Chinese and foreigners, predominantly from Eastern European countries, North Korea, and Vietnam; one was from Thailand. In the building where Wills lived, most of the residents were Chinese professors and teaching assistants. During his second year, he was assigned a Russian roommate named Sasha, and they conversed in Chinese. His next roommate, Per-Olow Leijon, was a Swedish student who remembered Wills as "thoughtful and clever." Leijon never spent the night in the same room with Wills since he was always with his girlfriend from Ceylon (now Sri Lanka) who lived in the same building.[26]

In August 1957, Wills spoke with several members of a visiting American youth group about living in the PRC. "Before coming to China," he told them over lunch in the university cafeteria, "I had some primitive ideas about the Chinese people wearing pigtails and acting the way they are portrayed in movies and comic strips." He had no definite plans for returning to the United States. "I like it here and like the people. I want to complete my studies." He was not concerned about his safety or that of the other former US soldiers still in China. The Chinese felt no hostility toward the average American, he said, "but they don't like the American government's policy toward socialist countries." As for romance, said Wills, "Chinese girls—and men—are more bashful than American ones. It just takes a little longer here."[27]

In 1958, Mao's ambitions to catapult China into the future led to a series of disasters, starting with the Great Leap Forward, a mass industrialization movement that, along with floods and drought, contributed to widespread famine. Food was rationed, and people from the countryside streamed into the cities. Wills was better off than most since he ate in a dining hall reserved for foreigners and had access to Friendship Stores where he could purchase goods unavailable to most Chinese citizens. People who knew him would drop by to talk about their hardships, how their children were starving, and would ask for his help. "I couldn't give things to everyone; it was impossible." Over the next three years, however, he bought and distributed at least a thousand cans of sardines.[28]

While at Peking University, Wills was introduced to eighteen-year-old Kaiyen Li, who was born in Guangdong, lived in Hong Kong after age ten, and had been sent to stay with her uncle in Beijing for high school. When Li and Wills persisted in seeing each other, she was arrested on trumped up charges of stealing from him—probably at the behest of the uncle, who opposed their relationship. Letters that Wills wrote to officials proclaiming her innocence were ignored. She was jailed, with no trial, in the nearby city of Tianjin, where she was held for ten months before being released. "She was very thin and frightened," he remembered. It was shocking that anyone "could be so brutal just because two people were in love." When they were married on November 22, 1961, the Red Cross Society organized a party for them. Whatever misgivings Wills may have had about China were amplified by Li's harsh treatment.[29]

Being Black in China

It was no accident that three of the POWs who went to China were African Americans: Clarence Adams from Memphis; LaRance Sullivan from Santa Barbara, California; and William C. White from Plummersville, Arkansas. (Sullivan returned to the United States in 1958 and White, who married a Chinese woman, left in 1965.) They were recruited to show the world that the Chinese Communist Party treated all people as equals. "White, Sullivan and I had our own reasons for going to China," wrote Adams. "We wanted to escape the racism we had suffered in our own country and in the military as well. We also wanted an education, a decent job, and to be treated with respect . . . . I wanted to be treated like a human being instead of something subhuman." He told Chinese cadres during his imprisonment in Korea, "I do not want to go back to America because I am hoping for better life than the one I left in the United States."[30]

China, in fact, had no legal system of racial segregation, no discriminatory Jim Crow laws, as in the United States. Minorities, who represent a very small percentage of the overall population, have equal rights under the PRC's constitution. Under Maoism, social prejudice and bigotry derived not from the color of one's skin so much as class background; peasants, workers, and soldiers were glorified, while landlords, business people, and intellectuals were vilified.

After two years at People's University, Adams transferred to Wuhan University in central China where he studied Chinese language and literature. He wanted a climate warmer than Beijing, he said, because of the pain of frostbitten toes from the Korean War. He was happy to find that instead of being scorned as an American who had been shooting at Chinese soldiers, he was accepted as a fellow student. "We would talk, sing songs, exercise, and take walks together," and during the first year or so there was a dance at the gym every Saturday night.

Adams thought of himself as a working-class man with no particular interest in ideology or politics, despite the fact that his presence served a political purpose. He spent time with cafeteria workers who would cook something, and then "we'd sit down and eat, drink, and tell jokes." He played sports, introduced students to softball, and became quite good at ping-pong. He enjoyed physical labor and cheerfully volunteered to go to the countryside with his Chinese classmates to help build a railroad. He recalled these as "the happiest years of my life."[31]

North Korean friends introduced Adams to Linfeng Liu, a graduate from Wuhan University who was teaching Russian at Wuhan Polytechnic University. She lived under a political shadow because her father had been a prominent military general allied with Chiang Kai-shek. After a year of courting, everyone in Liu's family was pleased when they decided to marry, except for the brother of her sister's husband, who was a dean at Wuhan University. "He had studied at the University of Chicago in the 1940s and had accepted the prevailing white attitudes toward blacks," wrote Adams. The brother told Linfeng, " 'If you really want to marry an American, at least marry a white man.' " A bureaucrat at her university was also opposed, but officials with the Red Cross Society intervened and they were married in a simple ceremony, followed by a big reception, in December 1957. (Until 1988, intermarriage between Chinese and foreigners required special permission from the government.)[32]

When Chinese friends heard the news that Linfeng was pregnant, they were curious about what the baby would look like. She was anxious as well, but Clarence assured her that he had seen many "mixed-blood" babies when he was stationed in Japan and "they all looked just fine." Their daughter Della was born in January 1959, toward the beginning of the devastating famine. Adams and his wife mostly ate vegetables and rice at the school cafeteria, and had difficulty getting milk for their infant. What he remembered best was the generosity of a farmer who gave them an egg and a fisherman who brought two fish for the child. Their son Louis was born in 1964.[33]

———

During the 1950s and 1960s, Beijing took advantage of racial discord in the United States to promote Communist China as a "non-white power that had suffered at the hands of foreign imperialism," as historian Gregg Brazinsky explains. Mao wrote two essays condemning racial discrimination and supporting the Black struggle for equality in the United States. Chinese propaganda aimed at Asian and African nations depicted the PRC as an inspirational alternative to the West. China could lead the way since it had triumphed over colonialism, imperialism, and racism.

Important foreign visitors were welcomed with gifts, free travel, elaborate banquets, and meetings with high-ranking Party leaders. Publications, films, musical performances, acrobatic troupes, trade delegations, and cultural exchange groups were sent abroad to foster an image of shared purpose with people of color and to convince them that China "was more worthy of their trust than the United States," writes Brazinsky. The US government, concerned about the success of Beijing's message, "urged the citizens of newly independent countries to envision themselves as part of a society of Free World nations while representing China as a threat." Washington also pointed out discrimination and unrest in the Chinese-controlled minority areas of Tibet and Xinjiang.[34]

The Chinese Communist Party made a special point of cultivating sympathetic Black American dissidents and civil rights leaders, the most distinguished of whom was W. E. B. Du Bois, one of the founders of the NAACP.[35] He and Shirley Graham Du Bois, his wife, toured China as honored guests for two months in 1959, and Clarence Adams was thrilled to meet with them in their hotel room when they visited the city of Wuhan. On that same trip, Dr. and Mrs. Du Bois had lunch with Mao Zedong at his villa near Wuhan's East Lake. Mao, in a lighthearted mood, proved to be extremely well-informed about US as well as international politics.[36]

In his autobiography, Du Bois extolled the virtues of Chinese socialism as compared with the exploitation of workers in the West. Those in America have more material goods, he admitted, but "the Chinese worker is happy. He has exorcised the Great Fear that haunts the West; the fear of losing his job; the fear of falling sick; the fear of accident; the fear of inability to educate his

Chairman Mao welcoming W. E. B. Du Bois at a villa near the East Lake in
Wuhan, April 1959.
Special Collections and University Archives, W.E.B. Du Bois Library, University of Massachusetts
Amherst.

children; the fear of daring to take a vacation . . . . I have seen the world," he
wrote. "But never so vast and glorious a miracle as China."[37]

For Du Bois, China's self-reliance stood as a shining example of independence for the oppressed peoples of Africa. In Beijing, on the occasion
of his ninety-first birthday, he addressed an audience of more than one
thousand at Peking University, expounding about China as an exemplar
for Africa.

China after long centuries has arisen to her feet and leapt forward. Africa arise, and stand straight, speak and think! Act! Turn from the West and your slavery and humiliation for the last 500 years . . . . You know America and France and Britain to your sorrow. Now know the Soviet Union and its allied nations, but particularly know China. China is flesh of your flesh and blood of your blood. China is colored, and knows to what the colored skin in this modern world subjects its owner . . . . Come to China, Africa, and look around . . . . Stand together in this new world and let the old world perish in its greed or be born again in new hope and promise.[38]

As part of its political and cultural diplomacy, the PRC provided scholarships for African students to study in China as an expression of "the eternal friendship of the African and Chinese peoples." But official regulations meant to protect and treat them as honored guests sometimes succeeded in driving them away. One especially disgruntled student was John Emmanuel Hevi, who arrived from Ghana in November 1960 and enrolled in Peking Medical School after one year of Chinese language study. From his perspective, political indoctrination, censorship, isolation from Chinese students (his "friends" were often informers), and the uniformity of socialist society (everyone wore the same blue clothing) made life alienating and "unbearably dull." He was uneasy about the preferential treatment of foreign students who, unlike the Chinese, had access to meat, fish, eggs, and milk. Hevi was especially indignant about anti-Black racism. He claimed that some Chinese women who dated African students were "packed off to prison or the commune farms for hard labor." Some of the students who shared Hevi's complaints organized demonstrations and hunger strikes protesting their treatment, but not much changed. By March 1962, unhappy with their lot, ninety-two of the 125 African students brought to China during the previous three years had cut short their studies and left for home.[39]

The Africans had discovered a yawning gap between China's rhetoric about the brotherhood of non-Whites and the attitudes of many ordinary Chinese. Lighter skin has long been prized as a sign of higher status in Asian cultures; darker skin is associated with peasants who toil in the fields. In the late-nineteenth century, prominent intellectuals who advocated for reform of the Qing government seized on social Darwinism and prejudices learned from the West to accept appalling stereotypes. Translator Yan Fu ranked Africans as the lowest race of human beings, and reformer Liang Qichao believed Africans were lustful of Caucasian women, slavish, backward, lazy, and stupid.[40] Such racist views persisted for decades, partly because of China's homogeneity and its lack of contact with outsiders.

Clarence Adams, by comparison, said that he experienced little in the way of overt discrimination. He did face some opposition to his marriage, and once when he was waiting for a public bus in Wuhan a young man walked up to him and—not realizing that Adams spoke Chinese—said loudly, "Look at how black this man is! All the soap and water in the world couldn't wash him clean!" After the man kept talking and reached out to touch his hair, Adams punched him in the face and knocked him down. Yet he dismissed this as an isolated incident. To admit that the Chinese were racist would have undermined his rationale for turning away from his own country. He wanted and needed to believe in China's claims to equality.[41]

Adams's passion for racial justice, which had brought him to China in the first place, still burned brightly. With access to magazines like *Time*, *Life*, and *Newsweek*, he was aware of anti–Vietnam War protests and the civil rights movement in the United States. In Beijing, in 1963, he likely would have attended a day-long rally of more than ten thousand people proclaiming solidarity with American Blacks a few weeks after Martin Luther King's "I Have a Dream" speech in Washington, DC. The progress of African Americans made him hopeful about returning home, although he also considered going to Ghana.

What was happening in Vietnam, on the other hand, was all too familiar to Adams. "The United States was fighting another war against communism in the name of freedom and democracy. I knew that once again many poor blacks would be sent to a remote foreign land to be slaughtered, just as I was." In August 1965, according to his own account, Adams went to the office of the Vietnam National Liberation Front in Beijing and without any guidance from the Chinese made two tape recordings that were broadcast on Radio Hanoi. He told Black American soldiers in Vietnam, "You are supposed to be fighting for the freedom of the Vietnamese, but what kind of freedom do you have at home?" He urged them return to the United States to fight for equality, "joining forces with people there who feel the Negro is equal."[42]

Disillusion and Departure

China was a proud and confident new nation when the American POWs arrived in the mid-1950s. The newly established PRC had fought the powerful United States to a standstill in Korea, albeit at a tremendous cost. (Mao's oldest son, Mao Anying, was killed in Korea.) Rampant inflation, corruption, and the social ills of drugs and prostitution had been curbed. People had enough to eat, healthcare improved, and literacy was growing. China was poor, but everyone seemed to be equally poor. There was a shared sense of common cause, dignity and pride, and optimism about the future. Harriet Mills marveled at "a remarkably effective and spontaneous code of public honesty, courtesy, and civic sense unknown in the old China."[43]

This period of hopefulness was not destined to last. "When I went to China," wrote Wills, "I had a vision of everyone there being completely, absolutely equal—which was one of the first things I discovered was not true . . . . I was terribly idealistic at the time: It was Utopia, not from the point of view of material things but from the point of view of relations between man and man. I felt I was part of the revolution and I wanted to help as much as possible and to educate myself along these lines." Unlike other foreigners, however, the former POWs were not dedicated revolutionaries, nor were they diplomats, journalists, or tourists. They were in a category unto themselves, and a degree of uncertainty and an element of suspicion always surrounded them. Wills believed he was quietly ostracized and never fully accepted by the long-term foreign expatriates because of his background.[44]

In the early 1960s, Adams, Wills, and William White, who had studied law at People's University, were assigned to work at the Foreign Languages Press, the Party's primary production center for a number of publications widely distributed to audiences overseas. The best known were *Peking Review*, *China Reconstructs*, and *China Pictorial*. About one hundred foreigners worked there, including a number of English, French, and Spanish speakers. White worked as a translator in the books and pamphlets department. His first job was to translate Winston Churchill's *Triumph and Tragedy* into Chinese. Adams, after completing his studies at Wuhan University in 1961, also worked in book publishing. Wills, who graduated from Peking University in 1962, translated, proofread, and polished articles for the English edition of *China Pictorial*, published monthly in nineteen languages with color photos of cheerful peasants and workers and smiling, rosy-cheeked children.

The three men lived with their families on the same floor of a building for foreign experts in the Foreign Languages Press compound. (Other staff lived in the Friendship Hotel, originally built for Soviet advisors in the early 1950s.) Travel within China was limited, normal contact with Chinese was rare, and the constant repetition of Marxist and Maoist rhetoric was mind-numbing.

Wills complained to his editors that patently obvious, wooden propaganda would be not be taken seriously by foreign readers, but his protests fell on deaf ears.

Adams, Wills, and White were well paid and lived comfortably by Chinese standards but received the lowest class of salaries since they lacked the political qualifications for higher ranks. All of them supplemented their incomes through black market operations, which Wills started doing at Peking University during the desperate years of the Great Leap Forward. Adams spent much of his free time socializing with diplomats at the embassies of Ghana, Guinea, Mali, and Cuba, which gave him the connections needed to obtain goods brought into China from Hong Kong via diplomatic pouch. Commercial attachés from Iraq and Ceylon were also active traders. The most popular items were new watches, pocket-size transistor radios, and wool cloth. When business was good, Adams could double his salary. White, who left for Hong Kong with his wife, son, and daughter in August 1965, was probably expelled from China because he refused to curtail his black market activities.[45]

The titles the Chinese used to address the former POWs provided one barometer of their declining status. They were called "comrade" (*tongzhi*) when they first arrived in China and "fellow student" (*tongxue*) at their universities. When xenophobia increased after the Sino-Soviet split, they were addressed as "friend" (*pengyou*) and then simply as "mister" (*xiansheng*). "As time went on," said Wills, "it became increasingly apparent that they didn't want me, that I was no longer useful to them, and the clearer this became to me, the more dissatisfied I became with the Chinese. By 1963 or so I felt useless. By the end, they just tolerated me." When his contract with the Foreign Languages Press ran out in June 1964, he was given a job teaching English to Chinese army officers and soldiers at a new language school. At this point, he believed the Chinese "didn't care anymore whether I stayed or not."

Officials did not stand in the way when Wills decided to leave. He asked the British embassy to arrange for entry to Hong Kong, and he and Kaiyen flew with their two-year-old daughter Linda from Beijing to Guangzhou, where the Canton Trade Fair was underway. From there they took a three-hour train ride to the border town of Shenzhen and walked across the bridge to the Lowu railway station on October 19, 1965.[46]

After returning to the United States, Wills wrote two lengthy articles for *Look* magazine explaining why he went to China and why he decided to leave. Obviously framed to redeem his reputation, they were, as historian Beverly

Kaiyen and Morris Wills crossing the Hong Kong border from China with their daughter Linda, October 1965.
Look Magazine Collection, Library of Congress.

Hooper points out, "masterly exercises in self-criticism, the technique Wills had learnt in ideological study sessions." He confessed he was "ashamed of going to China, of turning my back on the U.S. and my family." Writing in the midst of the Vietnam War, he was willing and able to confirm pervasive fears of communism based on his first-hand experiences. "I traveled a lot throughout China and finally realized that Chinese Communism is something that's intolerable for a Westerner."[47]

According to Adams, who was still in Beijing, the *Look* articles infuriated the Chinese, who felt betrayed after all they had done for Wills, and Adams came under suspicion since he and Wills were close and their wives were good friends. In addition, hostility to foreigners was growing and the atmosphere was increasingly tense as Mao's Cultural Revolution gathered force. Adams saw troops training all over the city, and even small children were being taught the use of rifles and spears. New Chinese staff at the Foreign Languages Press had poor language skills, but pristine political qualifications, and spent four hours a day studying the works of Chairman Mao. Adams said all of them came from poor peasant families with long revolutionary histories, and "they spoke almost entirely in Communist jargon."[48]

With a cloud over his head, Adams was politely informed that he was no longer needed at the Foreign Languages Press and was offered a factory job in the city of Jinan in Shandong where several other former POWs had worked. Uninterested, and realizing he was no longer welcome, he decided to leave. Adams arrived in Hong Kong with his wife and their two children on May 26, 1966. US and British officials and Hong Kong Red Cross representatives took them to a hotel where they stayed while arrangements were made for their travel to the United States. Adams told journalists in a press briefing that he wanted to see his ailing mother in Memphis for the first time since joining the US Army nineteen years before.[49]

Nicholas Platt, a young political officer with the US Consulate greeted Adams when he crossed the bridge marking the border between the PRC and Hong Kong, just as he had Morris Wills and William White. He asked each of them a series of questions to determine if they had done anything to in- validate their US citizenship. Had they served in the Chinese military, voted, or taken an oath of allegiance to a foreign state? Platt and others at the US Consulate debriefed the non-repatriates about their lives inside Red China and sent detailed classified reports to the State Department in Washington. Asked why they wanted to leave China, they told Platt that their families would have a better future in the United States. He concluded that their "decade plus in the PRC had convinced them that children of 'mixed blood' would have little chance in Chinese society."[50]

After Adams's departure, only Howard Adams and James Veneris remained from the original twenty-one who chose China. Both stayed to the end of their days. Veneris said he never regretted his decision, but Howard Adams told a friend he had lived for almost sixty years "as a traitor in the United States and a foreigner in China."[51]

Rediscovering America

Unlike many of the Korean War POWs who were treated with contempt when they returned from Communist China, Morris Wills had a relatively smooth re-entry into US society. Before leaving Beijing, he was invited to spend a year at Harvard University's East Asia Research Center to write about his experiences at Peking University. Wills "kept a low profile and seemed out of his depth," recalled Professor Ezra Vogel, who arranged a fellowship for Wills.[52] After Harvard, he took a master's degree in library science at

Columbia University, which seemed more practical than Chinese studies, and found work as the head cataloger at Utica College in central New York. Kaiyen Wills gave birth to two more children, Billy and Donna. Her world revolved around Utica's small Chinese community and her job at a Chinese restaurant.

Deborah Seiselmyer, a colleague of Wills at the Utica College Library for many years, remembers him as "private, quiet, and reserved." Being a librarian suited his personality, she said. "He was fastidious and methodical, always keeping to a set schedule. Morris was a decent person with a strong sense of justice. He was opposed to any form of racial discrimination, but avoided politics." He was suspicious of strangers and reluctant to talk about his years in Korea and China; Seiselmyer discovered his book *Turncoat* only by accident. Wills went back to China a few times to see friends and to discuss exchange programs for the college. He retired in 1995 and died in January 1999, at the age of sixty-five, after suffering a brain aneurism.[53]

Clarence Adams and his family traveled to the United States by ship from Hong Kong to San Francisco via Hawaii, where they took in the sights of Oahu and marveled at the abundance of meat in a supermarket. What impressed Adams most, reported the *Los Angeles Times*, was the diversity of the people, living together "in complete harmony, all colors blended together."[54] When they arrived from California by train in his hometown of Memphis in July 1966, he was optimistic about the improved racial situation in the United States after the passage of the 1964 Civil Rights Act. One journalist wrote that the thirty-seven-year-old was "amazed" at the changes made since he had left. "Things are moving now and I'm happy about it," he said when asked his feelings about relations between Blacks and Whites. He was impressed that the "Whites Only" signs had been removed from the Memphis train station. But he soon discovered that prejudice, including disapproval of mixed marriages like his, still existed. It was just less obvious than before.[55] Two years later, Martin Luther King was assassinated in Memphis while standing on the balcony outside his motel room.

A few weeks after returning, with little money and no job, Adams was called to appear before the House Un-American Activities Committee (HUAC) in Washington, DC. In closed sessions with four of its members, he was accused of collaborating with the enemy while he was a prisoner in Korea.

Clarence and Linfeng Adams arriving in San Francisco with their children,
Della and Louis, in July 1966.
AP Wirephoto.

He told the committee that he cooperated with the Chinese Communists for
the sake of his own survival. As a soldier, "I fought as hard as I could, but
I lost, and when I became a prisoner, I had to consider my own life. I think all
of you might well have done the same thing."

One Congressman asked why he chose to go to China, a Communist
country and enemy of the United States. Adams later wrote that he had
replied, " 'I had the right to go to any country that would honor my quest for
freedom, equality, education, and happiness'. . . . I responded by going into
great detail about how our white officers had sacrificed the all-black 503rd
Field Artillery just before I was captured, costing the lives of so many good
men . . . . I have been angry about this ever since." The most serious charge
against Adams was that he had disrupted the morale of US troops in Vietnam

and incited revolution in the United States with the radio broadcasts he made from Beijing. After several days of questioning, however, the charges against him were dismissed and he was free to go, although the FBI continued to keep him under surveillance.[56]

Adams applied to several universities to teach Mandarin Chinese but had no luck. In his search for work, the stigma of defecting to Communist China, which led to his dishonorable discharge from the army, was held against him. After months of looking, he finally found a job with a printing firm as a delivery truck driver and a linotype machine operator. He and Linfeng eventually saved enough money to start their own Chinese restaurants, including the Chop Suey House, known for its "Chinese soul food," and moved into a middle-class neighborhood. When the Chinese ping-pong team visited Memphis in 1971, they were invited to join the delegation for a cruise on the Mississippi River.

Adams died from emphysema at age seventy in September 1999 and his wife died two years later, never having returned to China. His autobiography, posthumously edited by his daughter Della Adams and historian Lewis Carlson, was not published until 2007. By the time he told his story, the Korean War was largely overlooked, the story of POW defections was not remembered, and the Cold War was long since over. In this changed world, Adams did not feel compelled to denounce communism, unlike his friend Morris Wills, and his assessment of his twelve years in the PRC was largely positive: "I sincerely believed that for the most part, China had treated me well."[57]

The twenty-one Americans who went China were collateral damage in a war that no one expected to fight. They were political pawns in the protracted negotiations over the fate of prisoners on both sides. Isolated and disillusioned by the stalemated conflict, their captors assured the young US soldiers of better lives in New China. For Adams and Wills, this proved to be true, at least at the outset. They were given the opportunity to master a foreign language, attend university, marry and have children, hold respectable jobs, and learn about a country that was forbidden territory. Since both were high school dropouts, a college education almost certainly would have been out of reach if they had returned to the United States after the war. Adams speculated that back in Memphis he "might have made it as a boxer, but only the few who reach the top make any kind of living. More likely, I would have gone back to hustling tips as a hotel porter or a room service boy."[58] Wills probably would have returned to work on his father's farm in upstate New York.

Clarence Adams and Morris Wills did not see themselves as deserters or traitors because, as Adams put it, "the U.S. had signed the agreement with the Chinese that gave me the right to go China if I wanted to." Yet they were caught in a web of contradictions and paid a high price for their self-imposed exile. They believed in the ideals of Chinese socialism but were disillusioned by the realities of political repression in the Communist state. To the Chinese they were symbols of American opposition to imperialism and racism, but to Americans they were victims of a mind-controlling nightmare called brainwashing. In China they were always outsiders, and in the United States they faced the guilt and shame of denying their nation. When their propaganda value was spent and anti-foreign sentiment grew, they left the PRC to start over in their home country. Instead of being welcomed as intermediaries, they spent the rest of their lives suspended somewhere between the two cultures, painfully aware that utopia was not to be found.

We next turn to two other Americans, Joan Hinton and Sid Engst, who were drawn to China more out of curiosity about the Chinese revolution than dissatisfaction with the United States. They were not combatants who suffered as prisoners like Adams and Wills. Unencumbered by the burdens of a war-scarred past, they accepted the PRC's idealistic goals with genuine enthusiasm.

3

Joan Hinton and Sid Engst

True Believers

Joan Hinton and Sid Engst found their way to China in the late 1940s not as Marxist revolutionaries but as inquisitive idealists. The two young Americans spoke no Chinese and knew very little beyond what they had heard from Joan's brother William Hinton, who was working in rural China, and from what they had read in Edgar Snow's dramatic account of the Communist leadership in his book *Red Star Over China*. They did sense that a transformation of historic proportions was underway and hoped somehow to be part of it. Yet neither of them expected to become ardent Maoists, nor did they think they would spend the rest of their lives in the People's Republic.

They were an unlikely couple. Joan was an experimental physicist and Sid was a dairy farmer. Her family was well off and his was poor. She was a bundle of nervous energy and he was calm and steady. On the other hand, both of them were open-minded, adventurous, practical, and independent. Like many Americans who had seen the suffering of the Great Depression, they shared progressive political views.

Hinton and Engst belonged to a disparate group of "international friends" who were allowed to stay in China when the new regime systematically rid itself of the vestiges of foreign influence after coming to power. The great majority of non-Chinese, including Catholic and Protestant missionaries who had lived there for decades, were forced to leave; some were detained or imprisoned on charges of spying. Only a small number of Americans and Europeans remained as technical experts, language teachers, translators, writers, or the spouses of Chinese citizens. As many as eleven thousand Soviet advisers arrived to help China to rebuild its economy, but pulled out abruptly after the Sino-Soviet split in 1960.[1]

"The overall profile of the long-term foreign resident community," writes historian Beverly Hooper, "was mostly middle-class and professional, including doctors, lawyers, journalists, economists and teachers (though some individuals had working-class roots)." It was "mainly but not solely

Anglo-American" and there was "a noticeable Jewish presence, reflecting the general Jewish involvement in leftist politics and, for some Europeans, displacement from their home countries by Nazism."[2] Some were Marxists, disillusioned by Stalinism and hopeful that Mao's form of communism would prove more humane. A few others left the United States because of McCarthyism, and twenty-one American soldiers—as described in the previous chapter—opted to live in the PRC after the Korean War.

Hinton and Engst never gave up their US citizenship, nor did they become became Chinese citizens or join the Communist Party; very few outsiders were allowed to do so. They also kept their distance from the polemics of Cold War politics, seeing themselves as humanitarians and internationalists. Walter Judd would have dismissed them as naïve dreamers and labeled them as apologists. Yet when it came to defending the righteousness of the PRC's transformation, their loyalties were unambiguous. Instead of rejecting communism as an oppressive, despotic system, they truly believed that China's path to the future would be humanity's salvation.

The Farmer and the Physicist

Erwin ("Sid") Engst grew up on farms near Syracuse in central New York. Born in 1918, the second youngest of ten children, it was a hardscrabble childhood. His father died when he was twelve, and the family struggled to get by, although there was always enough to eat. After an unsuccessful year in a pre-medical program at the University of Illinois, he transferred to Cornell University to study agriculture. Farmers were not subject to the draft during the Second World War, so he dropped out of Cornell a year before graduating to help support his mother, who lived in nearby Gooseville Corners. As much as Engst loved farming, however, he was thinking more and more about the problems of the world. He sold his cows and planned to join the army, but when the war ended, decided to go to China, where his knowledge of farming and animal husbandry opened doors in ways that he never could have anticipated.

Joan Chase Hinton's upbringing was much more comfortable financially, yet marked by tragedy, nonetheless. The youngest of three children, she was born in 1921 in Chicago, where her father, Sebastian Hinton, was a patent lawyer. He took his own life when Joan was two, but left the family with a good deal of money from his invention of the jungle gym. His wife, Carmelita

Hinton, never remarried. A Bryn Mawr College graduate who had worked at Jane Addams's Hull House in Chicago, she founded the progressive, co-educational Putney School in southern Vermont in 1935. She firmly believed that physical labor and play were just as important as classroom learning and taught Joan and her older siblings, Bill and Jean, to be free-thinking and creative, and to use their talents to make the world a better place. When Joan got to China, she would find Mao's ideas of learning through practice and striving to improve the collective good quite similar to her mother's philosophy of life.

A cheerful, robust teenager, Joan was an avid skier who also rode horses, loved hiking, and disdained lipstick and high heels. She had little interest in literature, being dyslexic, but excelled at science. At Bennington College, a small school for women in Vermont, she built a cloud chamber to track subatomic particles and graduated after three years. Because the chair of Cornell University's physics department refused to accept female graduate students—despite the fact that Hinton had done research there during two winter breaks—she went instead to the University of Wisconsin in Madison for a master's degree. One of her mathematics professors remembered her as "a good student, a rather eccentric girl, blonde, sturdy, good looking."[3]

Joan was completing her studies at Wisconsin when she was recruited to work for the top-secret Manhattan Project in Los Alamos, New Mexico on the design and construction of two reactors being built to enrich uranium for the world's first atomic bombs. When the bomb was detonated at daybreak on July 16, 1945 in the Jornada del Muerto Desert, 120 miles south of Santa Fe, she observed the mushroom cloud from a safe distance. "It was like being at the bottom of an ocean of light. We were bathed in it from all directions. The light withdrew into the bomb as if the bomb sucked it up. Then it turned purple and blue and went up and up and up."[4]

Three weeks later, she was shocked to learn about the total destruction of the Japanese cities of Hiroshima and Nagasaki. While Americans were relieved to know that the war with Japan soon would end, Hinton later commented, "There was no reason to use the bombs. Germany had already surrendered. They said they were using the bombs to save American lives. We know perfectly well that it was not to save American lives, but to keep the Soviet Union from coming into Japan."[5] (It should be noted that many historians believe the bombings were justified in forcing Japan to surrender; an invasion of the home islands could have cost millions of American and Japanese lives.)

A few years earlier, Bill Hinton had introduced his sister Joan to Sid Engst, his roommate at Cornell, and after the war ended, Engst—a lanky, easy-going, handsome fellow with a broad grin—hitchhiked to Los Alamos where Joan was still working. They visited the Grand Canyon, spent Thanksgiving together, and she invited him to join her family in Vermont for Christmas. Sid asked her to come with him to China and told his mother, "Joanie Hinton and I are going to get married—when I don't know."[6] She was tempted by the idea, but decided instead to study for a doctorate at the University of Chicago's Institute for Nuclear Studies with Enrico Fermi, a Noble Prize winner who had been one of the lead scientists at Los Alamos. She was hopeful that the establishment of the US Atomic Energy Commission would ensure that nuclear weapons and nuclear power would be under civilian rather than military control.

Encouraged by Bill Hinton, who was in China as an instructor for the United Nations Relief and Rehabilitation Administration (UNRRA), Sid Engst set off for Shanghai in May 1946 to work as an agriculture specialist with the same organization.[7] China's largest, most cosmopolitan city was reeling from the aftermath of eight years of war with Japan, and he was appalled by the "brutally basic relations between people—prostitution, begging, selling children, you name it." He was, in his own words, "an innocent upstate New York farm boy, and Shanghai was the den of iniquity in the world." The corruption, inefficiency, and politics of the Nationalist government were dismaying, and inflation was so extreme that "one needs a suitcase to carry his money in," he wrote home. "People living on a fixed income are having a desperate time making enough to buy food." Farms on the outskirts of Shanghai were very small scale and all the work was done by hand.

What Engst saw in the central province of Hunan that summer was far more disturbing. As a member of a small UNRAA team sent to investigate reports of a famine, he found six hundred refugees (left homeless by the war) in one camp living in tents with no sanitation and practically no water. "All but 100 were in the last stages of starvation. There is practically no flesh at all on their bones, and their heads had just the appearance of skulls with skin drawn over them . . . . A terrific stench pervaded the whole camp, and believe me after we left, we didn't go back directly to eat lunch." The conditions at another camp were not as ghastly, but "people are so hungry that banditry is common, and in many of the small villages a foreigner would get mobbed just by beggars if he didn't have a soldier with him."

Not long after experiencing the horrific human disaster in Hunan, Engst resigned from UNRAA, fed up with its bureaucracy and inefficiency, calling the relief agency "little more than a quartermaster corps for the Nationalist army." If an election was held, he told his mother, "Chiang Kai-shek and his gang wouldn't get enough votes to elect him as a village magistrate." He was increasingly critical of US support for the Nationalists' "rotten, feudal dictatorship." Americans had "a great reservoir of good will" after the war ended because of their help in fighting the Japanese, but "that is rapidly disappearing." To him, it was clear in the minds of "some four hundred million people that their only recourse is in the Communists . . . . You will never learn this from the *New York Times* or Henry Luce's *Time* magazine, but there just isn't any support from anyone any more for this [Nationalist] government."

Engst joined the China Welfare Fund, founded by Song Qingling—Sun Yat-sen's widow and older sister of Madame Chiang Kai-shek—who was an important liaison for the Communist Party in Shanghai. He hoped to be posted to an experimental farm in a "liberated" area in the northwest and in November 1946 flew from Beijing (then called Beiping) to the CCP's capital of Yan'an in Shaanxi Province, where he had his twenty-eighth birthday. Except for a few mud buildings, the city had been leveled by Japanese bombs. Most people lived in caves carved out of the hillsides, which were surprisingly comfortable: cool in the summer, warm in the winter.

The contrast with the dispirited Nationalist-controlled areas was striking. He found no begging in the streets, no evidence of prostitution, no starvation. Children at an orphanage were clean and well-fed, unlike the conditions he had seen in Hunan that summer "where the children were filthy and there was no organization at all." There appeared to be no very rich or very poor. Engst was impressed by the Eighth Route Army boys who had "their own blue-gray uniforms, their own home-made or captured Japanese weapons, and their own style of warfare, and believe me they are really proud of their army." He claimed that every soldier knew how to read and write. Outfitted in the same cotton-padded uniform as the soldiers, he wrote home, "I wish you could see me . . . . You wouldn't be able to tell me from any Chinese peasant."

Eager to gain international recognition for their revolutionary movement, the Communists treated the tiny foreign community in Yan'an as honored guests. Engst met all the "big shots," including Mao Zedong and Zhou Enlai, who invited the foreigners for dinners on Christmas and New Year's

Day. Zhou was very friendly, while Mao was more serious and asked many questions about the United States. Zhu De, the military commander-in-chief, was "a great big man with a big round face that always has a smile on it." The candor and informality of the Communist leaders led many Western visitors to conclude that the revolutionaries were democratic at heart.

Even though CCP propaganda made a clear distinction between US imperialism and the American people, a guard escorted Engst at first. "The peasants don't always know [the difference], and when they see American made planes bombing them and killing their people, they are apt to get pretty anti-American." His work on a nearby state farm to improve varieties of millet, wheat, and vegetables and to raise a herd of milk cows "is really the opportunity I've been waiting for." He was learning a lot. "When you see how these Communists work and live, you can realize what it means to give everything for the success of the working class movement." He had no idea how long he would stay.[8]

The Communists evacuated Yan'an in March 1947 when the Nationalists launched a military offensive in the region, and Engst spent the next several months in the surrounding mountains and valleys with a few men protecting a herd of about thirty black and white Holstein cows, the only dairy cattle in the entire area.[9] "The cows didn't care about the enemy soldiers and moved at their own pace," said Engst. During these months of deprivation, seeing what the Chinese, "who had nothing but millet and rifles, were able to accomplish, made me much more humble." He realized it was "not just a matter of teaching and respecting these men and women, but actually learning from them." This was when Mao's theory of learning through practice "really got into my bones."[10]

Sid's letters to Joan were full of enthusiasm for his new surroundings, and he urged her to join him while it was still possible to do so. She wrote back describing remarkable scientific discoveries of supernovas and black holes. (She was appalled to learn later that he had used her letters as toilet paper, having no better alternative.) His persistence finally paid off when she agreed to visit him, and she also looked forward to seeing her brother Bill and his wife Bertha Sneck, who were in north China. Joan, who was disillusioned about military control of nuclear physics research after learning that her fellowship was funded by the US Navy, decided to take a leave of absence from the University of Chicago. She told her colleagues, "I'm going to see what's going on, and I'll come back and finish the degree."[11] Her new life in China intervened and she never returned.

Sid Engst at the Chinese Communist headquarters in Yan'an in 1949.
Courtesy Fred Engst.

Hinton sailed from San Francisco for Shanghai in March 1948 with a slide rule, physics book, typewriter, sleeping bag, and her violin. With the Chinese civil war raging, it would take a year before she and Sid could see each other again. During her time in Shanghai, which was still under Nationalist control, she studied Chinese, taught English, and learned how to weld. She also contracted malaria and developed sprue (celiac disease), which further delayed her journey to the Communist stronghold in the northwest. In Beijing, not long before the People's Liberation Army seized the city on

January 31, 1949, she met members of the CCP underground who arranged her transportation into the interior by way of an old Dodge truck and a train. Along the way she stopped in Wenshui in Shanxi Province to see Bill, who was teaching tractor mechanics, and her sister-in-law Bertha.

When Sid got the news of Joan's arrival at Yan'an, he rushed back from the town of Waiyaobao, where he was helping to make irrigation pumps, cooking pots, and ploughshares with iron from unexploded bombs. Their Chinese hosts expected them to be married, and with little time to discuss or prepare, held a simple wedding ceremony for them on April 2.

Hinton's world had been turned upside down, and not just because she suddenly was Sid's wife. As a female scientist working with the best minds in the rarified world of nuclear physics, she had been at the pinnacle of her field in the United States. "But then I got into Yan'an, and suddenly the values are entirely different. Who cares about Fermi? Who cares about this little group of world-class physicists?" For too long, the Chinese told her, intellectuals in China had spent their time promoting themselves, refusing to roll up their sleeves and get their hands dirty.

She was astounded by the dedication of the people she met, people who didn't know how to read and write but knew more than she did. "I suddenly realized that I had to liberate myself from all this baggage. I had to relearn what life's about, what values are true values." Enthusiasm for what would be known as the Yan'an spirit (*Yan'an Jingshen*) was infectious. "I had the feeling of being part of something very, very big . . . . It was extremely exhilarating." She didn't feel isolated or alienated. "They treated me like a comrade, because they considered foreigners part of the revolution. They took me in as part of the world." Sid, who had proven himself during the evacuation of Yan'an, "was presented as a model to me. His feet were already over to the side of the people."[12] It would be a long and difficult process for her to follow in his footsteps.

Joan was loath to accept the idea that she had come to China just to get married. She knew how to fend for herself, having been a woman in a scientific field dominated by men, and kept her maiden name, which was the custom among Chinese women. She took the Chinese name *Han Chun*, meaning "Cold Spring." (Sid's was *Yang Zao*, "Early Sun.") She admired the Communists' determination to free women from the bonds of the old society. They had been subjugated by a male-dominated system for centuries; Confucius said women must obey their fathers before marriage, their husbands after marriage, and their sons when they are old. But under the

New Marriage Law of 1950, bigamy, concubinage, child betrothal, interference with the re-marriage of widows, and the exacting of money or gifts in connection with marriage were abolished. Marriage was to be based on the free choice of partners and equal rights for both sexes. With the sweeping new law, divorce was to be granted when husband and wife both desired it.[13]

Hinton was greatly impressed with these reforms, although there was no provision for equal pay for women or for sharing housework. Prior to the Cultural Revolution, rural women were not given leadership positions or taught to do technical work "because they would leave the village upon marriage," but this custom was changing, she wrote in 1976. "Now that young men often volunteer to move to their wives' villages, one of the obstacles to training women has been removed." A strong preference for sons over daughters was another source of inequality, but this too was shifting now that women could be "electricians, carpenters, masons, and even mule-cart drivers."[14]

After staying in Waiyaobao for six months, Party officials asked Hinton and Engst to relocate to Chengchuan, a walled town on the edge of the Ordos Plateau in Inner Mongolia: "a flat plane that stretches as far as you can see, and is interrupted only by sand dunes that rise anywhere from five to fifty feet high," wrote Engst, who had spent three weeks there on an previous trip in early 1947. North of the Great Wall, about seventy miles northwest of Yan'an, it was so remote that it took three weeks before they learned about ceremonies in Beijing's Tiananmen Square marking the founding the People's Republic on October 1. When a newspaper finally reached them, "we stayed up all night to sew the new flag and celebrated the following morning, marching around and shouting slogans."[15]

Their assigned job was to improve the breeding of cows, sheep, donkeys, and horses, and Hinton used her considerable mechanical skills to build a windmill and other machines. Sid charmed everyone with his folksy, Mark Twain–style sense of humor, and they spent many hours feasting, drinking, and singing at weddings and New Year's festivals. The local Mongolian people were friendly but didn't trust outsiders, and it took more than a year for the American couple to win their confidence. "We floundered in the sea of realities, in the ordinary everyday problems to which our theories gave no answers," confessed Hinton.[16]

The new Communist government confiscated opium, which Mongolian men smoked if they could afford it, and sent out work teams to destroy fields of poppies. Study sessions were organized to explain a raft of new regulations and a proclamation was issued to turn in guns. Public health clinics were organized and schools were set up for girls and boys. Unlike much of China, however, the "liberation" of Chengchuan did not involve land reform, which accounted for countless deaths in other parts of the country. Land reform was unnecessary because the land, which was too dry for farming, was used for grazing and was commonly owned.

Rather than landlords, the chief local obstacle to progress was a foreign Jesuit priest known as Father Ma. Virtually all Mongolians in the area were Catholics—there were also five Chinese priests and a few nuns—and regularly attended church services. "The people were being told that 'Communists cannot go to heaven,'" recalled Hinton. Moreover, "when we started inoculating cows against rinderpest, we sometimes met with the objection: 'If it's God's will, the cows will die.'" After it was alleged that Father Ma was behind a plot to murder the local Communist Party secretary, he was placed under house arrest, imprisoned, and deported to Hong Kong.[17]

Living with the Mongolians in the faraway grasslands was
completely different from the experience of other foreign residents in China, most of whom enjoyed the relative comfort of big cities like Beijing, Shanghai, and Guangzhou. With no electricity or running water, their one indulgence was ice cream in the winter, thanks to ample supplies of milk, cream, and snow. Yet instead of feeling exiled, Hinton and Engst relished the opportunity to live and work in a distinctive culture on China's periphery. "They loved the idea of working together to create a new society," said their son Fred, "not for self-interest but because it was the right thing to do."[18]

"The Atom Spy Who Got Away"

In 1952, Joan was pregnant with her first child. With a limited diet, poor healthcare, and very little heat during the long Mongolian winters, it was safer to give birth in Beijing where Bill Hinton and Bertha were now living; Sid stayed behind in Chengchuan. Soon after a two-week journey by donkey cart, trucks, and trains, Joan was invited to attend the Asia-Pacific Peace Conference, convened in Beijing in early October while the Korean War was still being fought on China's border.

She was pleased to join 470 peace activists and observers from nearly fifty countries, including ten Americans who were living in China. Learning of her background as a nuclear physicist, members of the Japanese delegation asked her to address the assembly. She accepted and spoke "in memory of the thousands upon thousands of innocent people, of the children, the old people, the men and women of every walk of life who were so ruthlessly murdered, so wantonly burned to death at Hiroshima and Nagasaki . . . . As a scientist who worked at the Los Alamos, New Mexico, atomic bomb project, as one who touched with my own hands the very bomb which was dropped on Nagasaki, I feel a deep sense of guilt and shame at the part I played in this crime against humanity as a whole, and this crime against the Japanese people in particular." She went on to question the idea that science exists in a vacuum, free of any moral implications.

> From as early as I can remember, I had an insatiable desire to know how the world was put together, and I determined to become a scientist. The more I studied science, the more I absorbed the philosophy of "science for science's sake." This philosophy is the poison of modern science . . . . I believed, as did many of my colleagues, that our job as scientists went only so far as to find out the truths of nature. Anything beyond this, anything to do with the application of the knowledge we scientists discovered, was of secondary concern to us. In our study of pure science, we had no time to concern ourselves with such trifles. The application of science must be left to statesmen and engineers. And I am ashamed to admit it took the horror of the bombings of Hiroshima and Nagasaki to shock me out of this ivory tower of complacency, to shock me into the fundamental realization that there is no such thing as "pure" science; that science has a meaning only in relation to its service to mankind; only in so far as it helps to create a rich and beautiful world.[19]

Peking Radio broadcast her passionate speech, reporting that it had received a "prolonged standing ovation," whereupon US newspapers picked it up and ran stories with lurid headlines: "Former A-Bomb Worker Speaks at Red Parley" and "Girl Cheered by Reds Had A-Plant Job."[20] A US government spokesman pointed out that Hinton held only a low-level laboratory position at Los Alamos, and one news article said that she and her husband were now running an animal breeding farm in Inner Mongolia. Despite these disclaimers, Ellis M. Zacharias, a retired US Navy admiral, wrote an article for *Real Magazine* on "The Atom Spy Who Got Away," claiming Hinton was a defector who had given secret information about the atomic bomb to the Chinese Communists. A cartoon with a mushroom cloud looming in the

Joan Hinton addressing the Asia-Pacific Peace Conference in Beijing,
October 1952.
Courtesy Fred Engst.

background portrayed her as a blond Mata Hari in a trench coat who had
"given her all to the reds."[21]

The improbable story drew further attention when Bill Hinton, who
returned from the PRC in 1953, was questioned by the Senate Internal
Security Subcommittee on two occasions. During both hearings he admitted
that Joan was living in Communist China but refused to say anything more
about her. His passport was taken, he was blacklisted from teaching jobs, and
his detailed notes on land reform were confiscated by US Customs. When his
papers finally were released in the 1960s, he wrote *Fanshen: A Documentary
of Revolution in a Chinese Village*, a classic study of the Communist takeover
in Shanxi Province.

Joan Hinton was never formally charged with espionage, but the hysteria
of McCarthyism and her brother's alarming experience with the US government dissuaded her from returning to the United States. Marni Rosner, the

daughter of Joan's sister Jean, remembered that FBI agents were frequently on their doorstep asking questions about her aunt. Because of the US embargo, no direct mail service existed with the PRC, so the family communicated through a cousin, Geoffrey Taylor, a physicist at Cambridge University in England, who forwarded letters and packages between the United States and China.[22]

Hinton said the idea that she had worked on China's nuclear program was laughable. There had been a couple of offers from universities to teach physics, which she politely declined, but she knew nothing about the PRC's ultra-secret project to construct an atomic bomb. Even if she had been asked, it is difficult to imagine she would have agreed to work on such a program, given her fierce opposition to atomic weapons. Russian advisors had provided some technical assistance, but after their withdrawal from the PRC in 1959–60, the CCP leadership was determined to be completely self-sufficient. A talented group of young Chinese scientists took charge, most of whom had obtained PhDs in nuclear physics in the United States during the late 1940s. China successfully tested an atom bomb in 1964 and a hydrogen bomb in 1967.[23]

Joan gave birth to a son on the final day of the Asia-Pacific Peace Conference. Named Fred, for Sid's father, his Chinese name was *Heping*, meaning "peace." It was not until May that Sid would see his child for the first time. Why he didn't go to Beijing to see Joan and the baby that winter is unclear, but travel was difficult and perhaps he was reluctant to disrupt the progress he had made in Inner Mongolia.

Both Sid and Joan wanted to stay in Chengchuan, but the government assigned them to the Caotan State Dairy Farm along the Wei River on the outskirts of Xi'an, which would be their home for the next thirteen years. The conditions were better for the Holstein cows that Sid and several Chinese herders brought from the north, but there was no electricity (a small gas-run generator provided refrigeration), and the road into the city, where milk was delivered every day, was unpaved and turned into sticky mud when it rained. Milk consumption increased steadily, especially since young mothers were being encouraged to join the work force and had less time to nurse their children.[24]

The only other American in the city of Xi'an was Jane McDonald Su, from Milwaukee, Wisconsin, who had been a lab technician at a Chicago hospital when she met Dr. Su Hongxi, a cardiovascular surgeon from China, who was working there. They married and moved to the PRC in 1957; "My husband was patriotic and thought he owed it to the Chinese people to return." Dr. Su was assigned to an army hospital in Xi'an, and Jane Su taught English at the Xi'an Foreign Language Institute. When Jane first met Joan Hinton in September 1958, because she needed milk for her child, they talked until two o'clock in the morning. Joan impressed her as "a dedicated revolutionary" who stayed true to her ideals and "helped me understand China." Su remembered that Hinton rejected any special privileges and was so strict with herself that she refused to go into the local Friendship Store where foreigners could buy goods that were not otherwise available on the Chinese market, viewing this practice, which the Chinese copied from the Soviet Union, as discriminatory and hypocritical.[25]

Joan and Sid's second son, named Bill after her brother, was born in 1955, and their daughter, Karen, arrived in 1956. Everyday life was not easy, but an older Chinese woman, an amah, cooked meals and helped raise the children, which allowed Joan to work on the farm. With no foreign playmates, the three children grew up speaking Chinese with a Xi'an accent at home and in school.

In 1962, when it was still illegal for Americans to travel to Red China, Joan's mother Carmelita Hinton was on a group tour with Americans in Moscow. Toward the end of the trip, she quietly made phone calls to arrange for a PRC visa, flew to Beijing, and took a train to Xi'an to see her daughter and her family. Joan, who was completely immersed in Mao's revolutionary rhetoric, had mixed feelings about her mother's arrival because of her "bourgeois" background. She needn't have worried. Ganny, as her grandchildren called her, quickly adapted to the new environment. Chinese officials treated her like a celebrity, praising her for ignoring the US blockade and for the dedication of her two children, Joan and Bill, to the revolutionary cause. Carmelita and Joan were invited to observe the October 1 National Day in Beijing, and the Chinese People's Association for Friendship with Foreign Countries arranged for them to tour the country as guests of the state. Carmelita stayed with Joan and Sid at their Caotan farmhouse for a year. Upon her return to the United States, her passport was seized, and it was ten more years before she could see her daughter again.[26]

Unshakable Maoists

Hinton and Engst were relatively untouched by the destructive movements that swept across China during the late 1950s and 1960s. They stayed

Joan Hinton and Sid Engst with their children (from left to right) Bill, Karen, Fred, and Joan's mother Carmelita Hinton (front row center) who visited them in Xi'an in 1963.
Courtesy Fred Engst.

steadfast in their commitment to Mao's leadership, which many Chinese began to question privately, although they criticized decisions made at the local level. There was considerable enthusiasm about the Great Leap Forward (1958–60) at the outset, remembered Engst, but "then people went too far, and many crazy things were done." Party leaders, fearful of making mistakes, insisted on "ridiculous" production goals for the farm, which now had fifty to sixty mature cows. Fortunately, the Caotan dairy farm was not compelled to build backyard iron furnaces, which had been mandated in other parts of the country, and communal kitchens, plagued by poor quality and considerable waste, lasted only for a couple of months. Many policies were unrealistic, but some actual progress was made: the dairy got electricity and a gravel road was built out from the city. Joan went about designing and building a more efficient, high-temperature pasteurizer.

The excesses of the Great Leap were followed by three hard years of widespread food shortages, now referred to as the Great Famine. Chinese and Western scholars estimate that between twenty and forty million people died of starvation due to a combination of mismanagement, drought, and floods—news that the government suppressed. Engst and Hinton said they witnessed no deaths in their area. "Around Xi'an there was malnutrition. You saw children with swollen stomachs," admitted Engst. Yet even after horrifying reports of the famine emerged during the post-Mao years, he refused to believe the extent of the disaster. In retrospect, he told Neil Burton, a Canadian academic, people "grossly exaggerate the shortcomings of that period, and grossly underestimate the achievements . . . . Putting the blame on Mao was tremendously unfair."[27]

After the disastrous Great Leap and devastating famine, Chairman Mao launched the Great Proletarian Cultural Revolution to reassert his control over the CCP and to implement his vision for a utopian socialist society. In his estimation, China was being held back by "reactionaries" with feudal thinking who sought to undermine the revolution. Not only was all-out class struggle the key to achieving a genuine communist society, but the Chinese people were told that capitalist roader enemies lurked everywhere. China was under siege by American imperialists, and any association with foreigners, no matter how loyal they appeared to be, was grounds for suspicion and fear.

Long-time "foreign friends" like Hinton and Engst, who prided themselves on being equals with their Chinese co-workers, felt the sting of xenophobia as early as the 1962 Socialist Education Movement, a precursor to the Cultural Revolution. They were no longer permitted to participate in meetings at the dairy, Engst was demoted from his position as vice manager, and their children were not allowed to wear the prestigious red scarves of the Young Pioneers. Their son Bill, who studied the violin with his mother, could not play for a school program because violins had become symbols of the bourgeois West. His brother Fred was interrogated by local Public Security officers who wanted to know why he had come to China, not realizing he was born there. The situation was so bad for some of Sid and Joan's Chinese colleagues that they committed suicide by hanging or drowning themselves.

The pressures on foreigners multiplied with the advent of the Cultural Revolution, and in April 1966 Party officials ordered Hinton and Engst to leave Xi'an and join other foreigners in Beijing for their safety. Tens of thousands of Chinese intellectuals and university students were being "sent down" to the countryside to learn from physical labor, while the two Americans, who had worked with their hands for fifteen years, were being "sent up" to the capital, which was full of youthful Red Guards from across the country, fervently worshipping Mao, the "Red Sun in Our Hearts."

The family was treated well in Beijing, but they were kept at a safe distance from ordinary Chinese. They lived in the Xinqiao Hotel where their children were amazed by the indoor plumbing but increasingly distraught over the disruption all around them. Fred was allowed to finish his school year in Xi'an and stayed to work in the fields picking corn that summer before finding a job in a wood factory near Beijing. Bill volunteered to work on a tea farm in the south.[28]

Sid and Joan were given desk jobs polishing English, which they detested. He was a foreign expert with the Bureau of Movie Distribution, and she was assigned to the Chinese People's Association for Friendship with Foreign Countries. A "minder" kept them under surveillance, but they refused to be driven to work in a car and rode their bicycles instead. Engst grumbled that they had been "put up in fancy hotels and given every convenience. Luxury and high salary were used to get [foreigners] to forget about the revolution. Joan and I, having been on the farm and used to living more simply and to living with the Chinese people, found this very hard to take. It was diametrically the opposite of what Chairman Mao teaches." Joan complained bitterly that the principles of the revolution were being subverted and that the whole reason for staying in China had disappeared.

Unwilling to keep silent, Hinton and Engst banded together with Ann Tompkins (a recently arrived American), Bertha Sneck (William Hinton's former wife who stayed and worked in China after he returned to the United States), and Bertha's sixteen-year-old daughter Carma Hinton (who was fluent in Chinese and would become a well-known documentary filmmaker and art historian), to write a big character poster (*dazibao*) protesting their treatment. In the political language of the day, they asked why it was that "foreigners working here at the heart of the world revolution are being pushed down the revisionist road?" and "What devils, demons, and snake spirits are behind the treatment of foreigners working in China?" Much to their surprise, the petition reached Mao himself, who agreed that "revolutionary foreign experts and their children should be treated exactly the same as the Chinese. No difference should be allowed."[29]

Mao's personal response was thrilling, but the situation only worsened for non-Chinese as the Cultural Revolution spun out of control. Several long-time Beijing residents—including David Crook, Israel Epstein, and Sidney Rittenberg—were accused of anti-revolutionary activities and without trials were sent to prison, where they languished in solitary confinement for years. Hinton and Engst avoided this fate but were fearful for themselves and their children. Their daughter Karen suffered a nervous breakdown and began throwing uncontrollable tantrums. When their jobs as copyeditors disappeared, they opened a shop to repair furniture and appliances for members of the international community. Engst briefly considered returning to the United States but was worried that Joan could not go back because she would be harassed as an "atomic spy." He also realized there was very little he could do in America. So much had changed that he no longer understood his home country, which was in the middle of its own cultural and political upheaval over civil rights, women's rights, and the Vietnam War.

After the United States lifted its embargo on travel to China in 1971, Bill Hinton returned for a visit, and Joan's sister Jean came the first time. Jean's daughter Marni arrived with a group of fifteen young Americans, and Joan and Sid arranged for them to work at a textile factory and a model commune for about nine months. In 1972, when the worst of the Cultural Revolution was over, Engst and Hinton were allowed to return to agricultural production, breeding livestock and designing milk-processing equipment at the Red Star Commune, an hour's bicycle-ride south of Beijing. (Going back to Xi'an or Inner Mongolia was not an option.) Living in three small rooms in a nondescript one-story building was difficult at first, but their circumstances gradually improved.[30]

In 1974, they felt confident enough to cross the border with Hong Kong and went to the US Consulate to renew their passports, which had expired two decades earlier. At the invitation of the US-China Friendship Association, Sid flew to the United States the following year, his first trip back since leaving in 1946. (Joan was sick at the time and unable to join him.) Traveling with his son Fred, he gave speeches and interviews in twenty-five cities, where audiences were eager to hear about Chinese day-to-day life and advances in agriculture. He also visited his relatives in upstate New York, where he was astounded by the paved roads and modern machinery, but noticed that small farmers were struggling to make a living.[31]

Joan was healthy enough to travel to the United States in 1977, where she also spoke in a number of cities as a guest of the Friendship Association. Her most memorable occasion was a reunion at Los Alamos with some of her former colleagues who had worked on the construction of the atomic bomb. They listened attentively to a presentation she gave on workers, peasants, factories, and communes in China. She also visited high energy physics laboratories in Berkeley, Chicago, and Stony Brook, Long Island, where she saw C. N. Yang with whom she had shared a lab at the University of Chicago (see

Chapter 4). They enjoyed reminiscing about their days together as graduate students, and he explained the operation of a low-temperature accelerator.

She was encouraged to find that American scientists "are worried about the direction of science, disarmament, ecology, planning, all the kinds of things that disturb me about the American future." As for life in the United States, Hinton commented with a broad smile, "there is too much of everything. Too much advertising, too much commercialism, and too much waste of food." No one recycled water, paper, or bottles. She was confident that China's "socialist road to progress is the fastest, certainly the fairest" as compared with the vast gap between rich and poor in the United States. As for personal freedom and individual rights, she said, "It is more important to be part of a system that is working for everybody's good. I believe that the good of the community is more important than that of a single individual."[32] Idealistic yet practical, she returned to China with a canister of liquid nitrogen holding straws of bull semen, worth thousands of dollars, for artificial insemination of Holstein cows. Thanks to some fast talking, she was able to transport the container as checked baggage on the airplane.

Hinton had abandoned a promising career in physics to marry a dairy farmer and spend the rest of her life enduring hardship in a distant land. When a reporter asked Carmelita if her daughter had any misgivings about staying in China, she replied, "Pure science and original research is what has most fascinated Joan. It has been a real sacrifice for her to give it up. I don't think she has ever missed the creature comforts, indoor plumbing, or central heat or even the luxury of privacy. I know she has never missed pretty clothes. Indeed, she might've been pleased to have so little choice and no indecisions about what to put on. But she very much misses the companionship of other scientists. She has missed the lab."[33]

In 1978, Sid needed a replacement heart valve and flew with Joan to Boston for the surgery. (Carmelita was now living in the Boston area.) The operation was successful, and one year later he and Joan accompanied twelve Chinese farmers on a six-week tour to study dairy mechanization in California, Wisconsin, Illinois, Pennsylvania, and New York. A *Los Angeles Times* reporter wrote that Joan Hinton "has found returning to the United States 'very pleasant, very warm, no hostility at all,' in contrast to the climate she says existed when she left for China more than three decades ago."[34]

They moved to the Xiao Wang Zhuang Dairy in Shahe, a suburb north of Beijing in 1980, where they would live out the rest of their days directing the construction of a modern, mechanized dairy for the production of high-quality milk. Aside from having the privileges of a government-provided car and driver and employing the services of a cook, they continued their spartan existence.

Mao's Revolution Betrayed

Engst and Hinton feared for the future of the Chinese revolution after the deaths of Zhou Enlai and Mao in 1976. Deng Xiaoping, who emerged as China's unchallenged leader, decided that Mao's short-cuts to communism had been disastrous; the impressive gains of the 1950s had been undermined by rigid centralized planning, and unbridled ideological struggle had produced a poor and weak nation. Deng convinced his Politburo colleagues that it was time to embrace economic pragmatism and unleash the private sector, famously saying, "It doesn't matter whether the cat is black or white, as long as the cat catches mice." The CCP would maintain its control of the government, and communism would still be the ultimate goal under a new hybrid state-run system called "socialism with Chinese characteristics." As we will see in later chapters, a significant part of the new route to wealth and power depended on the United States as a major source of trade, investment, and advanced training in science and technology. In opening up to the United States, Deng also gained access to the rest of the West, previously inaccessible behind the wall of containment.

The two Americans were deeply disillusioned with the unraveling of China's dream for a classless egalitarian society. As evidence, they pointed to the return of social ills from the pre-revolutionary past—corruption, drugs, prostitution, a growing gap between rich and poor—which came roaring back with a vengeance. From their perspective, Mao's vision had been betrayed. Yet they refused to blame Chairman Mao for the PRC's failures. They simply did not believe that his policies had resulted in millions of deaths; they had been in the countryside where they saw "malnutrition, not starvation," said Hinton. "Without socialism, we would have starved. We banded together, sharing grain coupons." She defended the Cultural Revolution as a crusade "to cure the disparity between the few and the many. How could that be wrong?"' That movement, said Engst, "identified the main problem, which is the dark side of the Party. It just didn't succeed in eradicating it."[35]

Mistakes had been made, to be sure, but self-serving local officials were responsible for the catastrophic Great Leap Forward. The conspiratorial Gang of Four, which included Mao's wife Jiang Qing, bore the guilt for the calamitous Cultural Revolution. Hinton insisted that Premier Zhou Enlai was flexible on tactics but never gave in on principles, and for this reason he "gained the respect of everyone who met him, regardless of whether they agreed with his politics or not." He understood that "you cannot really liberate yourself without liberating all mankind." She urged her son Fred to think for himself and "not just say something is so merely because China says it is so." Writing to him several months before Mao's death, she added, "I think you'll most of the time find that the Chairman has pretty good glasses."[36]

Steady economic development and a more liberal political climate did nothing to convince Hinton and Engst that Deng's policies were acceptable. In the spring of 1989, when thousands of students occupied Tiananmen Square protesting the Party's policies, Engst wrote to his sister that China was "a real mess .... Crime and corruption are rampant. Agriculture is going backwards .... All the time the people at the top are trying to convince both Chinese and foreign businessmen that everything is fine. They are scared to death that the foreign capitalists won't lend them money."

In the wake of Deng's order to clear the square in early June, an anguished Sid Engst wrote, "Forty years after the People's Liberation Army entered Beijing without firing a shot, and with practically the whole of [the population] out to welcome them, the PLA has to have hundreds of tanks and armored personnel carriers sputtering machine gun fire to shoot their way back into the city!! ... What happened on June 3 and 4th was just the logical outcome of the 'reform' that has been going on essentially since Deng came to power." Rampant inflation, exploding internal and external debt, unchecked crime and corruption, widespread prostitution and gambling proved that "Mao had been right about Deng Xiaoping" when he had imprisoned him as a capitalist roader. "My parents," said their son Bill, "were deeply upset and very disappointed. Something they believed in all their lives faded away."[37]

In the decades after China opened its doors wider to international trade and travel, Western journalists flocked to the dairy farm on the outskirts of Beijing to interview the American Maoist couple, who seemed to be living in a time-warp. Tom Ashbrook wrote for the *Boston Globe*, "Hinton's faded blue Mao cap seldom comes off her gray, short-cropped hair. Engst, craggy and balding in the blue work clothes of China's rural millions, talks to his cows in Chinese. Hinton and Engst are warm people, armed with an easy sense of American humor and quick to laugh at life's ironies." Politely but firmly, they defended the goals of the revolution: 'If you want to take China's mistakes,' said Engst, "sure you can write a very fat book. But there was a lot achieved in that time too—an awful lot.' "[38]

"Engst and Hinton say they have watched their socialist dream fall apart as millions of Chinese embraced Western-style capitalism," reported CNN correspondent Andrea Koppel. From 1949 to 1979, Hinton told a *New York Times* reporter, "there was very little stealing, there was great community spirit, there was a common goal. That's all been thrown away now, except for the memory." Joan Hinton "blasts all of the economic reforms beginning in 1978 and culminating with China's entry into the World Trade Organization [in 2001]—and its recent bid for market economy status—as betrayals of the socialist cause," wrote another reporter. She blames "capitalist roaders and imperialists" for any bloodshed during the Great Leap Forward or Cultural Revolution.

"The Western press and the Chinese powers are bragging about how well China is doing," Engst told his family in New York. "Of course, the Western businessmen and the Chinese ruling clique are doing very well indeed, but for about 90% of the ordinary Chinese, the situation is very difficult."[39] Hinton and Engst "remain ascetic Maoists," wrote *Newsweek's* Melinda Liu (see Chapter 10). "They are disappointed that 20 years of reform in China have handed over communal property to 'capitalist compradores,' and that dairy products from the station's 200 or so cows go to feed the customers of a distinctively American icon, McDonald's." Hinton complained that China had become "an altogether capitalist country . . . . China would have developed much faster with a leader like Mao . . . . He had all the people working to develop China. That's not true now. People just want to get rich."[40]

For some Chinese who were too young to remember the halcyon days of the 1950s when there was a shared sense of purpose, the old American leftists were like relics from another time and place. Their nostalgia was quaint and their refusal to acknowledge Mao as a tyrant seemed wrong-headed. They were respected as old friends but considered odd for refusing to move on and abandon such a deeply troubled past. Their stubborn defense of socialist values became a source of curiosity as well as a mild embarrassment to their friends and colleagues.

At the same time, however, their outspoken opinions resonated with tens of millions of Chinese who had been displaced by the reforms. For those men and women, the predictability and benefits of a socialist society—free health-care, free education, and relatively little corruption—had been exchanged for the corrosive pursuit of money. Community and a sense of belonging had

been replaced by loneliness and alienation, and the loss of purity and purpose that once had unified the Chinese nation was painfully real. Joan said
that their three children, who had moved to the United States, "probably
would have stayed if China were still socialist."[41]

When asked if he had any regrets about coming to China, Engst smiled and
answered, "No, because the first thirty years were so good."[42] After he died in
2003, Joan lived by herself on the farm until her death in 2010. Their ashes
were scattered on the Inner Mongolian grasslands where they had experienced the hard but hopeful early years of Communist rule. They remained
convinced that the traumas of land reform, the Great Leap Forward, the
Cultural Revolution, and other campaigns were essential to wrest China
from its miserable past. Tremendous improvements had been made in education, literacy, healthcare, and the emancipation of women. All of these
advances toward a more equal society, which they had personally witnessed,
proved the virtues of Mao's leadership. The Great Helmsman "was a terrific
person and he liberated all the people," said Hinton. "He was not a monster
at all."[43]

Engst and Hinton willingly left family and country behind to participate
in Mao's revolution, dedicating themselves to the betterment of the Chinese
people. Sid transferred his farming skills and Joan put aside a budding career
in a cutting-edge field of science for the uncertainties of a newly conceived
China. Chen-ning Yang, her Chicago graduate school colleague, whose story
is told in the following chapter, took the path she had forsaken. Destined to
become a world-class physicist, his international prestige put him in a unique
position to assist with the PRC's pursuit of greatness, an ambition he shared
with Hinton and Engst, but from a completely different perspective.

4
Chen-ning Yang
Science and Patriotism

Chen-ning (C. N.) Yang was "surprised and greatly honored" to learn, during his visit to Beijing in the summer of 1973, that Mao Zedong wished to speak with him. The fifty-year-old Nobel Prize winning physicist was the first Chinese American scientist to meet with the seventy-nine-year-old revolutionary. Yang spent an hour with Mao in his book-filled study in Zhongnanhai, the leadership compound adjacent to the Forbidden City. Premier Zhou Enlai and Zhou Peiyuan, a physicist who had studied in the United States and was president of Peking University, also attended.[1]

Mao did not come across as an overbearing, paranoid, self-absorbed tyrant. To the contrary, the conversation was "very relaxed and meandering" and "the Chairman had a very good way of putting me at ease," recalled Yang. To his amazement, Mao was "intensely interested" in the scientific laws governing the universe. "Mao clearly had been following some of the developments in contemporary high-energy physics, particularly the question of whether or not elementary particles are divisible. I told him that it was still being hotly debated without an explicit resolution thus far."

Yang was also surprised when Mao told him that ancient Chinese philosophers had speculated about the structure of matter. The Chairman was a poet who understood the sweep of history and had a vision for the future, opined Yang. He was a thinker, a leader, an extremely practical man, "one of the great men of the 20th century." A photograph of Mao meeting with Yang appeared on the front page of *People's Daily* one day after their conversation.[2]

Mao's unexpected audience with C. N. Yang had different layers of meaning. For one thing, China's leaders wanted to learn what it would take to create future Nobel prize winners who could bring international prestige to their nation. More importantly, Mao—the architect of anti-intellectual purges during the 1950s and 1960s—was sending a message that respect for science was once again acceptable. Even before the end of the Cultural

Revolution and several years before Deng Xiaoping's reforms, the meeting with Yang was a calculated signal to overseas Chinese that they were welcome to return to the motherland and assist with its development. The United States, a country with a long tradition of educating Chinese students, was the single largest potential source of advanced scientific training and expertise, and celebrated scientists like Yang could help to pave the way.

Yang had no experience as a politician and did not possess great oratorical skills, nor was he trained as a China specialist. Yet none of this stopped him from becoming the single most visible Chinese American spokesman for improved Sino-American relations. *Washington Post* correspondent Jay Matthews wrote in 1977 that the official Chinese media credited Yang as "the inspiration for the revival of theoretical scientific research in China." Beyond this accolade, Yang was quoted as saying, "I think that people who are at the higher levels in Washington are pleased that I am serving as sort of a bridge between the two countries . . . . I regard this as an important task for the future of the world."[3] From his distinctive perspective as a bicultural emissary, he was sure that the PRC's progress would benefit both nations.

Yang Chen-ning meeting with Mao Zedong in Beijing, 1973.
Alamy.

Following in His Father's Footsteps

In 1928, when he was six years old, Chen-ning Yang's mother took him to the Shanghai docks along the Huangpu River to meet his father who was returning on a ship from the United States. Wu-zhi Yang had spent five years on a Chinese government scholarship earning a bachelor of science degree at Stanford University and a doctorate in mathematics from the University of Chicago. He was a complete stranger to the boy, but they soon made up for lost time. "Father explained to me the structure of the solar system, using big and small balls to represent the sun and planets." He introduced his son to the Roman alphabet and arithmetic problems like the puzzle of chickens and rabbits, a children's introduction to algebra.

C. N. Yang would become a world-famous scientist, yet rather than teaching him geometry or calculus at an early age, his father had him memorize Tang Dynasty poems, the order of the Chinese dynasties, and the eight symbols of the I Ching. A tutor instructed him in the Confucian classics, and he learned to recite the works of major Chinese philosophers such as Mencius. Chen-ning also absorbed the key elements of traditional Chinese culture: loyalty, moral responsibility, and respect for authority—values that would guide him throughout life.[4]

The future physicist was born on September 22, 1922, in Hefei, then a small market town in Anhui Province, and grew up mainly in Beijing on the campus of Tsinghua University where his father was a professor of mathematics. His classmates called him "big head" and "science head." His pleasant, well-ordered life was disrupted, however, when Japan invaded north China in 1937. The Yang family, now with five children, left for the relative safety of Kunming in the southwest province of Yunnan, traveling for weeks by way of Guangzhou, Hong Kong, and Hanoi to get there. At the age of fifteen, Chen-ning enrolled in the Southwest Associated University and pursued his passion for mathematics and physics during the next six years, receiving bachelor and master's degrees. Equipment for experiments was limited because of wartime conditions, but he was able to do advanced work in theoretical physics since only chalk and a blackboard were required.[5]

Yang excelled in his studies—his undergraduate thesis was on group theory and the vibration of polyatomic molecules—and toward the end of the Second World War won a Boxer Indemnity Fellowship to study in the United States, following in his father's footsteps.[6] Traveling by way of Calcutta, he waited there for two months for a berth on a US military ship to New York

City. In January 1946, he enrolled as a graduate student at the University of Chicago to pursue a PhD with Enrico Fermi and Edward Teller, the world-famous physicists who had worked on the Manhattan Project to develop the first atomic bomb. (Yang and fellow grad student Joan Hinton worked to-gether in a lab, and he taught her a few words of Chinese before she left for China.) Colleagues who had difficulty pronouncing "Chen-ning" called him Frank, an English name he chose because of his admiration for Benjamin Franklin. He quickly adapted to American culture, but never forgot his Chinese heritage.[7]

Yang's success at Chicago led to an appointment at the Institute for Advanced Study in Princeton, New Jersey, directed by the renowned phys-icist Robert Oppenheimer. It was there at a Chinese restaurant that he met his future wife, Chih-li Tu, who was studying English in New York City. Coincidentally, she had been Yang's student in a mathematics class he had taught in Kunming in 1945. They were married in August 1950 and had two boys and a girl: Franklin, Gilbert, and Eulee.

Chih-li's personal history was complicated. Her father, Yu-ming Tu, was a prominent Nationalist Chinese general who had been captured by the Communists during the civil war, and her mother had fled to Taiwan and then to the United States with Chih-li. After ten years in prison, General Tu was released and made a member of the People's Political Consultative Conference, and his wife returned to live with him in Beijing in 1963. It seems possible he received special treatment because Beijing hoped to con-vince his famous son-in-law to return to the PRC.[8]

Yang left Princeton in 1966 to become Albert Einstein Professor of Physics and Director of the Institute for Theoretical Physics at the State University of New York Stony Brook on Long Island, where he worked for thirty-three years until his retirement in 1999. (The institute now bears Yang's name.) The Stony Brook campus was only twenty years old when he arrived, but was close to the Brookhaven National Laboratory where Yang had spent summers doing research. He declined offers from much more established programs at Columbia and Chicago, preferring the independence and chal-lenge of running his own show. He recruited new faculty, graduate students, and postdocs, and with support from the National Science Foundation and the Department of Energy built the Stony Brook Institute into a highly regarded enterprise. In his office was a framed photo of Einstein, whom Yang had met in Princeton. There was also a copy of a newspaper story from the 1930s denying the possibility of splitting the atom.

Yang's Adopted Country

Chen-ning Yang never intended to stay in the United States, but the turmoil of civil war and revolution in China convinced him the better option was to postpone his return. He was on a fast track and going back home would have to wait. It was a painful decision for a devoted son who was the eldest of his parents' children.

More than five thousand Chinese students and scholars were in the United States at the time of Mao's victory, most of them studying science, engineering, and technology. Inspired by the idea of rebuilding their homeland under its new government, about eight hundred soon returned to join their families, where the best and brightest of them took up key research and teaching positions. Others went to Hong Kong and Taiwan, but a majority, like Yang, stayed in the United States to complete their studies and continue their work.

US government policies concerning the Chinese students were wildly inconsistent. The Department of Justice issued orders for some to be deported, while the Department of State refused deportation orders. As many as 150 were barred from returning to Red China by the US Immigration and Naturalization Service as possible security risks, and the FBI's surveillance of students suspected of being Communist sympathizers increased after the outbreak of the Korean War. Caught in a legal limbo, they were unable to apply for permanent residence but were not permitted to leave the United States. The Refugee Relief Act of 1953 allowed two thousand Chinese to apply for residence as non-quota immigrants, but only a few were given the option of US citizenship. Late in 1955, the United States told those with expired visas to leave the country or face the possibility of being deported. The stranded students were understandably frustrated, confused, and angry.[9]

The most egregious case was Qian Xuesen (Hsue-shen Tsien), a brilliant scientist trained at the Massachusetts Institute of Technology and the California Institute of Technology, who was co-founder of the Jet Propulsion Laboratory in Pasadena. He wanted to visit his parents in China in 1950, but lost his security clearance and could not travel after being accused of having been a member of the American Communist Party. After repeated questioning by federal authorities, he was detained and not allowed outside the Los Angeles area for the next four years. Qian, his wife, and their two American-born children were finally authorized to leave the United States in 1955. Warmly welcomed in the PRC, Qian would become the celebrated head of the country's rocket and missile program, and to the end of his life, in 2009, would not consider setting foot in the United States again. His case is worth recalling today, in a time of heightened suspicions of Chinese scientists working in US universities.[10]

Eventually, some four thousand Chinese students stayed in the United States. They kept a low public profile, well aware of the country's long history of racism and discrimination against the Chinese. Their best course was to stay quiet, avoid politics, work hard, and blend into mainstream American culture.[11] C. N. Yang suffered no direct harassment or persecution, although he had reason to feel a degree of ambivalence about his adopted country. On one occasion in 1952, he considered leaving the United States when his wife had trouble getting a visa to return after visiting her mother in Taiwan. Later, in 1954, his family was prevented from buying a house in Princeton, New Jersey, because of their race. At the time, Yang felt "very unhappy and very surprised that such a thing should happen in Princeton, where people pride themselves on the liberal character of the town." He considered taking legal action, but decided against it and was able to purchase a house in another neighborhood "with absolutely no difficulty and very nice neighbors."[12] He was granted permanent US immigration status in 1953 but did not take US citizenship until 1964.

Winning the Nobel Prize in Physics

Chen-ning Yang and Tsung-dao (T. D.) Lee were catapulted to international fame in 1957 when the Royal Swedish Academy of Sciences announced they had jointly won the Nobel Prize in Physics. Both in their early thirties, they were the first Chinese scientists ever to receive the coveted award. Their research overturned the parity principle, one of the fundamental tenets of nuclear physics, and their theory was confirmed in experiments by a team of scientists at Columbia University led by Chien-shiung Wu, a woman who had done her undergraduate training in China. The Nobel Committee recognized Lee and Yang for a "stunning theoretical discovery" and praised them for ideas that "have led to a great liberation in our thinking on the very structure of physical theory." Their work shed new light on the behavior of the atom.[13]

T. D. Lee came from China in 1946 for graduate studies at the University of Chicago, where he met Yang, who was four years older. They became close friends—both men shared a fascination with traditional Chinese art and philosophy—and drove over 9,300 miles one summer in a 1941 Ford, exploring the western United States with two other students. "Yang was extremely bright," remembered Lee. "Often we would have different ideas and opinions and occasionally our discussions would become quite animated. That added a great deal of life to our student days." Jeremy Bernstein, a fellow physicist, wrote, "They take great pleasure in racing each other in calculations, and as they are both extremely fast thinkers, watching them or listening to them at work can be both an exhilarating and a somewhat exhausting experience."[14] Lee followed Yang to the Institute for Advanced Study in 1951 and two years later accepted a position at Columbia University, where he became the youngest full professor on the faculty. He taught at Columbia until his retirement in 2012.

How Yang and Lee would identify themselves at the Nobel ceremony in Sweden was unclear because neither was an American citizen at the time. Both of them carried passports issued by the Nationalist Chinese government on Taiwan. Lee's mother was in Taiwan (his father was dead) and Yang's parents were in Shanghai, which was under Communist control. It was not long after the first Taiwan Strait crisis and the Soviet Union's launch of Sputnik. When the two young men arrived with their wives at Stockholm's Bromma Airport on separate flights—Yang came by way of Copenhagen where he met with Niels Bohr, who had won the Nobel Prize in Physics in 1922—three representatives from the Chinese embassy were waiting to greet them and offer assistance. (Sweden officially recognized the PRC in 1950.) The Swedes, wanting to avoid an international incident, whisked the scientists away to a downtown hotel. At the award ceremony, to which all diplomats were invited, only the seat of the Beijing envoy was empty.[15]

After Swedish King Gustaf Adolf VI presented Lee and Yang with their gold Nobel Prize medals, Yang spoke before an audience of two thousand distinguished guests. He said very little about science and did not mention contemporary politics. Instead, he talked about China's prolonged struggle to come to terms with the West. He described the Boxer Uprising of 1900, a violent response to the expanding influence of Westerners, as "an emotional expression of the frustration and anger of the proud people of China who had been subject to ever-increasing oppression from without and decadent corruption from within." The demise of the Boxers, claimed Yang, settled "once and for all, the debate as to how much Western culture should be introduced into China." The Qing dynasty was forced to pay sizable reparations

Nobel Prize winners C. N. Yang (left) and T. D. Lee, Princeton, 1957.
Alamy.

to the Western powers and Japan, and the United States used much of the money to establish a fund to set up an English language institute, which grew into Tsinghua University, and to provide fellowships for Chinese students to study in America. "I was a direct beneficiary of both of these two projects," said Yang.

In accepting the prestigious Nobel award and acknowledging his debt to the United States for his education, Yang said he was "as proud of my Chinese heritage and background as I am devoted to modern science—a part of human civilization of Western origin—to which I have dedicated and continue to dedicate my work . . . . As I stand here today, I am heavy with an awareness of the fact that I am in more than one sense a product of both the Chinese and Western cultures, in harmony and in conflict."[16] Finding the right balance between China and America would be his life-long pursuit.

Yang and Lee had a falling out in the early 1960s after disagreeing over who deserved the most credit for their joint research on the parity principle. (There was friction between them at the Nobel ceremony when Yang insisted that he speak first because he was older, even though Lee's surname came first in the Roman alphabet.) Their collaboration "had always been one of equal partnership," said Lee at a symposium on the occasion of his sixtieth birthday. "The world has rewarded us with recognition and success. Shouldn't that be sufficient?" Yet the two scientists, once close friends and collaborators, went their separate ways and never reconciled.[17]

"A Turning Point in My Career"

While C. N. Yang's life in the United States was happy and rewarding, he had an abiding sense of obligation to his family in China, most especially to his father. No relationship was more important in traditional Chinese culture. Due to his son's growing prestige, Wu-zhi Yang was allowed to travel to Switzerland in 1957 to meet with him, Chih-li, and his grandson Franklin. It was an exceptional privilege for a professor of mathematics, now teaching at Fudan University in Shanghai, who had studied and had relatives in the United States. During periodic anti-US campaigns, the Communist Party branded others with similar backgrounds as traitors and spies.

The family stayed for six weeks in Geneva, where Chen-ning spent time at CERN (the European Organization for Nuclear Research), just a few months before the Nobel Prize was announced. At the time of their reunion, recalled Yang, "Father had . . . a sense of responsibility to convince me to go back to China," although he realized his son could do more advanced work in the West. The senior Yang's wholehearted enthusiasm for China's progress under Mao was a major influence on his son, who shared his father's conviction that the new nation was moving in the right direction and would eventually overcome the humiliation and exploitation of the past. He remembered how his father "wanted me to look far ahead, to clearly discern the sweep of history."

With his wife, their second son Gilbert, and C. N.'s brother Chen-ping Yang, who was now living in the United States, Yang was able to see his father as well as his mother in Geneva again in 1960, and for a third time in 1962. Two years later, Yang and Chih-li flew to Hong Kong to meet both of his parents and two of his siblings, brother Zhen-han and sister Chen-yu. (During that visit a crowd of about two thousand people waited for hours outside Hong Kong's City Hall to hear Yang give a public lecture.) Then, as the fury of the Cultural Revolution was unleashed, he lost contact with his father, who was criticized as an American-educated bourgeois intellectual. He was able to see his mother and brother in Hong Kong in 1970, but his father was too sick to make the journey.[18]

In the summer of 1971, Yang asked for permission to visit the PRC, now that the US travel ban was lifted. After picking up his visa at the Chinese embassy in Paris, he went to the American embassy to cancel the language in his passport that did not allow for travel to Communist China. He was elated when the pilot of his Air France flight announced they had entered Chinese air space: "My heart almost jumped through my throat."[19] He arrived in

Shanghai on July 19, two weeks after Henry Kissinger's secret trip to Beijing to lay the groundwork for President Nixon's visit in February 1972.

The immediate reason for Yang's trip was to see his father, who was seriously ill with diabetes, as well as his mother and siblings. During a month-long stay in China he gave lectures and visited universities, factories, and hospitals. At the Academy of Sciences in Beijing, he observed an atomic reactor and a low-energy accelerator constructed in the late 1950s with the help of Russian advisers. He also visited his hometown of Hefei and spent a day at Dazhai, a model commune in Shanxi Province where he was surprised and delighted to meet his good friend Joan Hinton.

Instead of being treated as a traitor who had turned his back on China, Yang was greeted as a prodigal son. There were reunions with scientists he had not seen in twenty years, including Huang Kun, who had studied in England and returned to China in 1951 to become a pioneer in the physics of semiconductors. Yang was especially happy to see Deng Jiaxian, who received his PhD from Purdue University and repatriated in 1950 to lead China's atomic and hydrogen bomb programs. When Deng told Yang that no foreigners were involved in the Chinese nuclear weapons program, aside from some minor assistance from the Soviet Union at the beginning, Yang was overcome with excitement to learn of Deng's "selfless and magnificent contributions," knowing full well that the PRC's self-reliance was essential for national unity and international respect.[20]

Yang's trip culminated in a dinner with Zhou Enlai. The ever charming, cosmopolitan Premier, who had studied in France as a young man, wanted to know all about life and politics in the United States—the student movement, the response to Nixon's plan to withdraw troops from Vietnam, attitudes toward Japan, the wages of carpenters, professors, and government officials. He was especially curious about the position of Blacks in American society.

Several of China's most prominent scientists who had trained in the United States also attended the five-hour banquet in Yang's honor. One of them was Qian Xuesen, the "father of Chinese rocketry" who had been deported from the United States. Others had studied at Harvard, Princeton, MIT, University of Chicago, and University of Illinois. Remarkably, about half of China's leading scientists had studied in America, and they would become some of the most effective promoters of future bilateral ties between the two countries.[21]

Upon returning to the United States, Yang called his journey "a turning point in my career." It was an "emotion-laden, soul-searching experience . . . that profoundly changed me." Full of admiration for the accomplishments of friends and colleagues who had left the West to offer their talents to New China, he must have experienced some pangs of guilt. What if he had answered his country's call and had gone back after the Communist victory in 1949? What might he have contributed to China's scientific modernization? Whatever the case, he now resolved to do everything he could to bridge the divide between the two nations that claimed his loyalty.

Yang told a reporter that the question of his returning to live and work in China never came up in his conversation with Zhou Enlai. At this point in his career, it would seem he was more valuable for what he could accomplish from the outside; his stature as a Nobel laureate gave him a prestigious international platform. It was apparent, moreover, that the PRC could count on the loyalty of Yang's parents. His father, who could have stayed in Europe or might have claimed asylum in the United States on any of his three trips to Geneva, had proven himself devoted not only to the Communist Party but also to the recovery of China's lost glory. Yang wrote after his father's death, "Circulating in my body is Father's blood, the blood of Chinese culture."[22]

Beijing was competing with Taiwan to win the political support of overseas Chinese and to attract their expertise and financial investments. Like C. N. Yang, many scientists in North America and other parts of the world had relatives as well as former classmates and teachers in mainland China, and beyond having a common language and culture they felt a responsibility to aid their motherland. The Chinese government had a special category for ethnic Chinese from abroad; it was typically easier for them to obtain visas and they paid less than other foreigners for train tickets and hotels, although more than local Chinese. With a mixture of curiosity, duty, and pride, many were eager to find opportunities to support China's development.[23]

During his early visits to the PRC, Yang discovered "a dramatically different country: still poor, but very, very different from the old fragmented China" whose tragic modern history had been a source of frustration and shame.

When I was a child, almost every year there was a drought or a flood in some province in which millions of people died. When these things happened, the peasants would drift away from where they lived. I was born in Hefei, a town of about ten thousand, and when these floods come, when these poor people came, they would camp in the squares and they would sell their daughters. You could buy a maid for a few dollars, and the maid became your property, and you could treat her any way you want, except if you killed her there might be some problems. But if you beat her no one would bat an eye. That was the state of China, and opium smoking was very common. Of course, the Western people would despise the Chinese. When the eight powers occupied Beijing [during the Boxer Uprising], they only had a few thousand troops, and yet they were able to occupy the capital of a huge empire. Why? Because China was down on her knees and there was nothing that China could do. Against such a background, everybody realized China was so weak . . . . Among other things this is because China had no modern science.[24]

The post-1949 transformation of China—previously ridiculed as the "sick man of Asia"—was nothing short of miraculous to Yang. Optimism and confidence had replaced a fatalistic acceptance of life's tragedies. China now was self-sufficient and proud, but not arrogant. It was "a country with a purpose" and "a pervading attitude that people should be moral." Crime in the streets, prostitution, alcoholism, and drug problems were "essentially nonexistent." There was "a spirit and discipline that American society lacks," he told a New York audience. "China says that American society is characterized by the principles of acquisition, competition and consumerism, and China does not want any of them."

From scientists in the PRC he learned that theory and practice always must go hand-in-hand since the purpose of education is to produce "a generation of young people dedicated to the service of Chinese society, not a new elite class." Research should "not be detached fundamentally from the needs of the whole society." In the Beijing area, reported Yang, students spend one month a year working in a small factory and one month on a farm. It was essential to "walk on two legs," according to the Maoist slogan. On the whole, he found that experimental science was more important than theoretical science, but work in his own field of high energy physics was not being neglected. He optimistically predicted, "I haven't the faintest doubt that China will play an extremely important role on every frontier of science and technology in the future."[25]

Yang, of course, did not experience the purges of intellectuals that took place during mass campaigns in the 1950s and 1960s. He was never criticized or forced to make confessions about being a counter-revolutionary because he had studied in the United States. He was not denounced and sent to the countryside for re-education. Some years later, he admitted that the

Cultural Revolution was a disaster for China, but confessed, "I didn't know it at that time because I was fed all sorts of information, and nobody, including my parents, [told] me the depths of devastation to China . . . . Part of it they didn't know, but . . . some things they knew they would not tell me." It was not until December 1979 that US-trained scientists who had been persecuted during the Cultural Revolution were officially exonerated. The government informed them that they had been "victims of frame-ups and false charges at the hands of Lin Biao and the Gang of Four," an acknowledgement that was hardly adequate compensation for their years of suffering.[26]

C. N. Yang was by no means the only foreigner to view the PRC through rose-colored glasses. The first two American scientists to visit since 1949 were Arthur Galston, a plant biologist at Yale University, and Ethan Signer, a professor in the genetics of bacterial viruses at MIT. Both men were anti-Vietnam War activists who were invited to Beijing in May 1971 after spending two weeks in Hanoi. Arriving two months before Yang, they met with Chinese counterparts, watched a demonstration of acupuncture anesthesia, enjoyed Chinese food, and were charmed by Premier Zhou Enlai. Similarly, Victor Sidel, an American medical doctor, and his wife Ruth Sidel, a psychiatric social worker, visited in the early 1970s and were greatly impressed by China's dramatic progress in providing medical care, especially through paramedical "barefoot doctors" in rural areas. They found "a country with a deep sense of mission and history, a nation trying all at one time to be daringly experimental, uncompromisingly doctrinaire, and unconstrainedly pragmatic."[27]

While many scientists of Chinese descent responded to the emotional pull of friends, relatives, and homeland, other US citizens had their own motives for wanting to connect with New China. Some, like Galston, Singer, and the Sidels, were disillusioned with Western society and the war in Vietnam and captivated by Mao's utopian rhetoric. Some simply wanted to explore a vast but forbidden land and be the first among their peers to see the People's Republic with their own eyes. And there were those with a more high-minded rationale who "believed profoundly in the power of science to transcend political boundaries," writes historian Mary Brown Bullock. "In this they were the heirs to the early twentieth century belief that modern science and the scientific method would introduce a progressive, modern society." They considered a field such as physics to be "a world science, a universal science, not a Chinese science nor an American science."[28]

Advocating for US-China Engagement

Chen-ning Yang completely agreed that science should not be held captive to politics, but this did not mean that he would sit back and simply watch events unfold. After 1971, he visited China annually and traveled widely, including trips to Xinjiang and Tibet. He not only knew the language and culture but had been introduced to China's leaders, unlike most China watchers in the United States. In addition to Mao and Zhou Enlai, he met with Hua Guofeng, Mao's designated successor, in 1976 and again in 1977, and with Deng Xiaoping in 1974, 1977, and 1978. After Zhou's death in January 1976, Yang delivered a eulogy to a crowd of more than 1,300 people in an auditorium in New York City's Chinatown. Speaking first in Chinese and then in English, he called the premier's passing a "gigantic loss to the people of China" and "to all the justice-loving people of the world."[29]

Yang was not the only Chinese American to engage in unofficial diplomacy, but he was especially persistent and effective. His first foray into a foreign policy issue concerned a seemingly obscure controversy over control of the Diaoyu Islands, a group of small uninhabited territories claimed by China but held by Japan, which calls them the Senkaku Islands. In May 1971, a dozen prominent Chinese Americans, including Yang, published a letter in the *New York Times* addressed to President Nixon and members of Congress asking them to "recognize Chinese sovereignty over these islands." Later that year, Yang testified before the Senate Foreign Relations Committee declaring, "the Chinese claim is irrefutable."[30] The contentious dispute remains unresolved to this day.

On university campuses across the United States, Yang gave lectures on Chinese science and education and also made the case for US diplomatic recognition of the People's Republic of China. Not every audience was receptive. Students at Northwestern University who were sympathetic to Taiwan took him to task for his uncritical views of Chinese Communism and questioned his qualifications for discussing US-China relations. They wrote tongue-in-cheek in the student newspaper, "We are thinking about inviting Dr. Kissinger to give us a lecture on Physics." But Yang was not dissuaded from speaking out. At the University of Maryland, he argued it was in the self-interest of Taiwan—where he noted he had relatives and friends, teachers and students—to "end the estrangement of Taiwan from its ancestral and cultural homeland." The island could not rely on the United States for its defense indefinitely because "the average American is less concerned about the long-range interests of the people in Taiwan than the average Chinese."[31]

Yang worked tirelessly to convince Chinese Americans that US recognition of the PRC was the right thing to do. In September 1977, he became president of the newly established National Association of Chinese Americans (NACA), a non-profit organization that lobbied for normalization between Washington and Beijing. "It is imperative that the two countries develop friendly relations. There are no other viable alternatives," said Yang. "As an ethnic group familiar with two cultures, we owe it to our country of origin, we owe it to our country of adoption, and we owe it to ourselves to work together to foster lasting understanding between the two peoples and to build a bridge of friendship between the two countries."

He also spoke out against racism in the United States. Addressing an audience of Chinese American students at the University of Buffalo, he encouraged them to make their voices heard; it was high time to come together to oppose mistreatment and discrimination. Anti-Chinese prejudice may have been "less blatant" in recent years, but this was due to the progress of the African American civil rights movement. "We are continuing to hold on to their coats. But it is time to begin to fight on our own to assert our rights. We cannot expect others to do this on our behalf."[32]

On February 27, 1977, five years after the Shanghai Communique was signed by Richard Nixon and Zhou Enlai, NACA took out full-page ads in the *New York Times*, *Washington Post*, and other newspapers urging President Carter to establish full diplomatic relations with the PRC. Yang and others who signed the statement asked, "Will the U.S. continue to isolate itself from its own allies by a China policy inconsistent with American interests and commitments?" A peaceful settlement of the Taiwan question cannot be achieved "by continued [American] military involvement with Taiwan, and by recognizing as the government of China a regime that was discredited and driven out by the Chinese people 28 years ago." Yang's lobbying was not without risk. His family received threatening letters and feared that packages sent to their Long Island home might contain bombs.[33] He did not necessarily speak for the Chinese community in the United States at large. They welcomed the prospect of family reunions, visits to home villages, and investment opportunities on the mainland, but generally preferred to steer clear of politics. Many remained intensely skeptical of communism.

After normalization was announced by Jimmy Carter and Hua Guofeng in December 1978 (see Chapter 5), NACA hosted a reception attended by Chai

Zemin, head of the PRC Liaison Office, at the Washington Hilton Hotel on January 1, 1979. On that occasion, Yang spoke confidently about increased opportunities for reunions between Chinese Americans and their relatives in China.

When Vice Premier Deng Xiaoping and his wife Zhuo Lin came to Washington a few weeks later, NACA cosponsored a banquet in their honor with the US-China People's Friendship Association, whose president was William Hinton. His mother Carmelita attended the dinner, and his daughter Carma, who had grown up in China, interpreted for Deng.[34]

In Yang's remarks at the banquet, he called Deng's visit "a watershed event of our times" that "will bring forth greatly increased exchanges in scholarly, cultural, commercial, and tourist activities." He noted that the Chinese American community had long been divided over the issue of Taiwan, but asserted that the "overwhelming majority" are "enthusiastically supportive of normalization."

> That there is only one China and Taiwan is a province of China is recognized by all Chinese as dictated by 4,000 years of Chinese history. We hope, for the long range interests of the residents of Taiwan and that of their children, that each and every one of them will recognize the inexorable development of history, will recognize their own historical responsibility, and will work for the reunification of the province with their 900 million brothers and sisters, with whom they share the same language, the same culture, and undoubtedly will share the same destiny in a world that will grow increasingly competitive. Because we are rooted in both the American and the Chinese cultures, we know that we bear a special responsibility in promoting the understanding and friendship between the two countries . . . . On this occasion, we re-pledge ourselves to continue to fulfill our responsibility in the task of the building of friendship between the peoples of the two nations, without which there can be no true peace and stability in the world.[35]

In Yang's judgment, bringing the United States and China closer together was his "most important contribution, far outweighing any other thing I have done."[36] That was a remarkable statement coming from one of the world's preeminent physicists, but entirely consistent with his determination to see China take its position as a respected member of the family of nations.

A Flowering of Scientific Exchange

From the Qing dynasty's self-strengthening movement in the late nineteenth century to the PRC's policy of "indigenous innovation" in the 2000s, China's leaders have generally seen science and technology—broadly defined to include national defense—as the key to wealth and power. Prior to the Communist revolution, the Chinese looked to Japan, Europe, and especially the United States for advanced education. In the 1950s, about one thousand Chinese scientists and thirty-seven thousand Chinese students went to the Soviet Union for training, and some eleven thousand Soviet advisors came to the PRC. After the Sino-Soviet split and the self-imposed isolation of the Cultural Revolution, China once again looked West. Ideology was rejected in favor of pragmatism in order to achieve the four modernizations: industry, agriculture, national defense, and science and technology. "Independence," said Deng Xiaoping, "does not mean shutting the door on the world nor does self-reliance mean blind opposition to everything foreign. Science and technology are a kind of wealth created in common by all mankind."[37]

During the 1970s, the Committee on Scholarly Communication with the People's Republic of China (CSCPRC)—an independent organization under the auspices of the National Academy of Sciences, American Council of Learned Societies, and Social Science Research Council—sponsored seventy-three academic delegations between the United States and China, mainly in the sciences. These month-long trips were useful in laying the groundwork for future long-term exchanges. Medicine, agriculture, and earth sciences were among the most promising fields for collaboration, and given China's size and its biodiversity, opportunities for research on the environment were especially attractive. The existence of certain historical documents was also enticing; there were, for example, records of solar spots and solar eclipses dating back more than two thousand years.

C. N. Yang offered encouragement and advice to the CSCPRC, but did not participate in its activities, perhaps because he wanted to maintain his own channels of communication rather than being part of a larger group effort. He also wanted to give special attention to high-energy physics, and masterminded a conference on that subject, the first attended by scientists from the PRC, at the State University of New York at Stony Brook in 1973.[38] Yang stepped down as NACA's president in October 1980, with the organization's mission of achieving normalization having been accomplished, and established the Committee on Educational Exchange with

China (CEEC) to raise money and identify placements for Chinese students at US universities. Yang was recreating his own experience—as well as his father's—of Chinese students coming to the United States for advanced training.

Stony Brook was eager to receive scholars from the mainland, and the first three to arrive on the campus in February 1979 included Yang's sister Chen-yu Yang, who was a physiologist from Shanghai. Twenty-one more came during the 1979–80 academic year and another twenty-eight in 1980–81, the majority supported by the Chinese government. Nearly all of the women and men were mid-career academics who had learned Russian during the 1950s; they needed training in English, and urgently wanted to make up for time lost during the Cultural Revolution when universities were shuttered. Those who joined Yang's Institute for Theoretical Physics could pursue research in field theory, super gravity, statistical mechanics, nuclear theory, astrophysics, and other subfields. In those early years, approximately 20 percent of the officially sponsored PRC scholars at US universities were in physics, more than any other field of study. Hard science was so highly regarded that Deng Xiaoping's son, Deng Zhifang, studied quantum physics at the University of Rochester, and the son of Jiang Zemin, Jiang Mianheng, received a PhD in electrical engineering from Drexel University.

Yang also gave attention to institution-building. He raised $1 million from Hong Kong for a new research institute at Zhongshan University in Guangzhou and helped to establish and fund a Center for Advanced Study at Tsinghua University in Beijing. In 1977, he correctly predicted that "in another twenty-five years, China will become one of the world's great industrial powers." Very few observers would have shared this view at the time, but his forecast was partly based on Beijing's decision to invest in basic research. The PRC's attention to mathematics and physics—which Yang, T. D. Lee, and other Chinese American scientists did so much to encourage—laid the essential groundwork for advances in semiconductors, quantum computing, and artificial intelligence, fields that would be crucial to the twenty-first century future of cyber technology.[39]

Cooperation and Crisis

A breakthrough in educational exchange came in August 1978, several months before full diplomatic relations were established, when Chinese officials proposed sending hundreds of scholars to the United States, a move that President Carter welcomed. In fact, when Frank Press, the president's science adviser went to China that summer to discuss longer-term academic exchanges, no ceiling was put on the number of Chinese who would come, so long as the US government would not have to pay the costs.

The honeymoon period that followed normalization after 1979 saw a flowering of scientific collaboration "led by a most remarkable network of Chinese-American researchers," according to the journal *Science*. As cultural intermediaries, they smoothed the way and hastened the process of educational exchange. Among them, "no researcher is regarded as more energetic and successful in furthering Chinese-American science ties than physicist Yang Chen Ning."[40] If the rapid expansion of Sino-American scholarly exchange was unexpected, the idea that hundreds of thousands of Chinese students would one day study in US universities was beyond anyone's wildest imagination. Unlike the tightly controlled centralized exchanges with the Soviet Union, a decentralized university-to-university approach was one big reason for its surprising growth.

In June 1989, however, the dream of a Western-inspired scientific and cultural renaissance turned into a nightmare after the bloody crackdown on protesters who had occupied Tiananmen Square. The US government imposed sanctions, the Fulbright scholar exchange was halted, and the National Academy of Sciences suspended almost all cooperation with China. American scholars faced a dilemma. Would continued engagement with China serve as an endorsement of a repressive regime? Or would withholding academic relations isolate and punish the very people they wanted to help? Yang took a long-term view, saying, "It is absolutely essential for the United States to keep traffic and intercourse with China going as much as possible. The best policy is to maintain scholarly exchanges as before. It is extremely important. It will benefit both countries . . . . If the United States imposes sanctions that are too strong, there is a danger that China will close its doors and the United States will have no influence on Chinese policies. That would be a disaster."[41]

Even before the Tiananmen crackdown, Chinese leaders were troubled about the corrosive appeal of Western ideas such as democracy. It was a longstanding quandary for China's modernizers: How could they import Western technology but resist liberal Western values such as freedom of speech? Fang Lizhi, an astrophysicist at the University of Science and Technology of China in Yang's hometown of Hefei, spoke out about the need to "look with humility at what others have to offer, and what is good we should try to incorporate. Complete openness, allowing the outside world to challenge our way of doing things, is the only way to change our society."[42] His opposition to Marxist orthodoxy inspired students to question the authority of the Communist Party, and in the aftermath of the June 4 uprising he was charged with counter-revolutionary crimes. After taking refuge in the US embassy in Beijing for more than a year (with the help of Professor Perry Link and Ambassador James Lilley), Fang and his wife were deported to the United States by way of Britain. Not wanting to burn his bridges with Beijing, C. N. Yang did not come to Fang Lizhi's defense. In his view, Chinese society operated on time-honored concepts of social relations, including loyalty and respect for authority, not Western definitions of individual human rights.

The Tiananmen crisis disrupted but did not destroy scientific and educational exchanges. The longer-lasting impact was brain drain—the fact that large numbers of Chinese students and scholars trained in the United States were not returning to the PRC. President George H. W. Bush's April 1990 Executive Order protecting some 50,000 Chinese students in the United States from deportation exacerbated the problem. (This policy was made permanent by the Chinese Student Protection Act, which was passed by Congress in October 1992.) Yang acknowledged the issue but took the hopeful view that many scholars would go back as conditions improved. "If you look at the presidents of the important universities in China," he later said, "the majority of them are the people that came to America and spent five or ten years and then returned to China. They are the leaders of Chinese higher education today."[43]

Coming Full Circle

Deep down, Yang always had been a Chinese patriot. When the British colony of Hong Kong reverted to Beijing's control on July 1, 1997, he was among four thousand people who attended the previous night's ceremonies in the gleaming new Hong Kong Convention and Exhibition Centre. Many Hong Kong citizens viewed the handover with trepidation, but for him it was source of enormous pride, marking a restoration of China's sovereignty and a "renaissance of the Chinese people." Had his father been alive, declared Yang, "he would have been even more moved than I." His son never forgot that Wu-zhi Yang lived through the height of the "humiliating exploitations" of the early twentieth century and "personally experienced pervasive racial discrimination" when he went to the United States in the 1920s. Lowering the British Union Jack and raising the PRC's flag over Hong Kong "proudly announced to the world: This is Chinese territory!" fulfilling a long-held desire of his father's generation. It was a day they had "dreamed of throughout their lives."[44] When asked on a local radio program about his greatest accomplishment in life, Yang replied, "It was to help the Chinese people to overcome a deep feeling of an inferiority complex. I still feel that is the meaning of the Nobel Prize."[45]

Two months after his wife's death in 2003, Yang's odyssey came full circle when he relocated to Beijing and took up a post at Tsinghua University, where he had spent eight years of his boyhood. In December 2004, the eighty-two-year-old physicist married a twenty-eight-year-old woman, Fan Weng, whom he first met in 1995 when she was a student at Shantou University in Guangdong Province. (Weng had been married and divorced by the time they met again.) Yang said their relationship, which created considerable controversy on Chinese social media, had given him a new lease on life.[46]

After more than a decade of living in Beijing and spending the winters at the Chinese University of Hong Kong, Yang quietly renounced his US citizenship and accepted PRC citizenship in 2017.[47] Doing so was a matter of convenience since dual citizenship is not allowed under Chinese law, but it was also a late-in-life expression of support for China's campaign to convince a new generation of Chinese scientists to return from abroad. His decision to apply for US citizenship in 1964 had not been an easy one. His father had studied in the United States for five years, recalled Yang, "yet I know, in one corner of his heart, he did not forgive me to his dying day for having renounced my country of birth." Yang spent most of his adult life in the United States. Even so, he explained, "the concept of leaving China permanently to emigrate to another country simply did not exist in traditional Chinese culture."[48] His life, as he said in his Nobel Prize speech in 1957, was "a product of both the Chinese and Western cultures, in harmony and in conflict."

Chen-ning Yang's determination to mobilize Chinese American opinion and to open the door for US-China scientific exchange was partly to redeem himself in memory of his father and partly to assuage his guilt for failing to join his fellow Chinese scientists who returned to the newly established People's Republic after 1949. His practice of informal diplomacy was effective and consequential, but until 1979 was limited by the absence of formal

US-China diplomatic relations. Accomplishing that goal, which was essential for more substantial change, would require the concerted effort of political leaders and diplomats. In the next chapter, we will see how Stapleton Roy, a US Foreign Service Officer with deep knowledge of China, would help to breathe fresh life into the longstanding hope of making China peaceful, stable, and friendly to the United States.

5

J. Stapleton Roy

The Art of Diplomacy

Stapleton Roy joined the US Foreign Service soon after graduating from college. "I didn't have a clue what diplomats did," he recalled, "but a State Department recruiter made the life sound exciting." The idea of living abroad was familiar since he had spent most of his youth in China, being the son of missionaries. His father had a dim view of diplomats as hard-drinking and too worldly, which only made him that much more curious about pursuing such a vocation.[1]

During a long and distinguished career, Roy would serve as US ambassador to Singapore, China, and Indonesia, and would hold high-ranking positions in the State Department. It was, however, his less visible role in helping to achieve full diplomatic relations between the United States and the PRC that stands as the single most important accomplishment of his professional life.

In 1978, when the two nations agreed to accomplish normalization, as it was called, Roy was deputy to Leonard Woodcock, head of the United States Liaison Office (USLO) in Beijing. The tough, taciturn former leader of the United Auto Workers in Detroit had no China background nor much experience as a diplomat, but he was a seasoned bargainer with a reputation for integrity and strong political connections with members of Congress. Woodcock chose Roy, a relatively junior Foreign Service Officer, as his right-hand man, and together they managed the final, crucial stages of the negotiations between Washington and Beijing.

Despite their completely different backgrounds and personalities, the two men proved to be an ideal match. Woodcock knew how to listen and when to push an issue, while Roy, who was fluent in Chinese and had served in Hong Kong and Taiwan, had a nuanced understanding of the political and cultural differences between Americans and Chinese. Woodcock tended to be an optimist, while Roy played the role of careful, cautious pessimist. His job, he said, was to anticipate problems and "try to look for things that could go wrong. I would always point out what I saw as potential stumbling blocks that still lay ahead. We never had a disagreement in terms of where we ended up."

Woodcock believed that "one of the best things that I did was choosing Stape to be the Deputy, because he was worth his weight in gold through the whole period." Roy, who had misgivings about amateurs doing diplomacy, returned the compliment. "What I liked about Woodcock was that he was truly a professional negotiator. He had an uncanny ability to sense where you were in a negotiation" and a talent for saying the right thing at the right time. Roy drafted detailed reports on their meetings with the Chinese for Woodcock's review and approval before sending them directly to the White House through a secret back channel.[2]

Throughout his career as a representative of the US government, Roy was obligated to defend American foreign policy interests without regard to his personal beliefs. Being clear-eyed and objective not only was necessary; it suited his personality. To him, China was *not* an unfathomable mystery or a people to be rescued. It was a geostrategic problem to be analyzed and solved. Moreover, his approach to US relations with the PRC was rooted in mutual respect and an understanding of differences, free of emotion and rhetoric, confident that this would lead to productive outcomes for both nations.

A Missionary Son in China

James Stapleton Roy—named after his maternal grandfather and known to his friends and colleagues as Stape—spent ten of his first fifteen years in China. His parents, Andrew Tod Roy and Margaret Crutchfield Roy, were graduates of Washington & Lee University and Vassar College, respectively. They met when both were traveling secretaries for the Student Volunteer Movement for Foreign Missions, the same organization that Walter Judd had worked for several years earlier. They married in 1928, studied theology in Edinburgh and Oxford, and sailed for China as Presbyterian missionaries in December 1930.

Andrew and Margaret were not hardcore evangelists. According to their son Stape, "They expressed their Christian faith through their behavior, by trying to help their fellow human beings. That was their general attitude. Both my parents were very practical, and I've inherited their disposition to think through issues logically."[3] While many foreigners were repelled by China's poverty, disease, and customs such as the foot-binding of young girls, the Roys learned to respect Chinese society. Andrew Roy wrote in his memoirs, "We believed we should look for the best, not the weakness, in another culture, or religion, or political system; that we should seek common ground, discover locally felt needs and people's hopes; then work together to move from the unsatisfactory to a more satisfying way of life, sharing our faith in the process.... We were where we wanted to be, doing what we wanted to do, and doing what we felt God wanted us to be doing, and we had fallen in love with China and its people."[4]

After eighteen months of language study in Beijing, Andrew took up a teaching position at Nanjing Theological Seminary in the capital city of Nanjing, and, in 1933, Margaret gave birth to their first son, David Tod Roy. Captivated by the written Chinese word as a teenager, David would become a professor of Chinese language and literature at the University of Chicago and the highly acclaimed translator of the famous Ming dynasty novel *Jin Ping Mei* (*The Golden Lotus*). Stape Roy—whose childhood nickname was *didi*, meaning younger brother in Chinese—was born at the Nanjing University Hospital on June 16, 1935.

One year later, the family sailed back to the United States on the *Empress of Russia* for a sabbatical in Princeton, where Andrew started his doctoral studies. The Roys returned to Nanjing in the winter of 1938, just after the city had been terrorized and brutally occupied by the Japanese military during the infamous "rape of Nanjing." They soon left, traveling by way of Vietnam to Chengdu in the southwest province of Sichuan, where they would live for more than six years. When the local Canadian-run bilingual school shut down, David and Stape were homeschooled by their mother and the wives of university professors from West China Union University, a consortium of refugee colleges where Andrew Roy taught. In spring 1939, Andrew undertook an eight-week trip in a broken-down Dodge truck to investigate conditions and deliver medical supplies to wounded Chinese soldiers in the northwest. Reaching the Communist headquarters in Yan'an, he was impressed by "an honest willingness to sacrifice personal interest for the common good."

One of Stape's boyhood memories from Chengdu was sitting in a backyard bomb shelter during Japanese air raids while his mother read stories to him and his brother. Later in the war it was exciting when American soldiers arrived in the area to establish four huge airfields for B-29 bombers to enable long-range attacks on Japan's home islands. The GIs would come on motorcycles and take the boys to their tent cities where they would eat chocolate bars, watch movies, and spend the night sleeping on cots. Stape watched in fascination as US fighter planes practiced their aerial maneuvers high in the skies over the city.

In the summer of 1945, shortly before the end of the war, the Roys flew to Calcutta (Kolkata) on a military cargo plane, heading back to the United States for a long-awaited home leave. From there they caught a train across India to Bombay (Mumbai) where they lingered for almost a month, waiting to board a ship to New York City. After visiting relatives in Pittsburgh, they spent the next three years at Princeton University, where Andrew wrote his PhD dissertation on modern Confucian social theory and its concept of change.

The family returned to China in September 1948, just as the Chinese civil war was accelerating. Andrew joined the philosophy department at Nanking University, one of thirteen private Protestant Christian colleges. The Nationalist government quietly pulled out of Nanjing on Saturday, April 28, 1949, and on Sunday morning, "we were wakened by the sound of steady marching. A long file of Liberation Army soldiers was passing our house .... All carried guns, but few were in uniform or wore military shoes. What struck me was their youth. They looked like a ragged file of high school kids, but their faces were grim and they seemed disciplined .... The city was calm, watchful and law-abiding."[5]

Stape, who was almost fourteen, enrolled at the Hillcrest School in Nanjing, but after it closed, went to Shanghai by himself on a US destroyer that was evacuating US citizens down the Yangzi River. After disembarking, he took a pedicab across town to the Shanghai American School where his brother was studying. Many in the foreign community were pulling out of China, but the school remained open and the two boys decided to stay on. The Battle of Shanghai began in early May and continued for about two weeks while students were having final exams. Roy has vivid memories of those days: "At night we'd climb out the windows onto the roof of the boys' dormitory and you could watch the tracer shells being fired into the city from the Communist forces that had surrounded the city."

After the People's Liberation Army occupied Shanghai in late June, Stape, his brother, and a classmate named Joan Smith, who was the daughter of missionaries, got permission to go back to Nanjing by train. During the following year, they were tutored by university professors, together with two Dutch teenagers, and lived normal lives, although the Nationalists sometimes conducted air raids on the city. "We'd go to church on Sunday and then we'd get a horse carriage and we'd go out to Purple Mountain, which is outside the city wall, and we'd visit the Sun Yat-sen Memorial out there and climb to the top of the mountain."[6]

Soon after the Korean War broke out in June 1950, however, Stape and David were sent by train to Hong Kong where they boarded the USS *General Gordon* for San Francisco and traveled from there to schools on the East Coast. Their parents stayed behind in Nanjing, wanting "to be with the Chinese people through this period of upheaval and change," explained their father. "We had promised not to interfere with whatever political and economic system the Chinese might adopt . . . . [W]e wanted to discuss issues at the heart of the faith and culture we were in, and not as alien outsiders." After the PRC entered the Korean War in October, China's intense hatred of the Japanese was transferred to Americans, and a diminished number of US citizens became the targets of a nationwide "Oppose America, Aid Korea" (*Kang Mei Yuan Chao*) campaign. Andrew and another American professor, Charlie Riggs, were accused of being imperialists, attacked in newspapers, forced to write confessions, and denounced in two mass meetings which they were not allowed to attend. (Andrew's situation was complicated by the fact that he had been required to teach a course on Marxist dialectical materialism, which none of his Chinese colleagues wanted to do.) When the accusations against them suddenly ended, Andrew and Margaret were granted exit permits, made their way to Hong Kong, and traveled back to the States early in 1951.[7]

The American missionary community was divided between those who supported the Nationalists, or at least tolerated them as the better of two evils, and those who favored the Communists. The Roys believed that foreigners had no right to judge the Chinese revolution. Instead of feeling betrayed, like some die-hard anti-communists, they were not embittered by their harrowing experience; they simply saw themselves as the nearest available targets to blame for US aggression in Korea.[8] Following their example, Stapleton Roy adopted a similarly pragmatic approach to Communist China, rooted in the facts of history rather than partisan politics or ideology. It was a philosophy that served him well during some of the most challenging phases in the US-China relationship. Unlike so many Americans, he was not inclined to be sentimental about the Chinese. As he explained,

I have always maintained that the advantage of being born in China, and growing up there as a child, is that it enables you to *not* see the Chinese in a romantic sense, but to see them as ordinary people. We lived on university campuses . . . . I grew up not glamorizing or dramatizing the Chinese but thinking of them as fellow human beings. My parents' closest friends were Chinese, and my playmates were their children. A lot of my colleagues, whose exposure to China did not occur until they were adults, got caught up in the fascination of the Chinese, tended to glamorize, or in some cases the opposite, and would think that all Chinese are dishonest. I've never subscribed to this mystique. On the other hand, having dealt with a lot of foreign cultures, I have always found that Chinese and Americans are very compatible. The Chinese have a sense of humor, and even when they're doing tough occupations, they don't become dour the way the Russians would. It's not difficult to form easy friendships with the Chinese.[9]

Becoming a Diplomat

After two years at Mount Hermon, a private school in Massachusetts, Stape Roy enrolled at Princeton University, where he had lived during his father's sabbaticals. Unsure of his ability as a writer, he spent his first two years of college studying engineering and did technical work at the Cleveland Electric Illuminating Company for a couple of summers. He learned to solve problems with logic and precision, yet finding that he lacked a talent for advanced mathematics, turned to the study of history. The prospect of producing a required 20,000-word senior thesis was daunting, but a breakthrough came when he wrote a paper for an English literature course critiquing T. S. Eliot's concept of the differences between prose and poetry. "I discovered that as long as it was something analytical, I could do it." His thesis on US policy preceding Japan's attack on Pearl Harbor won him a Phi Beta Kappa award. He graduated from Princeton *magna cum laude* and joined the Foreign Service that summer.[10]

After completing basic State Department training in Washington, DC, Roy attended the Foreign Service Institute in Taichung, Taiwan, in order to fulfill his language requirement. Becoming a China specialist was not necessarily the best way to advance one's career in the 1950s. Not only was the mainland off-limits to US citizens, but a previous generation of Foreign Service Officers who worked in China during the Second World War had been blamed for the "loss of China." Three of the most prominent men accused of harboring communist sympathies and being disloyal to the United States were John

Paton Davies, John Stewart Service, and John Carter Vincent. (Service and Davies were both China-born sons of American missionaries.) The purge of these men, who were demoted or dismissed from their jobs, hung like a dark cloud over the State Department for years. In 2000, in a speech commemorating the China Hands, Roy warned that "the factors that contributed to the tragedy continue to exist in human nature: the desire to suppress contrary views; the tendency to equate disagreement with disloyalty; the instinct to attack the bearer of unpleasant tidings; the willingness to put expediency ahead of principle; the propensity to reduce complex issues to black-and-white oversimplifications; and the use of political correctness as the yardstick of performance."[11]

Despite the obvious disincentives to becoming a China specialist, all of Roy's initial assignments involved China to one extent or another. In the early 1960s, he was a political officer with the US embassy in Thailand where he was responsible for collecting intelligence on Communist infiltration of Chinese ethnic groups. His next posting was in Hong Kong, processing visa applications at the US Consulate General; quotas were limited, and those with relatives in the United States were almost the only ones eligible to immigrate. (Occasionally he would go out to the New Territories and see the hills filled with refugees trying to cross the border into Hong Kong to escape famine in the PRC. Policemen attempted to block them, but large numbers entered illegally.) In 1962, Roy was transferred to Taiwan, where he was a political officer and aide to US Ambassador Alan Kirk for two years.

Anticipating that Mongolia's long borders with China and Russia would make it significant geopolitically, he then spent a year studying Mongolian at the University of Washington in Seattle. Nothing came of this venture after the United States decided against establishing diplomatic relations with Ulan Bator—until 1987. Roy's detour from a conventional career path raised a few eyebrows but did no lasting damage to his advancement. Personable, intelligent, and hard-working, he steadily moved up the ranks as he mastered the State Department's culture and bureaucracy, content to bide his time. "Since I started so young, I wasn't in a hurry to have senior positions. Some others who rose very quickly were promoted beyond their competence. I had time to prepare."[12]

After returning to Washington, Roy decided to change course and become a Soviet specialist. Prospects for a diplomatic breakthrough with Beijing seemed slim, and the US-Soviet relationship involved complex strategic issues that appealed to him, especially arms control. For the next three years, he served in the State Department's Office of Soviet Union Affairs and was able to avoid being drawn into the morass of the Vietnam War.

During this period, he met Elissandra ("Sandy") Fiore, a Vassar College graduate, as was his mother, who was working for the US Agency for International Development (USAID). The daughter of a US Army colonel who had frequently moved from place to place, she understood the itinerant life of a diplomat. She and Stape were married at St. John's Episcopal Church on Lafayette Square in January 1968. After six months, they left for Garmisch, Germany, where he studied Russian in preparation for a three-year posting with the US embassy in Moscow.

Roy continued to give some attention to Chinese affairs, gathering information on Sino-Soviet relations, although US and PRC diplomats could only meet unofficially at receptions. Henry Kissinger's secret trip to Beijing in 1971 "shocked the Russians to the core of their being," remembered Roy. "They had not anticipated this, and they did not think it was possible. They recognized instantly that this was a turning point in the Cold War, and they became absolutely focused on what the Americans were up to with China."

After Nixon's history-making trip to the PRC in 1972, Roy wanted to get back to East Asian affairs, but "I didn't have much marketability because the Asia people [in the State Department] looked on me as a Soviet specialist." He had not set foot in Asia since 1964. Waiting for the right opportunity, he returned to the Department's Soviet desk and spent time at the National War College (now called the National Defense University) in Washington. Then, thanks to the intervention of William Gleysteen, a deputy assistant secretary who was also the son of China missionaries, he landed a position as deputy director of the Office of the People's Republic of China and Mongolian Affairs. In April 1976, a few months after the death of Zhou Enlai, he made his first trip back to China as an escort officer for a large Congressional delegation and accompanied two more such delegations in April 1977 and April 1978. He recalled that each year their Chinese interlocutors "had to give us a completely different political line" because of the turmoil in the PRC's leadership. "It was a revelation about the difficulties of controlled systems which are in upheaval." It was also a waiting period for Sino-American relations: Nixon had not achieved normalization by the time he had to resign over the Watergate scandal, and his successor Gerald Ford, who failed to be elected president in 1976, lacked the necessary political clout.[13]

Solving the Normalization Puzzle

The 1972 Shanghai Communiqué signed by Richard Nixon and Zhou Enlai signaled an end to an era of mutual hostility, yet it would take seven more years for the United States and China to achieve full diplomatic relations. The sticking point was Taiwan. So long as the United States had an embassy in Taipei, and Taipei had one in Washington, the relationship with the mainland existed in a diplomatic limbo. Although liaison offices with small staffs were opened in Beijing and Washington in 1973, the scope of their operations was limited. It was not possible to set up full-fledged embassies and consulates, arrange aviation and shipping agreements, or establish long-term cultural and educational exchanges. The two governments could not negotiate trade deals, businesses could not set up offices, and journalists could not be in residence.[14]

It was as though the two nations were engaged to be married but could not agree on plans for the wedding. The Chinese were adamant: the United States would have to divorce Taipei in order to consummate its relationship with the People's Republic. Only after Jimmy Carter's election as president and Deng Xiaoping's rise to power—for a second time in the 1970s—did untying the Taiwan knot become possible.

Roy was extremely well prepared to serve as deputy to Leonard Woodcock, who headed the US Liaison Office in Beijing. During Roy's time in Washington, he had complete access to the classified records on Nixon and Kissinger's negotiations with Mao Zedong and Zhou Enlai, which served as a template for normalization. His apartment was not ready when he arrived in China in June 1978, so he lived in Woodcock's residence for a few weeks, which gave the two men the chance to get to know each other quite well. Sandy Roy joined him that fall, six weeks after the birth of their third child, Anthony, along with their two older sons, Andrew and David, seven and five years old, respectively.

Roy's brother David visited with a group of American China scholars in October, his first trip back since leaving three decades earlier. He noted that Stape made "a very favorable impression" on members of his delegation, who "remarked on how handsome and professional he looked, and on how good his Chinese was." David commented that Sandy "is still in the process of adjusting to life in a new environment. She finds Peking unexpectedly drab and I find that I have something of the same reaction. With the exception of the spectacular monuments from the imperial past it is not a particularly colorful city." Sandy, who had acquired a master's degree in applied linguistics in Washington, later helped to develop a Chinese government program for teachers of English. For entertainment, the family visited the Ming tombs, hiked in the Western Hills, and went ice skating during the winter months.[15]

The Carter administration threw a blanket of secrecy over the normalization negotiations, and only a handful of US officials were involved. By design, the most important discussions were held in Beijing, where it was easier to avoid publicity. Breaking the stalemate might prove impossible if opponents in Congress believed that Taiwan was being "sold down the river." Communications between the White House and the US Liaison Office were handled through the highly classified Voyager channel, an encrypted satellite relay system controlled by the CIA. Secretary of State Cyrus Vance and others at the State Department were kept informed, but the White House managed the process from start to finish. During periodic trips back to Washington, Woodcock coordinated with Zbigniew Brzezinski, the National Security Council (NSC) director, and Roy worked with Michel Oksenberg, the NSC's China specialist, who had been a professor at the University of Michigan.

After several months of preliminary discussions in Washington, New York, and Beijing, an agreement finally took shape in early December 1978. The initial breakthrough came when Woodcock and Roy met with Vice Foreign Minister Han Nianlong on December 4, 1978, in the Great Hall of the People. (Foreign Minister Huang Hua was in the hospital with flu and pneumonia.) Woodcock and Roy had no official interpreter of their own, but Roy, who took close to verbatim notes, was able to vouch for the accuracy of the translations.

Han informed the two US diplomats that the PRC was prepared to announce a joint communiqué on normalization on January 1, 1979, now that the United States had agreed to China's three conditions: to sever diplomatic relations with Taiwan, which the United States recognized as the Republic of China; to withdraw its military forces from Taiwan; and to abrogate its mutual defense treaty with Taiwan, which dated from 1954. The two sides agreed that the treaty would expire in accordance with its provisions, meaning that the United States had an obligation to defend the ROC for a year after Washington ceased to recognize Taipei. The vice minister agreed that the United States could continue "unofficial" people-to-people contacts with Taiwan and could maintain nongovernmental agencies, as Japan had done several years before.

But Han then raised a potential roadblock, telling Woodcock and Roy, "We have clearly stated our emphatic objection to the U.S. expressed intention of continuing its arms sales to Taiwan after normalization." He also made it clear that China would *not* make a commitment to a peaceful resolution of the Taiwan problem, as requested by the United States. How and when the PRC would "liberate" Taiwan would be China's decision.

The United States believed that continued arms sales to Taiwan were essential, not only to reassure opponents in Congress that an ally was not being ditched, but also to discourage China from invading Taiwan. In addition, the Carter administration reasoned that US military support would give Taipei the confidence to consider some form of unification with the mainland at a future date. China's leaders, on the other hand, were convinced that arms sales would only make unification more difficult and would increase the likelihood of their having to use force. Despite the impasse, Han told Woodcock and Roy that Vice Premier Deng Xiaoping, China's paramount leader, would like to meet them at an early date.[16]

Deng raised two substantive issues with Woodcock and Roy on the morning of Wednesday, December 13, in the Jiangsu Room of the Great Hall of the People. First, he strongly urged the United States to include an anti-hegemony statement—China's code word for opposition to the Soviet Union—in the communiqué announcing normalization. Second, he asked that no new weapons be sold to Taiwan during the one-year period while the US-Taiwan defense treaty had not been terminated. Nothing was stated by either side about arms sales *after* the one-year hiatus.

Woodcock cabled Brzezinski and Vance that the meeting "has launched us into a new and potentially decisive phase of the normalization process." Deng had "opted for movement rather than legalistic quibbling over details." Yet Woodcock's report, drafted by Roy, cautioned that Deng "did not explicitly confirm that we could resume arms sales once the Treaty [with Taiwan] had formally lost effect . . . . We cannot blithely assume that the Chinese have given us a green light for arms sales from 1980 on. Nevertheless, this was the distinct implication of Teng's [Deng's] comments." It seemed as though the pieces of the normalization puzzle finally were falling into place.[17]

After receiving further instructions from the White House, Woodcock and Roy met with the vice premier for a second time on Thursday, December 14, at 9 p.m. (Two Chinese officials as well as an interpreter and a note taker were present; Woodcock's secretary also attended this meeting.) Deng reviewed the text of the proposed joint communiqué and agreed to the draft with only minor changes. Woodcock confirmed that the United States would not sell any weapons or military equipment to Taiwan during 1979 while the Mutual Defense Treaty was being terminated, but stated that any arms or equipment already in the pipeline would be delivered. Deng agreed to this, and both parties left the meeting confident that the deal was done. Woodcock cabled Washington that Deng was "clearly elated by the outcome of our session, [and] called this a most important matter . . . . There is no doubt in my mind that we have clearly put on the record our position with respect to arms sales."[18]

However, after sifting through the record of discussions with the Chinese, the White House was concerned that Deng still did not understand that the United States intended to resume arms sales to Taiwan after a one-year hiatus. Woodcock and Roy were therefore instructed to arrange yet another meeting with Deng. They dreaded doing so, but had to agree that there was room for a possible misunderstanding. "We knew that Deng would not be happy," recalled Roy.

They met with the Chinese leader for a third and final time on Friday, December 15, at 4:00 p.m. Roy later recalled the outraged response when Deng was informed about the US position on providing military supplies to Taiwan. "He didn't just sit there. He actually stood up and stormed around for about ten minutes. He was truly upset. Here we were and we thought we'd come to the conclusion of these difficult negotiations, and all of a sudden we had reopened an issue which was a deal-breaker from his standpoint. It was only after he had calmed down when he turned to Woodcock and said to him, 'What should we do?' That's when Woodcock said he thought it would be easier to manage this problem from within a diplomatic relationship than without one. His judgment was that we should go ahead. That's when Deng said, 'Hao' (Okay)." As they walked to their car, Woodcock told Roy that he thought for a moment that they had failed and "everything was going down the drain."

"Looking back on it," says Roy, "you can assume that everything was going to fall into place. But that wasn't necessarily the case. Some people in retrospect say the Chinese were always prepared to let us continue arms sales, [that] they knew it had to happen. That's not true at all. I think Deng had sold the deal to his colleagues by saying that we would be stopping arms sales."

Later that night, Roy rode his bicycle—easier than getting a car and driver at a late hour—through Beijing's cold, dark, deserted streets to the Chinese Foreign Ministry. He provided the text of what President Carter would say, and the Chinese gave him what they would say in response. Roy cabled the NSC and returned to his apartment. "When I got back into bed around 3:30 a.m. and my wife woke up, that was the first time that I revealed to her what was going on." In Taipei, in the middle of the night, President Chiang Ching-kuo was shocked and angered when he was informed by US Ambassador Leonard Unger about the decision to sever ties with the ROC just a few hours before it was announced to the world.[19]

In Washington on Friday, December 15, at 9:00 p.m., which was 10:00 a.m. in Beijing on Saturday, December 16, President Carter went on television and radio to announce the establishment of diplomatic relations with the PRC. Hua Guofeng, Chairman of the Communist Party, held a press conference to inform the Chinese people, stating that the United States and the PRC would recognize each other's governments two weeks later, on January 1.

Carter said the decision to recognize the PRC as "the sole legal Government of China" marked the acceptance of a "simple reality" that would contribute "to the cause of peace in Asia and the world." He reassured his listeners that, "the American people and the people of Taiwan will maintain commercial, cultural, and other relations without official representation and without government diplomatic relations." The president also expressed the United States' interest in a peaceful resolution of the Taiwan issue—which China had refused to do—and did not specifically mention arms sales. Hua Guofeng, however, made an oral statement that China "absolutely would not agree" to the sale of weapons to Taiwan.[20]

Not everyone was pleased with the announcement. James Lilley, who was US ambassador to China from 1989 to 1991, wrote in his memoirs that the United States had rushed into a deal with Beijing and produced "a bungled, compromised agreement." In his view, America's prestige was diminished by an overly generous bargain that undermined Taiwan's security.[21] In fact, the Carter Administration, determined to maintain secrecy, had not prepared Congress for the break with the ROC. Members responded with the Taiwan Relations Act (TRA), overwhelmingly passed by Congress in April 1979, which authorized the United States to sell arms and provide training, conduct trade, lend money, recognize the passports of Taiwan citizens, and grant its diplomats immunity from US law. The American Institute in Taiwan, nominally unofficial, would represent US interests. The PRC viewed Washington's continued support for Taiwan as evidence of a conspiracy to block China's unification with the "renegade province" and to prevent the PRC's rise as a regional and global power.

Another affront to Beijing was the hasty transfer of the ROC's beautiful Twin Oaks embassy property in Washington to Taiwan interests for a nominal sum.

On the issue of arms sales, it seems that both sides heard what they wanted to hear. The announcement of the communiqué in mid-December, rather than January 1 as originally planned, added pressure to strike a bargain. Working under a tight deadline, Roy and Woodcock would have been exhausted by the nonstop, back-and-forth communications with Washington, which was thirteen hours behind Beijing. Operating in two languages added an additional layer of complexity and increased the likelihood of miscommunication, despite Roy's ability in Chinese and the skill of the Chinese interpreter, Ms. Shi Yanhua.

Yet if the Chinese were so strongly opposed to arms sales to Taiwan, why was Deng willing to go ahead with normalization after learning that the United States would suspend but not stop sales? Roy points to two factors that the US side was not aware of at the time. The first was a meeting of the Third Plenum of the CCP's Eleventh Central Committee from December 18 to December 22, where Deng consolidated his power and embarked on a plan of reform and opening-up (*gaige kaifang*) to modernize China's economy. To achieve his goals, he believed it was essential to have access to US science, technology, education, trade, and investment. The second factor was Deng's determination to use military force to "teach Vietnam a lesson," a decision triggered by Vietnam's occupation of Cambodia and a "Treaty of Friendship and Cooperation" signed by the Soviet Union and Vietnam on November 4, 1978 in Moscow. "There was a real risk that the Soviet Union might create problems on China's [northern] border if China attacked Vietnam," says Roy. "Having diplomatic relations with the United States would be a deterrent to the USSR."[22] China did attack Vietnam on February 17, 1979, and both sides claimed victory after a month of bloody fighting.

Carter shared the goal of containing the USSR's ambitions and wanted leverage to pressure Moscow into agreeing to limit its nuclear arms. He also believed that the PRC's economic development would make the Asia Pacific a more stable, peaceful, and prosperous region. Two additional factors made Carter's policy popular. First, Deng's determination to revitalize the PRC's economy dovetailed with an enduring US interest in a potentially vast commercial China market. Second, the idea of a China looking to the United States for assistance reawakened a deep-set American impulse to remake the world's most populous nation in its own likeness.

Stapleton Roy with Deng Xiaoping at Beijing Airport as Deng was leaving for
the United States in January 1979.
PRC Foreign Ministry.

When Leonard Woodcock accompanied Deng Xiaoping on his
barnstorming tour of the United States in late January and early February,
Roy stayed in Beijing to manage the Liaison Office, where he and his staff
worked day and night to prepare agreements for consular, cultural, and scientific exchanges. They also hammered out an arrangement for the PRC to
pay $81 million to settle the claims of US citizens and organizations for pro-
perty confiscated by the Communists after 1949. In return, the United States
opened its markets to Chinese exports. The Liaison Office quickly expanded,
and many new arrivals had to live in hotels since no apartments were available. Roy joked that getting diplomatic relations with China was "a piece of
cake" compared with the two years it took to set up the International School
of Beijing, a cooperative venture with the Australian, British, Canadian, New
Zealand, and American embassies.

As the senior diplomat in residence while Woodcock was awaiting Senate
confirmation as the new ambassador to China, Roy received Secretary of
the Treasury Michael Blumenthal—who had lived in Shanghai as a refugee
from Nazi Germany during the 1940s—when he represented President

Carter at the official opening of the US embassy on March 1. An admiring reporter noted that a "young, witty and untiring" Stapleton Roy "briefed Mr. Blumenthal on the negotiating style of the Chinese, how to raise subjects and how to give no offense when giving no ground . . . . Although Mr. Roy's gray hair and dark-frame eyeglasses tend to make him look like a college professor who is unremittingly serious, he is actually a bit of a cutup who can grin and pose for a photographer with instant animation, making wisecracks all the while." At the ceremony marking the occasion, Roy remarked on attending the last Fourth of July celebration at the American embassy in Nanjing in 1949 when he was a teenager, not long before the Communist victory.[23]

Ambassador to China in Turbulent Times

Historian David Hollinger observes that a number of American missionary children became US diplomats, having been raised with a strong sense of integrity, purpose, and an awareness of the world.[24] Among various Protestant denominations, the Presbyterians, with their Scottish roots, were well-known for being sensible, disciplined, and educated. It seems more than coincidental that three sons of Presbyterian missionaries have served as US ambassadors to China. John Leighton Stuart, born to missionaries in Hangzhou, was president of Yenching University in Beijing before Truman appointed him as ambassador in 1947. He had the dubious distinction of being in Nanjing when the Nationalists surrendered the city to the Communists; Mao wrote a biting essay on the occasion of Stuart's departure entitled "Farewell, Leighton Stuart!" Arthur W. Hummel Jr., born in Fenzhou, Shanxi, came up through the ranks of the Foreign Service and was ambassador in Beijing from 1981 to 1985. His missionary father, Arthur Hummel Sr., was an accomplished Sinologist who built the Chinese collection at the Library of Congress. Hummel, who escaped from a Japanese internment camp to fight with Nationalist guerrillas during the Second World War, was also ambassador to Burma, Ethiopia, and Pakistan. Stapleton Roy, whose parents spent decades as missionaries in China as well as Hong Kong, was US ambassador to China from 1991 to 1995.[25]

After leaving Beijing in 1981, Roy was assigned as deputy chief of mission in Bangkok, Thailand, one of the largest US embassies in the world, where he coordinated policies on narcotics and refugees. By the time he was appointed as ambassador to Singapore in 1984, he was the consummate diplomat. His manner was calm, deliberate, and thoroughly professional. He spoke in carefully measured words and backed up his statements with facts and figures. He was not a glad-hander and had limited patience for small talk, but had a quick sense of humor and a hearty laugh. Even more distinctive was a rare talent for looking beyond immediate issues and placing foreign policy in a larger historical context.

At first, he was perplexed by Lee Kuan Yew, Singapore's brilliant founding father and long-time prime minister. Lee had studied and practiced Western law in London but did not allow open democratic elections in Singapore. "Why would a Western-educated person like Lee feel this way?" wondered Roy. "It took me time to figure out that he genuinely believed in a Confucian style of government where the rulers have a responsibility to deliver good governance, but in response, if you deliver good governance, the people have a responsibility of loyalty to the ruler. To him this was the compact, and therefore the concept of a loyal opposition was an oxymoron in his mind because opposition was a sign of disloyalty."[26] Deng Xiaoping was attracted to Lee's Singapore model, which combined economic prosperity with one-party rule, and showed that reliable, predictable governance offered an attractive alternative to liberal democracy.

The US Senate confirmed J. Stapleton Roy as US ambassador to China in 1991, a position he held for four years under the George H. W. Bush and William Jefferson Clinton administrations. Yet twelve years after the normalization of Sino-American relations, interactions between two countries were anything but normal. In the aftermath of the fierce military crackdown on protesters in Tiananmen Square, American public approval of China plummeted, Congress imposed sanctions, and human rights became a priority for US diplomacy. With the exception of the business community, which still saw major opportunities in China, there was an enormous gap between predominantly negative perceptions, shaped by the Western media, and the actual conditions in China where Roy saw growing prosperity and much greater room for personal expression than in the past.[27]

What should have been the happy culmination of his career was instead punctuated by one crisis after another during Ambassador Roy's tenure in Beijing. Early on, he persuaded the Chinese foreign minister to give visas to three members of Congress—Nancy Pelosi (D-CA), Ben Jones (D-GA), and John Miller (R-WA)—who wanted to discuss amnesty for jailed Chinese dissidents. After they arrived, "Pelosi told me she was going back to the hotel

US Ambassador to China J. Stapleton Roy, 1991.
US Department of State.

to rest, and then she took a television crew down to Tiananmen Square and unfurled a human rights banner." It read, in Chinese and English, "To those who died for democracy in China." Chinese officials were humiliated and were truly angry, said Roy.[28]

President Bush's decision to sell 150 F-16 fighter jets worth $6 billion to Taiwan in 1992 marked another low point in Washington's relations with Beijing. Bush was up for re-election and needed political help in Texas, where the planes were built by General Dynamics in Fort Worth and thousands of jobs were at stake. According to author James Mann, Roy privately "argued that the sale seemed to violate the 1982 communiqué signed by the Reagan administration, which limited American arms sales to Taiwan to prior levels." After the announcement was made, Roy was summoned to the Chinese Foreign Ministry and was told that China might withdraw from international arms control talks if the sale went forward.[29]

Another calamity erupted in August 1993 when the United States intercepted the PRC container ship *Yinhe*, which was suspected of carrying illegal chemical weapons to Iran. President Jiang Zemin had personally assured Roy and a group of visiting congressmen that no such chemicals were on the ship. Roy urged Washington to take this seriously, but the US intelligence community was certain about its information. The *Yinhe* was boarded and inspected for a week at Dammam, Saudi Arabia, and no incriminating evidence was found. The incident was a fiasco for US diplomacy and a personal loss of face for the US ambassador.[30]

By far the most vexing problem for Roy was the Clinton administration's policy linking Most Favored Nation (MFN) status to China's human rights record. Whether to continue giving the PRC the lowest tariff rates for exports to the United States had become a contentious annual debate in Congress (see Chapter 9). Allowing human rights to dominate US-China relations did not make sense to Roy, who debated behind the scenes for a more balanced, less ideologically driven approach. When his protests fell on deaf ears, he gave vent to his frustrations in an interview with the *New York Times*. He acknowledged the continued "arrests and harsh treatment of political and religious dissidents," abuses that were likely to persist under the Communist Party, but argued that "the overall economic and social transformation under way in China should not be ignored." Chinese citizens enjoyed more "prosperity, individual choice, access to outside sources of information, [and] freedom of movement" than at any other time in the country's modern history.[31] There was more leeway to decide where to live and work, greater space to express personal opinions, and expanded opportunities for domestic and foreign travel.

Roy believed that dialogue on a range of critical issues, including human rights, would be more productive than single-minded attention to political repression. Positive political change, he thought, was more likely to come from continued economic growth than from outside pressure. On May 26, 1994, President Clinton announced that he would "delink human rights from the annual extension of Most Favored Trading status for China," confirming Roy's point of view. The policy had served its purpose, Clinton said, but "it is time to take a new path toward the achievement of our constant objectives. We need to place our relationship into a larger and more productive framework."[32] Roy's approach had prevailed, but not before the US-China relationship was damaged.

In yet another setback, not long before Roy's departure from China, the Taiwan issue resurfaced when the Clinton administration considered allowing Taiwan's president, Lee Teng-hui, to visit Cornell University, his alma mater. Beijing was adamant that doing so would be tantamount to official recognition of Taiwan. If a visa was granted to Lee, Roy told the Beijing press corps, "it doesn't matter whether we want a strong and prosperous China, or a weak and divided one. It interprets our actions on Taiwan as a reflection of the latter, in part because it doesn't see enough coherence in the way we are dealing with the region."[33] Under pressure from Congress, the White House relented and granted Lee a visa. Roy believes the PRC lost confidence that the United States was going to hold firm to a one-China policy and embarked on a sizable military buildup as a consequence. "They shot missiles into the [Taiwan] Strait, and began to threaten to use force against Taiwan if it continued to proceed on what the PRC considered to be an independence course."[34]

Roy quietly left the PRC in June 1995 to take up a new appointment as US ambassador to Indonesia. Robert Suettinger, who served on the NSC staff, writes that the China relationship "he had worked so hard to rebuild from its low point . . . was heading back downhill. His advice on how to improve the relationship had gone largely unheeded in Washington. He had watched in frustration as U.S. domestic politics repeatedly had misguided and damaged the bilateral relationship and what he considered larger U.S. strategic interests in the region."[35]

John Kamm (the subject of Chapter 9) was one of the last people to see Roy before he left Beijing. According to *New York Times* correspondent Patrick Tyler, Roy told Kamm that "the American ambassador had become a pariah and there was no sense in staying on. 'Why have an ambassador?' asked Roy, his tone conveying a sense of personal betrayal."[36] It would be a relief for him to be US ambassador in Jakarta, far from the never-ending controversies that plagued Sino-American relations.

Roy laments the fact that after he left China in 1995, not a single career Foreign Service Officer was chosen for the post until 2021 when veteran diplomat Nicholas Burns was nominated as ambassador to the PRC. A number of other countries, such as Japan, where the United States has significant strategic and economic interests, have not benefited from the experience of professionals. Too often, says Roy, appointments to these positions are the result of political patronage, which he calls an outrage. "We are using an eighteenth-century spoils system. The US military does not appoint generals from outside the ranks—you work your way up based on experience and accomplishments—and the Foreign Service should not be treated differently." There is a critical need for well-informed diplomacy, insists Roy, even in our modern media age. "There is no substitute for face-to-face communications."[37]

Entering the Private Sector

In 2001, after forty-five years with the State Department, Stapleton Roy was looking forward to a long-awaited vacation with his wife Sandy upon retiring from his final post as assistant secretary for intelligence and research.[38] That plan was deferred when Henry Kissinger called with an offer to work for his consulting firm, which had offices in New York and Washington. (Roy had impressed Kissinger during his visits to Beijing when Roy was ambassador.) He immediately accepted a position with Kissinger Associates as a managing director, advising clients on investment opportunities and government relations with China and other countries. He knew the former Secretary of State could be difficult, but respected Kissinger's ability to synthesize problems in a long-term historical context and agreed with him about the strategic importance of stable US-China relations. "There are very few people who are as interesting to discuss foreign affairs with," declares Roy. "It was challenging to work with him. He would come into your office and ask about what should be done in Yugoslavia. He didn't draw lines. He's interested in what's going on globally."[39]

In 2008, at the age of seventy-three, Roy was named the director of the newly established Kissinger Institute on China and the United States at the Woodrow Wilson International Center for Scholars in Washington, a position that provided a public platform for him to comment on critical issues. "Avoiding war is what diplomacy is all about," he said in one forum. "But the rising power versus established power syndrome is a particularly difficult one." Strategic rivalry between the United States and China was increasing, and "that is a pernicious cycle, because when defense establishments on each side are preparing for conflict with the other as the principal likely opponent, it creates a dynamic internally in each government that becomes difficult for leaders to manage. You need positive efforts to try and offset that."[40]

China faces a basic contradiction, notes Roy. It needs a peaceful environment to achieve its "Great Chinese Dream," but part of that dream is territorial integrity, which includes the recovery of Taiwan. For this reason,

Taiwan remains a dangerous source of misunderstanding and mistrust between China and the United States. To this day, as historian Steven Goldstein writes, "the fundamental issues that created confrontation and deadlock in the Taiwan Strait remain unsettled." Normalization "neither eliminated the Taiwan issue as a divisive element nor permitted the disentanglement of the United States from the legacy of the Chinese Civil War embodied in cross-strait relations."[41]

If anything, the Taiwan conundrum has grown more complicated since the island became a democracy in the 1990s. A majority of its population now consider themselves to be Taiwanese, not Chinese, which suggests they no longer accept the claim that Taiwan is a province of China. This implies that US policy—which acknowledges the position that "all Chinese on either side of the Taiwan Strait maintain there is but one China and that Taiwan is a part of China"—is effectively meaningless.

Taiwan is a political albatross as well as a beacon of freedom and democracy for the United States. Washington does not want the island to move in the direction of independence, which would provoke Beijing's retaliation and threaten peace in the region. Nor does it want China to absorb Taiwan so long as its population of nearly twenty-four million is opposed to uniting with the mainland. Some policy analysts have argued that continued US arms sales to Taiwan are merely symbolic, given the fact that China now has overwhelming military superiority. The idea that Taiwan can equal China's military strength is "fantasy," agrees Roy, but he holds that providing weapons is necessary, noting that Taiwan has no alternative sources for military equipment other than the United States.[42]

The larger unanswered question, Roy has said, is whether the US-China relationship will be "predominantly cooperative or predominantly competitive and even hostile . . . . In essence, we are precariously balanced between two alternative visions of China: Seeing China as the principal burgeoning threat to our position in East Asia and the world. Or, alternatively, seeing China as a country with whom we can cooperate in creating a new world order, despite the existence of strong elements of rivalry in the relationship . . . . The key challenge in US-China relations is how to limit costly and dangerous US-PRC strategic rivalry, especially in the military sphere."[43]

In July 2019, Roy was a lead author of an open letter addressed to President Trump and members of Congress expressing deep concern over "the growing deterioration in US relations with China, which we believe does not serve American or global interests."

China's troubling behavior in recent years . . . raises serious challenges for the rest of the world. These challenges require a firm and effective US response, but the current approach to China is counterproductive . . . . US efforts to treat China as an enemy and decouple it from the global economy will damage the United States' international role and reputation and undermine the economic interests of all nations . . . . The fear that Beijing will replace the United States as the global leader is exaggerated . . . . We do not believe Beijing is an economic enemy or an existential national security threat that must be confronted in every sphere; nor is China a monolith, or the views of its leaders set in stone. Ultimately, the United States' interests are best served by restoring its ability to compete effectively in a changing world and by working alongside other nations and international organizations rather than by promoting a counterproductive effort to undermine and contain China's engagement with the world.[44]

Stapleton Roy's China career has spanned extreme highs and lows, yet whether Sino-American relations have been hopeful or bleak, he has consistently advocated for objectivity and balance. Grounded in his knowledge of history and culture, he knows that China will follow its own path, which may or may not coincide with US national interests.

The normalization of US–PRC PRC diplomatic relations, which Roy helped to accomplish, ushered in an important new era of far-reaching interaction between individual Americans and Chinese, which is the focus of the second half of this book. Intrepid people like Jerome and Joan Cohen, whose story we turn to next, leapt at the chance to live and work in China, relishing their roles as mentors and intermediaries between two singular worlds.

PART II

FROM COOPERATION
TO COMPETITION

6

Jerome and Joan Cohen

Charting New Frontiers

Jerome and Joan Cohen were living in Berkeley, California, where he was teaching law and she was studying art, when they were drawn to China. Jerome—known to all as Jerry—was thirty, Joan was twenty-eight, they were raising two young boys, and a third child was on the way. They nonetheless abandoned a comfortable, predictable path for an unknown future. In the decades to come, their spirit of adventure would dramatically reshape their lives, and they in turn would enrich and promote American understanding of law and contemporary art in China.

The decision must have seemed foolhardy to their families and friends. It was 1960, Red China was closed to US citizens, and there was little chance that the situation would change anytime soon. Unlike most Asia experts at the time, they had no ties to the Far East, as it was then termed; they were not the offspring of missionaries, diplomats, or businessmen who had grown up in China, Korea, or Japan. Joan had traveled twice to Europe with college friends; Jerry had spent a year in Lyon, France, on a Fulbright fellowship. The rest of the world was terra incognita.

Yet China was not just another place. It was an idea, a cause, a revolution, a civilization. During the Cold War years, it also was forbidden fruit. Joan was eager to escape a prescribed, routine existence, and Jerry aspired to be a pioneer, charting unmapped territory. "I wanted to do something distinctive, but didn't know what," he recalled.[1] The Rockefeller Foundation's unanticipated offer of a four-year fellowship to train a younger scholar in Chinese law seemed like a possible answer. (Dean Rusk, then president of the Rockefeller Foundation, was thrilled when Frank Newman, dean of Berkeley's law school, proposed the idea.) Being the first venture of its kind, there was no roadmap, no idea where this might lead, no guarantee of success. Even so, the Cohens jumped at the chance.[2]

Whether he could gather enough evidence to make Chinese legal studies a legitimate academic field was uncertain, but Jerry was determined to try. He wanted to understand what rights Chinese citizens had under the country's new system of government. How was justice determined and administered in the PRC? How were lawyers trained and how much autonomy did they have? What was the relationship between traditional and contemporary law under the Communist Party?

Joan would face similar challenges in her investigation of the visual arts in the People's Republic. Mao had decreed that the sole purpose of art, music, dance, and literature was to motivate people to serve the goals of socialism and communism. She wanted to know how artists were trained and what their relationship was to the state. In what ways did artists draw upon China's vast heritage of secular and religious painting and sculpture? Were they influenced by Western schools of theory and technique? Was there any leeway to express their own ideas outside of official propaganda?

The Cohens' parallel investigations of art and law raised fundamental questions about human values and the freedom of ideas in China, questions they would pursue with dogged determination.

A Big Gamble on China

Jerry and Joan met when he was a senior at Yale and she was a freshman at Smith College. Joan remembered, "I took one look at him and said, I'm going to marry him."[3] Aside from being Jewish, their backgrounds were totally different. Joan Florence Lebold, whose father was a wealthy businessman—he invented the six-pack cardboard carrier for Coca-Cola—was born in 1932 and raised in the affluent Chicago suburb of Highland Park. She attended the Shipley School, an exclusive boarding school for girls in Bryn Mawr, Pennsylvania, and studied architectural history in college. Jerome Alan Cohen was born in 1930 and grew up in Linden, New Jersey, a blue-collar industrial town where his father was the city attorney. He attended public schools, went to Yale University on a scholarship, and graduated Phi Beta Kappa with a major in international relations. The only China connection he recalls from his youth is that his mother played mahjong.

Their upbringings aside, they shared a passion for education, an appetite for the unknown, and had outgoing, self-confident personalities. Charming and petite with short dark hair, Joan smiles easily and has an effervescent laugh. Jerry, more flamboyant, sports a large mustache, favors colorful bowties, and loves to tell humorous stories, often at his own expense.

The Cohens were married in June 1954, soon after Joan graduated from Smith. After a honeymoon in Mexico, they moved to New Haven where Jerry attended Yale Law School and Joan worked at the Yale University Art Gallery in the slide and photograph collection. She confessed, "I'd been so spoiled growing up that I didn't know how to do anything. So I had to learn fast. They don't teach cooking at Smith, you know."[4]

Jerry was a brilliant young lawyer. After graduating from law school, where he edited the *Yale Law Journal*, he held successive clerkships in Washington with Earl Warren and Felix Frankfurter, two of the most famous Supreme Court justices of the twentieth century, and served as an assistant US attorney with the Department of Justice. A subsequent stint doing corporate law with Covington and Burling was tedious and boring, says Cohen: "I longed for something that had social significance and social responsibility."[5] Joan had a "wonderful" job at the Corcoran Gallery of Art in Washington, as the registrar and as a curator, immersing herself in American art.

In 1959, Jerry took a position at the University of California's Berkeley Law School, known as Boalt Hall, offering courses on administrative and international law. After only one year, at a time in life when most young couples

Jerry and Joan Cohen, 1974.
Courtesy Peter Lebold Cohen.

would be looking to settle down, the Cohens abruptly changed course and took a huge gamble on China. It would be a dozen years, however, before they could see the Chinese mainland for themselves. Both of them took Chinese history and politics courses at Berkeley and started learning Mandarin Chinese. Gene T. Hsiao, who had studied the PRC's legal system in Taiwan, worked with Jerry as a research associate to compile a bibliography of the PRC's statutes, decrees, regulations, and legal literature. Jerry taught an experimental seminar on Sino-Soviet law with John Hazard, an early scholar in Soviet legal studies.[6]

A small number of Americans studied the Soviet legal system, but scholarship on Chinese law hardly existed in the West. Jerry gleefully recalled a conversation with Choh-ming Li, the director of Chinese studies at Berkeley, who later was the founding vice-chancellor of the Chinese University of Hong Kong. "'Confidentially,'" Li said to Cohen, 'we know there is no legal system in China. How do you spend your time?' Li thought I was a total fraud!"[7]

Choh-ming Li's dismissive comment betrayed a bias on the part of sinologists who failed to appreciate the significance of Chinese law. As William Alford at Harvard writes, many old-school scholars "subscribed to and helped perpetuate an image of imperial China in which law was seen as an inferior social instrument, and resorting to it was taken as an indication that the ruler and his delegates had failed properly to lead the people by moral suasion and exemplary behavior." The romanticized picture of a state based on a meritocracy, not coercion, appealed to Western enlightenment scholars like Voltaire and Montesquieu, and was perpetuated by academic studies of the Confucian gentry. To the contrary, argued Alford, modern social history proved that law played an active, vital role in Chinese society.[8]

Logic and experience told Cohen that ruling solely on the basis of high-minded idealism, arbitrary power, or even customary law was unsustainable for any government. China's dynastic and modern legal practices had been overlooked; there was an detailed system of law inherited from its long history, as well as more recent concepts and practices carried over from the Nationalist regime and imported from the Soviet Union. On the other hand, the PRC had abolished its Ministry of Justice in the late 1950s and the export of all legal books and journals was prohibited. Cohen admitted it was "a bit like researching imperial Roman law or deciphering developments on the moon" due to the lack of even basic information.[9]

The Cohens' first visit to Asia turned out to be a fluke. In the spring of 1961, one year into his Rockefeller Foundation fellowship, Jerry was invited to speak at the fiftieth anniversary celebration of the University of Hong Kong's founding. Perplexed, since he had not yet written anything on China, he and Joan nonetheless decided to accept and spent a week in Japan and another in Taiwan en route to Hong Kong, leaving their three sons in the care of close friends. The mystery of why he had been invited was soon revealed. "At the opening night's dinner," remembers Jerry, "several people congratulated me on the books I had written about China and Japan." Eventually, it became clear that the hosts had mistaken him for Jerome Bernard Cohen, a senior scholar at the City University of New York who was an authority on Japan's postwar economy.[10]

For the third year of the Rockefeller Fellowship, the Cohens moved to the British Crown Colony of Hong Kong with their boys, Peter, Seth, and Ethan, ages six, four, and two, respectively. They lived in a pleasant house at 12 Marigold Road in Kowloon, the peninsula across the harbor from Hong Kong Island. There was no telephone or car, but they did hire a cook and a housekeeper. Their Mandarin Chinese was of little use since Hong Kongers mostly spoke Cantonese; Taiwan would have been a better option for Chinese language study, but Jerry was determined to get as close as possible to the "real" China.

Beyond the mountains to the north lay the New Territories, mostly farmland in those days, and fifteen miles further was the border with Communist China. "Every part of the package was an adventure," recalled Joan, who enjoyed teaching the children of refugees in one of the public housing estates. There was little she could learn about Chinese art, however, since Hong Kong was not yet a significant cultural center, and was famously considered "a borrowed place on borrowed time."[11] Given its unpredictable future, the immediate goal for many Chinese, beyond survival, was to make enough money to emigrate to places like Australia, Canada, the United Kingdom, or the United States.

Hong Kong—which translates as "fragrant harbor"—was the point of entry for travel and the entrepôt for trade with the People's Republic. It was also a listening post for scores of diplomats, journalists, scholars, and spies. Working at the Universities Service Centre, which Jerry helped to establish, and the Union Research Institute, which held an extensive collection of mainland newspapers, he set about piecing together a picture of Communist China's criminal law code.

He relied mainly on interviews with Chinese refugees, spending many hours talking with thirty-eight informants to gain "a clearer understanding of the structure of China's legal institutions, how these institutions actually functioned and meshed, and how they related to the political, social, and economic systems." Most of the thirty-two men and six women were relatively young, educated, and lived in urban areas. Six had been police officials, three were judicial personnel, and five were students. Some were former CCP members, and others had been sentenced to reform through labor. Cohen discovered they had left China, legally or illegally, because of "poor economic conditions, unrewarding job assignments, and excessive regimentation," although some were simply rejoining family members in Hong Kong or abroad. "Pride in their nation's accomplishments seemed to mix with resentment and disillusionment."

The refugee interviews were a breakthrough for Cohen. "Here, instead of stacks of newspapers and magazines, were real people whose lives had only recently been caught up in what to me had previously been a fascinating but abstract academic puzzle. The goal of reconstructing 'reality' may well be unattainable," he conceded. "Yet a year in Hong Kong gave me the flavor of events, a feel for the stuff of Chinese life, that enhanced my zest for the quest."[12]

Instead of returning to Berkeley, the Cohens moved to Cambridge, Massachusetts, in 1964, where Jerry was a visiting professor at Harvard Law School and was offered a permanent appointment the following year. Joan studied Japanese art with Harvard Professor John Rosenfeld, taught Asian art at the School of the Museum of Fine Arts, and worked in the education department of the Boston Museum of Fine Arts. With support from the Ford Foundation, Jerry established an East Asian Legal Studies program at Harvard, the first of its kind at any US university. Rather than focusing exclusively on mainland China, he looked at interactions across the Confucian cultural world and recruited students from Hong Kong, Taiwan, South Korea, and Japan, many of whom became life-long colleagues and friends. Not content to be an armchair scholar, he used his Harvard platform to write opinion pieces, policy briefs, and book reviews, sometimes co-authored with Joan.

Based on his Hong Kong research, Jerry first major book, *The Criminal Process in the People's Republic of China, 1949–1963: An Introduction*, was published by Harvard University Press in 1968. He explained that in the PRC's early years, between 1949 and 1953, the criminal process was used as an instrument of terror to eliminate class enemies and consolidate power.

The framework for a formal judicial system, heavily based on a Soviet model, emerged in the mid-1950s. During the 1957 Anti-Rightist Campaign, the legal system was largely disbanded, and few published laws or court decisions were available. He concluded, "Although the leaders of the Chinese Communist Party (CCP) have made masterful use of persuasion, ideological incentives, social and administrative pressures, and other measures of control, and still at times predict that the state will wither away, they have never had illusions that they could dispense with criminal sanctions." As in traditional China, the interests of the state "have always prevailed over those of the individual." It was a society of rule *by* law rather than rule *of* law.[13]

Setting Foot on the Mainland

Americans tried various gambits to get into China during the 1960s. On one occasion, Jonathan Mirsky, a young Dartmouth College professor, jumped off a ketch at the mouth of the Yangzi River, hoping to be picked up by a nearby PRC patrol boat. The Chinese ignored him and cruised away. Jerry Cohen sent letters to Mao Zedong and Zhou Enlai asking for permission to visit the People's Republic but received no reply. Ever enterprising, he hoped his connection with the St. Louis Zoo—where Joan's uncle served on the board of directors—might win him a coveted trip. The zoo authorized him to pay a large sum of money for a Chinese panda, and he went to the office of a German trading company in Hong Kong that did business with the mainland. "'I said very simply that I had an offer to buy a giant panda,'" recalled Cohen. "The agent went through his list very soberly for five or ten minutes and then, I'll never forget it, he said very seriously: 'Zey do not haf any Ziant Pandaz for zale.'"[14]

On Cohen's first sabbatical from Harvard Law School in 1971, he and Joan decided to spend the year in Japan. With funding from the Guggenheim Foundation, he affiliated with Doshisha University in Kyoto, Japan's former imperial capital and the center of its cultural world, and spent much of his time learning Japanese. Joan happily immersed herself in traditional as well as contemporary Japanese art. "I focused on seeing every temple, every shrine, every festival that I could, to get a sense of what Japanese culture valued. It was as if I had died and gone to heaven." She also gave lectures on contemporary American art and studied Japanese. "I would get into a taxi with my formal, women's Japanese and the driver would get hysterical with laughter. He'd never heard anything like it."[15]

When Jerry wasn't learning about Japan, he was writing about US-China relations. Always interested in politics and never one to shy away from controversy, he backed the PRC's admission to the United Nations General Assembly as well as its claim to China's seat on the Security Council, which was held by the Republic of China on Taiwan. In an op-ed to the *New York Times* in April 1971, a few months before Kissinger's secret trip to Beijing, he argued in favor of a historic opportunity "to welcome new China into the family of nations," even though it would mean the expulsion of Taipei's delegates. It was time to jettison a "moribund policy" and deal with China on the basis of formal sovereign equality.[16] The PRC was admitted to the UN in October of that year.

Jerry also advocated for normalization of US-China diplomatic relations and wrote an article titled "Recognizing China" for *Foreign Affairs* in October 1971. President Nixon's decision to meet with Mao Zedong had ended two decades of public debate about the wisdom of engaging with Communist China, wrote Cohen. The question of *how* to do so, however, remained unclear. At the top of the list would be the problem of resolving the US alliance with Chiang Kai-shek's regime on Taiwan, since simultaneous recognition of both governments was unacceptable (see Chapter 5). In spite of this and other obstacles, including complex legal issues such as the resolution of seized assets and property claims Cohen concluded that it was imperative "to establish diplomatic relations with the real China and to complete the process of China's formal integration into the world community."[17]

With the prospect of better relations with Beijing, Cohen took the opportunity to lobby for the release of John Downey, one of his Yale classmates, from a Chinese prison. Downey had joined the CIA after graduation in 1951, as had a number of Yalies. During the Korean War, in November 1952, he and Richard Fecteau, another CIA agent, were flying a secret mission to airdrop seven Nationalist Chinese agents and supplies into northeast China as part of an effort to stir up anti-Communist resistance. The plane was shot down. Downey and Fecteau survived the crash, were convicted of espionage, and imprisoned; the Chinese captured with them were sentenced to death and executed. The State Department claimed the two US agents were army civilian employees whose flight went off course. Cohen testified before the Senate Foreign Relations Committee and wrote a *New York Times* op-ed urging the US government to "admit that it violated China's territorial integrity during a bygone wartime era, apologize for having done so and recognize China's sovereign right to punish offenses against its security." Fecteau was released in December, and Downey returned to the United States in February 1973.[18]

———

Only a handful of US citizens had entered China up to the point when the State Department lifted the ban on travel to the PRC in March 1971. After ping-pong diplomacy, a limited number of people-to-people exchanges were permitted, and securing a visa became the ultimate trophy for any China watcher, a highly sought-after confirmation of prestige and credibility. Those fortunate enough to cross the Hong Kong border and experience China first-hand were the envy of their peers.

Three months after Nixon's door-opening diplomacy in February 1972, the Cohens were among the early visitors to the People's Republic when they traveled with a group led by arms-control advocate Jeremy Stone, head of the Federation of American Scientists. While their boys stayed in Kyoto, they spent three weeks touring Beijing, Shanghai, and Guangzhou as well as the ancient capitals of Luoyang and Xi'an. Joan recalled flying one leg of the trip on a Russian-built propeller plane with folding chairs in the cabin. There was no food on board, so partway along the pilot landed on an airstrip in central China, and they were bussed to a restaurant for lunch. Their six-person delegation visited schools, factories, communes, street committees, medical clinics, and a May 7 Cadre School where intellectuals and officials did physical labor and studied Mao's writings. The head of the local Revolutionary Committee provided a twenty-minute "brief introduction" at each stop. "We were told that China had no disabled or handicapped people, and no one needed to lock one's bicycle because there were no thieves," remembered a skeptical Joan.[19]

Seeing the PRC with their own eyes brought China to life. Joan photographed families picnicking at the Great Wall, children swimming in the moat of the Imperial Palace, and soldiers playing basketball within the Forbidden City. The Chinese freely stared at the rare foreign visitors but were leery about interacting with them. In Beijing, Jerry awoke early one morning and decided to explore the neighborhood. He found a small eating place, bought a bowl of hot soy milk (*doujiang*) and fried bread (*youtiao*) for breakfast, and sat down at a table with three middle-aged workers. Unsure about talking with a foreigner, no one said a word when he nonchalantly asked,

"What's the name of this soup?" When Cohen persisted, one of them finally answered, "I'm not too clear about that."[20] The fear of disclosing even the most innocuous information to outsiders was still pervasive.

Lawyers and artists were always "unavailable" because they were being re-educated in the countryside. Art schools had been dissolved during the Cultural Revolution, and Jerry later told a reporter, "There were no legal institutions as we like to think of them—no meaningful prosecutors' offices or defense counsels or public notaries, few operating courts, except military ones, and virtually no legal education." Nonetheless, some experts were optimistic about these changes. Victor Li, a professor at Stanford University who had been one of Jerry's students, idealized the PRC's approach in his book *Law Without Lawyers*, writing about the benefits of relying on mediation, compromise, and community involvement rather than a cumbersome formal legal system.[21]

Joan was elated to see an archaeological exhibition on "Treasures Unearthed during the Cultural Revolution" at the imperial Forbidden City, which had been closed during the Cultural Revolution to protect it from rampaging bands of young Red Guards intent on destroying any vestige of China's feudal society. At the Peking Art Exhibition Center, she toured works commemorating the thirtieth anniversary of Mao's "Talks at the Yan'an Forum on Art and Literature." The art, she wrote, "illustrated the heroes and martyrs of the revolution, the struggles and accomplishments of the People's China." One room displayed enormous oil paintings of Chairman Mao showing him "with groups of peasants, workers, and soldiers, at factories and at farms, swimming, playing ping-pong, traveling in an airplane and a train." Other rooms featured large-scale paintings of workers in fields and factories, soldiers marching and fighting in battle, children in school, people drinking tea and resting from their labors. She found "no subtlety or detachment, no veiled metaphors in these works . . . . There is no place for the independent or negative artist in China. Any work that does not contain a positive demonstration of China's success is, by definition, unacceptable."[22]

The Cohens were in Guangzhou on the verge of exiting China when they were awakened at 2:00 a.m. with an invitation to return to Beijing. Joan declined—she needed to get back to their children in Japan—but Jerry accepted along with Jeremy Stone, his wife B. J. Stone, and Marvin Goldberger, a theoretical physicist. After meetings with Zhou Peiyuan, president of Peking University, and Vice Foreign Minister Qiao Guanhua, they were escorted to the Great Hall of the People where Premier Zhou Enlai hosted them for a four-hour banquet in the Anhui Room.

Cohen and his colleagues were joined at the dinner by six other Americans traveling in China: Harvard professor John Fairbank and his wife, art historian Wilma Fairbank; *New York Times* correspondent Harrison Salisbury and his wife Charlotte Salisbury; and Dick Dudman of the *St. Louis Post-Dispatch* and his wife Helen Dudman. Fairbank and Cohen were seated on Zhou's right and left, and Fairbank wrote in his memoirs that "between us we were soon reiterating how Harvard would welcome Chinese scholars under a variety of schemes, taking turns with our bright ideas, until the Prime Minister looked at his watch and opened up a more general discussion on Vietnam that he wanted to convey to the journalists." Cohen recalled, "Zhou deflected our efforts as well-meaning but premature . . . . He seemed to think that brief visits could soon be arranged but that study might better await the establishment of formal diplomatic relations between our two countries."[23] That is exactly what happened, nearly eight years later.

Different from a number of Americans who were mesmerized by New China, Joan Cohen felt "confused and let down" upon returning to Japan, overwhelmed by the drabness and austerity of life in the PRC. One of her biggest disappointments was learning that women in China, "in spite of much real progress at many levels, are still grossly under-represented in the highest levels of the Party and the government."[24] Jerry was neither depressed nor euphoric; his interviews in Hong Kong with refugees who shared their stories of hardship and deprivation had inoculated him against extreme views of the so-called people's paradise. Before leaving Japan several months later, Cohen's boundless curiosity led him and his family on a week-long trip to North Korea, making him the first US scholar to visit the Democratic People's Republic of Korea (DPRK).

Back in Cambridge, Joan and Jerry co-authored *China Today and Her Ancient Treasures*, a sizable volume published by Harry N. Abrams in 1974. Amply illustrated with Joan's color photographs of people, landscapes, art, and architecture, their book summarized Chinese history and culture from prehistoric times onward, and ended with a chapter on contemporary art in the PRC. Joan gave talks across the United States and in Europe, and reviewers welcomed the book as a candid, non-partisan report written for popular audiences.

Living and Working in Beijing

Soon after Washington and Beijing established diplomatic relations, the Cohens left their spacious Cambridge house, only six blocks from Harvard Law School, to live in a hotel in China's capital city for the next two and a half years. Arriving in February 1979, they knew it was a once in a lifetime opportunity.

Deng Xiaoping's headline-grabbing tour of the United States ushered in a period of considerable hope for the future of Sino-American relations. Because he was determined to modernize China's moribund economy with the help of international investment and trade, there was an immediate need for legal expertise in order for the Chinese to do business with foreign firms. "Deng believed you had to have institutions, and re-created the system they had under Soviet influence in the mid-50s. He didn't mean it for civil liberties and human rights, but for economic development," says Jerry Cohen. "The Chinese were recognizing that law was important, at least in principle. It was a very gratifying experience."[25] A functioning legal system was essential to reassure foreign businesses that the PRC would be a reliable and predicable partner. Law schools were reopening, and the Sino-Foreign Joint Venture Law was enacted in July 1979.

Cohen took a position with Coudert Brothers, an old-line New York firm, and recruited Stephen Orlins, who had studied with him at Harvard and was working at the State Department, to help set up the first American law office in Beijing. Corporate law was more exciting and challenging than either of them expected. Cohen explained, "You have to make a deal with those across the table, learn how to seek agreement, know their language and way of thinking, understand what documents are needed for approval, and how to deal with disputes."[26] Housing was at a premium, but they secured three suites at the Peking Hotel: one for Jerry and Joan, one for Orlins and his wife, and one for an office.

In the mornings, Cohen, Orlins, and Owen Nee, a Coudert lawyer based in Hong Kong, taught a seminar on international law, contracts, and dispute resolution for thirty mid-level Chinese officials. They spent long hours preparing Chinese language lectures since their interpreters lacked the necessary vocabulary for words like "depreciation" and "transferability." In the afternoons, they represented foreign companies seeking to build hotels, install elevators, or drill for oil. "Normally you negotiate a contract with case law and foundational law. But here we had to make it up from whole cloth, writing contracts in Chinese and English," remembers Orlins. Despite the fact that Cohen had no background in investment and joint venture law, it was not a case of the blind leading the blind. Rather, due to Cohen's remarkable attention to detail, says Orlins, it was "in the land of the blind, the one-eyed man is king."[27]

The Birth of Contemporary Chinese Art

Joan Cohen's arrival in Beijing coincided with a period of exhilarating intellectual ferment. Constraints on the arts were lifted in the aftermath of Mao's death, and the burst of artistic experimentation that followed seemed to be a harbinger of greater individual expression. She was in the right place at the right time to watch this drama unfold.

For centuries, Chinese art had been epitomized by glorious ink and brush paintings of lofty, mist-shrouded mountains and idyllic scenes of birds and flowers. Calligraphy, poetry, music, and painting were luxuries to be appreciated by those who could afford them. Sculptures and scrolls would be viewed in the privacy of one's home. Poetry and music were to be shared with friends while drinking wine. Public museums did not exist.

Until the downfall of the dynastic system in the early twentieth century, "the Chinese viewed their civilization as incomparable and found it unnecessary to look outside of China for any reason. Instead they looked backward," wrote Cohen.[28] To China's Communists, however, the purpose of art was to inspire the masses, not to entertain the ruling classes and wealthy elite. Mao followed Lenin's dictum that art and literature must exist for the working people to celebrate the accomplishments of real life. Art should be harnessed to build a modern socialist society, depicting the trials and victories of workers, peasants, and soldiers. Art, in other words, should serve politics, not anyone's private vision or personal fulfillment. There was no such thing as "art for art's sake."

As for China's renowned artistic heritage, the Party must "critically assimilate whatever is beneficial," said Mao, but "no revolutionary writer or artist can do meaningful work unless he is closely linked with the masses, gives expression to their thoughts and feelings, and serves them as a loyal spokesman."[29] Mao's pronouncements were pragmatic as well as ideological since the Communists needed every tool they could muster to win the support of ordinary people in the countryside.

Like the past, foreign ideas should serve China's needs, proclaimed Mao. They should be selectively employed to advance modernization. Yet this was easier said than done. "The problems confronting artists and the choices open to them are the very same ones that have been encountered by Chinese intellectuals in politics, economics, and other fields. What to conserve? What to import? How to adapt and absorb alien influences?"[30]

An earlier generation of Chinese had been exposed to Western intellectual movements in Paris in the 1920s and '30s, but this influx of "bourgeois" European ideas was repressed after 1949. Lacking a major revolutionary artistic tradition of its own, the Chinese Communist Party turned to Soviet Russian academic oil painting and socialist realism for inspiration during the PRC's first decade. Most artists were cut off from international movements beyond the Soviet bloc.

With the advent of the Cultural Revolution, all Western as well as traditional Chinese art was reviled as bourgeois and decadent. Mao's wife Jiang Qing "led a massive campaign to destroy . . . almost all existing art forms and make new, pure creations that were truly revolutionary," said Cohen. (In reality, the music, dance, and art of this period continued to reflect a heavy Soviet imprint.) Arts education came to a halt, except for propaganda paintings and posters, woodblock prints, and folk art. "In this process the great majority of the artistic establishment, policymakers as well as artists, were criticized, humiliated and sent to the countryside to 'learn from the peasants' or confined at their work units for a time." Some were beaten and tortured and committed suicide.[31]

By the time the Cohens arrived in Beijing in 1979, however, Mao's once ubiquitous images had disappeared from most public spaces, and art was resuming its role as an emblem of individual thinking. Joan seized the opportunity not only to investigate the changing arts scene but also to share information with Chinese audiences about modern and contemporary Western art, as she had done in Japan.

When the Central Academy of Fine Arts invited her to give a presentation, perhaps as many as nine hundred people crammed into the room for her illustrated lecture. It was the first time they had seen the work of artists like Jackson Pollock and Nicky de Saint Phalle, as well as abstract expressionists, surrealists, and minimalists. "The excitement was palpable," she said, and the response to Paul Klee, Franz Marc, the Blue Rider, Matisse, and Picasso was "thrilling." She also introduced the Bauhaus school, including Mies van der Rohe, Walter Gropius, and others who left Germany because of the Nazis, an observation not lost on her audience. The Party's gatekeepers were having second thoughts about China's fascination with the United States by the time Cohen gave a third lecture several weeks later. Her talk was relegated to a small room with about thirty students and no outsiders. When she offered to answer any questions after speaking, the professor in charge said, "Mrs. Cohen is very tired and she cannot take questions." She exclaimed, "I'm not tired!"

Joan was most interested in Chinese artists outside the state-run academy system who were pushing the boundaries of the politically acceptable. She was introduced to the Star Group in Beijing, independent avant-garde artists who had been denied admission to official art schools because they did not have the class backgrounds of workers, peasants, or soldiers. Wang Keping, who now lives in France, was a founding member, along with Ma Desheng, Yan Li, Li Shuang—the only woman—and others. Night after night, Joan met with them. "I would visit their quarters and often would find three of them living in a room. These places were so tiny and modest, and yet the artists were so eager to invite me for a meal and to share their stories." They were fascinated by the surrealists Miró and Dali and excited about Freud's book on dreams, which had been translated into Chinese. "It was as if the Chinese had no subconscious until then!"[32]

The first exhibition of American art in China, organized by the Boston Museum of Fine Arts and sponsored by the US government in 1981, included seventy paintings that spanned 250 years of US history. (No major permanent collection of foreign art existed anywhere in the PRC.) Four days before the show opened in Beijing, Chinese officials insisted that twelve abstract expressionist paintings be removed, including works by Helen Frankenthaler, Franz Kline, Morris Lewis, and Jackson Pollock as well as one nude. "Abstract art had been condemned by Communist art leaders for more than thirty years as being bourgeois and reactionary as well as incomprehensible," explained Cohen.[33] The Americans were adamant that the exhibition not be censored, and the full show went ahead as planned. Non-representational art was perplexing and confusing to many Chinese, but Qiu Deshu, an artist who saw the exhibit in Shanghai, wrote to Cohen that viewing the Pollock canvas "freed him from all the constraints that he had felt in his artistic life, and how he was given a new lease to explore and express more."[34]

As one Chinese artist introduced Joan to another, she traveled to cities outside of Beijing, meeting with faculty and students and lecturing with two slide projectors at arts academies in Guangzhou, Chongqing, Nanjing,

Portrait of Jerome Cohen by Chinese artist Kong Baiji, 1987.
Courtesy Jerome A. Cohen, Ethan Cohen Gallery, and Kong Baiji.

Hangzhou, Suzhou, Wuhan, and Xi'an. In this pre-internet age, "the most precious thing I could bring them from the outside would be art magazines. The younger generation had never seen Western art." The Xi'an group was especially experimental. "They were using old tires and wax and all kinds of materials, materials that were surprising at that time in China." But she was frustrated that meeting female artists was difficult; most of them were discriminated against and prevented from exhibiting their work.[35]

Cohen took thousands of photographs during her travels, some depicting mountains and trees veiled in mist to prove that the seemingly fantastic landscapes portrayed in Chinese paintings were real. She regularly wrote articles about China's artistic renaissance for *Art News*, a highly regarded magazine published in New York, and for the *Asian Wall Street Journal*, published in Hong Kong.[36] (Some of her stories were translated and circulated in the PRC.) She especially admired Yuan Yunsheng, who painted one of the boldest, most alluring works of this period: *Water Festival, Song of Life*—a spacious wall mural, one of more than a dozen works commissioned to celebrate the opening of the new Beijing International Airport on the occasion of the PRC's thirtieth anniversary on October 1, 1979. The mural depicted the annual spring water festival of the Dai minority in the southwestern province of Yunnan. Full of color, movement, and life, it featured tall, lithesome male and female figures—including two nudes—dancing, singing, bathing, and splashing water in a tropical setting. "The artist conveys the warm rich tones of these southern people in their verdant setting with absolute mastery, and with a flow that comes only with real genius," effused Cohen. She called *Water Festival* and other airport murals "the most inventive major development in Chinese art in 30 years—and the most controversial. The permissible styles now range beyond the former limits of official imagery. The results are works that are at the same time Chinese and international."[37]

At first, the airport murals were proudly featured in Chinese publications as a sign of modernity. Yet within a short period, the atmosphere changed and conservative officials claimed that the long-necked beauties were distortions and offensive to the Dai people. The two nudes were embarrassing and not in the Chinese tradition, so that section was curtained off, which sent crowds of Chinese and foreigners out to the airport to peek behind the veil. About a year later they were covered over with boards.

Yuan Yunsheng had found inspiration from the ancient Buddhist wall paintings of the Dunhuang caves, a centuries-old desert oasis on the Silk Road in northwest China. "Dunhuang was a mecca," says Cohen. "It was a departure from traditional as well as revolutionary Chinese art, but it wasn't about Western art, which was still risky." Yuan, who spent the Cultural Revolution exiled in Yunnan, told her that artists should not be like the proverbial frog in the well, thinking that the entire universe is contained in one small piece of the sky. "We have nothing to fear—we will not be overwhelmed by international currents. The idea is not to copy but to learn from them!"[38]

Periods of political and cultural relaxation alternated with crackdowns during the Socialist Morality Campaign (1981) and the Anti-Spiritual Pollution Campaign (1983–84), but the overall trend was in the direction of further openness. Robert Rauschenberg organized the first Western contemporary art exhibition at the National Art Gallery (now the National Museum of China) in Beijing in 1985. His use of multimedia and everyday ready-made objects prompted a number of younger Chinese artists to think beyond socialist realism and traditional art.

In December 1988, the National Art Gallery opened an exhibition, approved by the Ministry of Culture, that was devoted entirely to the study of nudes by Chinese artists. It attracted a crowd of 20,000 on the first day. "Some shook their heads in disbelief, while others gazed with clear appreciation," reported John Pomfret for the *Asian Wall Street Journal*.[39] An audacious avant-garde exhibition in Beijing followed in February, but this era of greater tolerance ended abruptly after the Tiananmen student movement was crushed in June 1989, and the pendulum swung sharply in the direction of censorship.[40] Private galleries were shut down and the National Art Gallery was closed for renovations. Approved artists were careful and unofficial artists went underground.

Joan made it her mission to promote contemporary Chinese art in the United States after she and Jerry moved to New York City in the fall of 1981. Around the same time, Chinese artists flocked to the United States in pursuit of freedom, fame, and fortune. "They were all looking for recognition and they wanted shows in galleries," she remembers, "and I tried to help them whenever I could. Some adapted very quickly and did very well." Their challenge was to bridge the gap between the formulaic art of the Cultural Revolution and more creative ways of representation, and to find the right balance between Asian and Western aesthetics. "If they went to art school in China, they already had their own style and were masters at making their paintings look real. Those with no classical training were freer to experiment."

Winning over converts to contemporary Chinese art was not easy. When Cohen tried to interest the Guggenheim Museum, "the curator would not see me, even the secretary wouldn't see me." To bring more attention to recent art from China, she mounted an exhibition at Smith College based on her own collection, which traveled to the Boston City Hall Gallery and the Brooklyn Museum. The problem for many viewers was that abstract and conceptual art from the PRC didn't look "Chinese."[41]

One person who did share Joan's enthusiasm for cutting-edge Chinese art was her youngest son, Ethan Cohen, who visited his parents in Beijing while he was in college. He was fascinated by the energy and dynamism of the artists he met and started collecting their work, which was not expensive at the time. Chinese artists wanted "to get out of China, come to America, be free, and just let their creative energies go," he recalled. Those who had experienced the Cultural Revolution wanted to make up for lost time. Some catered to Western expectations and became very commercial. Others looked more deeply into Chinese aesthetics.

Ethan founded a gallery on 52 Greene Street in New York in the mid-1980s and put on solo exhibitions for Yuan Yunsheng and Qiu Deshu. He also did projects with Ai Weiwei, including his first solo show, "Old Shoes, Safe Sex." (Ai, who lived in New York for twelve years, gambled in Atlantic City and did charcoal portraits of tourists on West 4th Street in the Village to pay his rent.) Cohen was helpful, but the Chinese wanted much greater visibility. "It was very tough to get galleries to even look at their work," he said. "People would laugh at us when we tried to promote Chinese art. The most common response I would hear was, 'It's so derivative!' "[42]

Chen Yifei was an exception. After arriving in the United States with very little English, he studied for a master's in fine arts at Hunter College. Already famous in China for his idealized portraits of Chairman Mao and grand panoramas of heroic soldiers, he changed his style when he realized Americans wanted romanticized Chinese scenes painted in a Western manner. "Chen's paintings of Suzhou and other Chinese canal cities are views of a Venice-like Orient," Joan wrote in a review. "Chen admires Chagall, a hero to many Chinese artists not only because of the quality of his work but because he never lost his Russian essence in the international currents. The Chinese are apprehensive that they will be co-opted into 'bourgeois internationalism' and will lose their cultural identity. Chen says, 'My work makes Chinese feel homesick.' "[43]

Other artists experienced more difficulties. When they came to New York, Paris, or Tokyo, they "had high expectations and were unprepared for the shock of having to fend for themselves," remembers Ethan. The language barrier was a problem, and many of them struggled to survive. In China, where rent was minimal, "they never thought about the economic side too much." In the United States, "they were free intellectually, [but] they were slaves economically."[44] Most had lived a privileged life in the PRC, where state-assigned jobs provided housing, medical care, and other benefits—the so-called iron rice bowl. "The Chinese artist's obligation to provide the state with a certain number of works per year requires only that he submit works that are acceptable in style and subject," wrote Joan. "There are no starving artists among those who work within the system."[45] Their exposure to Western capitalism came as a rude awakening—the pot of gold in America was not as shiny as they had thought—but it was good preparation for the burgeoning commercialization of art and culture back in China.

Joan Cohen's book *The New Chinese Painting, 1949–1986*, richly illustrated with her own photos and published by Harry N. Abrams, was a milestone in her goal to introduce China's new artists to the West. Historian Ralph Croizier praised her as "a supportive eyewitness to the outburst of creative activity and new honesty, mainly by younger artists, in the years between 1979 and 1983. It is her closeness to many of those young artists and unofficial art movements that makes this book so valuable as a source on that turning point of modern Chinese art and history. Indeed, no Western observer since 1949, and probably even before then, has been so well informed and so keen to act as an intermediary between the new Chinese art world and the West."[46] Most Americans, however, still had a fixed idea of Chinese art as timeless and unchanging, typified by museum collections of bronzes, porcelain vases, and silk scrolls. Despite Cohen's enthusiasm for the new wave, audiences for her book tour were sparse. She knew she had something good, but people simply were not interested.

Back in China, as its economy boomed in the 1990s, state subsidies to the arts were cut and many artists had to fend for themselves. Money became more important than politics, and lampooning the revolutionary past became a popular way to make a profit. Foreigners played a crucial role in cultivating a new movement of what was called Cynical Realism, hosting shows in their apartments and buying paintings and sculptures that satirized outdated Chinese propaganda, including shocking portrayals of Mao that would have landed artists in jail in previous years. Galleries proliferated in Beijing, Shanghai, and Hong Kong, and Western auction houses like Christie's and Sotheby's set up offices in those cities to sell contemporary as well as traditional Chinese works for enormous prices. New markets and new patrons turned dozens of Chinese artists into millionaires. But the shift toward commercialism meant that the paradigm of the independent artist standing up to the authority of a repressive state no longer carried as much weight.[47]

Fostering Legal Education Exchange

After leaving Beijing for New York, Jerry Cohen was made a senior partner with the law firm Paul, Weiss, Rifkind, Wharton, and Garrison, doing contract negotiations and dispute resolution. He regularly commuted to Hong Kong and Beijing, occasionally lectured on Chinese law at Harvard, and in 1990 became a professor and faculty director of a new US-Asia Law Institute at New York University. His efforts to share legal practices and principles matched Joan's cross-pollination of ideas in the arts.

By the late 1980s, scores of Chinese lawyers, law students, and legal scholars were coming to US law schools, and smaller numbers of Americans were teaching and studying Chinese law in the PRC. Many of these exchanges were organized under the auspices of the Committee on Legal Education Exchange with China (CLEEC), supported by the Ford and other foundations and chaired by Professor Randle Edwards at Columbia University. Cohen always tried to bear in mind that "the Chinese aren't interested in just transplanting other people's legal systems. They're trying to explore what's going to work for *them*. Right now," he told the *New Yorker*, "they're formulating new laws to govern the operation of a stock market, and they're getting into areas like bankruptcy. And, yes, the mortgage has come back to China. It's all immensely exciting, and law is leading the way to economic reform."[48]

In Cohen's mind, however, "transplanting other people's legal systems" did not mean that China should be exempt from international legal and ethical standards. He was well aware of the claim that China had no experience with the Western tradition of rights. It was said that traditional China emphasized "not law but morality, not rights but duties, not the individual but the group." Some observers, he noted, drew the conclusion that "it would be dangerously self-righteous demagoguery—indeed, cultural imperialism—to suggest that Chinese, like other people, might wish their government to observe minimum standards of fundamental decency in dealing with them." This reasoning, believed Cohen, was deeply flawed if China hoped to modernize. "So long as the fear of arbitrary action persists . . . one cannot expect officials to take bold initiatives, scientists to innovate, teachers and researchers to present new ideas, and workers to criticize bureaucracy and inefficiency. Choosing between economic development and individual rights is not an either-or proposition."[49]

The Chinese government did not officially acknowledge human rights until 1991, two years after the Tiananmen crisis. Yielding to international criticism, a lengthy white paper issued by the State Council voiced support for the ideals enshrined in the United Nation's Universal Declaration of Human Rights. In old China, wrote the authors, the people had been deprived of any such guarantees due to the oppression of imperialism, feudalism, and bureaucratic capitalism. Major progress had been made after the PRC's founding, and there was still much room for improvement. However, the white paper concluded, "owing to tremendous differences in historical background, social system, cultural tradition and economic development, countries differ in their understanding and practice of human rights." China's priority was "to secure the right to subsistence" under the guidance of the Party.[50]

Cohen rejected the claim that China was unprepared for individual political rights, asserting that neither socialist nor Confucian values should be used as an excuse to treat the PRC as an exception to international norms. As evidence, he pointed to Taiwan's transformation from martial law into a robust democracy. Taiwan's success proved there was nothing inherent in Chinese cultural DNA that should prevent the mainland from developing "credible rule of law."[51]

Consistent with his defense of universal values, Cohen fearlessly argued for the rights of lawyers and dissidents. As early as 1971, he spoke out on behalf of Peng Ming-min, a jailed Taiwan independence activist. Two years later, he lobbied for the release of South Korean opposition leader Kim Dae-jung, who later was elected as that country's president. In 1985, he intervened on behalf of Annette Lu, his former student and Taiwan's future vice president, who was imprisoned for five years for her role in promoting democracy. He advocated for various PRC dissenters, and in 2012 arranged for Chen Guangcheng, the blind Chinese human rights lawyer to come to New York University (see Chapter 10).

Cohen has been plainspoken in criticizing China, but unlike some foreign scholars has never been blacklisted or denied a visa by the PRC, perhaps, as Stephen Orlins suggests, because he is an old "foreign friend" who carries the aura of having met with the beloved Premier Zhou Enlai. Cohen explains, "All the problems I discuss are sensitive, whether they relate to criminal justice, the legal profession or good government. I try to play the role of a constructive critic, pointing out problems that require attention and suggesting possible improvements. Regarding China, I am neither pro- nor anti-communist but seek improvements in the government that exists."[52]

Art, Law, and Politics

Jerome Cohen retired from Paul, Weiss in 2000 and spent each fall in Beijing from 2002 to 2006 helping to train Chinese judges, lawyers, and police in a program jointly run by Temple University and Tsinghua University Law School. Joan Cohen met with artists, attended exhibitions, did interviews, and wrote articles for various publications. Their Chinese colleagues had far more personal liberty than in earlier decades, but constraints on free speech still existed. An exhibition Joan planned at Peking University in 2005 was cancelled, and when she was invited to give a talk at the Central Academy of Fine Arts, she found herself in an unmarked room with only a small audience. The school's dean politely introduced her and quickly excused himself, presumably because her presentation included three images of the Tiananmen protest movement. A celebration in her honor in 2012 left her badly disillusioned. Some Chinese friends were not told about the event, and others were frightened away when they heard she had invited Ai Weiwei after being assured that she could ask anyone she wanted to attend.[53]

Jerry's assessment of Chinese law is a mixed picture. "China has resurrected and strengthened its court system, restored the Procuracy and the Ministry of Justice, and has re-established the legal profession," he wrote in 2012. "Legal education has flourished; there are now almost 700 law schools and law departments, and several hundred thousand people take the bar examination each year. Law journals and books have proliferated. China has also expanded its international legal cooperation. It participates in many of the global multilateral treaties and organizations that it once shunned."

Nevertheless, he believes that China's legal system, still based on a Soviet-type model, is fundamentally flawed. The PRC's constitution guarantees freedom of speech, press, assembly, and association, but it is the Chinese Communist Party that dictates ideology, constitutional principles, legislation, and the design of legal education. The Party, writes Cohen, "has a stranglehold on the granular details: the selection, training, promotion, and removal of judges and other legal officials. There is also the licensing, restriction, disbarment, and prosecution of lawyers. And, of course, the Party can dictate outcomes in individual court cases . . . . Those who are perceived as a threat to the government are subject to arbitrary detention, house arrest and other forms of harassment, even when there is no legal justification."[54]

He points out that a crackdown on Chinese lawyers in recent years highlights a dilemma. Should they struggle for their rights using existing rules and regulations or try to upend Communist control over the legal system altogether? "One of the best-known human rights lawyers is Gao Zhisheng, a man who has suffered terribly," recalls Cohen. "In March 2006, I sat in a coffee shop in Beijing with him and nine or ten human rights lawyers discussing what is the proper posture for the future. Most of them agreed with me that if they want to go on fighting, the best strategy is to gradually opt for more reform within the existing parameters. That's the more realistic option. Gao said, 'We'll never have real rule of law unless the monopoly of the Communist Party ends, so we have to make that clear and fight for it.' I said, 'Of course you're right, but you're not going to be on the street within a year's time if you go on talking like that.' And that's what has happened." Gao was disbarred, detained, and imprisoned, and as of September 2021 his location was unknown.[55]

Cohen has described President Xi Jinping, who has taken China in an authoritarian direction since ascending to power in 2012, as a "bold, ruthless leader" who "wields greater domestic power than any Chinese leader since the heyday of Mao Zedong in the 1950s."[56] Xi, who faces no term limits as China's president, has used law to undermine the authority of local courts and centralize the power of the Communist Party. He has been adept at using rhetoric and symbols from the Maoist past to gain popular support and enforce Party discipline, calling, for instance, for a "people's war" to halt the spread of the coronavirus in early 2020.

Cohen has asked whether it was wrong-headed for Americans like him to help China, given that the PRC has become more repressive. At a University of Michigan conference in October 2019, he dismissed the idea that he and others were misguided and naïve. "We did not harbor the illusion that we were going to convert the Chinese Communists into emulating our system of government, including its legal premises and institutions." Rather, he saw an opportunity to learn about China and to assist with the "dramatic shift from class struggle to economic development," which would improve the lives of the Chinese people. He does not believe his efforts were futile, certainly not when it came to legal reforms that enabled China's economy to flourish. As for the rule of law, justice, and human rights, he argues that "the situation today, despite Xi Jinping's repression, is considerably better for most people—but surely not for Tibetans and Xinjiang Muslims—than it was in the dismal post-Cultural Revolution circumstances that we first encountered in 1979."[57] Cohen's analysis does not address a deeper question about Chinese political culture: Do a majority of Chinese people want Western-style rights, or do they prefer the stability of a one-party system?

————

The Cohens have been passionate advocates and effective intermediaries between China and the United States. The walls of their Park Avenue apartment in New York City are covered with contemporary Chinese art—including one piece installed on the ceiling—and Joan's stunning photographs of mountainous Chinese landscapes. Jerry's study is brimming with books and stacks of papers on Chinese law and human rights. "We didn't just observe art and law," he says. "We lived it!"[58]

When they embarked on their quixotic journey in 1960, they could not have foreseen the PRC's astounding social, cultural, and economic transformation. One constant challenge was anticipating and understanding which elements of Western law, art, and culture might be accepted and which rejected. Joan has no regrets but, like Jerry, laments the fact that the space for self-expression has contracted in recent years. In the era of Xi Jinping, artists are more cautious, agrees art historian Alfreda Murck. Criticizing China's consumer culture is permitted, in keeping with a vast anti-corruption campaign, but unapproved images of leaders and references to the Cultural Revolution, Red Guards, or Tiananmen have become unacceptable.[59]

Perhaps no one captures the issues at the intersections of art and politics, law and human rights better than the dissident artist Ai Weiwei, whom Ethan Cohen interviewed in 2015.

[Art] is about individuality, it's about personal freedom, and it's about freedom of expression, and all those qualities being considered as a political attitude or political principles that are not allowed in this kind of society—I would call it a totalitarian society, which is scared of this kind of practice . . . . Art can speak of the truth clearly, and can make complicated issues very simple and innocent, and that can be so powerful. That can destroy this kind of corrupted structure. So I think, being artists, we have a responsibility to make those very essential principles attractive, sexy, and understandable, and I think that is why I still can call myself an artist.[60]

The Cohens' pioneering spirit and their enthusiasm for building personal relationships helped pave the way for a multitude of exchanges in the arts and legal education, much as C. N. Yang had done for science. In the realm of China studies, Elizabeth Perry, the subject of the next chapter, opened up new pathways for scholars to think about modern Chinese history and politics. She would grapple with the essential question of whether the People's Republic has lived up to its revolutionary ideals.

7
Elizabeth Perry
Legacy of Protest

When she was in college, Elizabeth Perry joined a small study group to read the English-language version of *Quotations from Chairman Mao Tse-tung* , commonly known as the Little Red Book. The Chairman's aphorisms were inspiring and the teenage Red Guards, empowered by Mao to overturn China's establishment, seemed like kindred spirits to young Americans who were protesting for civil rights and against the Vietnam War. From a distance it also looked as though the Chinese had solved the problems of racism, sexism, crime, drugs, and poverty that plagued the capitalist West.[1]

Perry's youthful infatuation with the Chinese revolution—she had red Samsonite suitcases and a red car playfully nicknamed "Mao"—marked the beginning of an academic career that would influence a generation of scholarship on China. After completing her PhD and securing a teaching job at the University of Arizona, she became one of the earliest Americans selected to do research and fieldwork on the mainland. She was fortunate to be placed at Nanjing University, which was more open to foreigners than other institutions, partly because of its distance from political intrigues in the capital city Beijing.

She arrived in Nanjing the fall of 1979 with lofty expectations for what could be accomplished, only to realize that she was, in her words, "blissfully ignorant of what lay in store." (A fellow student remembered her as mature, knowledgeable, intense, and idealistic.) The Foreign Affairs Office had previous experience with international students, most of them from Vietnam and Africa, but no clear-cut category for dealing with a junior professor and no guidelines for handling her requests. "This lack of clarity proved to be an opportunity as well as an obstacle," says Perry. "Everything had to be negotiated, but virtually everything was negotiable."

She was unaware of any discrimination toward her as a woman. "For one thing, you were so strange as a foreigner, it was as though a pink panda had arrived. For a Chinese, it was so far from your own identity that whether you were male or female didn't really register. The position you had was more important than being male or female. If you were a visiting scholar from America, that's what you were."[2]

Her introduction to the People's Republic was clouded, however, by a disturbing experience when she and her mother—who had taught in China before the Communists took over—visited Shanghai in the spring of 1980. They toured the city and met with a group of her former students who insisted on hosting them for a lunch at the Xinya Restaurant on Nanjing Road, one of the few that was still in business. "It was a very nice occasion," recalled Perry, "except that several of those who were Christians had been severely crippled by beatings during the Cultural Revolution. Some of them were in wheelchairs as a result . . . . It was wonderful of them to do this for my mother, but it was extremely sad to see what had happened to her beloved students."

"Living in China fundamentally changed my views," confessed Perry, "not so much about the ideals of the Chinese revolution, but the tragic reality of it . . . . I also came to realize how unequal China was," despite the Communist Party's claims to the contrary. Before the year in Nanjing, she had portrayed the PRC in glowing terms in the courses she taught. "After I returned from a year of living in China, I had to completely revamp all my lectures."[3] No longer imagining Maoism as humanity's salvation, she would revisit her previous assumptions and ask fundamental questions about the true origins and meaning of the revolution.

Born in China, Raised in Japan

Christianity ran deep in Elizabeth Perry's family history. Her maternal grandparents were British missionaries in India and South Africa, who later ministered to the Sioux and Dakota Indians in the United States. Her paternal grandfather was an Episcopal minister in Troy, New York. Her parents spent nearly twenty years as missionary educators in Shanghai, where she was born in September 1948, the youngest of three children.

Her father, Charles Perry, graduated from St. Lawrence University in upstate New York, and was a warm, personable, quiet man with a wry sense of humor. Her mother, whose full name was Violet Carey D'Urban Coles, was kind, loving, and self-effacing. Known as Carey, she was born in England, came to the United States at the age of one, grew up on Indian reservations in the Dakotas, and studied at Kansas State Teachers College in Fort Hays (now Kansas State University).

After college, both Charles and Carey volunteered to teach in China. Like many well-educated, well-meaning young men and women of their era, they were eager to dedicate their talents to bettering the world. They traveled separately to Shanghai in 1932—they may have met briefly beforehand—under the auspices of the Episcopal Church. Charles taught Western and Oriental history at St. John's University, one of China's best known private colleges, and Carey taught mathematics and English at St. Mary's Hall, a prestigious Episcopal girls' school across the railroad tracks from St. John's. They fell in love and were married in July 1937, five years after first setting foot in China; their honeymoon in Japan marked the beginning of a life-long fascination with that country. But while there they were horrified by the news that the Japanese military had attacked Shanghai, the beginning of a devastating conflict that would last for eight years. The city fell to the Japanese in November, but life for most foreigners continued much as before, and their son, Charles Jr. (Chuck), was born the following year.

The 1940–41 academic year was spent in Cambridge, where Charles Perry pursued doctoral studies at Harvard before returning with his family to China. As the prospect for war between the United States and Japan grew, however, Carey and Charles Jr. left for Nelscott, Oregon, a small town on the Pacific coast where she had family. Her husband stayed behind and after Japan's surprise attacks on Pearl Harbor and the Philippines in December 1941, was interned along with 256 other US citizens at the Pudong Civilian Assembly Center, across the Huangpu River from Shanghai. After nearly two years in captivity, he was repatriated in a prisoner exchange and sailed back to the United States aboard the SS *Gripsholm*, arriving in New York on December 1, 1943. Charles once had the physique of a wrestler but in the prison camp had survived on just one meal a day and weighed only ninety pounds. After visiting with his parents in upstate New York, he traveled across the country to Oregon to reunite with his wife and now five-year-old son.[4]

While Charles was recovering from his ordeal in the camp, his first piece of mail came from the US government, ordering him to report for three months of duty at the US Navy Japanese/Oriental Language School at the University of Colorado at Boulder where he would study Cantonese. (He already spoke Mandarin, and until the atomic bombs brought an early conclusion to the war, US military planners thought it might be necessary to establish bases on China's southeast coast, where Cantonese was common, in preparation for an invasion of Japan.) Carey and Chuck joined him in Boulder, and the couple's second son, David, was born there. During the final months of the war, Charles was sent to China to patrol and map the Yangzi River on a US Navy ship.[5]

In April 1947, Charles and Carey sailed back to Shanghai with their two boys, via Manila, Cebu, and Hong Kong, to take up teaching posts at St. John's University. Elizabeth—who was called Liz—was born in September of the following year. The family lived peacefully in a roomy two-story house close to Suzhou Creek, but while the university was rebuilding and returning to normal, civil war between the Nationalists and Communists was raging.

The Perrys decided to abandon Shanghai a few weeks before Red Army forces took over the city in May 1949. "My father wanted to stay in China for as long as possible," says Liz, "even after the Communist takeover, but he was concerned about his family, and the Episcopal Church and American government both told him to leave."[6] It was a tearful parting with their amah and cook, a married couple, who wanted to go with them to the United States, but could not. The family spent several months in Hawaii, where Carey's sister was living, before heading for St. Lawrence University in Canton, New York, Charles' alma mater, where he was a visiting professor for the next year and a half.

Because foreign missionaries were no longer welcome in the new People's Republic, Charles and Carey decided to move to Japan, in spite of his having been imprisoned by the Japanese during the war. Liz was three years old when the family sailed from Seattle to Yokohama in September 1951. Her parents taught at Rikkyo (St. Paul's) University in Tokyo, an Episcopal school with red brick buildings designed in the style of an American liberal arts college. Japan was still struggling to recover from the devastation of the war, and it was the final year of the US military occupation.

Liz was homeschooled for two years, because her mother found the local kindergarten curriculum useless and boring. After attending the Christian Academy in Japan for elementary school, she went to the American School in Japan, a private day school founded in 1902. She was not an ardent student; "I played hooky as much as I possibly could, often with my parents' implicit approval."

Charles and Carey were liberals—they smoked, as was common in those days, drank alcohol, danced, and went to movies—but they were not Communist sympathizers. When they were living in China, "they were well aware that the Kuomintang [Nationalist Party] was very corrupt and understood why Chiang Kai-shek lost. On the other hand, they were pleased that a number of high-ranking Nationalist officials were Christians, and they realized the Communists were not as open to Christianity." She remembers her parents debating with friends the question of whether it was inevitable for China to have "gone communist." They would talk about the lessons that China's experience might hold for Japan. How strong was Japanese democracy? Was it possible that Japan might become communist? All of this was fascinating to their daughter, who would pursue similar questions as a scholar. From both parents she not only learned the value of independent thinking, but also absorbed the ability to navigate cultural boundaries.[7]

Happy and spirited, Liz was not a rebellious youth, but protest would be a steady theme in her personal as well as her professional life. She grew up hearing about political resistance in China, and was impressed at an early age by the power of popular movements in Japan. She has a sharp memory of her father coming home with his car window smashed after happening upon a May Day labor strike in downtown Tokyo in the late 1950s. In the spring of 1960, she skipped school with some American friends to participate in massive demonstrations opposing a renewal of the US-Japan Security Treaty. "My parents were fine with my doing that. It felt very safe and very festive."[8]

The Perrys grew to love Japan, but tragedy struck without warning on the evening of November 26, 1959, when they were celebrating Thanksgiving with a few friends at their home on the Rikkyo campus. Around 7:00 p.m. they heard their small dog barking, followed by the sound of breaking glass when a stone was hurled through one of their windows. Charles went outside to investigate and confronted two drunken Japanese students from nearby Daito Bunka University. When he chastised them and confiscated their identification cards, they yelled "stupid foreigner" and "Yankee go home," according to Peter Takuna, a colleague who joined him to see what was going on. One of the young men, who had studied karate, attacked Perry, bloodying his face and head and knocking him to the ground. Perry walked back into the house, refused medical attention, and laid down in his bed upstairs. He died one hour later from a cerebral hemorrhage. He was fifty-one; Liz was eleven years old.[9]

More than seven hundred people attended the memorial service at the campus chapel, and the university's president, Dr. Masatoshi Matsushita, expressed his profound regret over the incident: "Dr. Perry was a fine Christian, gentle and understanding. He loved Japan and was very popular among the students. I am deeply sorry that his death was caused by a Japanese and his love of Japan was betrayed."[10] Carey Perry, who took over some of her husband's classes, stayed at Rikkyo for three more years before moving with Liz and her brother David to Eugene, Oregon, where Chuck Perry was now a student at the University of Oregon.

Moving from the huge metropolis of Tokyo to a small city in central Oregon was a major adjustment for Liz, a teenager without much exposure to American society. As the child of missionaries—a "mish kid"—she was different from other students. South Eugene High School seemed bewildering at first, but she steadily overcame the culture shock and discovered her talents as a writer and an organizer. By her senior year she was editor of the biweekly student newspaper *The Axe*.

After graduating from high school in 1965, Perry received a full scholarship from William Smith College, a women's liberal arts school on Seneca Lake in Geneva, New York, founded by the Episcopal church. (Around this time it merged with Hobart College for men to become Hobart and William Smith Colleges.) But after only a week or so at William Smith, she phoned home to say she had to come back to Oregon. "I was so homesick that I couldn't take it."[11] After returning to Oregon for a short period, she went back to William Smith and quickly adjusted to college life. During her sophomore year, she and a friend led a successful protest against a restrictive dress code that did not allow female students to wear jeans. In October 1967, she took part in a huge march on the Pentagon to oppose the Vietnam War. The year 1968 was marked by the assassinations of Martin Luther King and Robert F. Kennedy, violent clashes between protesters and police at the Democratic National Convention in Chicago, and a silent protest against racial discrimination by two American Black athletes at the Summer Olympics in Mexico City.

Becoming a China Scholar

Perry's transition from activism to academia began in earnest in the summer of 1968 when she signed up with a group of thirty college students from several countries for a work-study program in Japan and South Korea, organized by the American Friends Service Committee (AFSC), a Quaker organization known for advocating world peace. After ten days touring Japan, including visits to the atomic bomb sites in Hiroshima and Nagasaki, the group made their way to Korea, sleeping on the deck of an overnight ferry to Pusan because the weather was so hot. They met with Korean students in Seoul and traveled by train to a very poor village near a coal-mining town in the northeast corner of the country, close to the future site of the 2018 Winter Olympics. They bunked in a schoolhouse—their first job was to dig a latrine—and set to work improving a road which was little more than a dirt track. Robert Snow, one of the Americans, recalled, "Our job was to use sledgehammers to break big rocks into little rocks." He remembers Liz, who became a life-long friend, as being "thoughtful, serious, and having a terrific sense of humor."[12]

Liz says one conversation during that grueling summer proved decisive. "I was spouting quotations from Mao, and had been teaching myself Chinese through tapes, but my Chinese was extremely rudimentary. A young Hong Kong woman in the AFSC group named Violet Tang, said to me, 'If you are really serious about this you have to go to Taiwan to learn Chinese.'" (Mainland China was off-limits to US citizens and Hong Kong, where the dominant language is Cantonese, was not a good choice for studying Mandarin.) "I took what she said very seriously and went to Taiwan after graduating early from college in 1969. And that was the start of my commitment to do Chinese studies." Taiwan was still under martial law, and intelligence agents questioned her about her background, possibly because she was born in Shanghai. The experience was unsettling, but in retrospect she saw it was good preparation for understanding life under the Communists, which was much more tightly controlled.

After several months in Taiwan, Perry enrolled as a graduate student at the University of Washington where she continued to protest the Vietnam War. She joined a radical antiwar group but soon dropped out after learning of their plans to bomb the ROTC (Reserve Officer Training Corps) building on campus, worried that even late at night a janitor—a member of the working proletariat—might be injured. After President Nixon ordered the US invasion of Cambodia to eliminate North Vietnamese sanctuaries in May 1970, strikes and protests broke out on campuses across the country. Perry took part in a march that blocked the I-5 interstate freeway in Seattle for hours. "I remember it being quite well-organized, and don't recall any violence. There was an extraordinary mood of solidarity."[13]

At the University of Washington, where she earned an MA degree, and the University of Michigan, where she continued her studies for a PhD, Perry was involved with the Committee of Concerned Asian Scholars (CCAS), a group of graduate students intensely opposed to the war in Vietnam and captivated by Maoist China. (The Chinese took note and hosted CCAS delegations in 1971 and 1972, although Perry did not join either one.) These young activists argued that US imperialism had been constructed around the racist assumption that the backward East needed to learn from the advanced West. James Peck, a graduate student at Harvard, made the case that modernization theory had been propagated by the United States as a Cold War alternative to Marxism and accused establishment figures like John Fairbank of complicity with government, foundations, and business. Some CCAS members gave up their academic studies after the Vietnam War ended in 1975, and the organization faded away.[14]

Perry avoided being drawn into acrimonious debates, but she did challenge the status quo as a woman in political science, a field dominated by men. "When I started at the University of Washington, the director of graduate studies told me that he had strongly opposed my being given a fellowship because he believed the place for women was in the kitchen and not in the classroom." At the University of Michigan, "I remember very clearly there were forty students in our incoming class, of whom four were women. We were told that about 10 percent of us could expect to get PhDs, which was about right. Because we were highly motivated, three of the four women succeeded." Fortunately, her advisor, Professor Michel Oksenberg, was supportive. "I never felt that there was a kind of weird [sexist] innuendo going on. I always felt it was about the ideas. He wanted to engage me intellectually." (As mentioned in Chapter 5, Oksenberg served on the National Security Council during the Carter administration and played an significant role in the normalization process.)

Having grown up in Japan, it would have been logical for Perry to become a Japan specialist, and she did take classes about Japan and studied the language. But China seemed more vibrant and dynamic even though American citizens still were unable to conduct research there. "There was much more controversy about China, and the Chinese revolution seemed like such a big question to try to explain." The study of Japanese politics, by comparison, was preoccupied with the application of Western social science theories about modernization and parliamentary democracies, which Perry found less exciting.[15]

Seeing China with Her Own Eyes

Elizabeth Perry was an up-and-coming young professor when she made her first trip to the PRC in the summer of 1979 as the scholar-escort on a

two-week trip with a delegation of thirteen American mayors jointly sponsored by the National Committee on United States-China Relations and
the US Conference of Mayors. The group was impressed with Chinese social services and community spirit. Their hosts, reported Perry, were open to
questions, frank to admit past mistakes, and curious about the United States.

In the course of their visits to Beijing, Nanjing, Hangzhou, Shanghai, and
Guangzhou, the mayors found substantial differences with their own cities.
Most obvious was the fact that Chinese mayors were not elected to office, although ordinary citizens could make suggestions and express grievances in
other ways. Chinese cities incorporated large rural areas and directly managed their economies; residents did not pay personal or property income tax;
and everyone was expected to participate in small groups to discuss current
issues and to assist with crime control and sanitation. A medical clinic in a
factory in Hangzhou dispensed contraceptives and performed sterilizations
and abortions free of charge. In Beijing, they were told that "China has no intention of encouraging private automobiles; resources will be invested in the
development of mass transit."

The major problem facing Chinese cities, said Perry, was a lack of adequate housing. "Strolling through back streets, one could hardly fail to notice
the shabby condition of many of the older dwellings—crowded and usually without plumbing."[16] She later recalled, "I was particularly shocked in
Shanghai because I had expected it to be livelier and more developed than
it was. I was taken aback by the poverty in China's richest city. In the early
mornings, people were crouched there cleaning their *matong* [chamber pots]
out on the street."[17] The Shanghai she had heard so much about from her
parents, who lived there prior to the Communist victory, had been much
more wealthy and urbane.

The short, guided tour she made with the mayors was what the Chinese
call "looking at flowers from horseback" (*zou ma guan hua*). It was completely
different from her experience as a visiting scholar at Nanjing University that
fall, where she lived for nine months in a dreary university dormitory with
communal bathrooms. Adjusting to life in Nanjing was physically, emotion-
ally, and psychologically exhausting for the half-dozen American students
and scholars. "We weren't eating well, we were all sick with colds, and we were
under enormous pressure." During the winter, heat would come on through
the radiators in their rooms for two hours in the morning and another two
hours at night. They held cups of hot tea to keep their hands warm while
sitting and reading documents, but were well-off compared with Chinese

students who lived in over-crowded dorm rooms and had no heat at all. Chinese were not allowed in the foreigners' dining hall, although foreigners could eat with the Chinese in their dining hall. The main diet consisted of fatty pork, cabbage, and rice, which often had pebbles in it because grain was dried along roadsides.

The Nanjing cohort experienced a roller coaster of emotions: hopeful excitement about what they might learn alternated with bleak despair over bureaucratic barriers and their grim living conditions. Americans at other institutions have vivid memories of those early days. Madelyn Ross, a Princeton graduate who studied at Fudan University in Shanghai, watched the campus recovering from the trauma of the recent past. Most Chinese students, who had spent years doing manual labor in the countryside, were in their late twenties and early thirties. They were eager to debate women's rights and happy to practice disco dancing with Ross in her dorm room. Tom Gold, a Harvard graduate student in sociology, also at Fudan, was struck by the importance of social relationships (*guanxi*) in getting anything done. This fundamental characteristic of traditional Chinese culture, which he had experienced in Taiwan, had not changed at all under communism. Charlotte Furth, who taught American studies at Peking University for the Fulbright Program, observed "no advertisements, neon signs, storefront displays, or billboards beyond a few giant Maoist propaganda posters already beginning to look a little derelict. After hyper-stimulated California, I found the absence of commercialism refreshing."[18]

There was tremendous curiosity about the young foreigners, and Perry and her colleagues were distressed to find they sometimes were objects of suspicion. Universities were recovering from the intense xenophobia and anti-intellectualism of the Cultural Revolution when any unsanctioned contact with Westerners—especially Americans—was dangerous. "China was waking up from a long period of terror," said Maryruth Coleman, a grad student from Harvard who was also at Nanjing University. She was quietly told that their dormitory had been used to imprison faculty members accused of being spies for an imperialist conspiracy. Little wonder that many Chinese were still cautious about speaking frankly with outsiders.[19]

When it came to doing research, the American scholars encountered another roadblock, said Perry. "Red Guard assaults had taken a toll on most libraries and archives; books had been burned, documents ransacked, and catalogues thrown into hopeless disarray . . . . As a consequence, librarians seldom knew what their collections still contained, let alone how to access particular items. Protecting the remaining holdings, rather than making them publicly available, was understandably their chief goal." Yet Perry's patience and persistence eventually paid off. After repeated requests, a packet of documents from the Number Two History Archives, which was not yet open to foreigners, was quietly delivered to her dorm room for her personal use.[20]

Studying China from the Ground Up

Perry entered Chinese studies just as a new wave of Western scholars was turning to "history from below" to explain social and political movements from the perspectives of ordinary people. Up to that point, most academics had analyzed contemporary China through the lenses of leadership, ideology, factionalism, and bureaucratic politics, an approach that reflected a Cold War preoccupation with totalitarianism. Doak Barnett, Chalmers Johnson, John Wilson Lewis, Robert Scalapino, Richard Walker, and others did groundbreaking work, but were severely limited by their inability to conduct research in China. As a consequence, comments political scientist Harry Harding, "the prevailing paradigms overestimated the unity of the country's leadership, exaggerated their control over China's society and economy, and underestimated the grievances and cleavages in both rural and urban areas."[21]

Initially, Perry planned to write her doctoral dissertation on the Cultural Revolution, but she remembers Professor Alan Whiting, who wrote a notable book on China's decision to enter the Korean War, saying, " 'You shouldn't do it. You feel too sympathetic to the Cultural Revolution and we really don't know very much about it.' " She accepted his advice and was grateful for it. Rather than tackling a contemporary topic, she took a highly unusual path for a political scientist at the time and studied the origins of the Nian Rebellion, an uprising in northern China from 1851 to 1868, which contributed to the collapse of the Qing dynasty in 1911. Rather than trying to decipher contemporary leaders and factions within the government and military, Perry focused on the historical roles of peasants in Chinese society, the very people who had carried the Communists to victory. Being an activist concerned with issues of social justice, it was natural for her to investigate marginalized groups. Other scholars, including Gail Hershatter, Emily Honig, Susan Mann, and Lisa Rofel would produce first-rate studies on the neglected role of women in Chinese society.

From a Marxist perspective, the Chinese Communist Party was the successor to earlier peasant movements, most notably the massive mid-nineteenth century Taiping Rebellion, whose leader Hong Xiuquan had called for a new social system with common property and equal rights for women and men. (The Taipings had been influenced by Christian missionaries and opposed foot-binding, prostitution, and gambling and banned the use of opium, as did the Communists.) Drawing on archival materials in Japan and Taiwan, which required a mastery of classical Chinese and official Qing dynasty documents, Perry concentrated on the Huaibei region, located between the Huai and Yellow Rivers in northern Anhui Province, one of China's poorest and most unstable regions. Why, she asked, did some areas produce rebellions while others did not? What links were there between religious beliefs and local uprisings? In what ways did these movements challenge the state's authority?

What Perry discovered—both for the Nian Rebellion and the early twentieth-century Red Spear Rebellion—contradicted the orthodox Marxist interpretation, which considered these uprisings to be logical and necessary precedents for the rise of communism. In her first book, *Rebels and Revolutionaries in North China, 1845–1945*, published by Stanford University Press, she found no evidence that insurrections in this region had been inspired by any particular belief system. She argued instead that the root cause of peasant violence was fierce competition for resources in an area subject to frequent flooding, periodic droughts, and high rents for small plots of land. Famine had turned the Nian people into plundering gangs. Local groups, moreover, were defensive and parochial and did not welcome outside agitators. While it was true that religious inspiration underpinned the Taiping Rebellion and the Boxer Uprising of 1900, Perry found tremendous variation and no single cause for historical Chinese rebellions. The idea of a smooth, seamless progression from peasant resistance to the Communist revolution was a convenient myth. It was only much later, during the patriotic War of Resistance against Japan (World War II), that the Communist Party was able to replace local secret societies and sectarian groups with its own mass organizations.

Not until Perry went to China in 1979 could she see the Huaibei region for herself. When she arrived as a visiting scholar at Nanjing University, she imagined that her proposal to study peasant rebellions would be easily accepted by the Chinese gatekeepers. "I did not fully appreciate the extent to which Cultural Revolution struggles had shaped and skewed historical interpretations of this subject. How a scholar analyzed a particular nineteenth-century rebel leader or practice was inextricably connected to his or her factional allegiances in very recent political conflicts." She also had no idea that northern Anhui, the area she had written about, had experienced severe drought and a devastating famine only two years before. Suspicious of her motives, the authorities turned down her application to visit the region.

Fortunately, Cai Shaoqing and Mao Jiaqi, professors and historians at Nanjing University who were also interested in peasant rebellions, intervened on Perry's behalf, and she was able to visit Anhui in the spring of 1980. "It was a sobering experience. We saw little kids suffering from malnutrition with swollen bellies and white hair." When she returned to the same area a few years later, she saw tremendous variation from one place to another. "In one county, trees had been planted all over the place and women were lined up outside the local clinic to volunteer for sterilization operations as part of the family planning program. They were each given a little transistor radio for volunteering for this operation. And right next door in another county, no trees had been planted and you saw many pregnant women out and about. It was like two completely different places because the local leadership was so different."[22]

Much of China's countryside was officially off-limits (*jinqu*) to foreign visitors, although Perry was able to visit remote parts of Jiangsu, Shandong, and Guangxi provinces on her research trips. In 1983, however, a moratorium was imposed on social science fieldwork, partly in response to the actions of Steven Mosher, a PhD candidate at Stanford University who was studying village life in Guangdong. He was married to a woman from that province and had given money to her family to build a house, and it was alleged that he bought a truck in Hong Kong and bribed local officials to bring it into China. The most damning accusation was that he had given photos of forced late-term abortions in China, without masking the identities of the women, to a Taiwan publication. For these and other reasons that were never fully disclosed, Mosher was dismissed from Stanford's anthropology department for "illegal and seriously unethical conduct."[23]

Beyond the Mosher incident, there were other factors that led Chinese authorities to curtail foreign research. First, US-China cooperation had deteriorated after Ronald Reagan announced as a presidential candidate that he wanted to improve relations with Taiwan. Second, China's ideological climate had tightened with the Anti-Spiritual Pollution Campaign, a conservative push-back to limit the effects of foreign influence. Third, and probably

Elizabeth Perry with Professor Cai Shaoqing (wearing a white shirt) and local officials in Anhui Province, 1980.
Courtesy Elizabeth Perry.

most important, the Chinese realized that reciprocity for US scholars to con-duct research at the local level in the PRC was not essential to their modern-ization plans. US universities were happy to accept large numbers of Chinese students in scientific fields, and the small number of Americans wanting study in the humanities and social sciences in China was not a priority for either country.[24]

In the late 1980s, Perry shifted her research focus from the Chinese coun-tryside to the city. Restrictions on fieldwork had eased, but she was ready for a change, and the door opened in this new direction thanks to Professor Zhang Zhongli, an old friend of her parents, who was slated to become pres-ident of the Shanghai Academy of Social Sciences (SASS). He had been a stu-dent of Perry's father at St. John's University and told her, "I remember when you were in your dad's arms, being carried around the campus. You were born in Shanghai. Why don't you work on Shanghai?" Zhang went on to say that the academy held a collection of more than two hundred interviews with Chinese workers and promised her access to them.[25]

When she arrived in Shanghai for the 1986–87 academic year, there were many more foreigners and the political atmosphere was more relaxed than it had been several years earlier. Libraries and archives were better organized, but widespread market reforms meant that outsiders promptly were seen as cash cows instead of being treated as honored guests. "Now that universities, research institutes, factories, and rural households were all on the lookout for additional ways of generating income," recalled Perry, "foreign researchers were subject to unpredictable charges for everything from scholarly affiliation and housing accommodations to copying documents and conducting interviews.... For foreigners, the costs of a year in China had skyrocketed to rival those of the most expensive venues in the world."[26]

Perry wanted to understand how urban labor protests and the Chinese revolution were connected, a variation on the question she had asked about peasant uprisings in the countryside. "Once again, I discovered that the issue was more of a political hot potato than I had anticipated." With the Party claiming to represent the working class, historiography on the Shanghai labor movement was fiercely contested, and the battles of the Cultural Revolution had left deep scars on this subject. "After I started writing about my results, I came in conflict with party hacks, who felt that I was misinterpreting the history of the Shanghai labor movement because I was not giving the Communist Party full credit for everything that had happened. Professor Zhang was very supportive of me and told the officials, 'The whole point of inviting foreigners to use these materials is that they're going to see these materials through different eyes. We don't expect them to interpret the materials the same way we've been interpreting them, and that's precisely why we want to encourage this kind of thing, and then we can have a discussion about what actually took place.'"[27]

Shanghai on Strike: The Politics of Chinese Labor, published by Stanford University Press, challenged conventional thinking about the role of Chinese workers in the revolution. Contrary to the standard Marxist interpretation, Perry found that labor was not an inchoate force that Communist organizers molded into a unified industrial proletariat. Nor could protests and strikes be explained simply as resistance to foreign control. The reality, wrote Perry, was "more complicated and fluid." In a city of immigrants, Shanghai workers typically coalesced around people from the same regions who shared the same professions: barbers, bankers, carpenters, or rickshaw pullers. When Perry examined the tobacco, textile, and transport industries, she found limited evidence of class consciousness. Differences in skills, wages, gender, and native place were more important factors than political allegiance. The Communist Party did have successes in organizing labor, but was constantly in competition with the Nationalist Party as well as secret societies and gangsters. *Shanghai on Strike* won the John K. Fairbank Prize of the American Historical Association for best book in East Asian history in 1993.

Based on the success of her first two books and a steady stream of journal articles and edited volumes, Perry quickly ascended the academic ladder. She received tenure at the University of Washington in 1982 and was made a full professor four years later. After a year as a visiting professor at National Taiwan University, she moved to the University of California at Berkeley—having declined job offers from the University of Chicago and the University of Michigan—and in 1997 accepted a position at Harvard University where she would become the Henry Rosovsky Professor of Government. She was reluctant to leave the temperate West coast for long winters in Cambridge, but Professor Roderick MacFarquhar used his considerable charm and persuasive powers to convince her to make the change. The *Harvard Crimson* reported that Professor Perry arrived "amid vehement protests over the lack of tenured women faculty."[28] She quickly settled into her new role at Harvard, where she met Nara Dillon, who also teaches Chinese politics there, and they were married in 2005 in the same Episcopal church where Liz's parents had worshipped during their furlough in 1940–41.

Explaining the Communist Victory

Unlike previous generations of Western scholars who studied China from the top down and the outside in, Elizabeth Perry was determined to get to the essence of the Chinese revolution from the bottom up and inside out, which led her to concentrate on local history based on empirical evidence drawn from Chinese language sources. She was by no means the only scholar to examine local level politics and society; others would study resistance to one-child campaigns, protests over land rights and environmental pollution, mistreatment of migrant workers, and much more. Perry encouraged and participated in these studies, but always kept her eye on the larger historical picture.[29]

Her early work on peasant rebellions and urban labor movements disputed the standard narrative of how the Communists had come to power. Ideology and class consciousness, she argued, were not necessarily the driving forces, nor was the revolution's outcome the result of historical inevitability. Yet if this was true, how could the Chinese Communist Party's (CCP) conclusive victory be explained?

Western and Chinese historians have pointed to various factors for the Communists' success. Nationalism was one. During the Second World War, the Red Army was able to fill its ranks with peasant soldiers in the cause of anti-Japanese resistance after Chiang Kai-shek's armies, which had been decimated by Japanese invaders, were forced to retreat to the southwest. A second reason was the popularity of the Party's social and political message. The masses were assured they would be liberated from the oppressive control of landlords and that land would be distributed equally. A third explanation was the charismatic personality of Mao Zedong, an inspiring visionary who understood the potential for communism to rescue China from its feudal past. A final reason for the Communists' success was the failure of the Nationalist government to overcome corruption, hyper-inflation, and political and military ineptitude.

Each of these theories had merit but left a nagging question in Perry's mind. "How did the intellectuals who founded the CCP manage to cultivate a large and loyal following among illiterate and impoverished peasants and workers, a stratum of the populace so distant from themselves?" Moreover, how were they able to repurpose a foreign ideology and institutions imported from the Soviet Union to fit Chinese circumstances?

Part of the answer, she speculated, was the Party's ability to appropriate existing symbols of religion, drama, and art for purposes of political persuasion. Mao, the son of a Hunan peasant, understood the strength of traditional practices and beliefs—ranging from festivals and operas to the martial arts—and knew that local culture was both an opportunity and an obstacle for revolutionary change. Perry suspected that the ability to convert existing sources of cultural power for new political purposes might shed light on the resilience and staying power of the Communist Party.

To test her ideas she decided, at the urging of Yu Jianrong, a leading sociologist at the Chinese Academy of Social Sciences, to investigate the history of Anyuan, a coal mine in the mountains of south-central China. It was there, only one year after the CCP's founding in 1921, that the Communists had their first major triumph in organizing a labor strike. Anyuan was located in a border region with a long history of rebellion, but the Communist-led strike was remarkable in part because it was nonviolent.

In the early 1920s, the mine and its associated railroad had a combined labor force of more than ten thousand workers. The miners' lives were desperate. They worked twelve-hour shifts in underground tunnels where temperatures were around 100 degrees. Black lung disease was widespread, and gas explosions and fires were frequent, accounting for 450 deaths over a fifteen-year period. Foremen were cruel and living conditions were wretched. "Meals consisted of low-grade rice and pickled vegetables. The dorms were infested with insects and vermin and reeked from poor sanitation." Such dire conditions made Anyuan ripe for revolt.

In the course of four research trips to the area, Perry learned that the Communists were able to win the trust of workers by providing schools for their children, setting up a cooperative store, and distributing economic benefits through a union. An uplifting message of change was conveyed through music, plays, dramatic lectures, and festivals. Rather than attacking and overthrowing the existing system, the Communists cooperated with local power holders, including a secret society called the Elder Brothers that held a virtual monopoly on mining jobs, not to mention gambling, smuggling, and prostitution.

The Anyuan experiment was formative for Mao Zedong, Liu Shaoqi, and Li Lisan, three of the CCP's most influential leaders. It was also a recruiting ground for some five thousand men who later joined the Red Army. For a brief period, Anyuan was a model for Communist-led movements in other parts of China. By the mid-1920s, however, the Party was forced to abandon its policy of moderation and restraint in response to the militarism of regional warlords and Chiang Kai-shek's ruthless campaigns to eradicate the Communists.

In recent years, writes Perry, "political posturing and cults of personality" have distorted and obscured the legacy of the Anyuan experiment. While short-lived, she believes it is worth remembering and retrieving as an effort driven less by violent class struggle and repression than by "the quest for human dignity through education and grassroots organization." The lesson of Anyuan is to suggest that ordinary Chinese, who face "glaring and growing inequalities," can gain a new perspective from this "more uplifting side of the Chinese revolution . . . . The Chinese people have paid too high a price, inspired by too hopeful a vision for their revolution *not* to be recovered and reclaimed."[30]

Explaining the Communist Party's Resilience

The blood-stained path of twentieth-century China gives considerable weight to Mao's famous dictum that "political power grows out of the barrel of a gun." Yet in the early spring of 1989 it seemed that a more positive and hopeful vision of the revolution might be "recovered and reclaimed." Then, after weeks of stalemate between protesters and the government, Deng Xiaoping's order to clear Tiananmen Square with military force defied the expectations of Western China experts. "Once again," wrote Perry, "the academic world has been forced to question many of its most basic premises about contemporary Chinese society and politics." Once again, she looked to the history of China's political culture for answers.

Perry believed that the firebrands who led the democracy movement ultimately had failed because they were unwilling and unable to make an alliance with urban workers who were suffering from the effects of inflation and rampant corruption generated by the post-Mao industrial reforms. Student leaders spoke with moral authority, as they had in the past, but kept the workers at a distance. Their myopia was a lost opportunity, in Perry's opinion. "Perpetuating a Confucian mentality that assigned intellectuals the role of spokespeople for the masses, students assumed that they were the only segment of society whose voice deserved to be heard. The disregard for peasants and workers was a prejudice that intellectuals share with state leaders."

A fatal flaw, she contended, was the inability of Chinese student leaders to imagine any alternative to a system dominated by the Communist Party. "Absent in China are the Catholic church of Poland, the old democratic parties of Hungary, or the dissident intellectual circles of the Soviet Union and Czechoslovakia," expressions of civil society that cultivated a measure of free expression in other parts of the world. Some aspects of the 1989 uprising, such as the hunger strike, seemed contemporary, said Perry, but the student movement was remarkably traditional in its core values. Despite the fact that the Party had achieved power by mobilizing workers and peasants to foment rebellion, "a special bond between state and scholar . . . was reconstituted under the socialist system" after the Communists assumed power, much like the old dynastic system of recognition and reward. Because the protesters framed their grievances "in officially approved terms in order to negotiate a better bargain with the authoritarian state," the Tiananmen movement failed to deliver on the promise of the revolutionary past.[31]

China continued to confound the experts, some of whom expected that the Communist Party was doomed after the June Fourth debacle, and during the 1990s the CCP "presided over the fastest sustained economic transition in world history," observed Perry. An explosion of wealth lifted millions out of poverty but spawned "growing income and regional inequalities, a flood of [internal] migration, and rampant popular protest." China scholars were confronted with entirely set of new questions: How was the CCP able to maintain its control and legitimacy? What explained the Party's resilience? Why did the regime only grow stronger after the collapse of communism in the Soviet Union and Eastern Europe?

Rather than looking to social science concepts and theories drawn from the West, Perry once again pointed to China's own history for answers. Contrary to authoritarian governments that typically grow rigid and out-of-touch over time, the CCP was surprisingly adaptable in the face of massive social and economic change. Perry and Sebastian Heilmann, a German sinologist, contended that the Party drew on its revolutionary tradition to promote experimentation at the local level. It employed Maoist-style strategies, including the use of managed campaigns, to popularize local models of governance and development. Another key explanation for the survival and vigor of China's Leninist system, said Perry, was the CCP's ability to "recruit, monitor, and reward the political elite."[32]

Leading the Harvard-Yenching Institute

It didn't take long for Perry's colleagues to take note of her talents as an administrator. She served as director of Harvard's Fairbank Center for East Asian Studies from 1998 to 2002, and was elected president of the Association for Asian Studies in 2007, an organization with some eight thousand members worldwide. Since 2008, she has divided her time between teaching in Harvard's Department of Government and directing the Harvard-Yenching Institute, an independent foundation established in 1928 with a bequest from Charles M. Hall, who invented an efficient method for producing aluminum.[33]

Before the Communist revolution, the Institute funded programs at Yenching University and other Christian colleges in China. However, instead of supporting Western learning, its purpose was to foster the study of Asian history, philosophy, language, literature, religion, and culture. This was unusual at a time when many intellectuals, including the Chinese Communists, were blaming traditional culture for China's backwardness and were seeking new creeds—ranging from democracy and Christianity to socialism and fascism—to recover their country's prestige and prosperity.

After Yenching University was absorbed by Peking University in 1952, the institute broadened its mandate to include other parts of Asia. With an endowment of $270 millionin 2020, Harvard-Yenching organizes training programs, workshops, and conferences and typically brings about fifty visiting fellows and scholars from East and Southeast Asia to Harvard each year. It also supports the *Harvard Journal of Asiatic Studies* and provides partial funding for the Harvard-Yenching Library, the premier university collection of East Asian materials in North America.

Perry has a spacious, book-filled office at 2 Divinity Avenue, a stately old building with large Chinese-style stone lions on either side of the entrance

Elizabeth Perry with scholars from China, Japan, Korea, and Taiwan at the Harvard-Yenching Institute's 90th anniversary in Shanghai, June 2018.
Courtesy Susan Scott.

that houses faculty offices, classrooms, and the library. Among other initiatives, she has led a program to train doctoral students from India in Chinese studies and has organized workshops in the PRC on new approaches to the study of Chinese politics. Her talent for networking and institution-building harks back to her early days as an activist when she once aspired to work for a non-profit organization.

For intellectual as well as emotional reasons, she relishes the Harvard-Yenching job. "I do feel a connection to my parents and the fact that their lives were devoted to higher education in Asia. I grew up on university campuses in Asia and in that sense, it feels like going home." Through the institute's programs, she has been able to introduce cutting-edge scholarship from Asia to Western audiences. "It is such a privilege to get to know the best minds of Asia," says Perry. "When I go to Vietnam or Thailand or someplace where normally I would just be a tourist, I can meet and talk with Harvard-Yenching alumni and with the presidents and vice presidents of our partner universities and learn a lot from them."[34]

Lost Promise of the Revolution

Elizabeth Perry represents the first generation of Americans since the be-ginning of the Cold War era who were able to study the PRC from the in-side. China, for her, was not an intellectual abstraction, as it had been for her mentors. After living in Nanjing as a young professor, her idealized views gave way to more nuanced and complex ideas; her romance with Maoism dissolved when she witnessed the harsh realities of social inequality and abuses of power. Yet rather than withdrawing from China studies in dismay, she set out to understand why her initial perceptions had been mistaken. She found that comparative Western theories about democracy, authoritar-ianism, and regime transition yielded few answers about the origins, trajec-tory, and longevity of the Communist revolution. China's unique heritage and its own political cultural offered better guides.

As for the future, one of China's greatest problems, believes Perry, is the willful suppression of historical memory. "The legitimacy of Chinese Communism rests, after all, not simply on alleged connections to an an-cient civilization, but also on a revolution that promised dignity for its most downtrodden citizens as well as for the nation as a whole. And that promise is susceptible to challenge not only by hyper-nationalists, but also by those who feel left behind by the post-Mao reforms . . . . Whatever the future may hold, the revolutionary past continues to haunt the political present in many unsettling ways."

Political legitimacy hinges on shared historical memory, but instead of calling for an honest accounting of the past, the Party has enforced a collective amnesia. The traumas of land reform, the Anti-Rightist Campaign of 1957, the Great Leap Forward, the Great Famine, the Cultural Revolution, and the role of Mao Zedong have been suppressed. The CCP advances alternative facts about Tiananmen, Taiwan, Hong Kong, and Tibet. Nationalism and the glories of a remote past are substituted for truth and reconciliation. "In no country," asserts Perry, "is the challenge of confronting the revolutionary past in order to chart the political future more problematic and less predictable than in the People's Republic of China."[35]

It could be that Chinese students trained in the West will become voices for a more honest appraisal of their nation's past. US higher education has had a tremendous influence in China, but Perry cautions that this does not mean Chinese universities have become laboratories for Enlightenment values and liberal democracy. The Chinese government has invested heavily in ensuring the loyalty of students and is determined to benefit from their talents, but resolute about avoiding protests like those that led to Tiananmen. Whether the absence of Western-style academic freedom will hamper the intellectual innovation needed for a twenty-first century knowledge economy remains to be seen.[36]

During the course of Perry's career, scholarly disciplines in China, as well as China studies in the United States and beyond, have been transformed through fieldwork, surveys, research, and exchange. Joint training projects between Chinese and American academics in anthropology, archaeology, economics, political science, sociology, and other areas have opened up a vast array of new perspectives. Regrettably, this window is closing as China moves in a more nationalistic and ideological direction under Xi Jinping. Access to archives has become more limited, and the room for discussion and debate on "sensitive" issues has become constricted. Looking ahead, this means that Perry's injunction to study China from the inside out and from the bottom up will be more difficult to follow.

With a steady deterioration in US-China relations, the excitement and enthusiasm of early Sino-American scholarly cooperation is giving way to disappointment and disillusionment. Even so, our countries are far from the mutual isolation and vast ignorance of the Cold War era. One only need point to the fact that many of the most talented young scholars teaching in US universities today are originally from China. Their bilingual and bicultural skills bring new levels of sophistication to American understanding of the PRC. Increasingly, it will be up to them and others outside of China to say what scholars inside cannot necessarily say for themselves, even at the risk of being denied visas.

Elizabeth Perry and Shirley Young, who is profiled in the following chapter, shared a deep appreciation and respect for China's past and worked for years to promote cultural and educational exchange. Beyond this, however, their stories diverge. Both were born in Shanghai, but Perry's career focused on China from the start while Young was a Chinese immigrant to the United States who reconnected with the land of her birth only later in life. Perry's mission was to unravel the history of the Communist revolution, while Young's initial goal as a businesswoman was to open the PRC's burgeoning consumer market to American investment.

8

Shirley Young

Joint Ventures

In 1995, when the General Motors Corporation (GM) signed a major joint venture deal with the Shanghai Automotive Industry Corporation, "few at GM were as instrumental in making it happen as Shirley Young," according to the *Wall Street Journal*.[1] While it wasn't the first American auto manufacturing agreement in China, it would be one the most successful in the history of modern US-China business relations.

Young, a GM vice president, never expected to play such an influential role in helping to open the China market. A Chinese American who grew up mainly in the United States, she had no knowledge of automotive engineering and was one of only three women in executive positions at GM. She had, however, been born in Shanghai and had an intuitive understanding of Chinese customs and culture, something that was crucial at a time when foreign entrepreneurs still had limited experience with the People's Republic. Added to this, her professional background in marketing and consumer behavior helped her to grasp the requirements for doing business in the PRC. Her family pedigree gave her another advantage: her father was a hero who had been executed by the Japanese during the Second World War, and her stepfather was an eminent patriot and diplomat.

In December 1998, four years after signing the joint venture agreement, a crowd of two thousand cheered GM's chairman, John F. Smith Jr., as he drove the first Buick Regal off the production line in Shanghai with Mayor Xu Guangdi sitting next to him. When the car would not move, Smith pulled a lever that opened the hood instead of releasing the emergency foot brake. It was not an auspicious beginning, but he laughed it off. A skeptical *New York Times* correspondent questioned whether GM's big gamble would succeed. "Demand may balloon one day in the distant future, but right now, the China market does not show a hunger for a high volume of high-end cars like Buicks."

To the contrary, Smith insisted, it was extremely important to get an early start: "This is going to be a huge market."[2] Thanks to the rapid rise of a large and prosperous middle-class, his prediction proved correct. Had it not been for sales in China, moreover, the largest automotive company in the United States might not have survived the 2008 global financial crisis. In 2010, GM sold more automobiles in the PRC than anywhere else in the world. In 2015, Chinese customers bought 3.6 million GM vehicles and the company earned $2.1 billion in operating profit, accounting for 37 percent of its global sales. In 2017, GM sold almost 35 percent more automobiles in China than in the United States. Sales declined to 3.1 million units in 2019 due to increased local competition, the growing popularity of ride-sharing services, and a slowing economy.[3]

Shirley Young's encounter with the People's Republic coincided with one of the biggest economic growth stories ever. From the start, she had understood that the fortunes of the Detroit company would depend on "a willingness to take a long view and to change our strategy to one of partnership." GM would have to have the patience to build relationships, negotiate cultural differences, find a suitable counterpart, and accept political and bureaucratic constraints. Equally if not more important was the company's ability to provide substantial direct investment and its willingness to share training and technology. "China's goal," said Young, "was not just to have one company. They wanted to build a modern industry."[4]

The Lure of the China Market

General Motors and Ford sold cars in China in the early twentieth century— and the United States sent fifteen thousand Dodge trucks during World War II—but sales were limited by a poorly developed road system and a relatively small number of customers outside of major urban areas. After the Communists took power in 1949, whatever ambitions US big business held for the China market came to a screeching halt. Foreign companies were driven out, the small domestic automotive industry was nationalized, and owning a private vehicle became an impossible luxury in a society where individual wealth was unacceptable. Government institutions and state-owned taxi companies owned the only cars, and travel was strictly limited to prohibit unauthorized migration from the countryside into cities. Motorcycles were rare, rickshaws were outlawed as symbols of colonial repression, and the average person walked or rode a bus, a pedicab, or a bicycle. (The durable, single-speed Flying Pigeon and Phoenix brands were the most popular.) Trains and trucks—primarily the Soviet-designed four-ton Liberation model—formed the backbone of the country's transportation system.

Only in the 1980s did the PRC begin to enter the modern automobile age as rapid economic growth created a surging demand for mobility. Thousands of vehicles, mainly Toyotas from Japan, were imported illegally by way of Hong Kong and Macau, and tens of thousands more came in through Hainan Island, which was not subject to the 260 percent import duty imposed on the rest of the country.[5] In response, the central government quickly understood that it was essential for China to design and build its own passenger cars.

Japan, South Korea, and Taiwan had developed globally competitive automotive, ship building, and electronics industries *without* foreign direct investment. The PRC, however, adopted a policy of large-scale joint ventures in order to accelerate investment, training, and technology transfer. Government ministries pitted foreign firms against one another to see which ones would offer the best terms. Foreign companies were not permitted to own a majority stake, and any profits would be shared, usually on a 50/50 basis. Some observers likened it to a forced marriage.[6]

Creating a modern automotive industry with technology from more advanced nations was comparable in some ways to the Qing dynasty's late nineteenth-century "self-strengthening" policy, which enlisted foreign assistance to manufacture arms, ammunition, and ships for defense against imperialist marauders. As Jonathan Spence has written, that attempt fell short. "The various projects undertaken . . . remained isolated phenomena. A real industrial breakthrough would have demanded either efficient governmental coordination of projects or courageous entrepreneurs with freedom of action and access to fluid capital."[7] Both factors were absent in the Qing's waning decades. After imperial China suffered an ignominious defeat at the hands of the Japanese in the brief war of 1894–95 and was humiliated by the Western powers and Japan during the Boxer Uprising five years later, the dynasty collapsed of its own dead weight in 1911. The PRC's leaders were determined to succeed where the ill-fated self-strengthening movement had fallen short.

The first Sino-foreign automotive joint venture of the new era, agreed to by American Motors Corporation (AMC) and a state-run subsidiary of the Beijing government in 1983, was designed to manufacture and export Jeeps. It had some success but ended mostly in failure. The French Peugeot brand, which opened operations in Guangzhou in 1985, was defunct twelve years later. Citroën did not fare much better in Wuhan. A 1989 GM joint venture to build two-door pickup trucks in Shenyang collapsed after only a few years. The sole exception to this string of defeats was a German Volkswagen joint venture to manufacture and sell the Santana, an outdated, no-frills sedan that was the mainstay of Shanghai's taxi fleet for decades. Japanese corporations, unwilling to give up advanced technology, chose to export their vehicles, not build them in China.

American automotive companies had high hopes for a potentially bound-less China market but were unprepared for a myriad of problems. Beijing was intent on acquiring advanced technology and management techniques, but not yet at the cost of increased unemployment and possible social un-rest. Inexperienced Chinese bureaucrats were inefficient and unpredictable. Import tariffs were prohibitive, and transferring foreign exchange out of the PRC was problematic. Labor was not expensive, but workmanship was er-ratic and the quality of local parts was poor, which meant that exporting cars built in China was not feasible. James Mann, who documented the Beijing Jeep story, reached the conclusion that romance and mystique about China, more than anything else, led to poor judgments on the part of Western busi-nessmen. "From the outside, China has always seemed malleable; from in-side it seems intractable, endlessly capable of frustrating change."[8] This dichotomy between outside and inside, illustrated across the chapters in this book, has been a persistent theme for American interactions with the People's Republic.

Oddly enough, the breakneck economic development that led to GM's success in China was linked to the collapse of Communist governments in Eastern Europe and the Soviet Union. From Deng Xiaoping's point of view, President Mikhail Gorbachev's fatal mistake in the Soviet Union was to put political reform (*glasnost*) ahead of economic reform (*perestroika*). The message was clear. The Chinese Communist Party's survival depended on sustained economic growth. The CCP took this to heart and, as economist Arthur Kroeber explains, Deng's famous southern tour in early 1992 "kick-started a new, aggressive reform phase. The next decade set China firmly on course to becoming a major industrial and trade power."[9] Foreign companies invested billions of dollars, much of it in export manufacturing, and firms like GM saw major opportunities in China's emerging domestic consumer market. Growth accelerated even faster after the PRC joined the World Trade Organization (WTO) in December 2001, which lowered trade barriers and provided Chinese firms with expanded access to international markets for imports and exports. Organizations like the US-China Business Council helped American companies to identify potential opportunities. The less visible role of Chinese Americans like Shirley Young, operating behind the scenes to construct relationships with Chinese state-owned entities, was no less important.

Becoming an American Chinese

Shirley Young gave little attention to her heritage after coming to the United States at the age of ten. Understandably, her goal was to fit into the mainstream culture, and being ethnically Chinese was not a big enough incentive to learn about China in high school or college. "My family spoke a few words of the Shanghai dialect at home, and I learned some Mandarin during a summer visit to Hong Kong," she said, but it was only many years later that she learned enough Chinese to give a speech or do a television interview. Nevertheless, a Chinese way of thinking and behaving was part of her makeup from the start.[10]

Young's parents belonged to Shanghai's cosmopolitan elite. Her mother, Juliana Youyun Yan, grew up surrounded by wealth and privilege and lived through a momentous shift toward more liberal thinking about the role of women during the transition from dynastic rule to republican government. She attended the Keen School in Tianjin, run by Christian missionaries, and then enrolled in Shanghai Baptist College. Finding the college too restrictive, she was one of the first women to study at Fudan University, which became one of China's top schools.[11]

Shirley's father, Guangsheng Yang, known as Clarence Young, came from a family of prosperous silk merchants. After graduating from Tsinghua University in Beijing, he went to the United States, spent a year at Colorado College, and received a PhD in international law and politics from Princeton University in 1924, writing a dissertation on "The Rights of Aliens in the United States." Charming, witty, and intelligent, he taught at Georgetown University and worked for the Chinese Legation in Washington, DC, before returning to China to join the Nationalist government's Ministry of Foreign Affairs.

The fashionable young couple married at the Majestic Hotel in Shanghai in 1929, and toured the United States en route to Clarence Young's diplomatic assignment in Europe. Their first daughter, Genevieve (Gene), was born in Geneva in 1930, and they moved to London the following year. After another posting in Switzerland with China's delegation to the League of Nations, they returned to Shanghai where Shirley was born in 1935. (She was named after Shirley Temple, the American child actress, whom her older sister Gene adored. Her Chinese name, *Xuelan*, was a transliteration of the English.) Early photos show her with the same round face and bright smile as her mother. She celebrated her third birthday in Paris, where her father directed China's Bureau of Information for Europe and where a third daughter, Frances, was born in December 1938.

The fate of the Young family, like so many millions of people around the world, was defined by the cataclysmic events of the Second World War. Clarence was sent to the Philippines as China's consul general, where his primary mission was to raise money from the wealthy Chinese business community to support the War of Resistance against Japan. Juliana and her three girls joined him in Manila a few months later, traveling with a Chinese cook, an amah, and a British nanny. The family lived on the outskirts of the city in a large house covered with bougainvillea and surrounded by flowering trees. Clarence and Juliana spent evenings dancing at the grand Manila Hotel, where one of their acquaintances was General Douglas MacArthur, commander of US forces in the Philippines, and his wife Jean.[12]

Their pleasant lives changed drastically after Japan's shocking attacks on Pearl Harbor and the Philippines, which was then a US colony, in December 1941. Manila was bombed, Japanese troops entered the city, and Filipino and US forces surrendered a few months later. The Youngs moved to the Manila Hotel for safety, and Shirley remembered the Sunday morning when the Japanese came for her father. "We were in the middle of breakfast which was being served around the dance floor of the hotel, which looked out on Manila Bay .... The soldiers were quite polite and the whole thing took place quietly and swiftly. Daddy went upstairs with the soldiers and left with a small bag of clothes. He must have been expecting them."[13] At first, the girls and their mother were able to bring him food in prison, but when Juliana received an envelope containing her husband's glasses and a lock of his hair, it seemed clear that he was not coming back. She later learned that Clarence and eight of his staff members had been executed by a Japanese firing squad in April 1942.[14]

Juliana and her children were left to fend for themselves. No longer a pampered diplomat's wife, the one-time socialite took charge and sheltered the wives and children of Clarence's colleagues in her own house. As Shirley recalled in an interview with Bill Moyers, "there was no more gasoline, so we had no more cars. So we went to horse carts. And then pretty soon, the water supply was cut, so we went to wells. And then there was no more electricity, so we went to candles and kerosene.... And then the garden became a farm. We had chickens and ducks and pigs." Despite their "increasingly impoverished circumstances," her memories of those days were happy ones. With nine children living in the house she was never without playmates. Most significantly, her mother's courage and perseverance in the face of adversity was a shining example that would shape her own life.[15]

By the time the Philippines was liberated by US and Filipino forces in early 1945, an estimated 100,000 civilians had been killed in the Battle of Manila, which destroyed much of the city. With her husband dead, there was little reason for Juliana to stay; neither did it seem promising to return to Shanghai, still occupied by the Japanese. The United States offered the greatest opportunities for her children, and on April 10, 1945, she and the girls sailed from Manila on the *Admiral E. W. Eberle* to San Pedro, California, traveling on diplomatic passports issued by the Republic of China. Among the two thousand passengers on board were Americans and Filipinos who had survived three years in internment camps.[16]

After spending the summer in San Francisco—where Shirley had an emergency appendectomy—the Youngs traveled across the country by train to New York City where Juliana had more friends. Ever the warm and gracious hostess, she became a protocol and liaison officer at the United Nations, a position she held for thirteen years. In 1947, she flew to Nanjing, the Nationalist capital, on a Pan American Airways Clipper with her daughter Gene to attend a state funeral honoring the deaths of Clarence Young and his staff, after their remains were exhumed in Manila. Gene returned to New York for school, and Juliana spent a month with her sisters and brothers in Shanghai. Two years before the Communist victory, it was the last time she would see her relatives. In 1959, Juliana married V. K. Wellington Koo, a family friend who was one of China's most distinguished diplomats, famous for defending his country's territorial sovereign rights. She died in 2017 at the age of 111, an avid mahjong player to the end of her remarkably long life.[17]

The three Young girls received scholarships to Abbot Academy, a private secondary school for young women that is now part of Phillips Academy in Andover, Massachusetts. Gene and Shirley went to Wellesley College and Frances attended Skidmore College. There were only five Chinese students in

Shirley's class at Wellesley, but she always felt welcome and remembered no racial discrimination.

The sisters were totally different. Gene, tall and elegant, made her career as a prominent book editor in New York's publishing world at a time when it included few women and even fewer Asians. Her marriage to Cedric Sun ended in divorce, and during the 1970s she married Gordon Parks, the famous African American photojournalist and filmmaker. Frances, cheerful, outgoing, and athletic, married and had four children with Oscar Tang, a handsome Chinese American financier, and tragically died of cancer at the age of fifty-three.

Shirley, the middle-child, standing five feet, four inches tall, was friendly, energetic, and self-assured. After graduating from Wellesley with Phi Beta Kappa honors in 1955, she and George Hsieh married and settled in New York. She applied for various jobs, but her liberal arts education had not prepared her for any specific occupation. "I wanted to do something important in the world. I didn't want to just be a housewife. I had, in my youth, always wanted to be a diplomat, like my parents, but at that time I wasn't an American citizen, so it wasn't an option."[18] She also experienced discrimination, not as an Asian, but as a woman. The only offers she received were for secretarial work, which she politely declined, saying that she couldn't type.

After six months of looking, she landed a job with Alfred Politz Research, an early leader in polling and opinion analysis, and in 1959, moved to Grey Advertising, a high-profile Madison Avenue agency, where she led the consumer marketing and research division. Young pioneered the use of attitudinal studies to explain consumer decision-making and worked with companies like Procter & Gamble, General Foods Corporation, and GM to understand the consumer: "What they want, not just what I want to sell them," she explained. "You always think about the other person's interests."[19] It was excellent preparation for bargaining with officials in China.

The business world was a good match for Shirley's competitive personality. "Living in an East 70's apartment in Manhattan," wrote one journalist, "Mrs. Hsieh is known to her friends as having a way to squeeze 48 hours of work in a day. 'If you have good health, a lot of energy, and a willingness to try, the things you can do are practically unlimited,' she commented."[20] In 1982, she was a founding member of the Committee of 200, an international organization of women entrepreneurs and corporate leaders. Ten years later, *Business Week* magazine named her as one of the top American women in business.

Young and her husband, who had studied engineering at MIT and was a master bridge player, had three sons, David, William, and Douglas, but George Hsieh's investments in the early stages of the computer industry ended in bankruptcy, and the marriage did not last. As they drifted apart, she met Norman Krandall, a high-ranking executive at the Ford Motor Company, another Grey Advertising client, during frequent business trips to Detroit. He saw that Young was "more than Grey's head of research. She was also the chief strategist for Grey, and one of the best brains in the agency . . . . I respected her grit, her analytical ability, and her capacity to be direct while not offending her clients." They came from completely different backgrounds—he grew up in the Slavic enclave of Hamtramck, Michigan and went to work for Ford after a stint in the US Navy—but they shared a passion for classical music. Their professional relationship became personal, and they were married in New York City's Madison Avenue Presbyterian Church. She was forty-three, and he was nine years older.

Like many Americans eager to see the PRC, Shirley and Norman traveled there as tourists with several friends in 1979, her first trip to the Chinese mainland since leaving at the age of two. In Shanghai they met some of her relatives, who were reluctant to talk about the hardships they endured during the Cultural Revolution. During that dark time, one aunt had all of her possessions taken away and was forced to live in a small space under a staircase. Krandall remembered that one of Shirley's relatives in Beijing "received us with strained cordiality, wanting to welcome us but clearly fearful of the consequences."[21] Only a few years earlier, contact with anyone in the United States would have been grounds for suspicion and possible persecution.

The trip must have reminded Young of how different her life would have been if her mother had not taken her and her sisters to the United States. Her brief visit did not lead her to imagine that her future career would be connected to China, which was in the very early stages of reopening its economy. Yet that is what happened fifteen years later.

GM's China Strategy

Shirley Young accepted a full-time job with GM as vice president for consumer marketing development in 1988. (She and Normal Krandall were divorced just before she took the new job.) It was a new, high-profile position, something like an ambassador without portfolio, that allowed her to interact with executives all across the company. But moving to Detroit was stressful. "I was not a man, not white, not a Midesterner. I was an Asian woman from New York. They almost had never hired anyone from the outside. I was like somebody from outer space." When she arrived, "there was clearly not a welcoming attitude . . . . You just could feel the hostility and suspicion . . . . They didn't believe in research and marketing," said Young. And they "never wanted to admit error." A *Business Week* reporter wrote, "Diminutive and genteel, she looks out of place in the clubby, male-dominated suites of Detroit."

Young's mandate was to redeem GM's battered image and improve its falling sales. Chevrolet, Pontiac, Buick, Oldsmobile, and Cadillac were famous brands but were losing market share due to a reputation for poor quality. The company's corporate culture was inbred and complacent, and its automotive divisions competed mainly with one other. Growing numbers of Americans considered Japanese imports—Hondas, Toyotas, and Datsuns— more reliable, affordable, and fuel efficient. Young pushed GM's marketing executives and advertising agencies to listen to the customers. "A lot of this job," she told a journalist, "is what I call persistent evangelism." Within two years, she launched a $40 million print and television ad campaign under the slogan "Putting Quality on the Road," a clear reference to the fact that GM's cars had failed to live up to buyers' expectations in the past.[22]

Young's introduction to doing business with China was serendipitous. A number of Chinese engineers and researchers who had come from the mainland to study at US universities in the 1980s had found jobs at GM's Tech Center in Warren, Michigan. When delegations from the PRC would visit Detroit, only to learn that GM's international division was in Zurich, Switzerland, "they would call on their Chinese friends and colleagues, and those colleagues would invite me to dinner with them on an informal basis," said Young. It was an awkward situation since she had no official reason to be involved. "I felt very uncomfortable because corporate structures really don't like interlopers." Yet these conversations proved to be an invaluable learning experience.

Eventually, Jack Smith, GM's chairman, wanted Young on his China team, and she liked the fact that he had a global perspective, having led the company's international business earlier in his career. In June 1995, he asked her to provide "strategic guidance and organizational support" to help establish an ambitious joint venture with the Shanghai Automotive Industry Corporation, which was owned by the Shanghai municipal government.

Young partnered with Rudy Schlais, president of GM China, who had set up a small office in Shanghai the year before, and they shuttled back and forth between the PRC and GM headquarters in Michigan. The Chinese were impressed that two high-ranking American executives were living and working in China, but the biggest challenge, said Young, was getting the attention of decision-makers in Detroit. "Everybody was busy doing their own thing. They wouldn't give any answers. My job was to tell the right people how important China was and get them involved." She agreed with Smith that the project made sense for GM, but others thought the China market was a total waste of time. "Nobody wanted the job," she remembered. "They would say, 'The Chinese make $1,000 a year. Who's ever going to buy a car? Why do we need to be there?' "[23]

Young's first step in formulating a plan with Schlais was to reconnect with some of the Chinese-born engineers working at GM and to bring them together as an advisory group. They explained the challenges of working in the PRC: developing relationships, learning how decisions were made, understanding the role of Party bureaucrats. They told her that personal connections (guanxi) were critical, state-owned businesses were closely connected to government ministries, and Communist officials did not make decisions quickly or independently. Working in China demanded patience, persistence, and an understanding that everything was connected. Young described it as a spider's web.[24]

According to Matt Tsien, who worked on the technical details of the new joint venture—and became the first Chinese American president of GM China in 2014—relatively few Americans worked in China in the early years, so "the cultural gap was wider and bridging it was essential."[25] Young coached GM executives on basic dos and don'ts. She explained that Chinese negotiators often are reluctant to reject a proposal outright because they choose to be respectful and polite. This was frustrating to Americans who expected a direct "yes" or "no" answer. The Chinese typically hosted a lengthy dinner before doing business, and some of GM's top executives thought these elaborate banquets were a waste of their time and money. Young would tell them, "There is a very real purpose, even if eating twenty courses is painful. It's a form of social interaction where people are making connections and developing trust as a basis for doing business." As a gesture of respect, she advised her colleagues to serve Chinese food to delegations who visited Detroit, instead of pizza or big pieces of meat. When the Americans bought presents from Tiffany's in New York, the distinctive blue boxes were wrapped in red ribbons instead of the normal white. GM also invested in public relations and charitable gifts. The company, for example, made a $125,000 contribution to the Shanghai Symphony Orchestra after Young joined its board. All in all, it was a comprehensive approach, sensitive to social and cultural differences.[26]

To convince the Chinese of GM's good intentions, Jack Smith made four trips to Beijing to meet with President and General Secretary Jiang Zemin, accompanied by Rudy Schlais, Shirley Young, and other GM executives. (The Chinese were impressed that Smith flew on a commercial airline instead of a corporate jet.) These high-profile visits helped to consummate the relationship at the highest levels of government.[27]

The GM team was slower to make connections between business and politics. When the Clinton administration gave Taiwan's President Lee Teng-hui permission to visit Cornell University, his alma mater, in June 1995, Beijing viewed the decision as a threat to its "one China" policy and conducted ballistic missile tests in the Taiwan Strait as a warning (see Chapter 5). Around this time, Young and two of her colleagues had a meeting at the State Planning Commission in Beijing where a minister asked what they were going to do about US-China relations. Stunned, they stammered that they had come only to talk about automobiles. The minister replied, "If you don't solve the problem of US-China relations, Americans are not going to get this project." They sat in their car after the meeting, suddenly aware that GM needed a plan for US government relations with China. "There was a big learning curve for our office in Washington, which was focused only on domestic US regulations," said Young.

Despite the vicissitudes of Sino-American relations, China's central government awarded GM a joint venture license in December 1995, a signal that Washington and Beijing were getting back on track. In a delayed ceremony at the Great Hall of the People in March 1997, Vice President Al Gore and Chinese Premier Li Peng celebrated a $2.4 billion agreement in contracts for GM and the Boeing Company.

GM's success was not guaranteed. At the outset of the negotiations, the company proposed selling the Chinese an existing plant "which would be depreciated, fully tested, no risk of quality or anything else," remembered Young. "We thought we were so brilliant. They could start making money immediately." But the Chinese side rejected the offer. If they accepted, they reasoned, China would always be several years behind the most advanced manufacturing. They preferred to wait longer, take more risks, and develop the capacity to compete at the highest levels of automotive engineering. GM

Front row, left to right: GM Chairman Jack Smith, President Jiang Zemin, Rudy
Schlais, and Shirley Young in Beijing, 1996.
Courtesy Rudy Schlais.

had to change its thinking in response. Young pointed out that the normal
approach in American business is direct: "You have a bullseye and you aim
straight for that target." The Chinese approach was different; they were
looking at a much bigger, longer-term goal. Instead of maximizing short-
term profits, GM needed to position itself as a reliable long-term partner if it
was going to succeed.[28]

GM then proposed building small sedans or minivans, but Chinese
officials at the Ministry of Machine-Building Industry wanted Buicks. It was

a car with a prestigious pedigree in China dating back to the early 1900s. The last emperor, Puyi, had owned two Buicks; Sun Yat-sen, founder of the Chinese Republic, was photographed riding in one; Chiang Kai-shek's Buick was on display in Nanjing; and Premier Zhou Enlai had a Buick when he lived in Shanghai for a short time in 1946. Coincidentally, Shirley Young's father and mother had driven Buicks in pre-revolutionary China.

GM and its Shanghai partner took advantage of this storied past and adapted the Buick to the local market. Chauffeurs still drove most cars in the 1990s, so the wheelbase was lengthened to give passengers more room in the rear seat where controls for heating and air-conditioning were added. The driver's cup-holder was redesigned for tall tea bottles. The suspension was strengthened for rough roads and engines were downsized to improve fuel efficiency. The most popular color was black, which signified power and authority.[29]

Ultimately, GM's commitment to provide the most modern technology and to keep it current gave the company an edge over its competitors. (GM was the first to put a catalytic converter on a car made in China.) A $750 million state-of-the-art factory in Pudong—a newly constructed city on the other side of the Huangpu River from Shanghai—represented the single largest US investment in China at the time. GM's total stake was $2 billion, mostly for auto parts. A *Los Angeles Times* story reported the Detroit company planned to invest $40 million in technology institutes, "with two already opened this year in Beijing and Shanghai to help pass on auto know-how."[30] A senior researcher at the Chinese Academy of Social Sciences told Young he had recommended General Motors over Ford. Both companies had good products, advanced technology, and strong finances, but he believed GM would be a better bet because everybody at the company understood the PRC's ambition not just to build cars with foreign assistance, but to develop its own advanced manufacturing capability.[31]

In addition to a willingness to provide technology, albeit with certain safeguards, GM instituted a long-term plan to make decisions and allocate resources locally. Bill Russo, an automotive expert with decades of experience in the PRC, explained, "The essence of GM's success is they ran a business in China for China. They didn't run a business by remote control as if it were just another market. Localization is the critical ingredient. As a result, they were able to source and develop a Chinese supply base to lower their costs and be more competitive."[32] Local manufacturing, in seventeen assembly plants around the country, was a less expensive approach so long

SHIRLEY YOUNG: JOINT VENTURES 201

as quality could be guaranteed. Chinese tariffs on imported auto parts also acted as a mechanism to spur local development.

Once the joint venture agreement was signed, Young's primary responsibility was marketing, distribution, and brand development for Buicks, something that previous joint ventures had not attempted with their cars. "Back then it was all fleet deals and government purchases," remembers Matt Tsien. "There wasn't any sort of mechanism for directly reaching out to the end consumer."[33] Young's job was to coach, counsel, and guide dealership development, and to make Shanghai General Motors a model for the industry. She concentrated on Beijing, Guangzhou, and Shanghai before extending the network to other cities. GM's joint venture, writes automotive consultant Michael Dunne, was preparing for the day when "more and more private individuals would have the money to buy their own cars . . . . Shanghai GM's management convinced dealers to invest millions of dollars to make the Buick showrooms the finest and most advanced. The dealerships featured expensive floor-to-ceiling glass, highly trained sales and service personnel, and state-of-the-art ordering and logistics systems." A showroom in Shanghai featured an antique 1913 Buick.[34]

———

GM's China strategy raised questions that have bedeviled US business leaders for decades: How much technology should their companies be willing to turn over in exchange for being able to enter the China market? How could they guard against intellectual property theft? What about the loss of manufacturing jobs in the United States? Young had colleagues at GM who asked why the company was taking such a big gamble. They believed the Chinese were "going to take our technology and come back and beat us." She quoted Jack Smith telling them, "Look, we are now ten or fifteen years ahead, and if we can't stay ahead, that's our problem. And if for some reason they catch up, we will have a share in what they are doing."

China's leaders confronted problems of their own as they entered into joint ventures with foreign manufacturers. How could they avoid dependence on outsiders in the process of modernization? What was the right balance between state command of the economy and private sector growth? Was it possible to protect state-owned enterprises (SOEs) and stimulate economic growth at the same time? How could the PRC maintain full employment and develop an industry that demanded automated technology?

After all, GM's objective was to build more cars with fewer people. "For example," said Young, "we had a plant in Eastern Europe where there were ten thousand people making one thousand cars. GM went in and a year later they were making ten thousand cars with one thousand people. It was a great success." But when the Chinese heard this story, they focused on the nine thousand people who lost their jobs. "They weren't concerned about profits and stock prices."[35] By the late 1990s, however, China's economic planners reversed course and instituted policies that led to millions of workers losing their so-called iron rice bowls. The imperative for rapid growth outweighed the potential for short-term political instability, and massive downsizing of state-owned and collective sector enterprises resulted in widespread protests and strikes.

For better or worse, urban Chinese, who transitioned from the bicycle age to the automobile era in a single generation, have bought into the American dream of individual mobility, making China the world's largest passenger vehicle market. "The development that we've seen over the past twenty years has gone well beyond our early imaginations," says Tsien. "It's almost been too successful when you look at the congestion and the environmental problems."[36] Vehicle ownership per capita is still fairly low, about 150 vehicles per thousand, but China has four times the population of the United States, with densely concentrated megacities like Beijing, Chongqing, and Shanghai. The PRC has responded to dangerous levels of air pollution with "a massive push into new-energy vehicles (NEVs), including hybrids, battery plug-ins, and most recently, hydrogen fuel cells," writes policy analyst Scott Kennedy, a move that has influenced GM's planning. The new industry has grown quickly, but is driven "less by consumer demand than government fiat and financing." Another worrisome fact is that "most of the electricity used to charge NEVs comes from fossil fuels, which is why some in China call NEVs 'coal cars.'"[37]

US corporations have made sensational profits in China. There is, however, ongoing concern over the theft of intellectual property and various unfair trade practices, including sizable Chinese government subsidies to some industries. Undoubtedly there is truth to these charges, but the reality is complicated. GM's advanced technology was not stolen; it was freely given as the price for admission to a lucrative China market. It is also worth noting that technology transfer is no longer one-sided; some innovations now come from Chinese engineers at GM's joint venture research centers in China. Almost all of the GM cars manufactured in China are sold in China and do not compete with vehicles made in the United States. On the other hand, many US companies buy less expensive automotive parts from the PRC, which has led to a net loss of American jobs.

The Politics of Inclusion

Shirley Young retired from GM in December 1999, at the age of sixty-four, although she continued as an advisor to the company and served on various corporate boards where she was almost always the only woman or Asian. She formed her own consulting firm and frequently traveled to Shanghai, where she maintained an office and a spacious apartment on an upper floor of the art deco Grosvenor House, part of the famous Jinjiang Hotel where Richard Nixon and Zhou Enlai signed the Shanghai Communiqué. During this phase of her career, she pursued a dual mission: advocating for Americans of Chinese descent and promoting cultural exchange between the United States and China.

When Young arrived in California with her mother and sisters in 1945, she was unaware of the painful history of anti-Chinese racism in the United States. She was not old enough to know about the impoverished laborers who came from southern China to work gold mines and build railroads in the American West during the nineteenth century, men who planned to make enough money to return home, buy land, and raise families. Those who stayed in the United States faced growing discrimination when the mines were played out and railroads completed and the US economy entered a recession. A virulent anti-Chinese movement, marked by lynchings and massacres, culminated in the first of a series of Chinese Exclusion Acts passed by Congress in 1882. Anti-Chinese legislation remained in force in various forms until its repeal in 1943, a change advocated by Congressman Walter Judd (see Chapter 1). Yet not until 1965 would a major reform of US immigration law lead to a significant increase in the number of Asians in the United States.

There was, however, a more positive, less-well-known narrative of inclusion represented by a small but steady flow of Chinese who came to the United States, not as laborers competing for jobs, but as students. Many of them, including Young's father and stepfather, looked to the United States as a model for reforming their country. The earliest endeavor was the China Educational Mission, a group of 120 boys who were sent to New England by the Qing government in the 1870s, a number of whom became leaders in various professions after returning to China. A second wave of American-educated students arrived during the early twentieth century, including some 1,300 men and women supported through the surplus of Boxer Indemnity funds that China had paid to the United States after the Boxer Uprising. The majority of students were funded by their families; others were sponsored by the Chinese government and a small number by Christian missionary boards.[38]

A third wave of educated Chinese came to the United States during the 1940s, most of whom stayed on because of civil war and revolution in their homeland. Many were from Shanghai, China's most international metropolis, and ended up in New York City. With good English and strong entrepreneurial skills, they preferred living on the fashionable upper east and west sides of Manhattan rather than downtown Chinatown, which was populated mainly by earlier generations of working-class Cantonese. Separated by only a few miles, there was relatively little contact between the two diasporas because of their different backgrounds as well as the fact that they spoke mutually unintelligible Chinese languages.[39]

The story of Oscar Tang, Shirley's brother-in-law, paralleled her own. His maternal grandfather was one of the boys who came to the United States with the China Educational Mission, and his father was a Boxer Indemnity Scholarship student at MIT. Tang was born in Shanghai, and his parents, who fled from the Communists for Hong Kong in 1949, sent him to a public school in Vermont when he was eleven. He then made his way through Phillips Academy, Yale University, and Harvard Business School, and co-founded Reich & Tang, a highly successful asset management firm in New York. He shared Shirley's passion for the arts, culture, and education, and became a generous patron of schools and universities, the Asia Society, China Institute, Metropolitan Museum of Art, and New York Philharmonic.[40]

Most Chinese Americans—whether they were educated or uneducated, wealthy or poor, legal or illegal, uptown or downtown—believed it was best to work hard, keep your head down, and avoid controversy. The Chinese were never interned, as were the Japanese during the Second World War, but they were well aware of the US history of racist "Yellow peril" propaganda, and they knew that politics could be a dangerous game. Because they kept to themselves and rarely protested or ran for office, the 1960s civil rights movement largely passed them by, and the mainstream media rewarded them with the label of "model minority." Successful professionals like Young and Tang never felt saddled by a sense of discrimination, and they saw little to be gained by entering the political arena. It was not until 1996 that Gary Locke, whose father emigrated to the United States from southern China, became the first American of Chinese descent to serve as a governor, elected in Washington State. President Obama chose him as Secretary of Commerce, and in 2011, he was appointed US ambassador to the PRC, another first for a Chinese American.

For well-to-do New Yorkers like Young, a transition from political apathy to activism was prompted not by discrimination of any kind, but by the PRC's brutal attack on Chinese protesters in June 1989. The most senior member of their elite circle was the world-famous architect I. M. Pei, who left China in 1935 to study in the United States. Tiananmen shocked him to the core, moving him to write in a *New York Times* op-ed, "The killing of students and citizens tore the heart out of a generation that carries the hope for the future of the country . . . . China will not be the same after this terrible tragedy." He found himself "besieged with calls from people wanting to know how Chinese-Americans felt about the crackdown," and was unsure about how to respond. Pei said, "There was no organization to turn to."[41]

Toward the end of June, Pei and others gathered in Shirley Young's Manhattan office on East 69th Street to establish a new organization called the Committee of 100 (C100), so named because they aimed to recruit one hundred members. The founding group included cellist Yo-yo Ma, scientist Chien-Shiung Wu (who had collaborated with C. N. Yang and T. D. Lee when they won the Nobel Prize in 1957), businessmen Henry Tang and Oscar Tang (not related), and Young, who served as their first chair from 1990 to 1996. The committee invited prominent Americans of Chinese descent to pursue a two-fold mission: advancing US-China relations and ensuring the full inclusion of Chinese Americans in US society. As an independent, non-profit organization, they made public statements and sponsored conferences, organized private discussions, and conducted opinion surveys in the United States and in China.

Pei insisted that the C100 should be "absolutely nonpolitical." No doubt he remembered the suspicions and scapegoating of Chinese during McCarthyism in the 1950s. He also wanted to avoid the trap of being either for or against China, since the Chinese community had been so bitterly divided between those who were loyal to the Nationalists on Taiwan and those who favored the Communists on the mainland. In addition, he believed the

Committee of 100 founders in New York City, June 1989. Front row from left: I. M. Pei, C. S. Wu, and Shirley Young. Back row from left: Yo-yo Ma, Henry Tang, and Oscar Tang.
Committee of 100.

Chinese government was wary of Chinese Americans. "They think our views are warped, that we are no longer Chinese," he told a reporter.[42]

The Committee of 100 has remained cautious about taking sides in disputes between Beijing and Washington. According to their website, "As American citizens, we believe that it is in the United States' interest to have peaceful relations with China and that this is the key to a stable and prosperous Asia." Members position themselves as bicultural intermediaries with the knowledge and connections to help the two countries understand one another, just as Shirley Young did in negotiating between GM and Chinese officials. They support constructive, cooperative engagement with the PRC and agree with official US policy that the Taiwan question should be settled by the Chinese themselves.

They have been more outspoken about racial discrimination in the United States, and in 2018 forcefully denounced "broad brush stereotyping and targeting of Chinese students and academics" by the FBI. "To target a whole group of people as being subject to greater suspicion, based purely on race and national origin, and in advance of any facts or evidence, goes against fundamental American ideals of the presumption of innocence, due process and equal protection for all. It also fans the flames of hysteria." There had been a "rush-to-judgment in the cases of Dr. Wen Ho Lee, Dr. Xiaoxing Li, and Ms. Sherry Chen—all Chinese American scientists or federal employees who were unjustly prosecuted based on suspicion of their ancestry, but who were later found to be innocent of wrongdoing, though not before having their lives ruined."[43] In 2020, C100 issued a press release denouncing racism directed toward Chinese Americans because of the coronavirus pandemic.

C100 has been greatly alarmed by racially charged slurs, actions, and violence against the Chinese American and Asian American community who were blamed because the virus originated in the city of Wuhan . . . . We are living in a once-in-a-lifetime crisis that calls for cooperation and collaboration, not finger pointing and recriminations. As we continue to be vigilant in preventing the spread of racism, to slow the spread of the virus and ultimately find a cure and vaccines, we must bring everything—and everyone—to the table, and not fuel anxieties and fears. Now is the time that we should all unite in a common goal of finding solutions to the shared challenges we face.[44]

Practicing Cultural Diplomacy

After retiring from General Motors, Young founded and directed the US-China Cultural Institute, based in New York and associated with the Committee of 100, to create bridges through the arts and education. "These are important means to bring the necessary human understanding between China and the West for peaceful world relations," said Young. "I always believed the way to get people to communicate was through the arts, which is not political and has no bias."[45] She had strong personal connections with China through GM, and now had the time and resources to practice cultural diplomacy.

Young, who was an accomplished pianist, threw her considerable energies into fostering joint ventures between Chinese and American arts organizations. Her Cultural Institute partnered with non-profit organizations, provided seed money and advice, and mentored young artists of Chinese heritage. As a trustee and philanthropist, she cultivated China relationships for the New York Philharmonic, National Dance Institute, and the Lang Lang Foundation. She helped to establish a partnership between Interlochen Center for the Arts in Michigan and the Shanghai Conservatory of Music. (Earlier in her career, she served on the boards of the Detroit Symphony Orchestra and the Detroit Institute of Arts.) She worked with the Beijing Philharmonic and China's Central Academy of Fine Arts and supported an exchange between violinist Itzhak Perlman's Music Program and the Shanghai Conservatory. "I'm the catalyst that develops the strategy and puts the ideas together," said Young.[46]

In collaboration with the National Dance Institute in New York City, Young's US-China Cultural Institute promoted a program that combined Western and Chinese dance and music for students in China, including the children of migrant workers. "The pedagogy is American, but the content is Chinese," explained Young. Led by the charismatic Jacques d'Amboise, the program became part of the curriculum in two dozen schools in the Shanghai area, and D'Amboise's month-long trip to China with Young was featured in a 2008 HBO documentary, "The Other Side of the World." "Dance is a universal language that transcends history and culture," he said. "It makes children feel special and believe that they can be successful."[47]

In January 2012, Young co-chaired a Chinese New Year gala hosted by the New York Philharmonic that featured Western and Chinese works, a children's choir from Mongolia, and a Chinese dragon dance. The goal, she told a reporter, was "to work with the American institutions in partnerships to make Chinese New Year something which becomes a universal cultural event that everybody can enjoy while learning something about Chinese culture."[48] The Lunar New Year was declared a public school holiday in New York City in 2016.

———

Shirley Young's New York office, tastefully decorated with traditional Chinese art, included a large screen depicting pine trees and long-legged black and white cranes, considered symbols of good fortune and longevity. A striking female Buddhist statue, painted gold and bathed in a spotlight, stood on a pedestal. The room's decor made a statement about the splendor of China's past, a past that is still critical, in her view, to understanding the present.

China is the result of five thousand years of history. It's not like somebody who just rode out of the desert. It's not new. China's leaders are heavily influenced by tradition. It still has a huge impact . . . . If things don't match what we think here in America, it's not necessarily bad or an aberration, but the result of a deep-seated past and therefore reasonable to consider. Their actions are based on a whole sequence of history which is different from ours. The United States is a young country. China looks at the past from a much longer timeframe. Communism was a revolution, but it still has a lot of Chinese pieces of history in it. For example, the education and testing system for children is rooted in the Confucian past; it is not something the Communist government imposed.

Because of China's completely different history, perspective, and cultural outlook, the idea that China would switch from communism to an American version of capitalism and democracy seems narrow and self-centered. The United States is an evangelical nation with a strong ideological belief that the American way is unique and is the beacon for the world. American exceptionalism has been a big piece of what drives our thinking about our role in the world. But in a global, multi-polar world, maybe that's not the way to think anymore because it creates frictions.[49]

Young recognized the PRC's shortcomings but subscribed to the view that the overwhelming majority of Chinese favor stability over disorder. "They don't want corruption or being treated unfairly, but people don't want Western type freedoms if it's going to create problems." She cautioned that it will take another generation to adjust to China's extremely rapid rise. "America was the big brother and all of a sudden this little kid called China is taller and stronger than before. It's a whole new situation that is very uncomfortable and creates a lot of misunderstanding." Patience, mutual respect, and continued engagement are required. "The important thing is to break down stereotypes that Americans have about China. We don't really understand how international and advanced China has become. What it takes is someone who is willing to listen to the other side."[50]

Shirley Young died in December 2020 at the age of eighty-five. Her proudest achievement, said her oldest son David, was serving as a cultural ambassador. Attesting to that claim, Yo-yo Ma, Lang Lang, and Renee Fleming gave performances at her memorial service. Her youngest son Douglas spoke about her hope for greater unity between China and the United States if we can learn to respect each other's differences.[51]

John Kamm, whose story is told in the next chapter, shares Shirley Young's admiration and respect for Chinese culture, and agrees about the need to "listen to the other side." Both of them had great success doing business in China, and both believed that Sino-American relations benefit from finding common ground. Yet where Young thought it was counterproductive for outsiders to interfere in China's internal affairs, Kamm fearlessly made it his mission to fight for the rights of individual Chinese.

9

John Kamm

Negotiating Human Rights

Midway through life, John Kamm abandoned a highly successful business career in Asia to become a human rights advocate. Kamm and his family had been living the expatriate dream in Hong Kong, complete with spacious apartment, company car and driver, maids, and country club memberships. All of this he traded for the frustration and uncertainty of working for the release of political prisoners in China.[1]

It was a bold and risky proposition. He knew a great deal about doing business in the PRC, but almost nothing about its criminal justice system. He had no background in law, nor any experience with non-profit organizations. Human rights groups were skeptical at first, given his lack of experience, but his dogged determination and the results he achieved eventually won them over. He did, however, have excellent Chinese language skills and a detailed understanding of how to navigate China's rules and regulations. He also knew that personal relationships (*guanxi*), built on goodwill and trust, were the key to the success of any endeavor.

Kamm brought two particular sensibilities to his encounter with the People's Republic: the pragmatism of a down-to-earth businessman and the high-minded idealism of a man of principle. He saw no contradiction between the two. Rather, he harnessed them in tandem. What made his approach unusual—and important to our understanding of US-China relations—was his steadfast conviction that cooperation would be more effective than confrontation, even on the divisive subject of individual freedom.

The Dui Hua Foundation, which Kamm established to advocate for improved rights in China, was based on the idea of identifying common interests, not lecturing or shaming Chinese officials publicly on their failings. (*Duihua* means "dialogue" in Mandarin.) By emphasizing shared concerns instead of differences, his aim is to avoid the persistent Chinese complaint that human rights is a Western concept too often imposed on non-Western developing countries. Knowing there are limits to what any outsider can accomplish, his distinctive approach has been to encourage reforms that are in China's own interest. Frequently it has been a matter of finding leverage. Early on, for example, his success in securing clemency for prisoners of conscience was due to his lobbying Washington to maintain the PRC's commercial ties with the United States.

When Kamm embarked on his quest, he was optimistic that improved treatment of political and religious prisoners would coincide with the PRC's desire for international respect. China, he argued, "wants to be seen as a great power, a country with a proud and ancient civilization that seeks to assume its rightful place in the community of nations. It increasingly recognizes that, to accomplish this, it needs to abide by international standards, whether those standards apply to trade, arms control, or human rights."[2] There certainly was truth to this assumption and considerable headway has been made. But with China's turn in an authoritarian direction in recent years, the hoped-for convergence of values between China and the West has proved more elusive than expected.

From New Jersey to Hong Kong

John Kamm has the confident, outgoing demeanor of a born salesman. "What I've been doing my entire career in China is selling," he says. His father, Arthur John Kamm, was a traveling liquor salesman who grew up during the Great Depression in Hoboken, New Jersey, and never graduated from high school. "As a little boy, he would sit me on a stool, and I could watch. I remember he would go into a bar and he'd give a few bucks to the guy sweeping the floor. He'd say, 'Take the little lady to a movie.' And I'd say, 'Hey, Dad, what are you doing giving money to the guy sweeping the floor.' And he'd say, 'John, the guy sweeping the floor today owns the bar tomorrow.' He always taught me you had to respect people."

When race riots broke out in Newark and Asbury Park in 1967, Arthur Kamm was possibly the only white man who ventured into the ghetto, and he never had a problem. "He kept a little book with names, birth dates, kids' names, what their favorite sports were. All the details about the people he was selling to, and he would get to know them personally. And that's been something I've relied on over the years. He taught me a lot about human nature."

Kamm also learned about human relations from his study of cultural anthropology. "Very often when I speak at colleges, and sometimes I've spoken to business schools, I tell the students, the best degree, in my opinion, for business, is not the MBA. It's anthropology. Anthropology teaches you to respect the culture, to learn the language, to learn the customs. It teaches you how to interview people, how to extract information from people. Business schools don't do that. Business schools don't teach you how to sell."

John Thomas Kamm was born on March 25, 1951, in Neptune City, New Jersey. He was raised as a Catholic, along with two brothers and a sister. As a teenager in the 1960s, he was inspired by the civil rights movement and the non-violent philosophy of Martin Luther King Jr. His large public high school was integrated—about 60 percent White and 40 percent Black—but race relations were tense. As editor of the school newspaper, Kamm spoke out against discrimination. Fights broke out, and he led a four-day strike that shut down the school. It was a foreshadowing of his determination to stand up for others.

His mother, Isabel Manes Kamm, was a high school French teacher who encouraged him to learn Chinese when he was admitted to Princeton University on a full scholarship. She told him, "You can always get a job with an exotic language." He created his own major in Chinese anthropology and, like Elizabeth Perry, was active in a strike against the university protesting the US invasion of Cambodia. After his sophomore year, he taught English at a Navajo high school in Ramah, New Mexico, in the summer of 1971. While the radio was on during dinner one night, he heard the news that Henry Kissinger had gone to Beijing. "Somebody at the table said, 'Hey, Kamm, finally you can use your Chinese!'"[3]

After graduating from Princeton a year early in 1972, he headed for Macau, then a Portuguese colony, to teach English through the Princeton-in-Asia program. The private school in Macau was in financial trouble, and a few months later he took a job as a tutor in the Sociology Department at the Chinese University of Hong Kong. It was there in one of his classes that he met Irene Chan, a student who was especially bright and talented in mathematics and statistics. Her father, a former officer in the Nationalist army, had escaped from China with his wife and two older children for Hong Kong, where Irene was born.

Kamm was considering an academic career and spent a summer doing research and writing a published essay on a walled village in Hong Kong's New Territories.[4] He then enrolled in Harvard University's Regional East Asian Studies MA program as a possible stepping-stone to a PhD. But instead of pursuing anthropology and a newfound taste for Cantonese opera, he studied Chinese economics with Dwight Perkins and audited a class taught by Jerome Cohen, who was pioneering Chinese legal studies in the United States (see Chapter 6). After his return to Hong Kong in July 1975, he and Irene Chan were married.

Kamm discovered he was in the right place at the right time to take advantage of China's budding economic opening. He wrote articles for the *U.S.-China Business Review* and other periodicals about a growing appetite for consumer goods and industrial supplies, including Swiss pocket knives and wrist watches, camera film, medicines, Albanian cigarettes, and Cuban cigars as well as raw materials and petrochemicals. In the process of doing research, he cultivated relations with official gatekeepers in Guangdong, next door to Hong Kong, since it was the most open province and he could speak Cantonese. Like Virginia Kamsky, who arrived in Beijing in 1978 to represent Chase Manhattan Bank, he learned that doing business in China demanded flexibility. She remembers the days when there was neither a joint venture law nor any law for wholly owned foreign enterprises. Many deals were creative barter transactions because China wanted technology and equipment but had very limited foreign exchange.[5]

A Sobering Introduction

John Kamm saw evidence of repression on his first trip to the Chinese mainland in January 1976 when he covered the China Feather and Down Garments Minifair in Shanghai for the National Council for US-China Trade. It was toward the end of the Cultural Revolution, and bureaucrats who were apprehensive about the restoration of "bourgeois capitalism" kept him at arm's length, giving perfunctory answers to questions. With time on his hands, he walked in the bitter cold to the International Seamen's Club, located in a grand old building on the Bund, the famous embankment that runs along the Huangpu River. It was one of very few places where a foreigner could buy a drink; the pre-revolutionary days when Shanghai was teeming with night clubs, bars, prostitutes, and opium dens were long since gone.

"I struck up a conversation with a young Hong Kong sailor who was working on a tramp steamer registered in Hong Kong and operated under the Chinese flag . . . . [He] told me of his life on a PRC-owned vessel. He complained about the incessant political study sessions he and his fellow seamen had to endure. I listened attentively. Apparently, others were also listening attentively." The following night, the phone rang in Kamm's room at the Shanghai Mansions. It was the young sailor. "He told me that he was leaving Shanghai early, and that I was not to try to contact him. He told me he would always remember our friendship. He rang off. A cold shiver ran up my spine."

Later that night Kamm heard loud voices and the sounds of fighting outside his window. He awoke the next morning to see the streets lined with military vehicles, and in the distance he could hear the somber music of a funeral dirge. A floor attendant, who was weeping, told him that Premier Zhou Enlai, much beloved by ordinary Chinese, had died. Two Australians also attending the trade fair returned from a walk and said the police had detained and questioned them for taking photographs of people reading newspapers that were posted on wooden bulletin boards.

Kamm went with a few other foreigners to the nearby Peace Hotel for lunch and noticed the waiters were wearing black armbands. "One of the young men came to our table and explained: 'We have been told not to commemorate Zhou Enlai's death, but we are doing so anyway. We are not afraid. Let them come and try to make trouble.'" The Gang of Four had warned the state media against memorializing Premier Zhou, concerned that his popularity would be used against them.[6]

Kamm made six more visits to the mainland that year, reporting on the spring and autumn Canton Fair in Guangzhou, China's oldest and largest trade fair, for business magazines in Hong Kong, and building up a network of contacts with Chinese buyers and sellers. "My memories of 1976 in Guangzhou are of grey buildings with huge red signs proclaiming the imminent liberation of Taiwan, dank interiors of run-down buildings that served as provincial headquarters for the state trading companies, the cold officiousness of the Public Security Bureau, and the omnipresent feeling of being watched. Foreigners were totally segregated from the local population and were accompanied everywhere by stiff and formal escorts."[7]

Kamm's introduction to the People's Republic was grim, but as the mainland opened up to trade and investment from the West, he pushed aside any thoughts about democracy. For the time being, he would concentrate on making money and raising a family. Based in Hong Kong, he went to work for Diamond Shamrock, a US multinational corporation and by 1980 had made $1 million (nearly $3.2 million in today's dollars) on commissions selling chemicals in China and other parts of Asia. The company was taken over by Occidental Chemical in 1985, and Kamm became the head of operations for all of Asia as well as Australia and New Zealand. On the road constantly, he was, like a number of expatriates who profited from East Asia's economic boom, living the exhilarating life of a well-to-do business executive. "In those days, those of us doing business in China, working in China, we were pretty optimistic that things were going to change, and China would be more open and tolerant and liberal."[8] Indeed, for several decades, this was the general consensus that guided US policy after Nixon's rapprochement with Beijing in 1972.

John Kamm at the Bookworm bookstore and restaurant in Beijing, 2018.
Dui Hua Foundation.

"A Shattering Moment"

John Kamm was hopeful about the outcome of peaceful protests demanding reform that went on for weeks in Beijing and other Chinese cities in the spring of 1989. The courage of demonstrators on the mainland inspired the people of Hong Kong and, for the first time since the 1960s, the city found its political voice. Margaret Scott, an American journalist, witnessed massive crowds at a rally in support of their "brothers and sisters" across the border.

> In late May, Hong Kongers held a jubilant fund-raiser for the students [in Beijing] at the Royal Hong Kong Jockey Club's Happy Valley racecourse. Wealthy entrepreneurs in Rolls-Royces, bankers, Queen's Counsels, students, secretaries and factory workers—all poured in by the hundreds of thousands to the "Concert for Democracy in China." When the legend "Chinese of the World Unite" flashed across the racecourse's vast video screen the cheers were deafening. After 12 hours, the scattered bins were full of red and green bank notes—about $1.5 million raised for the Chinese students. The mood was one of joyous hope: China would be reborn in Hong Kong's own image, and with time to spare before [the handover in] 1997.[9]

No one expected the People's Liberation Army to enter Beijing and slaughter unarmed civilians. "It was a shattering moment for me and so many other people," remembered Kamm. As the massacre unfolded, he happened to be on a business trip in the city of Zhuhai near Macau. He watched the coverage on Hong Kong TV, which was not censored, in a hotel with several Chinese officials. "Some of them were in tears, they were denouncing the government, and others were Party members who were very careful of what they said." As he traveled back to Hong Kong through Macau, he saw big character posters (*dazibao*) condemning the Chinese government and a run on the Bank of China. "People were panicking and trying to get their money out."[10]

In the coming days, Kamm, who was vice president of the American Chamber of Commerce (AmCham) in Hong Kong, successfully lobbied his business colleagues for a resolution condemning the violence, a statement that was published in several English and Chinese language newspapers.

Before the Tiananmen crackdown, the American public knew almost nothing about Chinese protesters, with the exception of Wei Jingsheng, a former Red Guard who gained international attention in 1978 when he posted a manifesto calling for democracy, which he termed the "Fifth Modernization." He was arrested for speaking out and sentenced to fifteen years in jail for counter-revolutionary crimes. Aside from Wei's case, advocates for political reform were anonymous. Unlike Aleksandr Solzhenitsyn and other Soviet dissidents, Chinese writers were not translated and published in English, and the internet did not yet exist. Besides, China was reaching out to the United States and there was good reason to be confident about the potential for improvements in PRC's legal and political system.

US foreign policy typically gave human rights a high priority—it was especially prominent on the Carter administration's agenda—but it was only after the suppression of protesters in Beijing that it became a central issue in US-China relations. Suddenly, the images from Tiananmen Square, broadcast live across the world, gave faces and voices to young Chinese dissenters. Hundreds of them were able to escape to Hong Kong, Taiwan, Europe, and the United States, while thousands more were arrested and imprisoned in the PRC. President George H. W. Bush worked behind the scenes to keep relations on an even keel, but the dismantling of the Berlin Wall in November 1989 and the demise of the Soviet Union in December 1991 undermined Washington's rationale for allying with Beijing as a strategic counterweight to the USSR. Now that the Cold War was rapidly fading, there was less political risk in confronting China, one of the few remaining communist states in the world.

Some members of the US Congress, including Representative Nancy Pelosi, whose San Francisco district included a large Asian American population, argued that China should be punished for its ongoing repression of dissidents. In her opinion, the Bush administration had not done enough to oppose Beijing's abuse of human rights. The most powerful tool available to Congress was a legal requirement to annually review and approve China's preferential trading status with the United States. Most Favored Nation (MFN) status, as it was known, first granted to China in 1980, set tariffs at a reasonable rate, providing greater access to the US market. This policy had been essential to China's export-driven economy and was also in the interest of numerous US companies. Congress seized on the annual renewal of MFN (which heretofore had been approved in pro forma fashion) in an effort to improve human rights in China. Kamm, now president of AmCham in Hong Kong, faced a tough balancing act: keeping the door open for American business while refusing to condone repression in the PRC.

Nearly one year after Tiananmen, in May 1990, Zhou Nan, China's senior representative in Hong Kong, hosted a banquet for the US business community to ask them to lobby the US Congress for the continuation of China's MFN status. Zhou was a tough and seasoned negotiator who had interrogated American POWs in Korea and had served as the PRC's ambassador to the United Nations in the early 1980s. From January 1990 to July 1997, when Hong Kong reverted to the PRC's control, he directed the New China (Xinhua) News Agency, which represented Beijing's interests in the British Crown Colony.

The banquet proved to be a turning point for John Kamm. As he and an American colleague were being driven to the Xinhua building in the Wanchai district, they heard a woman on a Hong Kong radio station pleading for the release of her son. Yao Yongzhan had been involved in protests in Shanghai and was arrested a few days after June 4 as he was boarding a plane to return to Hong Kong where his parents lived. His detention was part of a broader effort to intimidate Hong Kong's pro-democracy movement. "Of course, in those days we heard a lot of those kind of stories, so I was aware of the case," recalled Kamm. Listening to the mother's voice, though, triggered something in him. "It just stayed in my mind."

After drinking multiple shots of potent *maotai* liquor during the meal, Kamm praised Zhou Nan for his ability to quote from the prologue of Chaucer's *Canterbury Tales*. A self-satisfied Zhou raised a toast to thank Kamm for "everything you are doing for US-China relations." In his strong baritone voice Kamm asked in response, "What are you going to do for me?" Conversation in the room stopped dead. Zhou put down his glass and said, "All right, what would you have us do?" On the spur of the moment, Kamm told him he should arrange for the release of Yao Yongzhan, the young man being held in Shanghai.

"Zhou Nan went ballistic," says Kamm. "No one—especially a younger person like me—ever spoke to him like that." Kamm was well aware of the importance of respect for authority in Chinese society; he had broken the rules of etiquette and was unsure what would happen next. Zhou said, 'You have just committed an unfriendly act, a rude interference in China's internal affairs.' Finally, I said, 'Minister Zhou, whether or not you release Yao Yongzhan, I'm still going to Washington to testify in favor of keeping your trade status because I love Hong Kong. Do you love Hong Kong?' He said, 'All right, all right, all right. I'll see what I can do.'"

Kamm stood up and a waiter showed him the way to the men's room. Once they were out of earshot in a hallway, the man stopped, turned around, and looked at Kamm with tears in his eyes. "He grabs me, embraces me, and he says, 'Thank you for that.' That's when my life changed, right there." The next day, John told his wife what he had done. "She probably thought I had a little too much to drink."[11]

True to his word, he flew to Washington, DC about three weeks later and made an impassioned plea before a Senate committee to renew the PRC's trading status "for the sake of Hong Kong and for the reform movement in China." Stripping Beijing of MFN, he said, "will devastate Hong Kong economically and psychologically. Even the most forceful advocates of democracy in Hong Kong and reform in China support the renewal of MFN. They know the awful truth, that increasing China's isolation, undermining the reformers, and impoverishing Hong Kong will serve only to make those dark jail cells darker, the cries of their victims louder yet more difficult to hear."

Hong Kong, Kamm told the committee, was on the front line. "There are young Hong Kong people in Chinese jails. I take this opportunity to call once more for China's leaders to release them to their families. We, the American Chamber in Hong Kong, will continue to speak out and work as hard as we can to realize their freedom." He then promised, "Whatever capital we might earn by fighting further sanctions we will gladly spend in the effort to free all Chinese prisoners of conscience."[12] Kamm and other advocates were successful in convincing Congress to approve an extension of MFN for the PRC, which was made permanent in December 2001. (The United States imposed sanctions on Hong Kong in 2020 in response to the arrests of protesters and restrictions on elections in Hong Kong.)

When Kamm got back to Hong Kong, he was informed that Yao Yongzhan would be released from prison two days later. It seemed the Chinese government appreciated his support for trade rights and also was concerned about its negative image in Hong Kong. It was a small price for Beijing to pay, and Kamm had no idea if setting Yao free was anything more than a fluke. Whether a businessman-turned-activist could link trade benefits with human rights advocacy was an open question.

To test his newfound theory, he asked Western human rights organizations for the names of political prisoners and then approached officials in Guangdong and Beijing to provide information on two brothers from Hunan Province, Li Lin and Li Zhi, who had been active in the 1989 protests. As a result of his inquiries, as well as entreaties from former president Jimmy Carter and Human Rights Watch, the brothers won their freedom in July 1991. A week after their release, John and Irene had dinner with them in Hong Kong. They had been beaten, punched, and prodded with electric batons, and there were burn marks on their arms where electrodes had been attached. "They told me the day I got involved was the day their situation improved. I wept. That's when I started to think that I could talk to the Chinese about freeing prisoners, and they would do it."[13] At the age of thirty-nine, John Kamm had found his calling.

Irene supported his decision without complaint or reproach. Years later, she was in the audience when he publicly expressed his gratitude in a speech at Notre Dame University. "A mother with two young children, she watched her husband walk away from a secure job with many benefits for the uncertainties and dangers of a life spent going into prisons and cajoling the Chinese government into releasing political and religious prisoners, most of whose names are known but to God."[14]

Selling Human Rights

The modern human rights movement has been constructed around the concept of individual rights; freedom of speech, association, and religion are enshrined in the United Nations Universal Declaration of Human Rights, adopted in 1948. In keeping with these principles, Kamm believes the most effective means for moving forward is to focus on specific cases rather than long-term institutional change. "When it comes to human rights in China," he pointed out in a talk at the University of Southern California, "Americans and their elected representatives do not generally think in abstract terms about respect for rule of law and even religious freedom . . . . However, they do think in terms of human beings and the impact of Chinese policies on the lives of people." In his opinion, naming the names of lesser-known or entirely unknown prisoners is the single most effective way to promote rights because "doing so demonstrates in the clearest terms America's respect for the integrity and dignity of the individual. Showing concern for lowly and obscure prisoners, not just the 'big names' . . . tells the Chinese government a lot about our priorities."[15]

"Prisoners are first and foremost human beings," says Kamm. "Prisoners have rights—the right to due process, to medical care, to regular family visits, to be free from physical and mental abuse—and getting the Chinese government to recognize and better protect these rights contributes to greater respect for rule of law and a greater 'rights consciousness' which must gain hold if a better rights environment is to be achieved."[16]

It did seem that singling out individuals and making their names known could make a difference. According to a Human Rights Watch report issued three years after Tiananmen, there was a two-track system for jailing pro-democracy dissidents in China. "A small number of well-known intellectuals and student leaders—upon whom international attention tended to be most sharply focused—were held in relatively humane conditions and were by and large not subjected to gross ill-treatment." On the other hand, the "vast majority of lesser-known or entirely unknown pro-democracy detainees" were being held in conditions of "extreme overcrowding and inadequate sanitation and diet, and subjected to physical and psychological brutality at the hands of prison guards and other inmates."[17]

Drawing on his knowledge of Chinese society and his background in business, Kamm constructed what he called "a culturally acceptable, non-confrontational, non-threatening approach" to human rights. Instead of referring to political or religious prisoners, for instance, he spoke with Chinese authorities about political detainees or prisoners convicted of counter-revolutionary crimes. Rather than demanding the release of certain prisoners, he would inquire about their status and health. "In order to have a dialogue," he explained, "it's necessary to arrive at a shared language."[18]

His strategy was to convince officials that better treatment of prisoners was in China's best interest and should not be seen as giving in to the demands of foreigners. Rather than lecturing about international standards, he urged the Chinese to implement their own prosecutorial, judicial, and prison regulations. He identified reform-minded Party members, uncovered regulations governing physicians' access to prisoners, and encouraged discussions on issues such as the right to emigrate and freedom of religion.

During repeated visits to China, he met with government and Party officials at the provincial level as well as the Ministry of Justice, Ministry of Foreign Affairs, Supreme People's Court, Religious Affairs Administration, Chinese Academy of Social Sciences, and the Chinese People's Institute of Foreign Affairs in Beijing. It was his steadfast advocacy for MFN trading status that gave him an entrée to Chinese decision-makers. Li Baodong, vice minister of foreign affairs, who was the PRC's top human rights diplomat, later told New York Times journalist Tina Rosenberg, "Kamm is very critical of our policies, but his approach is acceptable to us. He loves China. He shows respect. He is constructive and realistic." Li told Kamm, "At China's most desperate moment, you gave up your career to work on the most sensitive issues, thereby making a great contribution to US-China relations. We will never forget this. We will always be grateful."[19]

At the outset of his crusade, there was considerable doubt that a businessman could be effective in the human rights field. Some experts treated Kamm as an interloper. Others asked whether leniency and the release of individuals imprisoned for their political and religious beliefs should take precedence over institutional reforms that could improve the lives of many more people.

Skeptics also found the idea of bargaining MFN trade rights for human rights distasteful. They questioned whether his approach involved too much compromise. Mickey Spiegel, a Human Rights Watch researcher, called the timing of Beijing's release of a few prisoners or even a single prominent prisoner ahead of major international meetings a "cynical charade." In bidding to join the World Trade Organization and to host the 2008 Olympics, wrote Spiegel, "China has raised hostage politics to an art form" designed to deflect criticism of its abysmal human rights record. "It is always a welcome development when a political prisoner is freed. But the release of one, two or even a few high-profile prisoners does nothing to address China's systemic rights crisis."[20]

Kamm met his critics head-on in testimony before the US Congressional-Executive Commission on China in 2002. "Some activists call working for the release of prisoners 'humanitarian work' and distinguish it from 'human rights work.' Getting a few people out of prisons is fine for those released and their family and friends, but such a result does nothing to change the system that put them in prison in the first place . . . . Pressuring the Chinese government is often compared to the odious business of 'hostage politics,' and those who engage in this work are sometimes referred to as 'hostage negotiators.' "

He fervently disagreed with this line of reasoning. "Far from being a side show, working to secure the release of political and religious detainees is the highest calling of human rights activism." It was precisely such people "who dare to expose corruption and otherwise speak truth to power." They included democracy advocates, labor organizers, religious leaders, scholars, and journalists. "To them belong the pain and glory of bringing change to China," declared Kamm, "but they can do little to reform the country if they are locked in prison cells together with tough and hardened criminals." He underscored the point that outsiders would not be the "principal catalysts" for civil and political rights.

> The agents of change will be found among the people of China. It was international pressure that saved the lives of Nelson Mandela, Kim Dae-jung, Lech Walesa and many others who eventually brought democracy and social justice to their countries. Yesterday's imprisoned dissident is today's leader of a democratic and free society. Does anyone believe that by passing another resolution or by running a few more seminars to train judges or by holding another legal exchange in which the sides do not discuss actual violations that more can be accomplished than what is accomplished by freeing from prison those who know the country best, who have suffered for their beliefs and who have thought long and hard of ways to bring about a better China?[21]

Unfortunately, Kamm's optimism about these dedicated "agents of change" has proven unrealistic. In a number of instances, Beijing has paroled a dissidents convicted of political crimes on the condition that they leave for other countries. (Kamm himself has helped a number of them to find refuge in the United States and Europe.) Once exiled overseas, most activists effectively lose their voices, and the Chinese government blacklists them from returning to China. Even very prominent critics—such as Wei Jingsheng, Fang Lizhi, and Wang Dan—fade into obscurity after they emigrate.

Making use of his growing credibility, Kamm made connections and shared information with the United Nations Human Rights Council (UNHCR), Human Rights Watch, and Amnesty International. He cultivated relationships with Congress, the State Department, and the White House. He urged Democratic and Republican senators and congressmen to write letters asking Beijing to provide information about specific prisoners, and lobbied to add names to lists that the United States submitted to the Chinese government. Xi Yang, a Hong Kong journalist; Jigme Sangpo, a Tibetan schoolteacher; and Yang Lianzi, who wrote protest songs and poems, were among them. Another was Zheng Yunsu, leader of a Christian evangelical group called the Jesus Family in Shandong, who was sentenced to twelve years in prison for disturbing the social order and fraud. Zheng was paroled in 1999, having served seven years of his term, after his case was raised during visits by senior US religious figures.[22]

Kamm made steady progress, but to his regret, his work on behalf of political prisoners garnered almost no support from the US business community. Kamm argued that "businesses are acting in their own self-interest when they actively promote respect for human rights." Not only would it be good for a company's image, but it went hand-in-hand with the development of law, which is essential for doing business. Yet when it came to individual rights, he reluctantly concluded that corporations "tread warily, afraid to offend, acting only when their interests are threatened."[23]

Christian Murck, who chaired the American Chamber of Commerce in China in 2001 and 2002, agreed that foreign companies should subscribe to the goal of legal reform. "They have focused on areas of commercial law and regulation where they have direct experience. The assumption has been that improving property rights, contract law, intellectual property rights, labor practices, etc. will help support a more general improvement in rule of law." He noted that businesses also worked to improve environmental standards, human resources, and labor practices for their employees, and accountability to their customers.

However, said Murck, foreign corporations have not raised the issue of political prisoners with Chinese authorities because they "do not have any direct knowledge of the circumstances of individual cases." For this reason, they "lack the capacity to make informed judgments about such cases, to prioritize one over others, to decide that the Chinese government either has not followed its own legal procedures or has faked the evidence given at trials, or to argue that a particular person should be released on medical or humanitarian grounds."[24] Kamm professed surprise and disappointment that the logic that seemed so obvious and compelling to him was unconvincing to nearly all of his former colleagues.

Creating the Dui Hua Foundation

Wanting to raise their two young sons, Jack and Rene, in the United States, the Kamms moved from Hong Kong to San Francisco in 1995, and John established the nonprofit Dui Hua Foundation there in 1999. Located on the ninth floor of an Art Deco building near Union Square, it has a staff of nine people, plus a representative in Hong Kong; Irene Kamm does the finance and accounting. Its first grants were from the Smith Richardson Foundation and the International Republican Institute. Over the years, support has also come from individuals and private foundations, the US State Department, and the governments of Switzerland, Denmark, Sweden, and Norway. With a budget of about $1.3 million in 2020, it is much smaller than international organizations like Amnesty International and Human Rights Watch.

Dui Hua will accept any case so long as the charges do not involve violence. Nothing else is off limits, including the arrests of Tibetans, Uyghurs in Xinjiang, labor activists, or members of the Falun Gong, an organization outlawed in China since 1999. Examples include Sun Xiongying, who gave pro-democracy speeches and defaced a bust of Mao during the 1989 demonstrations; Ngawang Oezer, sentenced to nineteen years in prison for translating and distributing the Universal Declaration of Human Rights in Tibetan; Liu Jingsheng, who has served more than ten years for trying to establish an independent trade union; Zhang Chengjian, jailed for more than eighteen years for attempting to form a political party; and Han Chunsheng, sentenced to eight years in prison for writing letters to Voice of America.[25]

The foundation's comparative advantage derives from detailed documentation of specific prisoners, many of them obscure, culled from open Chinese language sources: provincial newspapers, transcripts of radio broadcasts, police records, county gazettes, provincial sentencing records, legal dailies, and court websites. Information is gathered on the laws and regulations governing the treatment of detainees, including religious groups and national minorities. Kamm maintains that simply asking about prisoners can improve their lot. "Those who are forgotten, those who become prisoners without names, in cells without numbers, exist in a twilight world of unimaginable pain and despair."[26]

The records on prisoner cases were all on index cards when Joshua Rosenzweig, a graduate student in Chinese studies at the University of California, Berkeley, joined Dui Hua as a researcher in 2002. Over the next several years, he scoured library materials in China, Hong Kong, Europe, and the United States, gathering materials to assemble an extensive electronic database. "More sources eventually came online," recalled Rosenzweig. "Chinese courts started putting facts about their dockets on the internet, including a date, a crime, and a name. That's all we really needed. We were able to build a detailed picture not only of who was being incarcerated, but how the criminal justice system was being used against these people. I spent lots of time locating this information knowing full well that it might disappear.

Then we would present our information to the Ministry of Foreign Affairs or other Chinese officials and ask for updates on specific cases. What was the outcome if someone was arrested? Have there been any health issues? Were there any sentence reductions?"[27]

Kamm maintained a frenetic schedule, shuttling back and forth between China and the United States to bring attention to political prisoners. In 2002, he negotiated between the Prison Administration Bureau at the Ministry of Justice in Beijing and the Bureau of Democracy, Rights, and Labor at the State Department for the release of Ngawang Sangdrol, a Tibetan nun who was imprisoned for counter-revolutionary crimes in 1992. She and eleven other nuns secretly recorded songs praising Tibet and the Dalai Lama, which were smuggled out of prison and circulated overseas, an act of defiance that led to the extending of their sentences. With the approval of Chinese authorities, Kamm traveled to Lhasa to plead on her behalf. Soon thereafter, she was granted a medical parole and Dui Hua arranged for her to fly to the United States where she received asylum. According to Kamm, the quid pro quo for Ngawang Sangdrol's release was an invitation for Jiang Zemin to visit George W. Bush's Texas ranch, a rare honor for foreign leaders.[28]

As the Tibetan nun's case showed, securing the early release or reduction of sentences for political and religious prisoners was a transactional process. What was it the Chinese might want in exchange? As Kamm explained to a Congressional committee in 2002, prisoners will be released, lists answered, covenants signed, dialogues held, and rights delegations hosted for a number of reasons.

[Beijing] will sometimes release prisoners as gestures or even rewards to foreign leaders and governments, often in the run-up to a visit to China by a foreign politician or a visit to a foreign country by a Chinese leader. It also occasionally happens that prisoner releases are made to hint at a possible change in domestic or foreign policy. Thus, prior to negotiations with the Vatican on the normalization of relations in 1993, a number of [Catholic] clerics were set free to create a better atmosphere for the talks . . . . It is true that, if the Chinese government fears losing a trade privilege or if it fears losing a vote in the United Nations on its human rights record, it will seek to influence the outcome by making gestures like releasing prisoners or signing human rights treaties. But if it is confident of victory, the opposite is the case. Rather than making gestures, Beijing will hold off making releases

Tibetan nun Ngawang Sangdrol with John Kamm in Lhasa, October 2002.
Courtesy John Kamm.

and will often act defiantly, thereby demonstrating to its people that it is standing up to foreign pressure.[29]

One such example was the case of Guo Feixiong, a lawyer who was sentenced to six years in prison in Guangdong for criticizing the censorship of a newspaper. "He was on a hunger strike, protesting the prison's conditions," Kamm said. "They force fed him for over one hundred days. His wife had gone to Washington, had seen all kinds of people, and couldn't get anywhere. Now if you go to the Chinese and you say, 'You've got to do something about this,' it won't be useful." One can make progress, however, if there is something that can be bargained for. The G-20 Hangzhou summit in September 2016, which President Obama attended, provided the needed leverage. A Chinese official asked Kamm which cases would make a difference, and he explained that relocating Guo to a better prison would be helpful. He was soon moved and received improved treatment. "His wife says I saved his life."[30]

Contending with New Terms of Engagement

During the 1990s, Beijing acceded to international pressure on human rights in order to relieve sanctions, maintain advantageous trade relations with the United States and other countries, and increase its prospects for entering the World Trade Organization. The Chinese government established a human rights division in the Ministry of Foreign Affairs and agreed to bilateral dialogues with various European nations, Japan, and the United States. Beijing used these forums to fend off criticism and to present evidence that the protection of civil and individual rights was improving.

Discord in official US-China relations sometimes made any dialogue impossible. In 1995, Kamm had reached a promising agreement with the Ministry of Justice whereby he would submit lists of prisoner names and the ministry would provide written responses. Soon after providing the first list and receiving information on nineteen prisoners in return, Beijing indignantly suspended the arrangement after the Clinton administration bowed to Congressional pressure and allowed Taiwan's President Lee Teng-hui to visit Cornell University, an action that implied Taiwan's legitimacy in the eyes of the PRC. During ten successive trips to China over the next two-and-a-half years, Kamm was unable to see a single judicial or prison official. The deep freeze continued until President Jiang Zemin's visit to the United States in October 1997, when Jiang urged Americans and Chinese to seek common ground in the spirit of mutual respect, despite their differences. Just before Jiang's trip, the Ministry of Justice issued a list showing that many prisoners had received reductions in their sentences, parole, or better treatment.[31]

John Kamm, like Jerome Cohen, has the advantage of being considered an "old friend of China," a special category reserved for foreigners who are honored for their past contributions. "To this day," said Kamm in 2017, "when I go to China it is not uncommon for Chinese officials to thank me." But as China's need for assistance from outsiders has diminished, old foreign friends are increasingly rare. Sympathetic senior figures like Li Baodong have been replaced by younger men and women who have no memory of Kamm's history as an advocate for the PRC's trade privileges, and his contact with local and regional Party secretaries has become more limited. "Guangdong Province used to be very tolerant, very liberal," he says. "Now it's very difficult, one of the worst."[32]

The terms of engagement on human rights began to shift in the early 2000s. "As China grew wealthier and more powerful," wrote Kamm, "and as the United States' image as a human rights defender was tarnished by abuses committed in Iraq and elsewhere, China no longer feared sanctions and international censure . . . . Beijing eventually concluded that the Western governments needed the [human rights] dialogues more than China needed them."[33] He told a Congressional committee that senior members of the Communist Party and government "view the release of a high-profile opponent of the regime as a sign of weakness and even of humiliation. They oppose releases as craven concessions to foreign powers." Yet even as the door was starting to close, he appealed to Beijing to release political and religious figures with the argument that clemency "is not a sign of weakness, but a sign of confidence and strength."[34]

Kamm estimated in 2002 that for every ten letters or faxes he sent to the Chinese government, he received only one in return. "Sometimes I make a dozen phone calls over several days before I'm able to speak with the person I'm looking for." Faced with such resistance, Kamm decided the Dui Hua Foundation should lobby the Chinese government in somewhat less controversial areas while continuing to pursue individual cases.

Three topics seemed promising: juvenile prisoners, women in prison, and people awaiting execution. These initiatives dovetailed with the CCP's policy to improve governance, but getting results sometimes has proved challenging. A symposium on "Girls in Conflict with the Law," scheduled for April 2020 in partnership with the University of Hong Kong, was postponed because of the COVID-19 pandemic. On the flip side, Dui Hua successfully organized a series of eight international webinars on juvenile justice for girls between October 2020 and March 2021.

The number of women in Chinese prisons has increased significantly, possibly because of drug smuggling and a high poverty rate in Yunnan Province, but the Ministry of Justice has published no updated statistics since 2015. And despite a pledge to improve judicial transparency, a website operated by the Supreme People's Court has released fewer death penalty reviews during the past five years.[35]

Another of Dui Hua's tactics has been to give more attention to prisoners who are American citizens or who have a US connection, knowing that the US government cannot ignore them, although the Trump administration's general neglect of human rights was not helpful. According to Kamm, perhaps as many as two hundred US citizens were being deprived of their freedom in China as of 2021: "Some are held in detention centers, a few for long periods without adjudication; others are in prison, convicted and sentenced for offenses under China's criminal law; still others are forbidden from leaving the country because of commercial disputes or because a relative is suspected of a crime."[36]

Asian Americans have been especially vulnerable. One of them was Sandy Phan-Gillis, a Vietnamese American businesswoman who was traveling in China with a trade delegation from Houston in 2015. She was barred from leaving the country, detained, and placed under residential surveillance in an undisclosed location without access to a lawyer or any family members. Seven months later, in the southern city of Nanning, she was formally arrested on suspicion of stealing state secrets. The White House, State Department, members of Congress, and the Houston city government worked for her release. At the request of her husband, Jeff Gillis, Kamm raised her case in more than two dozen meetings with Chinese officials over a period of nineteen months. These efforts finally paid off in April 2017 when Phan-Gillis was released and deported to the United States after being tried and sentenced to three-and-a-half years in prison.[37]

Entering a Dark Forest

For more than thirty years, John Kamm has strived to gain greater respect for human rights, democracy, and rule of law in China. Since 1990, he has made over one hundred visits to China and Hong Kong and ten visits to Chinese prisons. He has intervened on behalf of some six thousand Chinese prisoners and has been able to help several hundred.

He estimates that less than 10 percent of the names of individuals arrested for political crimes are known. Anyone in this category is handled more strictly than ordinary prisoners, and rarely do they get sentence reductions or paroles. Borrowing from the opening lines of Dante's *Inferno*, he likens his journey to entering a dark forest much bigger and more savage than he ever imagined.[38]

It should be acknowledged that China has seen significant legal and judicial reform in recent decades. The category of counter-revolutionary crimes was abolished under the Criminal Procedure Law enacted in 1997, a new labor law provides more protections for workers, there is less use of "reform through labor," and the one-child policy was ended in 2015. Chinese citizens, moreover, generally are more aware of their rights and more willing to pursue legal measures to settle disputes.

Nevertheless, advocating for civil and political rights has become more difficult and dangerous since Xi Jinping took over China's leadership in 2012. One of his earliest institutional changes was the creation of a national security commission with the primary goal of stopping internal subversion. Widespread harassment and arrests of lawyers and their associates was orchestrated in July 2015 (see Chapter 6). Amnesty International reported that many of those arrested "made forced confessions obtained through torture and ill-treatment."[39] Chen Taihe, a law professor in the city of Guilin who advocated for adopting the jury system in China, was more fortunate than some. He was detained and placed under residential surveillance for inciting subversion of state power, provoking a serious disturbance, and embezzlement. Quite possibly because Chen had advocates outside China, including the Dui Hua Foundation, he was released and allowed to join his family in California in March 2016.[40]

By far the most horrifying abuse under Xi Jinping has been the treatment of hundreds of thousands of Uyghurs, Kazakhs, and other Muslim minorities sent to camps for political and cultural indoctrination in the northwest province of Xinjiang. Chinese authorities claim these "counter-extremism centers" provide useful Chinese language instruction and job training. Critics see massive internment as well as forced labor, birth suppression, and the destruction of cultural patrimony as clear-cut evidence of a massive human rights catastrophe that amounts to nothing less than a form of genocide.

In today's China, the authority of the state continues to take precedence over individual rights, and social and economic rights supersede civil rights. National unity and stability cannot and will not be sacrificed for the sake of democracy. Political prisoners still serve long sentences for "endangering state security," including subversion and "splittism," which means "splitting the country or undermining national unification." A law against leaking state secrets outside China has been used to silence journalists, intimidate lawyers, and harass campaigners for religious freedom. Those calling for greater autonomy in Tibet are treated as terrorists. Anything posted on the internet can be used as evidence of criminal activity. Kamm has testified before Congress that those who speak out against one-party rule, those who attend house churches and practice banned religions, and those who organize so-called "mass incidents" are "treated as a group apart, a group to whom basic rights are denied."[41] These cases almost never result in acquittals, and a majority are sentenced to long prison terms. Meanwhile, Hong Kong's freedoms have been restricted under a national security law enacted by the National People's Congress in June 2020. In the face of such limitations, Kamm openly admits to falling short of his goals.

> At an event at the University of Southern California, I was asked about the cases I was working on and my most recent successes. I said, I can talk to you about a few, but there is something you need to understand. My failures are many. They are legion. I have failed, and failed badly, and have wept bitter tears about some of these, including people who have been executed or have died in prison. Despite my efforts, I was unable to help Tenzin Delek, a Tibetan lama who died in prison in 2015, and Wo Weihan, who was accused of being a Taiwan spy and was executed by a gunshot to the head in 2008. And in 2016, the death of Peng Min, the democracy advocate who was serving a life sentence in Hubei Province. Sometimes I get notice too late to do anything.[42]

In spite of multiple setbacks, Kamm simply refuses to give up. Although diagnosed with diabetes and now walking with a cane, he continues to fight. He remains confident, as he once said, that "focused persistent efforts to engage the Chinese government in a discussion on human rights and the situation for prisoners, undertaken in professional and sensitive ways, can yield positive outcomes. Done the right way, intervention works. Not in every case, not all the time, certainly not at the pace we would like to see, but my experience tells me that if we find out their names, if we learn as much as we can about them, and if we raise their cases at every opportunity, the chances are that prisoners will be afforded some measure of relief and possibly early release."[43]

He has no regrets about leaving a profitable business career. "I made a commitment. I promised I would use all the capital that I gained by helping save China's access to the US [markets] to press for the release of political prisoners. I promised that, and I've done my best to fulfill it." He believes his quixotic journey has been far more rewarding than selling tons of chemicals.[44]

Kamm's contributions have not gone unrecognized. The MacArthur Foundation gave him a prestigious $500,000 "genius" grant in 2004, and he has received two major awards from the US government. Sophie Richardson, China director at Human Rights Watch, who was puzzled by John at first, grew to admire him. "He's been an extraordinary role model for this kind of work. It's not just the depth and the breadth of his knowledge and experience—when you ask him how a particular case might play out, you can see the vast database in his brain ticking over to assess the different variables in dozens of similar cases. It's also the thought and care that goes into developing a strategy to free a particular person, and the incredible tact and support to that person's family and friends. And even when there aren't family and friends to answer to, John is answering to a broad historical record."[45]

Kamm has a big personality, but is humble about the limits of what any outsider can accomplish. "The United States can help, but we can determine neither the cause nor the timing of change in China. We can help by promoting transparency and accountability, a strengthened legal system that safeguards due process, and humanitarian treatment for those in prison who seek change through non-violent advocacy. And we can trade with and invest in their companies, bringing with us those core American values for which we as a people are respected around the world."[46]

John Kamm's largely quiet, behind-the-scenes work on behalf of Chinese prisoners of conscience contrasts with the more public persona of Melinda Liu, a journalist whose story we turn to in the final chapter. Both of them have taken personal risks in defending the right to free expression. Both have learned how to deal with the contradictions between American ideals and the PRC's realities.

10
Melinda Liu
Reporting the China Story

If Melinda Liu dressed like an average Chinese citizen, she did not stand out like other foreigners in Beijing, although her shoes gave her away. The problem in the early 1980s was that if you looked Chinese, people assumed you must be able to speak the language fluently. Growing up in the Midwest, she had learned a few words of Mandarin from her mother, and she had taken one semester of beginning Chinese in college. But it was only after graduation that she took the language seriously, after winning a two-year Michael C. Rockefeller Memorial Travelling Fellowship to study Peking opera in Taiwan.

When Liu arrived in Taipei in 1973, "people treated me as if I were handicapped—and, truth be told, I *felt* handicapped. Even with helpful interpreters, I couldn't hold a heartfelt conversation. I couldn't understand political debates. I didn't even know the really juicy Chinese curse words. If my goal was to learn about Peking Opera, I certainly couldn't succeed without speaking the language." That's when she decided to live with a family who spoke no English and started an intensive study of Mandarin Chinese.

Because she needed money to make ends meet, it was also in Taiwan that she embarked on a journalism career. She cut her teeth as a stringer for *Newsweek*, the *Washington Post*, and CBS News. She also wrote for *Echo*, a local English-language magazine that featured articles on history, culture, and everyday life in Taiwan. The work suited her outgoing, down-to-earth personality. She reported on Taiwanese dissidents who opposed the government's martial law, Communist pilots who defected from the mainland, and Generalissimo Chiang Kai-shek's death in 1975. Because trade with the Communists was illegal, she once was reprimanded after writing that traditional herbal medicines and Shanghai freshwater crabs could be bought in Taipei markets. No one could envision that the economic relationship with China would be transformed in the years to come. By 2018, hundreds of thousands of Taiwanese citizens, many of them factory managers, were living on the mainland, and the value of cross-strait trade was $150 billion; the Chinese market accounted for 35 percent of Taiwan's trade.

After a few years in Taiwan, Liu joined the staff of the *Far Eastern Economic Review*, a well-respected weekly magazine published in Hong Kong, and covered the expanding Chinese economy. Her big break came in April 1980, when she was tapped to open the Beijing bureau for *Newsweek*, the first US news magazine to be credentialed in the PRC.

Unlike most foreign correspondents, who typically stay in a country for only a few years before moving on to a new assignment, Liu has spent much of more than four decades reporting on China. A thorough understanding of the language and culture has opened her eyes to "how differently Chinese might view the world and their place in it, their relationships, their government. It brings a much deeper appreciation of the vast scale of the nation, and the huge regional differences *inside* China. If I had an interpreter constantly glued to my side, it would be easier to perceive China's 1.3 billion people as a monolithic bloc—everyone feeling the same feelings, dreaming the same dreams."[1]

Being a journalist gave Liu a front-row seat on China's post-Mao transformation and its subsequent rise on the global stage, one of the modern world's great stories. Reporting on China was alternately exhilarating and perplexing, inspiring and exasperating. But it was never boring.

Unplanned Sino-American Encounters

Melinda Liu grew up without much interest in her Chinese heritage, never expecting to be involved with China. Born in Minneapolis in 1951, she and her brothers, Tom and Sheridan, grew up in Kettering, Ohio, a White, middle-class suburb where her family had no Asian neighbors. She graduated from Fairmont West High School—she was the only Chinese American in her class—and attended Radcliffe and Harvard, majoring in sociology and making a film on second-generation Chinese in Boston for her senior thesis.

As was true for C. N. Yang and Shirley Young, the events of the Second World War determined Melinda's family history. After the Japanese occupied Beijing (then called Beiping) in 1937, her mother and father met on a train as they evacuated with their fellow Tsinghua University students. They spent time in Changsha in central China before heading on to Kunming, in faraway Yunnan Province, where they attended National Southwest

Associated University (known as *Lianda*), a consortium of three refugee schools: Tsinghua University, Peking University, and Nankai University. After graduation, they were married at a YMCA in Shanghai's International Settlement.

In April 1942, Melinda's father, Tung-sheng ("Tom") Liu, was in Zhejiang Province on his way to Guilin, where he expected to work in a newly built aircraft factory. While waiting for transportation, a Nationalist officer asked him if he spoke English and would be willing to act as an interpreter for a crew of American airmen who had been discovered in the area. They were members of the Doolittle Raiders—named for their commander Colonel Jimmy Doolittle—eighty men who flew sixteen B-25 bombers from an aircraft carrier in the Pacific on a daring mission to bomb Tokyo and other Japanese cities. The attack inflicted relatively little damage, but was a huge shock to Japan and a major psychological boost for the United States. The planes flew on to China—one went north to Soviet territory—but unable to find a designated airfield on a dark and stormy night, the crews bailed out or crashed landed.

The Chinese greeted the Americans as heroes and did everything possible to help them evade the Japanese. Tung-sheng Liu and local Chinese guerillas accompanied five of the fliers for the next two weeks, traveling at night through the mountainous region to avoid enemy patrols. Carl Wilder, one of the airmen, later wrote that Melinda's father "had risked his neck for us and had seen to it that we had the best of care. Under Liu's guidance, our treatment was superb." Wilder was sure that Tung-sheng would have been tortured and executed if he had been captured.[2]

After the war, Melinda Liu's parents decided to study at the University of Minnesota, where her father pursued a master's of science in aeronautical engineering, and her mother, Man-ming Wang Liu, took an MA in English literature. In 1948, Tung-sheng, who then was an instructor and research scientist at the university, read in a local newspaper that the US airmen he had known in China planned to hold a reunion in Minneapolis. They greeted him with open arms when he showed up at their hotel, and he was later named an honorary Doolittle Raider in recognition of his bravery, the only ethnic Chinese given this distinction. It was a defining experience for the entire Liu family, all of whom attended annual reunions commemorating the historic raid on Japan for decades to come. Melinda has kept the memory alive, making a short documentary film, working to build a memorial hall in Zhejiang Province, and organizing trips for the sons and daughters of the

Raiders to places where their fathers were rescued in 1942. The famous history has been a vital bridge connecting her American and Chinese identities.

After several years in Minneapolis, Melinda's father took a job as a civilian aeronautical engineer at Wright-Patterson Air Force Base in Dayton, where he was the system engineering director for the C-5A, a massive military transport aircraft built by Lockheed. Like many Chinese students and scholars in the United States, the Lius had decided against returning to their homeland while civil war was raging between the Nationalists and Communists. It was an agonizing decision because they had left their first-born child with Manming's parents in Suzhou when he was three years old, expecting to return from the United States in a year or two. During their separation, they sent letters and transferred money through Hong Kong to family members in the PRC, but it would be more than thirty years before they could see their son again.

Melinda met her eldest brother for the first time when she visited Suzhou in January 1979. Guangyuan, whose name meant Distant Light, was thirty-seven and she was twenty-six. He lived with his wife, two daughters, and mother-in-law on Jade Phoenix Lane. It was a sobering experience for her. "Their home was a single rectangular room, divided by a massive wardrobe into two areas, each 12 feet square, and their toilet was a chamber pot." Her brother, "a bookish, soft-spoken optimist who worked the graveyard shift at a silk factory for the equivalent of $26 a month, considered himself lucky: his home had a wooden floor, a ceiling overhead and a small courtyard where he could keep a few chickens. His big regret was his loss of the family library during the anti-intellectual rampages of the Red Guards in the Cultural Revolution."[3]

After several days in Suzhou, Melinda took a train to Shanghai to meet her father's brother, Liu Guansheng. "He had once been a public-health official, but during the Communists' first wave of witch hunts in the 1950s he was condemned as a 'rightist' and banished to Xinjiang province, at the edge of the Gobi Desert. He returned home a broken man in 1964, only to have his old 'crimes' trotted out again. Members of his family were forced to denounce him." Her uncle had been politically rehabilitated by the time she saw him, and the authorities had pasted a bright red certificate on his front door declaring that his pension had been reinstated. "A neighborhood public-health center had even offered him a job teaching hygiene classes."[4] Learning through her relatives about the dark side of life under communism opened Liu's eyes to realities unseen by most Western journalists.

Melinda Liu (right) with her brother Liu Guangyuan (left) and his family in Suzhou, 1979.
Courtesy Melinda Liu.

Newsweek Arrives in Beijing

Newsweek did not hire women as reporters until the early 1970s, and Liu was the rare female correspondent. "Melinda had polish and panache," says Carroll Bogert, who worked with her in Hong Kong, China, and the Philippines. "She thought big and had a big personality. And she was beautiful."[5] At a time when print and television dominated the media landscape, working for *Newsweek* or its rival *Time* was a highly enviable job.

By the time Liu was assigned to Beijing, she had strong Chinese language skills, which gave her an edge over most foreign journalists. She recalled that it was advantageous with official interpreters "who would translate Chinese into the most boring English-language platitudes imaginable—but virtually ignore the most interesting bits . . . . I can't tell you how many times I've collected catchy anecdotes, colorful details, jokes, even insults because I could understand what was being said in Chinese."[6]

American journalists who covered China in the 1930s and 1940s, before the Communists took power, were more diverse and less professional than those who came later. Those early reporters, writes historian Stephen MacKinnon, "were refugees from the Great Depression, attracted by the promise of adventure in a mysterious country and rumors of job opportunities. Jobs were especially important to women because the chances of breaking into journalism in China were much better than in Europe."[7]

After 1949, China was unknown territory to virtually all US citizens, who were limited to watching and "reading the tea leaves" from Hong Kong. In early 1957, William Worthy, a Black journalist with the *Baltimore Afro-American* and two reporters from *Look* magazine, Edmund Stevens and Phillip Harrington, defied a State Department ban against visiting and had their US passports revoked upon returning to the United States. The only other early exception was Edgar Snow, who had written sympathetically about Mao Zedong and other Communist leaders in his famous *Red Star Over China*. Because of McCarthyism, he left the United States to live in Switzerland, and made trips to the PRC as an honored guest in 1960, 1964, and 1970. With permission from the US government, several American journalists traveled with the ping-pong team on their visit in 1971, and a sizable entourage of correspondents accompanied President Nixon on his trip in 1972. In both cases, they were captives of carefully scripted schedules arranged by their Chinese hosts, as were others who went on guided tours during the next several years.[8]

After the United States and China established diplomatic relations in 1979, American wire services, newspapers, news magazines, and television networks were more than eager to set up offices in Beijing. The relationship between the Western reporters in residence and Chinese bureaucrats tasked with managing them was uneasy from the start. Accustomed to controlling the media, the Chinese were ambivalent about the recently arrived correspondents. If their stories were positive, it would encourage tourism and investment. But if the outsiders painted a negative picture, it would damage China's interests. The best approach was to politely cultivate journalists as "friends" while keeping them at arm's length. It was a well-established policy for dealing with foreigners of all kinds. It was also an approach that sowed suspicion and mistrust.[9]

Melinda Liu and other reporters were assigned to live and work in the Qianmen Hotel, not far from the Temple of Heaven, where her eighth-floor room was infested with bats. Just filing a story was laborious. She would ride her bicycle to the public telegraph building a few miles away, retype the copy on a telex machine, plead with a clerk to send it out, and patiently wait until the transmission ended. Her editors in New York had little appreciation for the obstacles she faced. On one occasion they asked for a panda story within twenty-four hours, not realizing how long it would take to reach a preserve in far-off Sichuan Province. Except for going to the nearby port city of Tianjin, traveling outside of Beijing meant applying for a permit ten days in advance.[10]

Officials treated basic information, including economic statistics, as national secrets, and Liu was occasionally questioned by police and wrote self-criticisms apologizing for over-stepping boundaries, but was never expelled or denied a visa. On one trip from Hong Kong to Beijing in 1980, she made an unauthorized stop in Fuzhou and was immediately taken aside upon arriving in the capital city. Of course, local Chinese staff were more vulnerable than anyone with a foreign passport, and there was always the risk of endangering her sources. "If you revealed identities or said too much about someone, that person was going to be detained and interrogated."[11]

Some Americans who had been waiting for years to report from China "got there and it wasn't the paradise they thought it was going to be," recalled Liu. "They felt betrayed and became cynical and disillusioned. It was almost as if they were jilted lovers."[12] Fox Butterfield, with the *New York Times*, admitted that he had to "unlearn" many supposed facts about China: that the PRC was a revolutionary society that offered great equality and social mobility, that the socialist system had eliminated special privileges and corruption, that the thirty-eight million Communist Party members were all atheists. He was startled to discover that Party officials had their own exclusive network of markets, bookshops, hospitals, and resorts, "which provides them with food and services unavailable to the 'masses.'" There actually were two Chinas, wrote Butterfield: the official version that featured "cardboard cutouts" who were "always smiling, selfless, and dedicated to the cause," and the other China that "was partially hidden, an inner universe whose one billion inhabitants had gone through three decades of cataclysmic change, sometimes for the better, but often . . . involving brutality, waste, and terrible personal suffering."[13]

Liu was younger than most correspondents and had fewer preconceived notions about the People's Republic. Unlike Elizabeth Perry, who was three years older, she had not been involved in Vietnam War protests in college and was never captivated by Mao's revolutionary aura. Her only exposure to the mainland prior to 1980 was a short trip to Shenzhen, then a sleepy village on the other side of the border with Hong Kong, and her 1979 visit to Suzhou and Shanghai to meet her brother and uncle. She was, however, "one of the best prepared reporters," according to Jaime FlorCruz, a Filipino student at Peking University who fled martial law in the Philippines in 1971 and worked for Liu. (He later became the Beijing bureau chief for *Time* and CNN.) "She knew Chinese culture well enough to pick up the nuances and used her dual Chinese American identity to her advantage."[14]

Liu's stories for *Newsweek* described a society awakening from the bleak desperation of the recent past. "Western advertising is no longer an oddity," she wrote in one of her first dispatches from Beijing, "and shops are beginning to stock an assortment of popular consumer items—wristwatches from Switzerland, color-television sets from Japan and radios and sunglasses from Hong Kong . . . . Love stories, crime thrillers and sitcoms have replaced the dreary, doctrinaire productions shown for years in local movie houses." Yet her excitement about China's opening was tempered with a measure of disbelief. "Despite the changes, many Chinese question whether the new freedoms will endure. They are wary of the government's official backtracking on liberalization and still remain far from convinced that the future will live up to its advance publicity."[15]

She also voiced skepticism when many journalists reported on the dismantling of the people's communes as an undisputed victory for capitalism. "I ran into initial resistance from my editors when I said we should also mention some of the challenges that China's tiny family farms would face in the future, since they would be so labor-intensive." To *Newsweek*'s credit, her story quoted agricultural economists who warned that "some individual families might have difficulty harvesting large rice fields and handling irrigation systems down the line—to the point where a certain degree of 're-collectivization' might be called for."[16]

The top story of 1980, wrote Liu, "was the trial of the Gang of Four—Mao's imperious widow, Jiang Qing, and three male sycophants—on charges of instigating the Cultural Revolution's many crimes against the Chinese people in the decade before Mao's death in 1976. The defendants were accused of framing, purging, and persecuting more than 700,000 Chinese, including 34,800 victims who died. This was no sunlit South Africa-style 'truth and reconciliation' process. No foreign media or independent monitors sat with the 900 carefully screened observers who were allowed into the courtroom," although millions watched the spectacle on television. Looming over the trial were unanswered questions about Mao Zedong's culpability.[17]

During this period of reassessment, Beijing's streets were full of petitioners, "people camping out who had serious grievances left over from the Cultural Revolution. These were people who were desperately poor, horribly abused, and had very little recourse." Witnessing these personal tragedies gave Liu a deeper appreciation of the rights and freedoms that Americans take for granted: being able to travel, having access to education, not having to worry about where your next meal is coming from. She said it made her feel more American.[18]

Deputy Foreign Minister Zhang Wenjin and Melinda Liu at a reception in the Great Hall of the People in Beijing, 1981.
Courtesy Melinda Liu.

244 AMERICANS IN CHINA

Covering the Tiananmen Incident

Liu relocated from Beijing to Hong Kong in 1983 as *Newsweek*'s Asia regional editor and was the magazine's diplomatic correspondent in Washington, DC, from 1992 to 1998. While continuing to write about China, she reported on hotspots around the world: the Soviet Union's occupation of Afghanistan, US military interventions in Somalia and Haiti, and the Persian Gulf War. During the US invasion of Iraq in 2003, she watched the "shock and awe" bombing of Baghdad from the balcony of her room in the Palestine Hotel.

She made multiple trips to the Philippines in 1986 to report on the "People Power" revolution that would topple the corrupt and dictatorial President Ferdinand Marcos. (*Newsweek* had a big budget in those days, and she stayed in a suite in the luxurious Manila Hotel.) After weeks of demonstrations, she joined a huge throng outside the Malacanang Palace around midnight on February 24. "There were soldiers," remembered Liu, "but there was also something of a carnival atmosphere . . . . Some idiot let off firecrackers, which can sound like gunshots, and before you know it, these soldiers are shooting at the crowd." Liu was wounded in the right leg and was taken to a hospital. A bullet fragment had passed through her knee, but the damage was not severe; others around her were more seriously wounded.

The incident only added to her reputation as a rising star at *Newsweek*, remembers her colleague Carroll Bogert, but Liu's dispatches made no mention of her injury. Too many major events were unfolding in the days that followed: the sudden collapse of the Marcos regime, his escape from the Palace by helicopter, the new government formed under Corazon Aquino, the hunt for Marcos's enormous hidden wealth, and the sensational discovery of his wife Imelda's three thousand pairs of shoes.[19]

By comparison, very few foreign correspondents covered a fierce military crackdown on demonstrators in the streets of Rangoon, the capital of Burma (Myanmar), in August 1988. Liu arrived at the airport just as other reporters were leaving. The following morning, "my photographer and I dodged potholes and bullets to visit an ancient city hospital, whose wards were like something out of Hieronymus Bosch. Piles of feces lay in the hallways. The worst part was counting mangled bodies in the morgue, including the corpse of a young teenager missing most of his head."[20] As many as three thousand people had died. Yet because there were no television or video images, the horrific news provoked relatively little outrage outside Burma.

The international response to massive protests in Beijing in 1989 was completely different because of live television coverage, which was possible only because the Chinese government had given permission for CBS and CNN to bring in their own satellite up-links for the impending visit of Soviet leader Mikhail Gorbachev. The uprising and massacre that followed, which no one anticipated, was "a perfect television story," wrote journalist Mark Hertsgaard, "filled with action, compelling visuals, nail-biting suspense and easily identifiable heroes and villains." Protesters "played to the cameras relentlessly. With signs and slogans in both English and French, the students clearly saw the international press corps as an ally. Television—through its magical ability to transport images across the globe and to tens of millions of TV sets simultaneously—helped create immense public sympathy for the protestors."[21]

Liu's experiences in the Philippines and Burma made her realize that "often it's the moment when you're the most tired, you're the least able to see how anything is going to change and you most want the story just to fizzle away and be done with that is the most dangerous moment." When she landed in Beijing on May 3 to supervise *Newsweek*'s coverage of the demonstrations, which had begun on April 15, she knew that the outcome would be unpredictable. "There were protesters all over in Tiananmen Square and it felt like low tide. There was no energy from anywhere. Negotiations didn't go anywhere. Students had cursed the leaders on TV. It just seemed like nothing was happening. Everybody was exhausted, and most of my reporters and photographers wanted to leave."[22]

Liu was present on the square when a military crackdown ordered by Deng Xiaoping began on the night of Saturday, June 3. Hundreds of Chinese were killed, both protesters and bystanders, mainly to the west of Tiananmen. In the aftermath, as gunfire continued to erupt across the city, thousands of foreigners—tourists, students, businessmen, diplomats and their dependents—made their way to the airport and got out of the country, fearful that the situation would devolve into all-out civil war.

Liu stayed in Beijing for nearly two months before returning to Hong Kong where she wrote one of the first comprehensive accounts of the unprecedented movement and its bloody denouement for a book of photographs by twin brothers David and Peter Turnley. In *Beijing Spring*, she chronicled an upheaval that was "remarkable in scope and seismic in intensity." The protests, she explained, were driven more by economic discontent than demands for democracy. Deng's policy of dismantling the communes and allowing farmers to manage their own plots of land had created substantial new wealth in the countryside, but this sudden prosperity produced rampant political graft, nepotism, and other forms of corruption among government and Party officials. Meanwhile, the wages of urban residents not only were stagnant but were being eaten away by inflation. In April, the funeral of Hu Yaobang, the CCP's former secretary general and an outspoken advocate for reform, was a catalyst for mass demonstrations.[23]

When Gorbachev arrived in mid-May, a million people converged on Tiananmen Square. "Every morning, more and more protesters poured out of the Beijing railway station from the provinces. Sympathetic train conductors had allowed them to ride for free," wrote Liu. Some three thousand students took part in a hunger strike, an unprecedented event in China's modern history. Liu spent a night with them, where "moonlight illuminated a patchwork of multicolored protest flags and banners fluttering in the breeze. *I need food but I'd rather die for democracy*, read one in English." She grew fearful as she listened to their demands. "With memories of Burma still fresh, my eyes welled with tears."

The demonstrators were not seeking to overthrow the government, but China's leaders had been deeply humiliated and were afraid the situation might spin out of control. A thirty-three-foot tall "Goddess of Democracy," erected in the Square on May 30, was possibly the final straw. Liu witnessed the brutal suppression of the largely peaceful protests, which were labeled "counter-revolutionary." As she approached the square, she saw "a ragged crimson stain spread across a man's white shirt. I reached for his arm to try to help, but three men appeared, frantically tossed him onto a three-wheeled cart and wheeled it away." Civilians were beating a flaming armored personnel carrier with sticks and metal rods "as if it were a living beast." She was sure that a row of troops pointing their machine guns in her direction would never fire into a crowd of civilians. But then they did. "I had to dive for cover in a pedestrian underpass to keep from getting hit." The world watched in disbelief as the People's Liberation Army cleared the square.

From the safety of the Peking Hotel in the "grim, gray dawn" that followed, Liu and Carroll Bogert saw a convoy of about fifty military vehicles roaring down Chang'an Avenue, smashing through barricades. It was later that same morning that the iconic image associated with the Tiananmen massacre was recorded: a lone man standing in front of a line of tanks, refusing to give way as the lead tank attempted to maneuver around him.

Even as the violence began to wane, Liu described " a nightmare world of grief and destruction. At hospitals and makeshift morgues, relatives sobbed over the dead and dying. Burned city buses and other wreckage littered major crossroads. West of Tiananmen Square stretched a wasteland of gutted military vehicles, including dozens of mangled trucks and more than sixty torched armored personnel carriers." At one university, a white vertical banner of the kind displayed at funerals asserted: "A generation of younger heroes has gone to an early death." Liu tried to see hope amid the despair. Even if demands for a more democratic system of government had been rejected, she believed the Chinese people "were convinced that the mandate of heaven had shifted that spring in Beijing, and that it was now just a matter of time before Deng's reign came to an end." He did step down from his official positions, but remained powerful until his death at the age of ninety-two in 1997.[24]

———

Reports about Chinese dissidents appeared more frequently in the US media in the aftermath of June Fourth, reinforcing a storyline of courageous individuals willing to sacrifice themselves in the face of a repressive authoritarian regime. Western journalists sometimes found themselves walking a thin line between personal advocacy and objectivity, a quandary Liu faced with the case of Chen Guangcheng.

She first met Chen, a blind lawyer from Shandong Province, in a Starbucks coffee shop in Beijing in 2001 when she was researching a story on "barefoot lawyers." He told her how he had taught himself law and had become an advocate for the rights of the disabled in rural China, before fighting to close a paper mill that was polluting the water in his village. "In 2005," wrote Liu, "Chen took up another cause, this time against family-planning authorities who forced people to have abortions and sterilizations in a draconian pursuit of the country's one-child policy. Even though Chinese laws ban such brutal measures, thousands of rural women were forced to undergo even late-term abortions; those who escaped were detained and tortured." Chen launched a high-profile campaign to publicize the abuses and filed a class-action lawsuit on the victims' behalf.

The following year he was charged with "willfully damaging property and organizing a mob to disturb traffic" and spent the next four years in prison. After his release, Chen and his wife were confined to their farmhouse for two years. In April 2012, the blind activist made a daring escape in the middle of the night and fled to Beijing where he sought refuge in the US Embassy compound. "After six intense days of negotiations between American and Chinese authorities, a deal was struck," Liu reported for *Newsweek*. "Chen and his family would stay in China but relocate to the coastal city of Tianjin, where he could formally study law, something I knew he'd always dreamed of—and authorities would leave him alone." Chen emerged from the embassy on May 1, smiling, and walking with a crutch, accompanied by US Assistant Secretary of State Kurt Campbell and holding hands with Ambassador Gary Locke. Secretary of State Hillary Clinton, who had just arrived in Beijing for high-level talks, praised the deal as one reflecting "his choices and our values."

Then, fearing for the safety of his family, Chen suddenly changed his mind about staying in China, even though he realized his celebrity would quickly fade if he became an exile. "When I spoke to him on the phone," Liu recounted, "he pleaded with me to help get him out," even though it was not within her power. After tense negotiations, Jerome Cohen arranged a fellowship for him to study law at New York University and Chen was granted a US visa. Happy to be rid of him, the Chinese government quickly allowed Chen to leave with his wife and their two children.[25]

Because of Liu's access to Chen—she referred to him "my longtime friend"—she was able to tell a riveting tale, but worried that their personal relationship might have compromised her impartiality. She admired his "great persistence and will and energy, but his personality was mercurial. Maybe I should have written something that showed him less as this all-around hero, and more of a human being with his own failings and his own quirks."[26] Liu's sympathy for Chen highlighted the perils of becoming too closely involved with a source. Her experience also exposed the limits and pitfalls of applying her own cultural expectations to China's realities.

"Fervent Nationalism"

Throughout most of the 1990s, American perceptions of China were filtered through the prism of Tiananmen. "It is," wrote David M. Lampton, "like looking at China through a straw. The view provided is real, but there is no peripheral vision."[27] US public opinion was overwhelmingly negative, and Congressional debates over the PRC's trade status during this period hinged on Beijing's human rights record, an issue that John Kamm leveraged to improve the treatment of political prisoners.

Liu believes the Tiananmen crisis hastened the process of China's astounding growth in the years that followed. "Internationally ostracized and worried that his economic reforms might stall, Deng pushed industrial growth at any cost, short of giving up one-party rule. Investors kept pouring in from Hong Kong and Taiwan, unfazed by questions of human rights, to build factories and take advantage of cheap migrant labor from the hinterlands." The new mood was summed up in the slogan, "To Get Rich is Glorious." In order to maintain control, she wrote, the regime effectively co-opted the Chinese people with "an even more powerful weapon than tanks: astonishing economic growth," which continued without interruption for the next three decades. "To inspire fresh loyalty to the Party, the regime also disseminated a new ideology to replace communism: fervent nationalism."[28]

US news coverage of China swung in a more positive direction as the result of presidential summits between the two countries in 1997 and 1998, the first talks between Chinese and American heads of state since the Tiananmen crisis. As an outcome of President Jiang Zemin's trip to Washington and President Clinton's return visit to Beijing, the PRC made concessions on human rights and the United States affirmed that it did not support Taiwan independence.

But one year later, anti-American riots erupted in China after US planes bombed the PRC's embassy in Belgrade during the Kosovo war, killing three Chinese journalists. American officials declared that the bombing was a terrible mistake, but no Chinese believed this. "As the mob in Beijing pelted the US Embassy with rocks and paint, protests ignited in more than 20 other cities," reported Liu. An enduring image was the photograph of a somber Ambassador James Sasser looking through a shattered window of the US embassy. "China's media stoked the anger by delaying news of the US apology for two days. Jiang Zemin praised the anti-American demonstrations as a sign of China's 'great patriotism and cohesive force' and proclaimed that 'the People's Republic of China can never be bullied.' "[29]

In spite of the bombing and other frictions, there was encouraging news about Sino-American cooperation on economic, humanitarian, and security issues, including a shared concern about North Korea's nuclear ambitions. "China was like a whole new world," Liu exclaimed when she returned to Beijing as *Newsweek*'s bureau chief in 1998. "It was moving out of its own past and had begun to embrace the future." A more confident, prosperous nation was rising before her eyes, evidenced by the glass and steel towers that dotted the horizon. Modern air terminals and extensive subway systems were being constructed in cities across the country.[30]

The changes were not only physical; more money and mobility meant more room for individual expression, which had been tightly controlled not so long ago. "Indeed, the Chinese are taking control of their private lives," wrote Liu. "In the past, the party meddled in everything from marriage to hairstyles. To be sure, it still wields a heavy hand in family planning. But now many citizens just try to ignore the government, even pushing against official taboos . . . . Snooping party hacks used to ensure that everybody conformed to the social norm; now yesterday's misfits are popping out of the closet. 'Comrades' are no longer old revolutionaries; today the word is slang for 'homosexuals' . . . . So here is China's new rule of play: stay out of politics, and you can do almost anything."[31]

Back in 1980 when Liu set up *Newsweek*'s bureau, "China was an immense ruin of enforced ignorance and abject poverty, the psychic rubble that remained after Mao's misconceived attempts to reshape Chinese society. The distance from there to the present is even greater than it seems, since the trajectory has been anything but straight. That journey is usually described in hard figures: dollars and cents, millions of people, tons of concrete. But the changes are even more startling when you look at them in human terms."[32] Hundreds of millions of Chinese were no longer destitute, but the explosion of new wealth produced a widening gap between rich and poor, rampant corruption, and misuse of power. It opened the door to drugs, prostitution, and other menaces that had been eliminated under Mao.

One tool the Party deployed to deflect public opinion from such problems was the recovery of Hong Kong, a territory ceded to the British after the First Opium War of 1848. Melinda's father insisted on joining her when she covered the handover on July 1, 1997. In his eyes—and in the view of C. N. Yang, who also was there—the ceremony ended a "century of humiliation" that China had experienced at the hands of Western colonial powers. A drenching rain did nothing to dampen his enormous pride in the historic occasion. Melinda noted that Secretary of State Madeleine Albright's presence affirmed Hong Kong's importance to the United States. "Washington's interest goes well beyond geopolitics: 40,000 American expats in Hong Kong far outnumber their British counterparts, and US-Hong Kong trade exceeds $24 billion a year."[33] (By 2020, 85,000 Americans and 1,300 US companies were based in Hong Kong.) To reassure investors about a smooth transition, Beijing promised that Hong Kong could maintain its way of life for fifty years under the formula "one country, two systems." Beijing's harsh crackdown on protesters in 2020 and 2021 have undermined that pledge.

As China entered the new millennium, Liu's articles chronicled a growing list of major accomplishments. The PRC's first astronaut, Yang Liwei, who launched into space in 2003, demonstrated the country's technological prowess. (China successfully landed spacecraft on the moon in 2013, 2019, and 2020.) A massive high-speed rail project, announced in 2008, efficiently connected cities throughout the country. The 2010 Shanghai World Expo, the biggest and most expensive world's fair ever, attracted seventy-three million people. The Three Gorges Dam, highly controversial because of environmental risks and the displacement of more than 1.5 million people along the Yangzi River, opened in 2012 to control flooding and to produce hydroelectric power.

As China's wealth and power grew by leaps and bounds, Liu reflected on the PRC's ambitions in a talk she gave at Stanford University when she received the 2006 Shorenstein Journalism Award for outstanding reporting on the Asia-Pacific region. "After decades of isolation, after twenty-five years of trying to catch up with everyone else, Chinese are finally beginning to see themselves, quite comfortably now, as citizens of the world, connected, globalized, traveling overseas, buying foreign goods, drinking Starbucks coffee, eating McDonalds."[34] Internationalization and economic prosperity, it seemed to Liu and many others, would lead naturally to a more liberal society.

Liu and Jaime FlorCruz, *Time* magazine's Beiing bureau chief, were optimistic that the Chinese news media "have become increasingly open and responsive to public demand" in response to market forces. After Tiananmen, wrote FlorCruz, "the press was muzzled, allowed only to churn out rosy propaganda." A decade later, "the vibrancy and enterprise of newspapers, magazines and television shows reflect growing diversity—and Beijing's inability to control it . . . . Publishers think not only in terms of politics, but of advertising, making them more responsive to their audiences' changing tastes and expectations." He recognized that direct criticism of high-level leaders was still impossible, but investigative reporting of wrongdoing and malfeasance by officials "serves the interests of Beijing, where officials fear that unchecked graft and corruption could spark social unrest." Of course, the commercialization of news invited other problems such as cash bribes in exchange for positive stories. FlorCruz also realized that Beijing's leaders "have no intention of unleashing a totally free press. The unspoken threat of punishments—fines, reprimands, even prison terms—creates a chilling effect of self-censorship that is planted in the journalist's subconscious."[35]

In addition to the potentially salutary effect of new market forces, foreign reporters were extremely hopeful that the advent of the internet would make it more difficult for censors to control the flow of information and might lead Chinese society to be more open and transparent. "Suddenly," wrote Liu, "e-mail and social media gave people unfettered and instantaneous communications, a nightmare scenario for autocrats." She later came to realize that contrary to such rosy predictions, "the Chinese regime has proved itself adept at mastering its digital toolkit—often employing Western technology—to profile, control, and intimidate its citizens through facial recognition and internet surveillance, the Great Firewall and armies of nationalist trolls."[36] Keyword filtering software was used to monitor and block any mention of human rights, democracy, Taiwan independence, the Dalai Lama, and other topics deemed politically problematic. Foreign news websites, including the *New York Times*, *Wall Street Journal*, and Voice of America were blocked, as were all Google services and most Hong Kong and Taiwan newspapers. Proxy servers, or virtual private networks (VPNs), allowed users to circumvent these restrictions and gain uncensored access to the web, but only small numbers of people had the time and money to do this. Instead of operating as a vehicle for free expression, the internet became an instrument of social control. "We lost sight of the fact that technology is just a tool without values," lamented Liu.[37]

Standing Up for Journalists

The treatment of journalists and their access to information became Melinda Liu's primary concern when she was elected president of the Foreign Correspondents' Club of China (FCCC) in 2005. The PRC's booming economy had been paralleled by a steady expansion of the foreign press corps. In 2002, there were 199 resident overseas media organizations and 353 accredited foreign journalists in China; by 2007, there were 363 media organizations and 760 journalists. Some previous restrictions had been lifted: correspondents could live where they wished and could choose their own assistants without approval from the Ministry of Foreign Affairs.

Liu regularly raised concerns about the treatment of the international press corps with Chinese authorities, although her gravest worry was the welfare of Chinese news assistants, translators, photographers, and support staff. Without the protection of foreign documents, they were far more likely to be threatened, detained, beaten, and imprisoned. It is "a very big issue for us," she said. "There are some stories we just won't do because we feel it's too dangerous. But if we were to be 100 per cent careful in every case, we would simply not be able to do our jobs. Sometimes you are going to make the wrong call. It is a huge dilemma."[38]

Much of her attention was focused on the regulations that would govern reporting on the 2008 Beijing Summer Olympics. In order to win the games, which would be covered by some 20,000 foreign journalists, the Chinese promised to allow free press coverage and full internet access. International opinion was divided between those who thought the Olympics would be a powerful incentive for the PRC to become more open—as was the case with 1988 Olympics in South Korea—and those who echoed Walter Judd's dire warnings that the Communists would never change and should not be "rewarded." (Similar calls for a boycott of the 2022 Beijing Winter Olympics have been made in response to China's alleged human rights violations.)

More relaxed but temporary guidelines for foreign media were announced in January 2007, including a provision that journalists would no longer have to request permission for travel and interviews. Liu was skeptical: "I'm certainly not rushing out to test them," she told Agence France-Presse. "It's a welcome development, but if grassroots officials are not well-briefed or actively drag their feet, there will still be problems."[39] The FCCC would continue to ask its members to report any problems.

In March 2008, violent protests erupted in Lhasa after demonstrators disrupted the Olympic torch relay in London, Paris, and San Francisco in a bid to bring international attention to repression in Tibet. Contravening its earlier commitment, the Chinese government instituted a ban on foreigners attempting to travel to the affected areas. After ten days, the Foreign Ministry relented and allowed a small group of foreign press to visit the Tibetan capital where they would interview "victims of the criminal acts and also visit those places that were looted or burned." Liu complained that the limited access violated the new regulations. "Clearly this is not only not in keeping with the spirit of the guidelines, but it falls far short of what the international community expects from an Olympic host nation."[40]

Then, in May, Chinese officials backtracked and permitted extensive international coverage of a devastating 8.0 magnitude earthquake in Sichuan Province that killed nearly 70,000 people. This time there was no news blackout. "In a rare display of civic action," said Liu and her colleague Mary Hennock, "volunteers are driving from as far away as Beijing, Shanghai and Hangzhou with donations of food, medicine and clothing." Instead of restricting outside involvement, the government accepted relief supplies and gave access to rescue personnel from a number of international organizations. The tragedy gave Beijing "a chance to repair the country's battered image."[41]

The spectacle of the Olympics opening ceremony, commencing on the eighth minute of the eighth hour of August 8, 2008, "took my breath away," wrote Liu. (In Mandarin the word for eight (ba) is considered lucky because it rhymes with good fortune (fa).) "The sheer precision of thousands of performers moving intricately as one" was astounding. Chinese inventions—from gunpowder to paper to the compass—were celebrated. A dramatization of movable type "morphed into a vast sea of undulating cubic shapes, simulating a giant computer keyboard."[42] The People's Republic was now positioned to recover the Middle Kingdom's lost glory. The message that China had arrived as a global power was unmistakable.

Except for a short ceremony to raise the PRC's national flag, any reference to the Chinese Communist revolution was entirely missing from the stunning performance in the Bird's Nest stadium. Ignoring the recent past spoke volumes about the CCP's troubled relationship with its own history (see Chapter 7). In its place, an ancient era embodied by the legacy of Confucius was displayed to reinforce President Hu Jintao's call for a "harmonious society." The Confucian revival, designed to promote virtuous, responsible social relations, was heavy with irony. In the early twentieth century, Liu explained, "the Communist Party catapulted into power by attacking the Confucian order, which it said perpetuated inequality. Indeed, Confucius is credited with promoting a social hierarchy in which roles are strictly defined: students defer to teachers, kids revere elders, wives serve husbands, and citizens obey rulers—unless they become abusive, in which case citizens are justified to rebel."[43]

Nonetheless, Confucianism proved too distant and abstract to serve as a solid substitute for the country's fading allegiance to Marxism and Maoism. The real glue holding Chinese society together would be national pride. China was no longer the poor, backward, isolated "sick man of Asia" which previous generations of Westerners had disparaged. From Beijing's perspective, China was on the rise and the United States' global dominance was in decline.

The more lenient rules for journalists granted during the Olympics did not last. Restrictions were reimposed in early 2011, when reporters covered a so-called Jasmine Revolution, small pro-democracy protests in over a dozen cities in response to Arab Spring revolutions in the Middle East. "Parallels between Tahrir Square in 2011 and Tiananmen Square in 1989 haven't been lost on China's media censors," noted Liu. "Chinese authorities see the political turmoil in the Middle East as a continuation of the so-called color revolutions that toppled authoritarian post-Soviet regimes in Georgia, Ukraine, and Kyrgyzstan, and that made Beijing wary about pro-democracy spillover."[44] In Beijing, two American reporters were beaten and a number of others were questioned by the Public Security Bureau.

The climate worsened after Xi Jinping assumed power in 2012. Foreign reporters who dared to shine a negative light were unable to renew their visas and a few were expelled. Stories on mass incarcerations of Uyghurs and other Muslim minorities in Xinjiang were especially sensitive. Chinese investigative reporters, once lauded by the government for exposing corruption and abuse of power, faced great dangers. They had been "rare voices of accountability and criticism in a society tightly controlled by the ruling Communist Party, exposing scandals about babies sickened by tainted formula and blood-selling schemes backed by the government," wrote Javier Hernandez for the *New York Times*. "But under President Xi Jinping, such journalists have all but disappeared, as the authorities harassed and imprisoned dozens of reporters and as news outlets have cut back on in-depth reporting."[45]

The perennial struggle between the CCP and foreign journalists escalated sharply in 2020. Three correspondents with the *Wall Street Journal*—one of whom had been reporting on the outbreak of COVID-19—were expelled in February. The US State Department responded by limiting the size of five Chinese news organizations in the United States, after which China's Ministry of Foreign Affairs revoked the credentials of US citizens writing for the *New York Times*, *Wall Street Journal*, and *Washington Post*. (Several other media companies, including CNN, NBC, CBS, Bloomberg News, and the Associated Press were not targeted.) Beijing seemed determined to silence Americans who questioned the regime's official narrative and Washington was adamant about creating a "level playing field." (By 2021, only thirty-nine US journalists were left in China, and those in Hong Kong were feeling increased pressures.) The blow-for-blow actions, in the middle of a global pandemic, were symptomatic of a serious worsening of US-China relations, exacerbated by an ongoing trade war. The FCCC warned, "There are no winners in the use of journalists as diplomatic pawns by the world's two pre-eminent economic powers."[46]

The Struggle to Control the Message

"The cardinal sin committed by American news organizations in covering China is to portray it, always, in one overly simplistic frame," writes James Mann, a former correspondent for the *Los Angeles Times*. "Stories in the American media tend to be governed at any given time by a single story, image or concept."[47] During the 1950s, the Chinese people were depicted as mindless automatons enslaved by their communist overlords. Under Mao in the 1960s, China was a land of revolutionary madness. After Nixon's trip in 1972, the Chinese were perceived as virtuous citizens. During the 1980s, Americans were giddy with hope that China would embrace capitalism. (Deng Xiaoping was featured as *Time*'s "Man of the Year" in 1985.) The over-whelming image in the 1990s was a repressive, authoritarian China. Since 2000, China has been portrayed as an expansionist threat.

US news coverage of China has made enormous strides since the days when Cold War propaganda molded public opinion and journalists had no physical presence there. Major events like Tiananmen, the Beijing Olympics, and China's economic rise have been covered extensively, as have disputes between the United States and China over issues like Taiwan, Tibet, and the South China Sea. Articles on the details of the trade war launched by the Trump administration multiplied because American farmers, businesses, and consumers had vested interests in the outcome. Stories generally are more nuanced and often quote Chinese scholars and policy analysts.

China nevertheless is still a distant, perplexing subject to most Americans, partly because of fundamentally different views about the role of the media in our two nations. Freedom of the press, enshrined in Article 1 of the US Constitution, guarantees the expression of different beliefs and helps to en-sure the accountability of government. No such tradition has evolved in China, where the media's purpose is to support and promote the goals of the state. "Chinese officials," writes David Lampton, "do not value, indeed fear, a free flow of information, having been brought up in a system in which access to information was a privilege, not a right."[48]

For years, Chinese officials have objected that Western reporting presents an incomplete, unfair picture of the PRC. They think that disproportionate attention to individual rights has prevented a more realistic understanding of Chinese society. From their perspective, a constant barrage of negative news undermines good relations between the United States and China, and the true aim of such reports, says the Foreign Ministry, is to undermine China's peaceful rise. Accepting this line of reasoning, Xi Jinping has treated the foreign press as an enemy, while demanding the loyalty of state media and silencing the voices of independent Chinese journalists. Free and open expression on issues deemed "sensitive" is more constrained than at any time since the aftermath of Tiananmen. "For a regime obsessed with controlling what appears in the media," observes Liu, "Beijing can be strangely blind to how badly its heavy-handed tactics tarnish its image abroad."[49]

More often than not, the Chinese government's default position has been to cover up bad news. Information about AIDS, as well as the SARS and bird flu epidemics, was suppressed until Chinese medical specialists and foreign journalists got the word out. The initial response to the coronavirus that erupted in the city of Wuhan in December 2019 was to keep it secret and to detain the doctors who first sounded the alarm, one of whom subsequently died from the virus. As the disease surged, the government acknowledged the crisis and enforced unprecedented restrictions on the movement of millions of citizens to slow its spread.

The pandemic was an enormous test of leadership for Xi Jinping, who was confronted with a public health emergency as well as a sudden contraction of the economy. Writing from Beijing, where normally crowded streets were almost empty, Liu felt as if she had "stumbled onto the set of a post-apocalyptic film." She saw the government's heavily enforced quarantine of cities and entire regions as a familiar response to other issues. "The Great Firewall of China and censorship protocols isolate most Chinese online users from ideas such as free speech and universal suffrage . . . . To counter ethnic unrest in the majority-Muslim Xinjiang region, Beijing officials threw a security cordon around it, restricted internet usage inside the zone, and forcibly interned those perceived to be potential troublemakers in camps. When the government decided to experiment with free market principles in the post-Mao era, it built special economic zones to ring-fence the quasi-capitalist enclaves from everywhere else."[50] The Communist Party believes such measures ensure stability; whether they inspire the trust and confidence of the Chinese people is unknown.

Ordinary Chinese are not demanding Western-style democracy, says Liu, but they "are getting used to the idea of determining their economic circumstances." In June 2018, for example, a massive strike by truckers protesting high fuel prices and low fees blocked highways in as many as nine provinces. It was a grievance, but did not give rise to some type of political movement. Outrage over the twenty-year-old cover-up of the rape of a woman who committed suicide after no one would listen to her allegations against a Peking University professor resulted in millions of posts on social media before censors could delete them. These things "bubbled up for a while, and now it's quiescent again. It suggests that there is a lot of liquid magma down there under the surface somewhere. It might not be erupting, but it's there. Every once in a while there might be some sulfur fumes escaping, and at the right moment, who knows what could give it an excuse to erupt?"

Liu continues to live and work in Beijing, although she talks about moving back to the United States one day. In the meantime, China is still one of the great stories and she wants to see for herself how it will turn out. Considerable uncertainty lies ahead. The grand bargain of prosperity in exchange for unquestioned acceptance of one-party political control may not be sustainable: "I think it can last for a certain amount of time, but I don't think it can last forever. No one knows for sure, but maybe Xi Jinping feels that the status quo is fast reaching its use-by date. It could be that his clamping down on corruption and consolidating power is one thing he can do to try to ward off the inevitable."[51]

Conclusion

The Search for Common Ground

Americans have been confounded by China time and time again. The success of the Chinese Communist revolution was unexpected, China's entry into the Korean War was unpredicted, the Cultural Revolution was unforeseen, and the Tiananmen massacre was unimaginable. Americans were taken aback to learn that Mao Zedong was not a romantic idealist, Deng Xiaoping was not a progressive democrat, and Xi Jinping was not a reform-minded technocrat. No one believed that such an impoverished, ideologically driven nation could become the world's second largest economy in a matter of a few decades. Little wonder that observers have been perplexed and confused.

After the Communists assumed power in 1949, the PRC attained national unity, instituted land reform, advanced the rights of women, and improved healthcare, education, and housing. All of this even while fighting a major war with the United States in Korea. Starting in the late 1970s, the government decollectivized agriculture, instituted economic and legal reforms, and opened its centralized system to foreign trade and investment. Joint ventures transferred technology, and a massive export economy created vast new wealth. The PRC joined the UN Security Council, World Trade Organization, International Monetary Fund, and World Bank. Hundreds of millions of people were lifted out of abject poverty.

China's leaders and its people have determined the course of its transformation, not foreigners. Even so, the long-lived American yearning to change China—or at least to help, influence, or gain something—persisted. During the Cold War, the relationship was framed as a contest to determine the superiority of one system over the other. Many agreed with Congressman Walter Judd that communism was a scourge that prevented the Chinese people from attaining their natural desire for freedom and democracy. Mao's regime, allied with the Soviet Union, was perceived as a dire threat to the United States. Yet a twenty-year policy of isolation and sanctions did nothing to alter the Communist Party's grip on power.

In the early years, after most Westerners had left China, information about the PRC was limited to anecdotes and fragments gleaned from newspapers, radio reports, and refugees in Hong Kong. Only a few Americans dared challenge Washington's embargo on travel. Korean War POWs Clarence Adams and Morris Wills took a leap of faith, testing the idea that New China had succeeded in achieving liberty and justice for all, only to find it was not the utopia they were seeking. Adventurers Joan Hinton and Sid Engst defied conventional wisdom by declaring themselves fervent adherents to Mao's egalitarian vision, yet were deeply dismayed when his successors turned toward capitalism. Elizabeth Perry was hopeful that China could offer inspiration for an imperfect United States, but disheartened when she learned about the human toll inflicted by Chinese communism. These cycles of keen hope followed by profound disillusion have been replicated throughout the history of modern Sino-American relations.

Breakthroughs came slowly through the efforts of people like C. N. Yang, who rallied support for scientific exchange, and Stapleton Roy, who helped to accomplish diplomatic relations between Washington and Beijing. Once the door to China finally opened, a number of Americans, including those profiled in the second part of this book, helped to write new rules for an era of engagement. Optimistic about change, Jerome Cohen, Joan Cohen, John Kamm, Elizabeth Perry, and Melinda Liu nurtured the seeds of legal reform, artistic expression, human rights, academic freedom, and freedom of the press that lay within Chinese society. C. N. Yang, Stapleton Roy, and Shirley Young took a long-term view, confident that China would follow its own course and cautious about the ability of Americans to enact any external agenda.

Chinese Americans like Yang, Young, and Liu played essential yet largely unheralded roles as bicultural ambassadors fostering dialogue between the two societies. They faced the advantages and disadvantages of being considered insiders and outsiders at the same time. In China they were expected to be patriotic, while in the United States they sometimes were suspected of being disloyal.

All of the Americans profiled in this book faced difficult choices in coming to terms with China. From the Communist Party's perspective, there was no middle ground: foreigners either were friends of China and or they were not. For this reason, they faced the dilemma of whether to compromise their own values in light of the PRC's principles. Was it better to abide by Chinese standards, taking into account China's unique history and culture? Or should individual civil and human rights be defended as universal? Might the arts be a source of individual creativity, free of politics? Or was the state's policy of art in the service of politics more suitable for China? Was it wise for US companies to give up advanced technology in exchange for access to China's burgeoning consumer market? Or was it best to protect intellectual property and refuse the demands of Party-state capitalism?

Regardless of their positions on these and other issues, the Americans profiled in this book played significant roles as emissaries who expanded and deepened human ties on both sides of the Pacific. Their lasting contributions have been two-fold: establishing pathways for exchange, debate, and discussion between China and the United States; and observing, reporting, interpreting, and explaining China to Western audiences. They have played an important part in shaping the contours of the relationship and showing how we have arrived at the current juncture.

Assessing US Relations with China

After normalization in 1979, it seemed that China would move steadily in the direction of Western liberal values, not because of US pressure but because it was in China's self-interest. The idea that the PRC would lean in the direction of the United States appeared convincing, almost inevitable. Social and political reform would flow from economic progress, just as it had in other parts of East Asia. Moreover, if the PRC's continued growth depended on foreign capital and innovation, it seemed self-evident that any restrictions on access to investment and information from the West would be counterproductive. If China needed to maintain smooth relations with the rest of the world for the sake of its development, why would it run the risk of antagonizing the United States with aggressive behavior? Successive Republican and Democratic administrations accepted the thesis that a secure, non-hostile China was a better alternative than a poor and unpredictable nation-state with the world's largest population.

The popularity of Coca-Cola, McDonalds, Kentucky Fried Chicken, Starbucks, and Walmart made it look as though the Chinese people wanted nothing more than to imitate the United States. Melinda Liu wrote about a new middle class that rushed to buy US-brand cars to reach restaurants and malls on American-style highways. There was more freedom to practice religion, including Christianity, and hundreds of foreign faith-based non-governmental organizations (NGOs)—World Vision, American Friends Service Committee, and Habitat for Humanity among them—sponsored programs in underserved areas of China.[1] Chinese universities added courses on religion, human rights, public administration, international finance, international law, gender issues, and the environment. Numerous non-profit organizations, including Shirley Young's US-China Cultural Institute and foundations like the Harvard-Yenching Institute, directed by Elizabeth Perry, fostered exchanges in the arts and education. More audacious was John Kamm's conviction that dialogue could improve the rights of political prisoners though his Dui Hua Foundation.[2]

To be sure, there were skeptics who questioned the premise of an uninterrupted march toward Western values. James Mann predicted in his 2007 book *The China Fantasy* that the PRC would neither collapse nor would it liberalize in ways that Americans might hope; democracy was not inevitable and international trade would not bring an end to China's one-party political system.[3] Yet so long as business, tourism, education, and cultural exchange were booming, the United States seemed justified in seeking areas of mutual benefit and maintaining a policy of cooperation. The Clinton administration called it "constructive engagement."

With the advent of the twenty-first century, however, America's optimism about China's peaceful trajectory was shaken by an unexpectedly powerful PRC willing to confront the United States on various fronts, from the South China Sea and Taiwan to trade practices and intellectual property rights. Beijing began to challenge US dominance in the fields of robotics, artificial intelligence, quantum computing, 5G communications networks, and biotechnology. The PRC deployed a state-dominated economic model to extend its influence across Central and Southeast Asia to the Middle East and Africa through massive Belt and Road Infrastructure (BRI) projects.

Domestically, China reverted to earlier methods of political indoctrination to enforce obedience to the Party. This shift in the direction of authoritarianism under President Xi Jinping, with increased restrictions on individual liberties and the repression of minorities in Xinjiang and Tibet, convinced a growing number of Americans that earlier assumptions about China were naïve and misguided. Despite the determined efforts and considerable progress made by the Cohens, Kamm, Liu, Perry, and scores of others, it was apparent that the PRC still lacked an independent legal system, adequate protection of human and labor rights, genuine freedom of expression, and the capacity to confront the grievances of its own history.

A growing sense of alarm about the gulf between American desires and Chinese realities led to a fundamental re-examination of US policy. In 2018, Kurt Campbell and Ely Ratner wrote in *Foreign Affairs* arguing that Washington "once again put too much faith in its power to shape China's trajectory."

> Neither carrots nor sticks have swayed China as predicted. Diplomatic and commercial engagement have not brought political and economic openness. Neither U.S. military power nor regional balancing has stopped Beijing from seeking to displace core components of the U.S.-led system. And the liberal international order has failed to lure or bind China as powerfully as expected. China has instead pursued its own course, belying a range of American expectations in the process.[4]

Stapleton Roy took issue with Campbell and Ratner, arguing that Richard Nixon's intent was "not to turn China into a democracy but to gain a geopolitical advantage for the United States in the competition with the Soviet Union . . . . The wisest approach would be to continue engaging with China while focusing on advancing U.S. interests."[5] Roy's realism notwithstanding, the wisdom of engaging with China was widely doubted for the first time since the Tiananmen crisis of 1989.

A New Cold War?

The coming years loom as a precarious time for US-China relations. Despite the goodwill and hard work of so many Chinese and Americans, the larger problem of how to adjust to China's rapid economic and military growth is unanswered and the perennial question of Taiwan's status remains unsolved.

Disputes that had festered for years over unfair trade practices, the theft of US technology, and the loss of American jobs became much more contentious during the presidency of Donald Trump. After taking office, his administration imposed hefty tariffs on imports from China to rectify a massive trade deficit. Beijing reciprocated and US-China relations entered a downward spiral, exacerbated by the eruption of the deadly coronavirus in Wuhan in December 2019. Trump accused China of failing to control the spread of the disease, dubbing it the "China virus." An outbreak of racist attacks on

Asian Americans in the United States was one consequence of his rhetoric as the pandemic took its toll on the United States.

The US government went further, resurrecting the acrimonious Cold War debate over the wisdom of any form of cooperation with Communist China. The Trump administration identified China not just as a competitor but as an adversary, calling for "decoupling" the United States from the PRC's economy. The White House and Republicans in Congress took a series of actions to "disengage" with China. Educational and cultural exchanges were targeted in 2020: the Peace Corps was withdrawn from China, the Fulbright Program was suspended for the PRC as well as Hong Kong (though it continues in Taiwan), and the FBI and Justice Department increased investigations of Chinese students and scholars in the United States. US universities were warned about the dangers of Confucius Institutes, which offer Chinese language training with funds from the Chinese government. On the diplomatic front, the US government abruptly ordered China to close its consulate in Houston, accusing PRC diplomats of espionage and theft of intellectual property. Beijing responded by shutting down the US consulate in Chengdu.

These and other actions by Beijing and Washington had worrisome implications for the future. China imposed restrictions on foreign NGOs, and the PRC's national security law, passed in 2020, made it more difficult for journalists and human rights organizations to operate in Hong Kong. Increased US government scrutiny of Chinese students and scholars studying in the United States had a chilling effect on American universities. The coronavirus pandemic added more uncertainty by disrupting visas and travel for business, students, and tourists as well as exchanges in the arts, sports, nonprofits, and education.

Official Sino-American relations reached a tipping point as the US consensus for treating China as a strategic partner broke down. Public opinion dipped to its lowest point in years, Beijing's suspicions of the United States expanded, and both sides increasingly foresaw a zero-sum contest of strength. The US assault on China was crystallized in a July 2020 speech given by Secretary of State Michael Pompeo at the Nixon Library in California on "Communist China and the Free World's Future." With dissidents Wang Dan and Wei Jingsheng in the audience, Pompeo declared an end to "the old paradigm of blind engagement with China."

We opened our arms to Chinese citizens, only to see the Chinese Communist Party exploit our free and open society. China sent propagandists into our press conferences, our research centers, our high-schools, our colleges, and even into our PTA meetings. We marginalized our friends in Taiwan, which later blossomed into a vigorous democracy. We gave the Chinese Communist Party and the regime itself special economic treatment, only to see the CCP insist on silence over its human rights abuses as the price of admission for Western companies entering China.

We, the freedom-loving nations of the world, must induce China to change . . . because Beijing's actions threaten our people and our prosperity. . . . We must start by changing how our people and our partners perceive the Chinese Communist Party. We have to tell the truth. We can't treat this incarnation of China as a normal country, just like any other.

Pompeo concluded with bellicose language that echoed that of Walter Judd: "If the free world doesn't change, communist China will surely change us. There can't be a return to the past practices because they're comfortable or because they're convenient."[6]

In Beijing, Chinese Foreign Minister Wang Yi issued a forceful yet carefully calibrated response to Secretary Pompeo's speech. "The assertion that U.S. policy of engagement with China has failed is just a rehash of the Cold War mentality. It turns a blind eye to all that has been achieved in China-U.S. relations over the past decades, shows ignorance of the historical process and lack of respect for the Chinese and American peoples. This is a political virus which is understandably questioned and rebuked by people in the United States and the international community."

Wang added, "It is neither necessary nor possible for the two sides to change each other." Some American politicians want to "drag China and the U.S. into renewed conflict and confrontation and plunge the world into chaos and division again." He called for dialogue and cooperation based on mutual respect, warning that the United States "must abandon its fantasy of remodeling China to U.S. needs. It must stop its meddling in China's internal affairs, and stop its irrational cracking down on China's legitimate rights and interests."[7]

Underlying Minister Wang's words is the fact that many members of China's political elite distrust the United States for several reasons. Chinese officials have long been suspicious of US motives and regularly accuse American officials of conspiring to prevent China's peaceful rise. The Tiananmen upheaval and more recent protests in Hong Kong are blamed on a US plot to undermine the PRC. Worse, from Beijing's point of view, is

Washington's continued arms sales to Taiwan, which proves that the United States seeks to keep China divided by opposing its unification.

In the past, the PRC leadership welcomed foreign assistance for modernization, but was always was determined to do so without undermining the Communist Party's monopoly on political power. Today, as a major world power, the Chinese are far less inclined to accept foreign advice, assistance, and demands. US-China relations have entered a period of wariness, and the CCP treats the ideas highlighted in this book—transparent business practices, open scholarly and cultural expression, unfettered rule of law, authentic human rights, and true freedom of the press—as potential threats to its own existence. To allow a foreign state to impose its will on China would be evidence of weakness, tantamount to treason.[8]

The China Challenge

US relations with China have never been equivalent. When the United States was becoming an industrialized nation, China was undergoing a prolonged agrarian revolution. While America was growing strong and confident, the once-great Chinese empire was divided and weak. Missionaries went to China to teach and convert, while Chinese students came to the United States to study and learn. This lopsided equation generated paternalism and pity on the part of Americans, matched by a mixture of envy and resentment on the part of the Chinese. The PRC looked to the United States as a partner for reform, but was careful of dependency and critical of America's ills, regularly citing inequality, racial discord, gun violence, and the "chaos" of democracy as evidence of weakness and decline. Yet China does not endeavor to change the United States so much as it seeks to protect its own interests.[9]

The United States is profoundly unsure if a formidable China will be friend or foe. Now that the two nations have entered a period of insecurity and diminished confidence in their relationship, the basic question for the United States is whether to accommodate the PRC's new status or to oppose its rise as an existential threat. A key issue for China's leaders is whether a less aggressive foreign policy and a more open society can be pursued as an expression of strength, not weakness. Lurking behind these macro questions is the question of how Taiwan is to be integrated into China's mainland, no less an issue now than in the past.

Kurt Campbell and Jake Sullivan have warned against the mistake of "assuming that competition can succeed in transforming China where engagement failed—this time forcing capitulation or even collapse. Despite the many divides between the two countries, each will need to be prepared to live with the other as a major power." They call for a "steady state of clear-eyed coexistence on terms favorable to U.S. interests and values."[10]

President Joe Biden, more consistent and less ideological than Trump, has avoided Cold War rhetoric about changing China but continues to see the PRC as a threat. His administration is coordinating closely with traditional allies, including Japan and South Korea, and seeks to work with the PRC on issues of common concern, including climate change and the environment, global health, and the nuclear programs of North Korea and Iran. At the same time, he is opposed to China's coercive and unfair economic practices as well as its oppression of Muslim minorities in Xinjiang and human rights abuses in Hong Kong. "Most important is that we lead once again by the power of our example," Biden has said. "America's commitment to universal values sets us apart from China . . . . That is how to project a model that others want to emulate, rather than following China's authoritarian path."[11] In order to serve as a beacon of light, the United States must restore its moral authority and stand up for principles beyond self-interest.

Regardless of whether US influence is applied through isolation or engagement, genuine reform will, of course, come from within China, not from external sources. As a starting point, the Communist Party, as Elizabeth Perry has urged, must reckon with its own history, painful as that may be, if it is to recover its founding ideals. A tentative first step emerged during the 2010s with a neo-Maoist movement that advocated for the revival of egalitarian socialism. Its spokesmen were motivated by more than nostalgia; they were hopeful that Xi Jinping, who celebrated Mao's legacy in his speeches, would rectify the injustices of state-led capitalism. Instead, concludes Jude Blanchette, they learned that "for all its many platitudes about upholding socialism, the CCP still has little tolerance for actual socialists."[12]

Externally, the precipitous deterioration of nation-to-nation relations between China and the United States has made engagement more difficult, rendering individual relations that much more important. People-to-people exchanges are transmission belts for information, ideas, and opinions; they provide a vital human dimension. The success of foreign policy, joint ventures, and scholarly and cultural exchange depends on personal relations, mutual understanding, and trust. However, as Stapleton Roy realized in practicing diplomacy, Shirley Young learned from doing business, and John Kamm saw in his human rights work, both sides need to gain something.

Fortunately, for vast numbers of Americans, China is no longer an inaccessible land of mystery. The two societies are intertwined in ways that defy calls for "decoupling," and a deep reservoir of understanding and respect exists despite the animosity between our governments. More than 70,000 US companies do business with the PRC, thousands of US citizens live and work there, and many more visit as tourists. Cultural, sports, and academic exchanges abound, Chinese language programs are no longer unusual in US schools, and American families have adopted more than 80,000 children from China. Science and education, music and the arts are forces without national boundaries, engines for interaction and innovation that supersede politics. Engagement, which helped to propel China's incredibly rapid economic development, is an ongoing reality.

Perhaps the most positive harbingers are the millions of PRC students who have attended universities in the United States during the past forty years— including the children of China's top leaders—and the smaller number of Americans who have studied in China. These young women and men are the next generation of change agents, taking the place of the pioneers who explored the limits and defined the terms for Sino-American relations. Their future encounters represent our best hope in the indispensable search for common ground.

America's bond with China is volatile, unpredictable, and complex. Racism coexists with altruism, conflict alternates with cooperation, optimism collides with fear. Still, we have learned a great deal about one another and are able to see our differences more clearly thanks to individual personalities who had the courage, determination, and skill to see China not as a projection of American hopes and dreams, but as a different reality. They discovered, as did the Westerners in Jonathan Spence's To Change China, that false hopes only lead to disappointment and disenchantment. They learned that progress comes in fits and starts, through an interactive process of shared learning, negotiation, and compromise. They found that principles cannot be prescribed, norms cannot be enforced, values cannot be imposed. They realized that change is inevitable but often happens in ways that you never expect.

Notes

A Chronology of US-China Relations

1. See Robert Sutter's *Historical Dictionary of United States-China Relations* (Scarecrow Press, 2006) for a more detailed chronology and historical overview.

Introduction

1. "U.S. Warns 48 Youths Planning China Trip," *Los Angeles Times*, August 13, 1957; "Red China Sets Propaganda Trap by Invitations for U.S. Youth Visit," *Los Angeles Times*, August 11, 1957.
2. Max Frankel, "41 Defy Warning, Set Off for China," *New York Times*, August 15, 1957.
3. David Chipp, "41 U.S. Youths Reach Peking Amid Cheers," *Washington Post and Times Herald*, August 24, 1957. Twenty-nine delegates from several other countries arrived on the same train but the Americans "stole the show." Five of the Americans disagreed with the statement about free interchange, saying it would be used for propaganda purposes.
4. "Discussion with American Youth Delegation" (official Chinese transcript), September 7, 1957, Wilson Center Cold War International History Project, www.digitalarchive.wilsoncenter.org/document/260511.
5. Eighteen US correspondents were invited for a month-long trip to China in mid-1956, but strong US government opposition persuaded them not to accept. Other countries that had no diplomatic relations with the PRC allowed their journalists to make trips during the 1950s, including Australia, Canada, Japan, and France.
6. Email and phone conversation with Robert C. Cohen, April 29, 2020. Cohen's 1957 film "Inside Red China," which he showed on university campuses across the country, can be viewed on YouTube.
7. David Chipp, "China Visitors Clash Over U.S. Prisoners," *Washington Post and Times Herald*, September 10, 1957; "U.S. Prisoner in China Lectures Touring Youths," *Los Angeles Times*, September 20, 1957; "Americans Visit 3 U.S. Prisoners in Shanghai," *New York Times*, September 30, 1957; "Ex-G.I. in China Talks to Visitors," *New York Times*, August 28, 1957.
8. "14 Americans, in Soviet, Would Visit China Again," *New York Times*, October 6, 1957. US immigration officials seized the passports of those who returned directly to the United States, although some refused to hand them over.

9. Ruth Eckstein, "Ping Pong Diplomacy: A View from behind the Scenes," *The Journal of American-East Asian Relations* (Fall 1993), 327–42; Guoqi Xu, *Olympic Dreams* (Harvard University Press, 2008), 117–62. Xu's book includes a full account of the table tennis exchange.

10. Quoted in Eckstein, "Ping Pong Diplomacy," 336.

11. Harold R. Isaacs, *Scratches on Our Minds: American Views of China and India* (John Day Co., 1958; M. E. Sharpe, 1980); Irv Drasnin, *Misunderstanding China*, CBS News broadcast, February 1972. Pearl Buck's novel *The Good Earth* was published in 1931 and the film was released in 1937.

12. Jonathan Spence, *To Change China: Western Advisers in China, 1620–1960* (Little, Brown & Company, 1969), 289–90.

13. See Beverley Hooper, *China Stands Up: Ending the Western Presence, 1948–1950* (Allen & Unwin, 1986).

14. Spence, *To Change China*, Introduction.

15. Walter Judd, "What Should We Do in China Now?" *Town Meeting of the Air*, broadcast January 6, 1948, Judd Papers, Box 34.13, Hoover Institution Archives.

Chapter 1

1. Walter H. Judd, quoted in Lee Edwards, *Missionary for Freedom: The Life and Times of Walter Judd* (Paragon House, 1990), 271, 320. Edwards worked closely with Judd as secretary of the Committee of One Million Against the Admission of Communist China to the United Nations.

2. Interview with Lee Hamilton, Washington, DC, March 15, 2010.

3. Walter H. Judd, "What is the Truth About China?" *Congressional Record*, March 15, 1945.

4. Paul Hopper, "Interview with Walter H. Judd on Dwight D. Eisenhower," Washington, DC, August 29, 1968," in *Walter H. Judd: Chronicles of a Statesman*, ed. Edward J. Rozek (Grier, 1980), 3.

5. See Terrill E. Lautz, "The SVM and Transformation of the Protestant Mission to China," in *China's Christian Colleges: Cross-Cultural Connections, 1900–1950*, eds. Daniel Bays and Ellen Widmer (Stanford University Press, 2009), 3–21. By the twentieth century, the Social Gospel—teaching Western science and culture, building schools and hospitals, and doing relief work—was widely thought to be more effective than direct evangelism.

6. Interview with Lee Edwards, Washington, DC, May 27, 2010; Victor Cohn, "The Congressman's Scars of Courage," *Coronet* (July 1960), 31–34.

7. Miss Cushing, "Memo re. Walter Judd," April 2, 1929, and Robert E. Chandler, "Remarks about Dr. Walter H. Judd," April 11, 1938, ABCFM Archives, 77.1, Box 38, Houghton Library, Harvard University. Cushing and Chandler were with the American Board of Commissioners for Foreign Missions (ABCFM) which was headquartered in Boston.

8. Judd, October 14, 1925, quoted in Yanli Gao, "Judd's China: A Missionary Congressman and U.S.-China Policy," *Journal of Modern Chinese History* (December 2008), 203.

9. The Andover Harvard Theological Library holds useful information on the early history of the Shaowu Mission in the ABCFM Records.

10. Quoted in Edwards, *Missionary for Freedom*, 27–28.

11. Judd, *Student Volunteer Movement Bulletin*, January 1927, 100; Judd to Reverend William Strong, March 24, 1927, Yale Divinity School Archives, quoted in T. Christopher Jespersen, *American Images of China, 1931–1949* (Stanford University Press, 1999), 8–9.

12. Anne-Marie Brady, "Introduction," in *A Foreign Missionary on the Long March: The Memoirs of Arnolis Hayman of the China Inland Mission* (MerwinAsia, 2010), xi–xxxviii; "Chinese Reds Free Two American Women," *New York Times*, December 4, 1930

13. Quoted in Hopper, "Interview with Walter H. Judd," 17. Judd may well have been reading Cold War politics into his retrospective comments on the Communists.

14. Bliss returned to Shaowu after Judd's departure in 1931 and left in late 1932 when Communist troops advanced on the city. Edward Bliss Jr., *Beyond the Stone Arches: An American Missionary Doctor in China, 1892–1932* (John Wiley & Sons, 2001), 189, 213, 217.

15. Judd, "A Philosophy of Life that Works," 390–91.

16. Miriam Barber Judd, *Miriam's Words: The Personal Price of a Public Life*, ed. Mary Lou Judd Carpenter (Miriam's Legacy Publishing, 2013), xi, 15.

17. Miriam Judd, *Miriam's Words*, 48–49.

18. Donald G. Gillin, *Yen Hsi-shan* [Yan Xishan] *in Shansi Province, 1911–1949* (Princeton University Press, 1967), 8, 220–27, 264–71. After joining Chiang Kai-shek's army to fight the Communists, the warlord general allied with the Communists when Japan invaded China in July 1937.

19. Ibid., 70.

20. Miriam Judd, *Miriam's Words*, 111–12.

21. Gillin, *Yen Hsi-shan*, 264.

22. Fox Butterfield, "A Missionary View of the Chinese Communists (1936–1939)," in *Papers from Harvard Seminars*, ed. Kwang-ching Liu (Harvard University East Asian Research Center, 1966), 253, 296.

23. Judd to Rowland M. Cross, February 20, 1938, ABCFM Archives, 77.1, Box 38, Houghton Library, Harvard University.

24. Quoted in Hopper, "Interview with Walter H. Judd," 11.

25. Judd to Madame Chiang Kai-shek, January 28, 1943, Walter Judd Papers, Box 163.17, Hoover Institution Archives.

26. Walter H. Judd, "Let's Stop Arming Japan!" *Reader's Digest* (February 1940), 41.

27. Quoted in Hopper, "Interview with Walter H. Judd," 13.

28. Charles Hirshberg, "Walter Judd Never Met a Communist He Trusted," *Washington Post*, January 24, 1988.

29. Miriam Judd, *Miriam's Words*, 331. During their years in Washington, Miriam Judd volunteered with the Red Cross, YWCA, church groups, the Congressional Club, Mount Holyoke College, and her girls' schools.

30. Judd, "How Can We Win in the Pacific?" *Congressional Record*, February 25, 1943. John W. Dower's *War Without Mercy: Race and Power in the Pacific War* (Pantheon, 1987) is an important study of the horrific caricatures produced by US and Japanese propaganda machines during World War II.

31. Miriam Judd, *Miriam's Words*, 188–89.

32. Judd, "How Can We Win in the Pacific?"

33. Judd, "Dare We Believe Today in Our Historic American Principles—Freedom and Equality?" *Congressional Record*, October 20, 1943. The McCarran-Walter Act of 1952 included Judd's amendments to eliminate racial discrimination from immigration and naturalization laws, although comprehensive reform did not come until 1965.

34. See Meredith Oyen, "'Thunder without Rain': ARCI, the Far East Refugee Program, and the U.S. Response to Hong Kong Refugees," *Journal of Cold War Studies* 16, no. 4 (Fall 2014), 189–221.

35. Judd, "U.S. At War: Our Ally China," *Time*, June 18, 1945.

36. Judd, "What is the Truth About China?"

37. "China's Judd," *Washington Post* editorial, November 29, 1947.

38. Judd, "What Should We Do in China Now?" *Town Meeting of the Air* radio broadcast, January 6, 1948, Judd Papers, Box 34.13, Hoover Institution Archives.

39. Judd to A. N. Larson, June 3, 1947, Judd Papers, Box 234.2, Hoover Institution Archives.

40. Judd to Don F. Reed, July 6, 1961, Judd Papers, Box 234.2, Hoover Institution Archives. See Terry Lautz, *John Birch: A Life* (Oxford University Press, 2016) for the story of the missionary-turned-soldier for whom the John Birch Society was named.

41. Judd to Nancy B. Morrell, December 20, 1957, Judd Papers, Box 234.2, Hoover Institution Archives.

42. See Ross Y. Koen, *The China Lobby in American Politics* (Octagon, 1973). Koen's book was suppressed after it was first published in 1960.

43. Joyce Mao, *Asia First: China and the Making of Modern American Conservatism* (University of Chicago, 2015), 60.

44. Charles T. Morrissey, "Oral History with Walter H. Judd," Washington, DC, January 26, 1976, 48. Available at the Harry S. Truman Library, www.trumanlibrary.gov.

45. Judd to Harry S. Truman, October 7, 1953 and Judd to J. F. Krammer, June 25, 1955, Judd Papers, Box 179.3, Hoover Institution Archives; Judd, "Mao's Government Threatens World Peace," *U.S. News & World Report*, January 15, 1954.

46. See Stanley Bachrack, *The Committee of One Million: "China Lobby" Politics, 1953–1971* (Columbia University Press, 1971); Judd to Mark Crassweller, November 1, 1957, Judd Papers, Box 179.3, Hoover Institution Archives.

47. Nancy Bernkopf Tucker, *The China Threat: Memories, Myths, and Realities in the 1950s* (Columbia University Press, 2012), 183–84.

48. Edwin O. Reischauer, *Wanted: An Asian Policy* (Alfred A. Knopf, 1955), 232–49.

49. Judd to Josephine Schletty, November 28, 1949, Judd Papers, Box 179.3, Hoover Institution Archives.

50. "Energetic Keynoter: Walter Henry Judd," *New York Times*, July 26, 1960.

51. For the National Committee's early history, see Jan Carol Berris, "The Evolution of Sino-American Exchanges: A View from the National Committee," in *Educational Exchanges: Essays on the Sino-American Experience*, eds. Joyce Kallgren and Denis Simon, (Institute of East Asian Studies, University of California, Berkeley, 1987), 80–95.

52. Richard M. Nixon, "Asia After Vietnam," *Foreign Affairs*, October 1967, 111–25.

53. Miriam Judd, in *Miriam's Words*, 326; Morrissey, "Oral History with Walter H. Judd," 47.

54. Hirshberg, "Walter Judd Never Met a Communist He Trusted."

55. Morrissey, "Oral History with Walter H. Judd," 41. Walter and Miriam Judd visited the offshore island of Quemoy (Jinmen) in 1961.

56. Judd, "President Chiang Kai-shek: His Faith and His Work," *Asian Outlook*, October 1986, 12; Morrissey, "Oral History with Walter H. Judd," 41, 47.

57. Judd remarks at Georgetown University, July 18, 1989, quoted in Edwards, *Missionary for Freedom*, 323.

58. Hirshberg, "Walter Judd Never Met a Communist He Trusted."

59. Judd, "What is the Truth About China?"

60. Remarks at the Presentation Ceremony for the Presidential Medal of Freedom, October 9, 1981. Judd received honorary doctorates from twenty-eight colleges and universities.

61. Morrissey, "Oral History with Walter H. Judd," 48.

Chapter 2

1. Possibly another 4,300 American POWs died in captivity, as many as were released. Seven thousand are still missing in action. One thousand British prisoners returned to the United Kingdom, and one British marine, Andrew Condron, went to China with the twenty-one US soldiers. He returned to England with his Chinese-French wife and their son in October 1962. Two Belgian soldiers also went to the PRC.

2. Virginia Pasley, *21 Stayed: The Story of American GI's Who Chose China* (New York: Farrar, Straus & Cudahy, 1955).

3. *Renmin Ribao* (*People's Daily*), January 28, 1954.

4. Clarence Adams, *An American Dream: The Life of an African American Soldier and POW Who Spent Twelve Years in Communist China*, eds. Della Adams and Lewis H. Carlson (University of Massachusetts, 2007), 12–13, 17.

5. Ibid., 18, 22.

6. Ibid., 28, 32–33, 46, 49.

7. Morris R. Wills, *Turncoat: An American's 12 Years in Communist China*, as told to J. Robert Moskin (Prentice-Hall, Inc., 1968), 25.

8. Ibid., 41, 47, 49.

9. Ibid., 52, 58–61.

10. William Cowart, quoted in Pasley, *21 Stayed*, 48.

11. Charles S. Young, *Name, Rank, and Serial Number: Exploiting Korean War POWs at Home and Abroad* (Oxford University Press, 2014), 65. Before any resolution of the POW issue was achieved, South Korea's President Syngman Rhee allowed some 27,000 anti-communist prisoners to "escape."

12. David Cheng Chang, *The Hijacked War: The Story of Chinese POWs in the Korean War* (Stanford University Press, 2020), 357, 362. Chang's carefully documented study describes an anti-communist indoctrination program organized by the Americans with the help of translators provided by Chiang Kai-shek to persuade Chinese POWs not to return to China. Ha Jin's brilliant novel *War Trash* (Vintage, 2004) paints a vivid and deeply disturbing picture of the terror inflicted on Chinese prisoners held in the south.

13. See Charles Young, *Name, Rank, and Serial Number* for a well-informed discussion of the germ warfare charges. He concludes (p. 68), "It is unlikely that the United States used any bacterial weapons in Korea."

14. Adam J. Zweiback, "The 21 'Turncoat GIs': Nonrepatriations and the Political Culture of the Korean War," *The Historian* (Winter 1988), 345–62. Eleven of the 4,300 US POWs who chose repatriation were tried and convicted for collaboration with the enemy.

15. "Korean Puzzle: Americans Who Stay," *U.S. News & World Report*, October 9, 1953; "Inside Story: Why Prisoners Balk at Coming Home," *U.S. News & World Report*, December 25, 1953, 24–25.

16. Virginia Pasley, *21 Stayed*, 227.

17. Steven Lee Myers and Chris Buckley, "In Xi's Homage to Korean War, a Jab at the U.S.," *New York Times*, October 23, 2020.

18. Wills, *Turncoat*, 18–19.

19. Harriet Mills, "Thought Reform: Ideological Remolding in China," *The Atlantic Monthly*, December 1959, 71–77. Mills received a PhD from Columbia University after returning to the States and taught Chinese language and literature at the University of Michigan for many years. Robert Jay Lifton's *Thought Reform and the Psychology of Totalism: A Study of "Brainwashing" in China* (Norton, 1961) is a classic study based on interviews with Korean War prisoners.

20. Wills, *Turncoat*, 77, 81.

21. Ibid., 71; *Renmin Ribao* (*People's Daily*), February 25, 1954.

22. Adams, *An American Dream*, 74.

23. Wills, *Turncoat*, 72–73.

24. Ibid., 85, 91.

25. Henry R. Lieberman, "3 Turncoats, Out of China, Condemn Communist 'Hell,'" *New York Times*, July 11, 1955.

26. Wills, *Turncoat*, 93–94; Per-Olow Leijon, interview with Beverly Hooper, Paris, March 27, 2008. I am grateful to Professor Hooper for sharing this interview.

27. "Ex-G.I. in China Talks to Visitors," *New York Times*, August 28, 1957.

28. Wills, *Turncoat*, 105.

29. Ibid., 113, 115, 119.

30. Adams, *An American Dream*, 66, 68.

31. Ibid., 76–79

32. Scott Rush, another former POW living in Wuhan, married a Chinese woman in 1956. He worked in a state-run textile factory and left the PRC with his wife and child in September 1963.

33. Adams, *An American Dream*, 84–91.

34. Gregg A. Brazinsky, *Winning the Third World: Sino-American Rivalry during the Cold War* (University of North Carolina Press, 2017), 133–34, 150, 152.

35. Gordon H. Chang provides an excellent summary of African American views about China in *Fateful Ties: A History of America's Preoccupation with China* (Harvard University Press, 2015), 209–15. Those attracted to Mao's messianic message included Du Bois, Paul Robeson, Robert F. Williams, and Huey Newton.

36. Tracy B. Strong and Helene Keyssar, "Anna Louise Strong: Three Interviews with Chairman Mao Zedong," *The China Quarterly* (September 1985), 491–97.

37. Du Bois, *The Autobiography of W. E. B. Du Bois: A Soliloquy on Viewing My Life from the Last Decade of Its First Century* (New York: International Press, 1968), 51–53.

38. Du Bois, "China and Africa," *Peking Review*, March 3, 1959, 11–13.

39. John Emmanuel Hevi, *An African Student in China* (New York: Praeger, 1963), 20–21, 51, 79, 119, 131. Based on declassified official Chinese files, Philip H. Liu confirmed many of Hevi's complaints in his article "Petty Annoyances? Revisiting John Emmanuel Hevi's *An African Student in China after 50 Years*," *China: An International Journal* Vol. 11, no. 1, (April 2013), 131–145.

40. Frank Dikotter, *The Discourse of Race in Modern China* (Stanford University Press, 1992), 68, 82.

41. Adams, *An American Dream*, 81.

42. Ibid., 103–104; "Made 2 Red Broadcasts, Turncoat Says," *Los Angeles Times* (AP), May 27, 1966.

43. Mills, "Thought Reform," 73.

44. Wills, *Turncoat*, 120. He writes that he heard rumors that an American woman fitting the description of Joan Hinton was involved with China's nuclear project. Her story, told in Chapter 3, shows no evidence of this.

45. Debriefings of Clarence Adams (May 1966), Record Group 59, General Records of the Department of State, Central Foreign Policy Files, 1964–66, Box 302, National Archives at College Park (NACP), College Park, MD, hereafter referred to as RG 59, Box 302, NACP.

46. Wills, *Turncoat*, 154–55.

47. Morris R. Wills, "Why I Chose China," *Look*, February 8 and 22, 1966; Beverly Hooper, *Foreigners Under Mao: Western Lives in China, 1949–1976* (Hong Kong University Press, 2016), 71.

48. Debriefings of Clarence C. Adams, Record Group 59, Box 302, NACP.

49. "American Turncoat Reaches Hong Kong," *New York Times*, May 26, 1966.

50. Nicholas Platt, *China Boys: How U.S. Relations with the PRC Began and Grew* (Washington, DC: Vellum, 2010), 36–37; interview with Nicholas Platt, New York City, December 3, 2018. Platt traveled with Nixon to China in 1972 and served with the US Liaison Office in Beijing in 1973. After a distinguished diplomatic career, he was president of the Asia Society in New York.

51. Quoted in Hooper, *Foreigners Under Mao*, 74. Suibo Wang, a Canadian Chinese, told the story of James Veneris in his 2005 documentary, *They Chose China*.

52. Interview with Ezra Vogel, Cambridge, MA, May 1, 2017.

53. Interview with Deborah Seiselmyer, Utica, NY, October 9, 2018.

54. "Hawaii Proves Wonderland to Turncoat," *Los Angeles Times* (UPI), July 1, 1966.

55. "Turncoat Finds Hope in U.S. Racial Scene," *New York Times*, July 10, 1966.

56. Adams, *An American Dream*, 124–27.

57. Ibid., 110.

58. Ibid., 141.

Chapter 3

1. Prior to the Communist victory, there were about three thousand Americans in China, including missionaries, businessmen, journalist, aid workers, diplomats, and their children. *Foreign Relations of the United States*, Document 1306, July 20, 1949. For an excellent account of this period, see Beverly Hooper, *China Stands Up: Ending the Western Presence, 1948–1950* (Allen and Unwin, 1986). Hooper makes the case that the decision to force foreigners out of China was made well before the Korean War.

2. Beverly Hooper, *Foreigners Under Mao: Western Lives in China, 1949–1976* (Hong Kong University Press, 2016), 12.

3. Stanislaw Ulam, quoted in Ruth H. Howes and Caroline L. Herzenberg, *Their Day in the Sun: Women of the Manhattan Project* (Temple University Press, 1999), 52.

4. Hinton, quoted in Ibid., 56.

5. Julian Ryall, "Mother of the Bomb Who Recoiled at Its Power and Rejoiced in Mao's China," *South China Morning Post*, August 17, 2008. Hinton visited Hiroshima and Nagasaki for the first time in 2008.

6. Sid Engst to Edna Engst, September 30, 1946, Sid Engst Papers, Rare Books and Manuscripts, Cornell University.

7. William (Bill) Hinton went to China toward the end of the war to work for the US Office of War Information in Chongqing, the Nationalist government's capital, and stayed on after Japan's surrender as an UNRAA instructor, first in Nationalist-controlled areas in the northeast and then in Communist-held areas in the northwest.

8. Sid Engst to Edna Engst, May 21, July 13, and July 23, 1946; November 2 and 11, 1946; and January 2 and February 11, 1947. These family letters are posted on www.joanhinton.com. Sid Engst, interview with Neil Burton, Shahe, China, February 11, 1987.

9. The Holstein cows, originally imported from overseas by General Yan Xishan, were captured from the Japanese by the Communist Eighth Route Army.

10. Dao-yuan Chou, *Silage Choppers & Snake Spirits: The Lives and Struggles of Two Americans in Modern China* (Ibon Books, Quezon City, Philippines, 2009), 96. Chou was a Chinese American who spent five years with Hinton and Engst on their farm near Beijing.

11. Joan Hinton, interview with Neil Burton, Shahe, China, February 1987.

12. Ibid.; Chou, *Silage Choppers & Shake Spirits*, 128–29. Hinton and Engst explain their reasons for staying in China in "Cold Spring, Morning Sun," a 1988 documentary film produced and directed by Chris Haws, an Independent Communications Associates Production.

13. Joan Hinton, "Marriage Law Brings Happiness," *China Reconstructs* (July–August 1952), 48–52.

14. Joan Hinton, "Politics and Marriage," *New China* (June 1976), 32–34.

15. Sid Engst, interview with Neil Burton, February 1987. Burton taught at the University of British Columbia.

16. Joan Hinton, interview with Neil Burton, February 1987.

17. Sid Engst, interview with Neil Burton; Chou, *Silage Choppers and Snake Spirits*, 150. Joan Hinton, "Northwest Breeding Station," *China Reconstructs* (November–December 1952), 45–49. Belgian missions were established in Inner Mongolia in the late nineteenth century, mainly under the jurisdiction of the Congregation of the Immaculate Heart of Mary or the Scheut Fathers.

18. Interview with Fred Engst, Beijing, June 20, 2018. For a comprehensive photo history with Chinese language text, see Fred Engst and Li Weimin, *Life and Times of Two American "Reds": Joan Hinton and Erwin (Sid) Engst in China* (Jixie Gongye Press, Beijing, 2018).

19. Quoted in Chou, *Silage Choppers & Snake Spirits*, 183–84. See Rachel Leow, "A Missing Peace: The Asia-Pacific Peace Conference in Beijing, 1952 and the Emotional Making of Third World Internationalism," *Journal of World History* (June 2019), 21–53. Leow suggests the conference might be seen as a bid to create an alternative to the United Nations, which the PRC was excluded from until 1971.

20. The Associated Press and United Press wrote stories on Hinton's speech that were carried in the *Los Angeles Times*, *Washington Post*, and other newspapers. The US reports referred to "Peiping Radio" since Peking (or Beijing) means "northern capital," which would have conferred legitimacy on the PRC.

21. Ellis M. Zacharias, "The Atom Spy Who Got Away," *Real Magazine* (July 1953), 33–35.

22. Interview with Marni Rosner, Putney, Vermont, September 9, 2017.

23. For an in-depth account of China's atom bomb program, see John W. Lewis and Xue Litai, *China Builds the Bomb* (Stanford University Press, 1988).

24. Cows' milk has a long history among Mongolians and other nomadic peoples but was not widely consumed in China, Korea, or Japan. See Andrea S. Wiley, "Milk for 'Growth': Global and Local Meanings of Milk Consumption in China, India, and the United States," *Food and Foodways* (February 2011), 11–33. Wiley writes that China's

diary industry has boomed in recent years because milk products have been promoted as a source of national strength.

25. Interviews with Jane Su, Beijing, June 18 and 19, 2018.
26. Chou, *Silage Choppers & Snake Spirits*, 295–306. The US State Department lifted the travel ban on the PRC in 1971.
27. Sid Engst, interview with Neil Burton, February 12, 1987.
28. Interviews with Fred Engst, Beijing, June 20, 2018, and Bill Engst, Shanghai, June 21, 2018.
29. Sid Engst and Joan Hinton, interviews with Neil Burton, February 1987.
30. Marie Ridder, "Leaving the Science of Destruction Behind," *Washington Post*, March 12, 1978; Chou, *Silage Choppers & Snake Spirits*, 465.
31. The US–China Friendship Association, founded in 1974, was sympathetic to the Chinese revolution and worked to cultivate positive relations with the PRC through lectures, conferences, publications, and tour groups to China. William Hinton was its first chair. Chou, *Silage Choppers & Snake Spirits*, 437–38.
32. Ridder, "Leaving the Science of Destruction Behind."
33. Chou, *Silage Choppers & Snake Spirits*, 448–55; Ridder, "Leaving the Science of Destruction Behind."
34. Jeanne Lesem, "American Couple Look Back on 31 Years in China," *Los Angeles Times* (UPI), November 22, 1979. Joan made another trip to the United States in 1982 to care for her mother, who died the following year in Concord, Massachusetts.
35. Quoted by Seth Faison, "History's Fellow Travelers Cling to Mao's Road," *New York Times*, August 28, 1996.
36. Joan Hinton to Fred Engst, January 17, 1976, Sid Engst Papers, Cornell University.
37. Sid Engst to Verda Hunt, May 22,1989 and Engst to his sister Bernice, July 26, 1989, Erwin Engst Papers, Cornell University. Interview with Bill Engst, Shanghai, June 22, 2018.
38. Tom Ashbrook, "For Two American Veterans of China's Revolution, The Flame Still Burns," *Boston Globe*, May 3, 1984.
39. Andrea Koppel, "Leftist Americans in China Grieve Shift to Capitalism," *CNN*, October 1, 1996; Catherine Rampell, NBC News, August 13, 2004; Sid Engst to Verda Hunt and Helen Engst, March 29, 1994, Engst Papers, Cornell University.
40. Melinda Liu, "A Cold War 'Mata Hari'?" *Newsweek*, March 21, 1999; Ryall, "Mother of the Bomb."
41. Catherine Rampell, NBC News. Fred Engst moved back to Beijing in 2007 to teach at the University of International Business and Economics. Guo Shuhan, "American Calls Chinese Birthplace his Real Home," *China Daily USA*, July 1, 2011.
42. Jan Wong, *Jan Wong's China: Reports from a Not-So-Foreign Correspondent* (Toronto, 1999), 156; Rob Gifford, "Yankee Maoist Still Committed to the Revolution," National Public Radio, September 3, 2002.
43. Peter Alford, "Woman Who Worked on First Atomic Bomb Pays Tribute to 'Terrific' Mao, *The Australian*, August 19, 2008.

Chapter 4

1. Zhou Peiyuan had studied physics and worked in the United States before returning to the PRC in 1947. He played a leading role in revitalizing scholarly exchanges between China and the United States after the normalization of diplomatic relations in 1979. See Mary Brown Bullock, "American Science and Chinese Nationalism: Reflections on the Career of Zhou Peiyuan," in *Remapping China: Fissures in Historical Terrain* eds. Gail Hershatter et al. (Stanford University Press, 1996), 210–23.

2. *People's Daily*, July 18, 1973; Yang Chen-ning, "A Thinker, A Leader, and Extremely Practical Man," *New China* (Spring 1977), 12–18. T. D. Lee, Yang's former collaborator, met with Zhou Enlai in October 1972 and had a one-on-one meeting with Mao in May 1974. T. D. Lee, *Symmetries and Asymmetries* (University of Washington Press, 1988), xii.

3. Jay Matthews, "China, Taiwan Woo Nobel Scientists of Chinese Descent," *Washington Post*, October 7, 1977.

4. Chen-ning Yang, "Father and I," December 1997, in *Selected Papers II, C. N. Yang* (World Scientific Publishing, Singapore, 2013), 221, 226. Yang's father, Wu-zhi Yang, was also known as K. C. Yang.

5. John Israel's book *Lianda: A Chinese University in War and Revolution* (Stanford University Press, 1998) is an authoritative history of the Southwest Associated University, which was a consortium of Peking, Tsinghua, and Nankai universities.

6. The Boxer Indemnity Scholarship Program, established in 1908 with excess funds from the Boxer Indemnity, provided funding for Chinese students to be educated in the United States.

7. A detailed chronology of Yang's life can be found at the C. N. Yang Archive located at the Chinese University of Hong Kong (CUHK). See also *Guifan yu Duichen Zhimei: Yang Chen-ning Chuan*, ed. Chiang Tsai-chien (Tianhsia Yuanjian Press, Taiwan, 2002) .

8. General Tu Yu-ming attended the televised banquet that Zhou Enlai hosted in President Nixon's honor in Beijing in 1972.

9. See Meredith Oyen, *The Diplomacy of Migration: Transnational Lives and the Making of U.S.-Chinese Relations in the Cold War* (Cornell University Press, 2015). After 1945, the US State Department funded 3,636 scholarships through the China Students' Aid Program.

10. The best English-language biography of Xuesen Qian is Iris Chang's *Thread of the Silkworm* (Basic Books, 1995).

11. Two well-informed accounts of the travails of Chinese students stranded in the United States are Zuoyue Wang, "Transnational Science during the Cold War: The Case of Chinese/American Scientists," *ISIS*, Vol. 101, no. 2 (June 2010), 367–77, and Nick Waldrop, "Educating the Enemy: Chinese Students and the Sino-American Cold War, 1948–1955," MA Thesis, Iowa State University, 2016.

12. C. N. Yang, *Selected Papers 1945–1980, with Commentary* (W. H. Freeman: San Francisco, 1983), 56–57; unidentified newspaper story in the C. N. Yang archives, CUHK.

13. "Nobel Prize in Physics Awarded to Two Chinese Working in U.S.," *New York Times*, November 1, 1957. Around 1954, Yang and his student Robert Mills did work on gauge fields that provided the basis for modern quantum theories, but its importance was not recognized until the 1970s.

14. Jeremy Bernstein, "A Question of Parity," *New Yorker* (May 12, 1962), 96.

15. Felix Belair Jr., "Swedes 'Protect' Two Nobel Winners: Chinese Physicists Arrive from U.S.—Red Embassy Aides Are Fended Off," *New York Times*, December 9, 1957; "'These Chinese Choose," *Newsweek*, December 23, 1957.

16. Chen-ning Yang: Banquet Speech," www.nobelprize.org. Between 1976 and 2009, six more ethnic Chinese who claimed US residency or citizenship would receive the Nobel Prize. It was not until 2015 that a PRC citizen, Youyou Tu, a female biologist, received a Nobel Prize. See Zuoyue Wang, "Transnational Science during the Cold War: The Case of Chinese/American Scientists," *ISIS*, Vol. 101, no. 2 (June 2010), 367–77.

17. T. D. Lee, "Reminiscences," in *Thirty Years Since Parity Nonconservation*, ed. Robert Novick (Birkhauser, 1988), 154, 164.

18. Chen-ning Yang, *Studying and Teaching for Forty Years* (Joint Publishing Co., Hong Kong, 1985), 71. Chen-ping (Alfred) Yang, came to the United States in 1948 to study at Brown University and continued graduate studies Harvard and Princeton. He taught physics at Ohio State University and died in 2018.

19. C. N. Yang, "Father and I," 237.

20. C. N. Yang, "Modern Physics and Warm Friendship," (1990) in *Selected Papers II*, 147–153 and "Deng Jiaxian," (1993) in *Selected Papers II*, 197–204.

21. "Dr. Yang Feted by Chou En-lai," *South China Morning Post*, August 20, 1971; "A U.S. Scientist Greeted in China," *New York Times*, August 23, 1971; Kathlin Smith, "The Role of Scientists in Normalizing U.S.–China Relations: 1965–1979," *Annals New York Academy of Sciences* (December 1998) 130.

22. Yang, "Father and I," 238.

23. See Zuoyue Wang, "Chinese American Scientists and U.S.-China Scientific Relations: From Richard Nixon to Wen Ho Lee," in *The Expanding Roles of Chinese Americans in U.S.-China Relations: Transnational Networks and Trans-Pacific Interactions*, eds. Peter H. Koehn and Xiao-huang Yin (M. E. Sharpe, 2002).

24. "Yang Finds Chinese 'Miracle,'" *Newsday*, September 22, 1971.

25. Chen Ning Yang, "Education and Scientific Research in China," *Asia* no. 26 (Summer 1972), 74–84. See also Gloria Lubkin, "C. N. Yang Discusses Physics in People's Republic of China," *Physics Today* 24, no. 11 (November 1971): 61–63; "Physicist Tells of Visit to China," *New York Times*, September 23, 1971; "Inside the Laboratory," *New China* (Fall 1975), 28.

26. Simons Foundation interviews with C. N. Yang, 2011, Part 21, www.simonsfoundation.org; "State Council Bureau Exonerated U.S. Trained Scientists," *Xinhua News Agency*, December 27, 1979.

27. See Sigrid Schmalzer, "Speaking about China, Learning from China: Amateur China Experts in 1970s America," *The Journal of American-East Asian Relations* (Winter

2009), 313–52; Victor W. Sidel and Ruth Sidel, *Serve the People: Observations on Medicine in the People's Republic of China* (Beacon Press, 1973), 5.

28. Mary Brown Bullock, "The Influence of the CSCPRC on Educational Relations with China," in *Bridging Minds Across the Pacific: U.S.-China Educational Exchanges, 1978–2003*, ed. Cheng Li (Lexington Books, 2005), 50; Bullock, "American Science and Chinese Nationalism," 217.

29. Eleanor Blau, "1,300 Turn Out in Chinatown for a Memorial Tribute to Chou," *New York Times*, January 19, 1976.

30. Full-page ad in the *New York Times*, May 23, 1971; Testimony before the Senate Foreign Relations Committee, October 29, 197, in the C. N. Yang Archive, CUHK.

31. "We Want Answers Dr. Chen Ning Yang," *Daily Northwestern*, May 25, 1972; Chen Ning Yang, "Speech on United States-China Relations," University of Maryland, April 21, 1977 in the C. N. Yang Archive, CUHK.

32. "Nobel Laureate Wants to Organize Chinese-Americans," *Reporter* (University of Buffalo), May 18, 1978. C. N. Yang's National Association of Chinese Americans (NACA) competed with the Organization of Chinese Americans (OCA), a national group founded in 1973 to defend the civil rights of their members in the United States. OCA, which had thirteen chapters and about 1,700 members in 1978, avoided taking a position on the divisive "two Chinas" issue.

33. Marjorie Sun, "U.S.-Chinese Scientists See Dreams Imperiled," *Science*, June 9, 1989.

34. "Private Dinner—for 700," *Washington Post*, January 31, 1979. Established as a non-profit US organization in 1974, the US-China People's Friendship Association organized lectures, distributed publications, and organized group trips to China.

35. C. N. Yang, "Remarks Welcoming Deng Xiaoping," January 30, 1979, located in the C. N. Yang Archive, CUHK.

36. Quoted in *Harmony* (Stony Brook magazine), March 3, 1977.

37. Deng Xiaoping, "Speech at Opening Ceremony of National Science Conference," March 18, 1978.

38. Interview with Anne Keatley Soloman, New York, NY, May 26, 2018; Yuegen Yu, "The Bond of an Enduring Relationship: United States-China Scientific Relations, 1949–1989," PhD Dissertation, West Virginia University, 1999, 257. The first group of Chinese scholars arrived in the United States in December 1979.

39. T. D. Lee, who shared the Nobel Prize with Yang, organized the China-U.S. Physics Examination and Application (CUSPEA) program, an alternative admissions system which screened a large number of Chinese graduate students for study at US universities.

40. Marjorie Sun, "Soul-Searching after China Crackdown," *Science*, August 4, 1989.

41. Quoted by Marjorie Sun, "U.S.-Chinese Scientists See Dreams Imperiled," *Science*, June 9, 1989.

42. Fang Lizhi, *Bringing Down the Great Wall: Writings on Science, Culture, and Democracy in China*, ed. and tr. James Williams (W. W. Norton & Co., 1992), 163; Simons Foundation interviews with C. N. Yang, Part 22.

43. Simons Foundation interviews with C. N. Yang, Part 29.

44. C. N. Yang, "Father and I," 239.

45. Interview with C. N. Yang, *Harmony*, March 3, 1977; Simons Foundation interviews with C. N. Yang, Parts 27 and 30.
46. "Chen Ning Yang, 82, to Marry a 28-year-old Woman." *China Daily*, June 21, 2017.
47. Kathleen McLaughlin "Two Top Chinese-American Scientists Have Dropped Their U.S. Citizenship," *Science*, February 24, 2017; Xinhua News Agency, February 21, 2017, www.xinhuanet.com. Andrew Yao (Qizhi Yao), who won the Turing Prize in computer science and moved to Tsinghua University, also gave up his US citizenship.
48. Chen Ning Yang, *Selected Papers, 1945–1980, with Commentary*, 56.

Chapter 5

1. Oral history with Stapleton Roy, Association for Diplomatic Studies and Training (hereafter referred to as ADST Oral History), Foreign Affairs Oral History Project, March 15, 2013; J. Stapleton Roy, "The China Hands: Profiles in Courage and Lessons for the Future," Open Forum of the Secretary of State, April 25, 2000, www.freerepublic.com.
2. Telephone interview with Stapleton Roy, September 14, 2016; Leonard Woodcock Oral History, Tape 14, February 9, 1982, Michel Oksenberg Papers, Bentley Library, University of Michigan.
3. Interview with Stapleton Roy, Washington, DC, August 10, 2016.
4. Andrew T. Roy, *Never a Dull Moment: A Memoir of Family, China & Hong Kong* (Self-published, 1994), 71, 120, 130–31.
5. Ibid., 60, 94. Nanking University, known in Chinese as Jinling University, was founded by US missions in 1888. It was absorbed by the government-run Nanjing University in 1952.
6. ADST Oral History, July 25, 2013.
7. Roy, *Never a Dull Moment*, 99, 102, 105, 110. In 1954, Andrew and Margaret Roy went to Hong Kong, where he taught at Chung Chi College, now part of the Chinese University of Hong Kong, until 1972.
8. See William Inboden, *Religion and American Foreign Policy, 1945–1960* (Cambridge University Press, 2008), 157–89.
9. Interview with Stapleton Roy, August 10, 2016.
10. Interview with Stapleton Roy, Washington, DC, August 9, 2016.
11. Stapleton Roy, "The China Hands: Profiles in Courage and Lessons for the Future," April 25, 2000.
12. Interview with Stapleton Roy, August 10, 2016.
13. ADST Oral History, July 25, 2013. The 1976 Congressional delegation met with Zhang Chunqiao, one of the notorious Gang of Four.
14. Policy analysts, scholars, and various participants, including President Carter, have written about the normalization process. Some of these draw on declassified papers that were made available through the Jimmy Carter Library circa 1999. The State Department's Office of the Historian published the most comprehensive and

authoritative record in 2013, edited by David P. Nickles and Adam M. Howard in the *Foreign Relations of the United States* (FRUS) series.

15. David T. Roy, "Journal of a Trip to China, October–November 1978," unpublished journal. I am grateful to Douglas Spelman for sharing this with me. "A China Hand: Young, Witty, and Untiring," *New York Times*, March 19, 1979.

16. *FRUS*, Vol. 13, Document 159.

17. *FRUS*, Vol. 13, Documents 166 and 167. Deng Xiaoping's surname was rendered as Teng, based on the Wade-Giles Romanization system then used in the United States.

18. *FRUS*, Vol. 13, Document 168. Roy recalls two meetings with Deng on December 14, but the *FRUS* documents show evidence of only one meeting that day. Richard C. Bush provides an excellent analysis of the joint communiqué and ancillary documents in his book *At Cross Purposes: U.S.-Taiwan Relations Since 1942* (M. E. Sharpe, 2004).

19. Telephone interview with Stapleton Roy, September 14, 2016; Leonard Woodcock Oral History.

20. Quoted in Richard C. Bush, *At Cross Purposes*, 138–41.

21. James Lilley, *China Hands: Nine Decades of Adventure, Espionage and Diplomacy in Asia* (Public Affairs, 2004), 211–12.

22. Telephone interview with Stapleton Roy, September 14, 2016. Vietnam's December 25, 1978, invasion of Cambodia (Kampuchea) to overthrow the Khmer Rouge made Deng even more determined to "teach Vietnam a lesson."

23. "A China Hand: Young, Witty and Untiring," *New York Times, March 19, 1979.*

24. David A. Hollinger, *Protestants Abroad: How Missionaries Tried to Change the World but Changed America* (Princeton University Press, 2017).

25. William Gleysteen, the son of Presbyterian missionaries in China, served as ambassador to South Korea and Indonesia; Edwin Reischauer, whose missionary parents were Presbyterians, was born in Japan, became a pioneer in Japanese studies at Harvard University, and was US ambassador to Japan; and James C. Thomson Jr., who served in the Kennedy and Johnson administrations, was the son of a Presbyterian missionary who taught at Nanjing University.

26. Interview with Stapleton Roy, August 10, 2016.

27. The most reliable account of this period is Robert Suettinger's *Beyond Tiananmen: The Politics of U.S.-China Relations, 1989–2000* (Brookings Institution Press, 2003). Suettinger was director of Asian affairs on the NSC from 1994 to 1997.

28. ADST Oral History, November 18, 2013; Uli Schmetzer, "Americans' Tiananmen Protest Derided by China," *Chicago Tribune*, September 6, 1991.

29. James Mann, *About Face: A History of America's Curious Relationship with China, from Nixon to Clinton* (Vintage Books, 2000), 264–73; Thomas Friedman, "China Warns U.S. on Taiwan Jet Deal," *New York Times*, September 4, 1992.

30. Patrick Tyler, *A Great Wall: Six Presidents and China* (Public Affairs, 1999), 396–99; Suettinger, *Beyond Tiananmen*, 174–77; Kai He, *China's Crisis Behavior: Political Survival and Foreign Policy after the Cold War* (Cambridge University Press, 2016).

31. Patrick Tyler, "Rights in China Improve, Envoy Says," *New York Times*, January 1, 1994.

32. Quoted in Suettinger, *Beyond Tiananmen*, 197.

33. Quoted in Tyler, *A Great Wall*, 415.

34. Telephone interview with Stapleton Roy, April 17, 2017.

35. Suettinger, *Beyond Tiananmen*, 221.

36. Quoted in Tyler, *A Great Wall*, 416. In 1996, Roy was confirmed by Congress for the rank of Career Ambassador, an honor bestowed only a few dozen times since it was created in 1955.

37. Interview with Stapleton Roy, August 10, 2016. Roy admits that Leonard Woodcock, who was not a professional diplomat, was an exception.

38. Roy resigned one month before his retirement from the State Department in December 2000 to protest Secretary of State Madeline Albright's decision to suspend Donald Keyser, his deputy director, whom she held responsible for the disappearance of a laptop computer with classified information.

39. Telephone interview with Stapleton Roy, April 17, 2017. Roy was a managing director and then vice chairman of Kissinger Associates, Inc. from 2001 to 2008, when he became a senior advisor to the firm.

40. "Five Former U.S. Ambassadors to China Discuss U.S.-China Relations," National Committee on US-China Relations forum, June 9, 2014, www.ncuscr.org.

41. Steven Goldstein, *China and Taiwan* (Polity Press, 2015), 66, 69.

42. Interview with Stapleton Roy, April 17, 2017.

43. J. Stapleton Roy, "The Heart of the Matter: Reassessing the Foundations of U.S.-China Relations," Wilson Center conference, October 7, 2015.

44. "China Is Not an Enemy," Open letter published in the *Washington Post*, July 2, 2019.

Chapter 6

1. "Life, Law and Asia: Jerome A. Cohen's Video Memoirs, with Comments from Joan Lebold Cohen," produced and edited by Vanessa Hope, New York University, Part 1, placed online December 8, 2009, www.jeromecohen.net/video-memoirs.

2. Dean Rusk, Inter-office Correspondence, March 22, 1960, Rockefeller Foundation, SG 1.2, Series 200, Box 564, Rockefeller Archive Center.

3. Interview with Joan Cohen, New York City, May 26, 2016.

4. Ibid.

5. "Life, Law and Asia: Jerome Cohen's Video Memoirs," Part 1.

6. Rockefeller Foundation, SG 1.2, Series 200, Box 564, Rockefeller Archive Center.

7. Interview with Jerome Cohen, New York City, May 26, 2016.

8. William P. Alford, "Law, Law, What Law? Why Western Scholars of Chinese History and Society Have Not Had More to Say about Its Law," *Modern China* 23, no. 4 (October 1997): 402.

9. Jerome A. Cohen, "The Missionary Spirit Dies Hard," in *My First Trip to China*, ed. Kin-ming Liu (Hong Kong: East Slope Publishing Limited, 2012), 157.

10. Jerome A. Cohen, "Hong Kong in 1963–64: Adventures of a Budding China Watcher," *Hong Kong Law Journal* 47 (2017), 292.

11. Interview with Jerome Cohen, New York City, May 21, 2019.

12. Jerome Alan Cohen, "Interviewing Chinese Refugees: Indispensable Aid to Legal Research on China," *Journal of Legal Education* 20, no. 1 (October 1967): 36, 42. 53, 59.

13. Jerome A. Cohen, *The Criminal Process in the People's Republic of China, 1949–1963: An Introduction* (Harvard University Press,1968), 5, 50–51. Another pioneering work is Jerome Cohen and Hungdah Chiu, *People's China and International Law: A Documentary Study* (Princeton University Press, 1974).

14. Quoted in Jay Matthews, "The Strange Tale of American Attempts to Leap the Wall of China," *New York Times*, April 18, 1971.

15. "Life, Law and Asia: Jerome Cohen's Video Memoirs," Part 12. The Cohens ruled out living in Tokyo because of its heavy air pollution at that time. Interview with Joan Cohen, May 26, 2016.

16. Jerome A. Cohen, "China—The U.N. Issue," *New York Times*, April 24, 1971.

17. Jerome Alan Cohen, "Recognizing China," *Foreign Affairs* (October 1971), 30, 43. In 1968, Cohen was one of several scholars who sent President-elect Nixon a memorandum recommending talks with the PRC.

18. Jerome Alan Cohen, "Will Jack Make His 25th Reunion?" *New York Times*, July 7, 1971. With Cohen's encouragement, Downey attended Harvard Law School after coming home and later became a Connecticut Superior Court judge.

19. Joan Lebold Cohen, "My First Trip to China," unpublished essay, 2011.

20. Jerome A. Cohen, "The Missionary Spirit Dies Hard," 158–59.

21. Victor H. Li, *Law Without Lawyers: A Comparative View of Law in China and the United States* (Stanford University Alumni Association, 1977).

22. Joan Lebold Cohen, "Art—For Whom?" *Smith College Alumnae Quarterly*, August 1974, 19–20.

23. Jeremy F. Stone, *Every Man Should Try: Adventures of a Public Interest Activist* (Public Affairs, 1999), 123–29; John King Fairbank, *Chinabound: A Fifty-year Memoir* (Harper & Row, 1982), 423; Jerome A. Cohen, "The Missionary Spirit Dies Hard," 169. Fairbank, the leading US scholar of modern China, considered Jerry Cohen "the only promoter of Chinese studies I know more persistent than myself."

24. Joan Lebold Cohen, "My First Trip to China"; Glenda Daniel, "Equality, Chinese Style, Lopsided," *Quad-City Times*, May 18, 1975.

25. Interview with Jerome Cohen, May 26, 2016; "Life, Law and Asia: Jerome Cohen's Video Memoirs," Part 11.

26. "Life, Law and Asia: Jerome Cohen's Video Memoirs," Part 16.

27. Interview with Stephen A. Orlins, New York City, October 20, 2017. Orlins is president of the National Committee on US-China Relations.

28. Joan Lebold Cohen, *Painting the Chinese Dream: Chinese Art Thirty Years after the Revolution* (Smith College Museum of Art, 1982), 3.

29. Mao Zedong, "Talks at the Yan'an Forum on Literature and Art," 1942. *Selected Works*, vol. 3 (Beijing Foreign Language Publishers, 1985), 81, 84.

30. Joan Cohen, *Painting the Chinese Dream*, 1.

31. Ibid., 6.

32. Joan Cohen, Interview with Jane DeBevoise, New York City, October 31, 2009, www.china1980s.org.

33. Joan Cohen, *Painting the Chinese Dream*, 10. France had sent an exhibition of nineteenth–century European landscape painting to China in 1978.

34. Joan Cohen, Interview with Jane DeBevoise, Smith College, January 26, 2017, www.aaa-a.org; Meredith Palmer, "When Public Policy Made a Difference: American Paintings in China in 1981," *Washington Post*, December 23, 2011; Eva Cockcroft, "Abstract Expressionism, Weapon of the Cold War," *Artforum* (June 1974), 43–54, argues that the US government promoted abstract American art as an alternative to communist Social Realism.

35. Joan Cohen, Interviews with Jane DeBevoise, 2009 and 2017.

36. Cohen used a Japanese Nikon camera and film had to be processed in Japan or Australia. Her slides are now housed at the Asia Art Archive in Hong Kong.

37. Joan Lebold Cohen, "Murals Challenge China's Art Orthodoxy," *Asian Wall Street Journal*, August 11, 1980.

38. Interview with Joan Cohen, May 21, 2019; Joan Cohen, *Painting the Chinese Dream*, 24. The frog in the well metaphor comes from the famous Daoist philosopher Zhuangzi.

39. John Pomfret, "Nude Painting Exhibition Raises Eyebrows in Beijing," *Asian Wall Street Journal*, January 2, 1989.

40. "1989 China/Avant-Garde Exhibition," Asian Art Archive, Hong Kong, www.aaa.org.hk.

41. Interview with Joan Cohen, May 21, 2019; Joan Cohen, *Painting the Chinese Dream*.

42. Ethan Cohen, interview with Jane DeBouvoise, New York City, October. 15, 2009, www.china1980s.org.

43. Joan Lebold Cohen, "Braving the Currents of 'Bourgeois Internationalism,'" *Art News* (January 1984), 11.

44. Ethan Cohen, interview with Jane DeBouvoise.

45. Joan Lebold Cohen, *The New Chinese Painting, 1949–1986* (Harry N. Abrams, Inc., 1987), 151.

46. Ralph Croizier, "Art and Society in Modern China—A Review Article, *Journal of Asian Studies* (August 1990), 593–94. Interview with Joan Cohen, May 21, 2019. An exhibition of contemporary painting from the PRC, focused on modern interpretations of traditional ink and brush painting, was organized by Lucy Lim, director of the Chinese Cultural Center of San Francisco, and toured the United States from 1983 to 1985.

47. Two excellent studies on the complex relationship between art and commerce are Jane Debevoise, *Between State and Market: Chinese Contemporary Art and the Post-Mao Era* (Brill, 2014) and Richard C. Kraus, *The Party and the Arty in China: The New Politics of Culture* (Rowman & Littlefield, 2004).

48. "Talk of the Town: Law and China," *New Yorker*, January 17, 1987, 26.

49. Jerome Alan Cohen, "Due Process?" in *The China Difference: A Portrait of Life Today Inside the Country of One Billion*, ed. Ross Terrill (Harper & Row, 1979), 239–40, 259.

50. "Human Rights in China," Information Office of the State Council, November 1991, Beijing.
51. Jerome A. Cohen, "The U.S.-China Consular Convention: Need for Greater Protection for Individuals," *South China Morning Post*, August 18, 2010.
52. Ibid.
53. "Life, Law and Asia: Jerome Cohen's Video Memoirs," Part 16; interview with Joan Cohen, May 26, 2016.
54. Jerome Alan Cohen, "Courts with Chinese Characteristics," *Foreign Affairs* (October 11, 2012), www.foreignaffairs.com.
55. Interview with Jerome Cohen, May 26, 2016.
56. Jerome Cohen, "Xi Jinping Sees Some Pushback against His Iron-Fisted Rule," *Washington Post*, August 2, 2018
57. Jerome A. Cohen, "Was Helping China Build Its Post-1978 Legal System a Mistake?" University of Michigan Conference on Chinese Law, October 11–13, 2019.
58. Interview with Jerry Cohen, May 21, 2019. Among other tributes to Cohen, see James V. Feinerman, "Pioneering the Study of Chinese Law in the West," *The American Journal of Comparative Law* 65, no.4 (December 2017), 739–44.
59. Interview with Alfreda Murck, New York City, June 27, 2019.
60. Quoted in Ethan Cohen, "Ai Weiwei: A Conversation," *Social Research: An International Quarterly* 83, no. 1 (Spring 2016), 156, 163. Ai and his family left China for Berlin in 2015, moved to England in 2019, and was living in Portugal in 2021.

Chapter 7

1. See Paul Hollander, *Political Pilgrims: Travels of Western Intellectuals to the Soviet Union, China, and Cuba, 1928–1978* (Routledge, 4th ed., 2017).
2. Interview with Elizabeth Perry, Cambridge, MA, September 8, 2016. Perry received a fellowship though the Committee on Scholarly Communication with the PRC.
3. Hanchao Lu, "Narrating the Past to Interpret the Present: A Conversation with Elizabeth J. Perry," *The Chinese Historical Review* 22, no. 2 (November 2015): 163–64.
4. Telephone interview with Chuck Perry, May 16, 2018; New York, Passenger Lists, 1820–1957, www.ancestry.com.
5. In addition to Mandarin and Cantonese, the Navy Language School taught the Amoy and Fujian dialects, spoken in coastal provinces of southeast China. I am grateful to David M. Hays at the University of Colorado Boulder Libraries for this information.
6. Interview with Elizabeth Perry, Cambridge, MA, February 24, 2017.
7. Interview with Elizabeth Perry, Cambridge, MA, April 6, 2018. For an excellent study of how the daughters and sons of missionaries became cosmopolitan advocates for liberal values, see David A. Hollinger, *Protestants Abroad: How Missionaries Tried to Change the World but Changed America* (Princeton University Press, 2017).
8. Hanchao Lu, "Narrating the Past," 163–64.

9. "College Students Beat American Teacher to Death," *Japan Times*, November 26, 1959. Morita was tried and convicted of Perry's murder in March 1960. Because he was a minor at the time of the crime, he was sentenced to only three years of hard labor.

10. *Japan Times*, November 28, 1959; telephone interview with Chuck Perry, May 16, 2018.

11. Interview with Elizabeth Perry, February 24, 2017; telephone interview with Chuck Perry, May 16, 2018.

12. Telephone interview with Robert Snow, April 24, 2018.

13. Interview with Elizabeth Perry, Cambridge, MA, May 22, 2018.

14. For a detailed history of the Committee of Concerned Asian Scholars see Fabio Lanza, *The End of Concern: Maoist China, Activism, and Asian Studies* (Duke University Press, 2017).

15. Interview with Elizabeth Perry, September 8, 2016.

16. Elizabeth J. Perry, "Report on the Mayors Delegation to the People's Republic of China," *Urbanism Past & Present* (Summer 1980), 21–28.

17. Hanchao Lu, "Narrating the Past," 163.

18. Interview with Madelyn Ross, Syracuse, NY, October 5, 2017; interview with Tom Gold, Berkeley, CA, January 20, 2017; Charlotte Furth, *Opening to China: A Memoir of Normalization*, 1981–1982 (Cambria Press, 2017), 19 .

19. Telephone interview with Maryruth Coleman, January 28, 2019.

20. Elizabeth Perry, "Remembering the First Decade of American Research in China," *China Exchange News* (Spring 1996), 9–12.

21. Harry Harding, "The Evolution of American Scholarship on Contemporary China," in *American Studies of Contemporary China*, ed. David Shambaugh (M. E. Sharpe, 1993), 20.

22. Hanchao Lu, "Narrating the Past," 163.

23. Interview with Halsey Beemer, Washington, DC, October 31, 2016. Beemer was on the staff of the Committee on Scholarly Communication with the PRC, which funded Mosher's research.

24. Mary Brown Bullock makes this point in "Scholarly Exchange and American China Studies," *American Studies of Contemporary China*, 292.

25. Interview with Elizabeth Perry, September 8, 2016. Zhang Zhongli wrote a seminal study of the role of the Chinese gentry in nineteenth-century society when he was a visiting scholar at the University of Washington in the early 1950s. He was also an authority on the business history of Shanghai capitalism.

26. Perry, "Remembering the First Decade of American Research in China," 9–12.

27. Interview with Elizabeth Perry, September 8, 2016.

28. "Three Professors Appointed in Social Sciences," *Harvard Crimson*, June 3, 1997.

29. For example see Elizabeth Perry and Mark Selden, eds. *Chinese Society: Change, Conflict, and Resistance* (Routledge, 2000).

30. Elizabeth J. Perry, *Anyuan: Mining China's Revolutionary Tradition* (University of California Press, 2012), 46, 28–29, 121; Elizabeth J. Perry, "Reclaiming the Chinese Revolution," *Journal of Asian Studies* 67, no. 4 (November 2008): 1158, 1161–62.

31. Elizabeth J. Perry, "Casting a Chinese 'Democracy' Movement: The Roles of Students, Workers, and Entrepreneurs," in *Popular Protest and Political Culture in Modern China: Learning from 1989*, eds. Jeffrey Wasserstrom and Elizabeth Perry (Westview, 1992), 3, 151, 159–160; Elizabeth J. Perry, "A New Rights Consciousness," *Journal of Democracy* 20, no. 3 (July 2009): 20.

32. See Elizabeth J. Perry and Sebastian Heilmann, eds. *Mao's Invisible Hand: The Political Foundations of Adaptive Governance in China* (Harvard University Asia Center, 2011); Elizabeth J. Perry, "Studying Chinese Politics: Farewell to Revolution?" *The China Journal* 57 (January 2007): 9.

33. The author is a former trustee and chair of the Harvard-Yenching Institute.

34. Interview with Elizabeth Perry, May 22, 2018.

35. Elizabeth J. Perry, "Cultural Governance in Contemporary China: 'Re-Orienting' Party Propaganda," Harvard-Yenching Institute Working Paper Series, 2013; Perry, *Anyuan*, 292–93, 296.

36. Elizabeth J. Perry, "Higher Education and Authoritarian Resilience: The Case of China, Past and Present," Harvard-Yenching Institute Working Paper, 2015.

Chapter 8

1. Gabriella Stern, "GM Executive's Ties to Native Country Help Auto Maker Clinch Deal in China," *Wall Street Journal*, November 2, 1995.

2. Charlotte Craig, "General Motors Tries Novel Approach in China," *Edmonton Journal*, December 4, 1998; Seth Faison, "G. M. Opens Buick Plant in Shanghai," *New York Times*, December 18, 1998.

3. See Statista at www.statista.com. After the 2008 financial crisis, the Shanghai Automotive Industry Corporation (SAIC) made a major loan to GM that was paid off when the company emerged from bankruptcy.

4. Interview with Shirley Young, New York City, November 3, 2016.

5. Eric Harwit, *China's Automobile Industry: Policies, Problems, and Prospects* (M. E. Sharpe, 1995), 29.

6. Arthur R. Kroeber's *China's Economy: What Everyone Needs to Know* (Oxford University Press, 2016) provides a first-rate overview.

7. Jonathan Spence, *Western Advisers to China: To Change China* (Little, Brown, 1969), 154.

8. James Mann, *Beijing Jeep: The Short, Unhappy Romance of American Business in China* (Simon & Schuster, 1989), 308. Eric Harwit includes a case study of the Beijing Jeep venture in *China's Automobile Industry*, 67–91.

9. Kroeber, *China's Economy*, 48.

10. Interview with Shirley Young, November 3, 2016.

11. Juliana Young Koo with Genevieve Young, *My Story* (Oddi Printing, Iceland, 2008), 24. A Chinese language edition of Koo's book was published under the title *109 Springtimes: My Story* (New World Press, Beijing, 2015).

12. Genevieve Young, "My Father: A Personal Memoir," unpublished manuscript, n. d. Gene Young passed away in February 2020 at eighty-nine years of age.
13. Shirley Young, quoted in Koo, *My Story*, 95.
14. Genevieve Young, "My Father: A Personal Memoir."
15. Bill Moyers interview with Shirley Young, "Becoming American: The Chinese Experience," PBS Television Production, 2003; Koo, *My Story*, 101.
16. Ibid., 121; California, Passenger and Crew Lists, 1882–1959, www.ancestry.com.
17. Wellington Koo, like Clarence Young, came from a wealthy Shanghai family and undertook graduate studies in the United States at Columbia University. He served as Nationalist China's ambassador to France (1936–40), Great Britain (1940–46), and the United States (1946–56). James Barron, "Juliana Young Koo, Chinese Immigrant Who Published Her Life Story at 104, Dies at 111," *New York Times*, June 8, 2017.
18. Interview with Shirley Young, November 3, 2016. Soong Mei-ling (Madame Chiang Kai-shek), who was also from Shanghai, graduated from Wellesley College in 1917, making the school famous in China.
19. Interview with Shirley Young, November 3, 2016.
20. Diane Ying, "Shanghai Sisters Travel Two Routes to Success," *Christian Science Monitor*, September 29, 1969.
21. Norman Krandall, *Rustbelt Odyssey: Tales of a Motor City Dissident* (New Alexandria Press, 2010), 217, 220, 257, 264.
22. Bill Moyers interview with Shirley Young, 2003; Mark Landler, "Shirley Young: Pushing GM's Humble Pie Strategy," *Business Week*, June 11, 1990.
23. Interview with Shirley Young, November 3, 2016.
24. Bill Moyers interview with Shirley Young, 2003; Eric Thun's *Changing Lanes in China: Foreign Direct Investment, Local Governments, and Auto Sector Development* (Cambridge University Press, 2006) is the most authoritative study of the automotive industry in the PRC.
25. Interview with Matt Tsien, Shanghai, June 25, 2018.
26. John L. Graham and N. Mark Lam, "The Chinese Negotiation," *Harvard Business Review* (October 2003), 2–11.
27. Telephone interview with Rudy Schlais, May 5, 2020.
28. Interview with Shirley Young, November 3, 2016.
29. William J. Holstein, *Why GM Matters: Inside the Race to Transform an American Icon* (Walker and Company, 2009), 173–74, 180–81.
30. Maggie Farley, "GM Poised to Win $1-Billion Auto Contract in China," *Los Angeles Times*, October 25, 1995. Beijing has frequently used buying sprees to improve political relations with other nations.
31. Bill Moyers interview with Shirley Young, 2003.
32. Interview with Bill Russo, Shanghai, June 25, 2018.
33. Interview with Matt Tsien, June 25, 2018.
34. Michael J. Dunne, *American Wheels Chinese Roads: The Story of GM in China* (John Wiley & Sons, 2011), 102.
35. Interview with Shirley Young, November 3, 2016.
36. Interview with Matt Tsien, June 25, 2018.

37. Scott Kennedy, ed., *China's Uneven High-Tech Drive: Implications for the United States* (Center for Strategic & International Studies, 2020), 1. Despite enormous progress in the Chinese domestic auto manufacturing industry, a majority of the cars sold still are foreign brands from Japan, South Korea, Europe, and the United States.
38. See Edward Rhoads, *Stepping Forth into the World: The Chinese Educational Mission to the United States, 1872–81* (Hong Kong University Press, 2011). Weili Ye writes about the second wave in *Seeking Modernity in China's Name: Chinese Students in the United States, 1900–1927* (Stanford University Press, 2001).
39. Helen Zia describes the mass exodus from China's wealthiest city in *Last Boat Out of Shanghai: The Epic Story of the Chinese Who Fled Mao's Revolution* (Ballantine Books, 2019).
40. Interview with Oscar Liu-Chien Tang, New York, NY, April 21, 2017.
41. I. M. Pei, "China Won't Ever Be the Same," *New York Times*, June 22, 1989. Fox Butterfield, "Building a Voice for Chinese in the U.S.," *New York Times*, June 22, 1991. Pei neglected to mention the Organization of Chinese Americans and other such groups.
42. Fox Butterfield, "Building a Voice for Chinese in the U.S."
43. Committee of 100 press release, posted February 16, 2018, www.committeeof100.org. Wen Ho Lee was a scientist at Los Alamos who was arrested by federal authorities in December 1999 and held in solitary confinement for nine months; Xiaoping Li taught at the University of Pennsylvania; and Sherry Chen worked at the National Weather Service.
44. Committee of 100 press release, posted March 25, 2020.
45. Shirley Young, "Dancing into the Future," Asia Society program, June 3, 2014.
46. Interview with Shirley Young, November 3, 2016. Her cultural work followed in the footsteps of Chou Wen-chung, composer and Columbia University professor who founded the US-China Arts Exchange in 1979 and arranged for stars such as Luciano Pavarotti and Isaac Stern to visit China.
47. Jacques d'Amboise, "Dancing into the Future," Asia Society program, June 3, 2014.
48. Pia Catton, "The Right Dragon for the New Year, *Wall Street Journal*, January 26, 2012.
49. Interview with Shirley Young, November 3, 2016.
50. Ibid.
51. David Hsieh and Douglas Hsieh, memorial service for Shirley Young, Church of Heavenly Rest, New York City, January 9, 2021. Posted on www.shirleyyoung.com.

Chapter 9

1. Tina Rosenberg, "John Kamm's Third Way," *New York Times Magazine*, March 3, 2002.
2. John Kamm, Congressional Testimony on Accession of China to the WTO, May 3, 2000. Most Favored Nation (MFN) was changed to Permanent Normal Trade Relations (PNRT) in 1998.
3. Interviews with John Kamm, San Francisco, CA, January 17 and July 7, 2017.

4. See John T. Kamm, "Two Essays on the Ch'ing Economy of Hsin-An," *Journal of the Royal Asiatic Society Hong Kong Branch* 17 (1977): 55–84.

5. John Kamm, "The Market in China for Foreign Consumer Goods," *U.S.-China Business Review*, March–April 1975; interview with Virginia Kamsky, New York City, December 7, 2017.

6. John Kamm, "Shanghaied at the Feather and Down Minifair," in *My First Trip to China*, ed. Kin-ming Liu (East Slope Publishing Limited, Hong Kong, 2012), 222, 224–26.

7. John Kamm, "Reforming Foreign Trade," in *One Step Ahead in China: Guangdong Under Reform*, ed. Ezra Vogel (Harvard University Press, 1989), 338.

8. Interview with John Kamm, January 17, 2017.

9. Margaret Scott, "Hong Kong on Borrowed Time," *New York Times*, October 22, 1989. The author attended the Happy Valley rally with her.

10. Interview with John Kamm, San Francisco, February 11, 2019.

11. Interview with John Kamm, January 17, 2017.

12. Statement of John Kamm for the US Senate Committee on Finance Hearing on Extending Most-Favored-Nation Status for China, June 20, 1990. Kamm also testified before the House Foreign Affairs Committee and the Trade Subcommittee of the House Ways and Means Committee.

13. Quoted by Deborah Herndon, "The Business of Human Rights," *Princeton Alumni Weekly*, April 7, 1993, 14. The Li brothers were granted political asylum in the United States two months after returning to Hong Kong. The last known Tiananmen prisoner was released in October 2016.

14. John Kamm, "Civil Rights, Human Rights: The Struggle for Social Justice in the United States and China," Lecture at Notre Dame University, March 15, 2005.

15. John Kamm, "The China Card: Politics vs. Policy," Lecture at University of Southern California, September 29, 2016; Kamm, Testimony before the US House Committee on Ways and Means, Hearing on Accession of China to the WTO, May 3, 2000.

16. Kamm, Testimony before the Congressional-Executive Commission on China, April 11, 2002.

17. *Human Rights Watch World Report 1992: Events of 1991*, New York, 368.

18. Herndon, *Princeton Alumni Weekly*, 14; Sophia Woodman interview with John Kamm for Human Rights in China, October 16, 2000, www.hrichina.org.

19. Tina Rosenberg, "John Kamm's Third Way," *New York Times Magazine*, March 3, 2002.

20. Mickey Spiegel, "China's Game with Political Prisoners," *International Herald Tribune*, December 6, 2003.

21. Kamm, Testimony before the US Congressional-Executive Commission on China, April 11, 2002.

22. "John Kamm Remembers: Resurrection: The Jesus Family," *Dui Hua Digest*, May 15, 2021, www.duihua.org.

23. John Kamm, "The Role of Business in Promoting Respect for Human Rights in China," *International Business Ethics Review* (Fall/Winter 1997), 1, 6.

24. Email with Christian Murck, January 17, 2017.

25. Kamm, Testimony before the US Congressional-Executive Commission on China, April 11, 2002.

26. Kamm, Speech at Notre Dame University, March 15, 2005.

27. Interview with Joshua Rosenzweig, Hong Kong, June 28, 2018. In 2013, China's Supreme People's Court launched China Judgements Online, a massive database of court decisions, but information on sensitive cases is limited.

28. "John Kamm Remembers: The Singing Nuns of Drapchi," *Dui Hua Digest*, March 5, 2017, www.duihua.org.

29. Kamm, Testimony before the US Congressional-Executive Commission on China, April 11, 2002.

30. Interview with John Kamm, January 17, 2017.

31. Sophia Woodman interview with John Kamm, October 16, 2000; Kamm, Speech at Notre Dame University, March 15, 2005.

32. Interview with John Kamm, July 7, 2017

33. John Kamm, "What Future for Human Rights Dialogues?" in *China In and Beyond the Headlines*, eds. Lionel Jensen and Timothy Weston (Rowman & Littlefield, 2012), 335.

34. Kamm, Testimony before the US Congressional-Executive Commission on China, April 11, 2002; "Door on Freedom of Prisoners 'May be Closing,'" *South China Morning Post*, March 30, 2014.

35. Dui Hua Foundation 2018 Annual Report. A new Foreign NGO Law which took effect in January 2017 has increased the risks for international organizations working on human rights, workers' rights, and rule of law.

36. Email with John Kamm, September 17, 2021. .

37. Interview with John Kamm, July 7, 2017; "China Sentences Phan Phan-Gillis, U.S. Businesswoman, in Spying Case," *New York Times*, April 25, 2017.

38. Kamm, "Separate and Unequal: State Security Detainees in China," Testimony before the US House Committee on Foreign Affairs, November 3, 2011; interview with John Kamm, January 17, 2017.

39. "China: Torture and Forced Confessions Rampant amid Systematic Trampling of Lawyers' Rights," Amnesty International, November 11, 2015.

40. "China Lets Rights Lawyer Flee to U.S. After Release," *New York Times*, March 8, 2016.

41. Kamm, Testimony before the US House Committee on Foreign Affairs, November 3, 2011.

42. Interview with John Kamm, January 17, 2017.

43. Kamm, Testimony before the US House Committee on International Relations, April 30, 1998.

44. Interview with John Kamm, January 17, 2017.

45. Email with Sophie Richardson, March 8, 2020.

46. Kamm, Testimony before the US House Committee on Ways and Means, Hearing of Accession of China to the WTO, May 3, 2000.

Chapter 10

1. Melinda Liu, "Reasons You've Never Thought Of: Why Studying Chinese Made a Difference," Princeton in Beijing conference at Princeton University, October 22, 2016.
2. Carl R. Wilder, quoted in Carroll V. Glines, *Doolittle's Tokyo Raiders* (Van Nostrand Reinhold Company), 151; "War 'Brothers' Reunite: Doolittle's Raider Says Chinese Man Saved His Life," *The Joplin (Missouri) Globe,* n.d. (1991?).
3. Melinda Liu, "Mao to Now: China Is Thousands of Years Old but Has Been Made Anew in the Last Three Decades, and My Family with It," *Newsweek*, December 31, 2007/January 7, 2008. Her brother came to the United States with his family in 1982 and after working for a Taiwan-owned company near Los Angeles, retired in his hometown of Suzhou. By then, his old house had been torn down to make way for a shopping mall.
4. Liu, "Mao to Now."
5. Telephone interview with Carroll Bogert, September 4, 2019.
6. Liu, "Reasons You've Never Thought Of," October 22, 2016.
7. Stephen MacKinnon, "Covering China: The 'Romantic' Generation," *Media Studies Journal* 13, no. 1 (Winter 1999): 26. Also see Stephen MacKinnon and Oris Friesen, *China Reporting: An Oral History of American Journalism in the 1930s & 1940s* (University of California Press, 1987)..
8. "3 Newsmen in Red China Face Action," *Washington Post & Times Herald* (UPI), December 29, 1956. One of the best accounts of the press coverage of Nixon's trip is found in Margaret MacMillan's *Nixon and Mao* (Random House, 2007).
9. Anne-Marie Brady's *Making the Foreign Serve China: Managing Foreigners in the People's Republic* (Rowman & Littlefield, 2003) is a penetrating study of the PRC's foreign affairs (*waishi*) system.
10. Interview with Melinda Liu, Washington, DC, November 1, 2016. She was able to rent an office for the *Newsweek* bureau in the Jianguomenwai Diplomatic Compound in 1981.
11. Telephone interview with Melinda Liu, August 5, 2019.
12. Melinda Liu's interview in "Assignment: China," University of Southern California U.S.-China Institute, written by Mike Chinoy, produced by Clayton Dube, September 30, 2015. This excellent series of interviews with US journalists who have covered the PRC is available online.
13. Fox Butterfield, *China: Alive in the Bitter Sea* (Times Books, 1982), 6–9.
14. Interview with Jaime FlorCruz, Beijing, June 19, 2018.
15. Melinda Liu, "No Shutting the Open Door," *Newsweek*, April 14, 1980.
16. Email with Melinda Liu, February 17, 2020.
17. Liu, "Mao to Now." Jiang Qing was sentenced to life imprisonment and committed suicide in 1991. The Party later would judge Mao as having been 70 percent right and 30 percent wrong.
18. Interview with Liu, November 1, 2016.
19. Ibid.; telephone interview with Carroll Bogert, September 4, 2019.

20. Liu, "Mao to Now."
21. Mark Hertsgaard, "China Coverage: Strong on What, Weak on Why," *Rolling Stone*, September 21, 1989.
22. Interview with Liu, November 1, 2016.
23. Melinda Liu, with photos by David and Peter Turnley, *Beijing Spring* (Stewart, Tabori & Chang, 1989), 25, 27, 31.
24. Liu, "Mao to Now;" Liu, *Beijing Spring*, 41, 43.
25. Melinda Liu, "Chen Guangcheng's Blind Injustice," *Newsweek*, May 7, 2012.
26. Interview with Melinda Liu, November 1, 2016.
27. David M. Lampton, *Same Bed, Different Dreams: Managing U.S.-China Relations, 1989–2000* (University of California Press, 2001), 278.
28. Liu, "Mao to Now;" Melinda Liu, "How Tiananmen Changed China," *Newsweek*, June 3, 2014.
29. Melinda Liu, "Wounded Pride," *Newsweek*, May 23, 1999.
30. Melinda Liu interview in "Assignment: China," University of Southern California U.S.-China Institute, September 30, 2015.
31. Melinda Liu, "Crackdown Cabaret," *Newsweek*, February 7, 1999.
32. Liu, "Mao to Now."
33. Melinda Liu, "Beijing's New Babysitter," *Newsweek*, July 13, 1997.
34. Melinda Liu, Shorenstein Journalism Award Speech on "China in the World: A View from Beijing," February 16, 2006. The audio for her talk is available through Stanford University's Asia-Pacific Research Center.
35. Jaime A. FlorCruz, "Chinese Media in Flux: From Party Line to Bottom Line," *Media Studies Journal* 13, no. 1 (Winter 1999): 82.
36. Melinda Liu, "30 Years After Tiananmen: How the West Still Gets China Wrong," *Foreign Policy*, June 4, 2019.
37. Interview with Liu, November 1, 2016.
38. Liu quoted in "Dangers of Working with Foreigners," *South China Morning Post*, October 19, 2005. Todd Carrel, an ABC News correspondent, was severely beaten by Chinese police and suffered serious head and spinal injuries while visiting Tiananmen Square on the third anniversary of the protests in 1992.
39. Liu quoted in "Foreign Reporters Skeptical about New China Openness," Agence France-Presse, January 3, 2007.
40. Liu quoted in "China to Bring Foreign Media to Lhasa but on Short Leash," Agence France-Presse, March 25, 2008.
41. Mary Hennock and Melinda Liu, "China's Tears: The Sichuan Earthquake Could Change the Way Chinese See Their Leaders," *Newsweek*, May 26, 2008. The 1976 Tangshan earthquake killed some 225,000 people and was kept secret.
42. Melinda Liu, "The Olympics Opening Ceremony and China's Past," *Newsweek*, August 7, 2008.
43. Melinda Liu, "Confucian Comeback: China Remains Divided over Reviving Its Ancient Sage," *Newsweek*, September 10, 2012.
44. Melinda Liu, "China Censors Egypt Coverage," *Newsweek*, February 6, 2011.

45. Javier C. Hernandez, "'We're Almost Extinct': China's Investigative Journalists Are Silenced under Xi," *New York Times*, July 12, 2019.

46. "China Banishes U.S. Journalists from Wall Street Journal, New York Times and Washington Post," *Wall Street Journal*, March 18, 2020.

47. James Mann, "Framing China: A Complex Country Cannot Be Explained with Simplistic Formulas," *Media Studies Journal* 13, no. 1 (Winter 1999): 103–04.

48. Lampton, *Same Bed, Different Dreams*, 269.

49. Melinda Liu, "China's New Crackdown," *Newsweek*, September 18, 2006.

50. Melinda Liu, "How Do You Keep China's Economy Running with 750 Million in Quarantine?" *Foreign Policy*, February 24, 2020.

51. Interview with Melinda Liu, Beijing, June 20, 2018.

Conclusion

1. See Xu Yihua, "Religion in Current Sino-U.S. Relations," in *The United States and China: Mutual Perceptions*, ed. Douglas Spelman (Woodrow Wilson Center, 2011), 111–20. Amity Printing in Nanjing produced twelve million Bibles in 2012, two-thirds of them for export.

2. For an overview of US-China public and cultural diplomacy, see Terry Lautz, "The Cultural Relationship," in *Tangled Titans: The United States and China*, ed. David Shambaugh (Rowman & Littlefield, 2013), 211–33.

3. James Mann, *The China Fantasy: How Our Leaders Explain Away Chinese Repression* (Viking, 2007).

4. Kurt Campbell and Ely Ratner, "The China Reckoning: How Beijing Defined American Expectations," *Foreign Affairs* (March/April 2018), 61.

5. Stapleton Roy, "Engagement Works," *Foreign Affairs* (July/August 2018), 185–86.

6. Michael R. Pompeo, "Communist China and the Free World's Future," Speech at the Richard Nixon Presidential Library and Museum, July 23, 2020, . Pompeo's address was the culmination of earlier speeches on China by National Security Advisor Robert O'Brien, FBI Director Chris Wray, and the Attorney General WilliamBarr.

7. Wang Yi, interview with Xinhua News Agency, August 5, 2020, www.xinhuanet.com/english/2020-08/05. In August 2020, Secretary of Health and Human Services Alex Azar became the highest-ranking US official to visit Taiwan in four decades when he met with President Tsai Ing-wen and praised her handling of the coronavirus pandemic. Under Secretary of State Keith Krach followed in September, representing the US government at former President Lee Teng-hui's funeral.

8. See Kenneth Lieberthal and Wang Jisi, *Addressing U.S.-China Strategic Distrust* (Brookings Institution, 2012).

9. See Jing Li, *China's America: The Chinese View the United States, 1900–2000* (State University of New York Press, 2011).

10. Kurt M. Campbell and Jake Sullivan, "Competition Without Catastrophe: How America Can Both Challenge and Coexist with China," *Foreign Affairs* (September/October 2019), 97.
11. Joe Biden, "The Presidential Candidates on China and Human Rights," Council on Foreign Relations, July 30, 2019.
12. Jude D. Blanchette, *China's New Red Guards: The Return of Radicalism and the Rebirth of Mao Zedong* (Oxford University Press, 2019), 161.

Suggested Readings[*]

1. United States–China Relations: History and Diplomacy

Chang, Gordon H. *Fateful Ties: A History of America's Preoccupation with China*. Harvard University Press, 2015.

Christensen, Thomas. *Useful Adversaries: Grand Strategy, Domestic Mobilization, and Sino-American Conflicts, 1949–1958*. Princeton University Press, 1996.

Cohen, Warren I. *America's Response to China: A History of Sino-American Relations*. 5th ed. Columbia University Press, 2010.

Cohen, Warren I. *The Asian American Century*. Harvard University Press, 2002.

Diamond, Larry, and Orville Schell, eds. *Chinese Influence & American Interests: Promoting Constructive Vigilance*. Hoover Institution Press, Stanford University, 2018.

Fairbank, John K. *The United States and China*. 4th ed. Harvard University Press, 1983.

Foot, Rosemary. *The Practice of Power: U.S. Relations with China since 1949*. Oxford University Press, 1997.

Garver, John W. *China's Decision for Rapprochement with the United States, 1968–1971*. Westview Press, 1982.

Harding, Harry. *A Fragile Relationship: The United States and China since 1972*. Brookings Institution, 1992.

Kennedy, Scott. *China Cross Talk: The American Debate over China Policy since Normalization*. Rowman & Littlefield, 2003.

Kirby, William, Robert Ross, and Gong Li, eds. *Normalization of U.S.-China Relations: An International History*. Harvard University Asia Center, 2005.

Lampton, David M. *Same Bed, Different Dreams: Managing U.S.-China Relations, 1989–2000*. University of California Press, 2001.

Lieberthal, Kenneth, and Wang Jisi. *Addressing U.S.-China Strategic Distrust*. Brookings Institution, 2012.

Lilley, James. *China Hands: Nine Decades of Adventure, Espionage, and Diplomacy in Asia*. Public Affairs, 2004.

Madsen, Richard. *China and the American Dream: A Moral Inquiry*. University of California Press, 1995.

Mann, James. *About Face: A History of America's Curious Relationship with China from Nixon to Clinton*. Alfred Knopf, 1999.

MacMillan, Margaret. *Nixon and Mao: The Week That Changed the World*. Random House, 2007.

Murray, Jeremy, Perry Link, and Paul Pickowicz. *China Tripping: Encountering the Everyday in the People's Republic*. Rowman & Littlefield, 2019.

---

[*] These suggested readings follow the themes covered in this book. It is not a comprehensive list, and only some of the titles mentioned in the text are included.

Pomfret, John. *The Beautiful Country and the Middle Kingdom: America and China, 1776 to the Present*. Henry Holt and Company, 2016.

Ross, Robert S. *Negotiating Cooperation: The United States and China, 1969–1989.* Stanford University Press, 1995.

Ross, Robert S., and Jiang Changbin, eds. *Re-examining the Cold War: U.S.-China Diplomacy 1954–1973*. Harvard University Press, 2001.

Schaller, Michael. *The United States and China: Into the 21st Century*. Oxford University Press, 2002.

Shambaugh, David, ed. *Tangled Titans: The United States and China*. Rowman & Littlefield, 2012.

Shewmaker, Kenneth. *Americans and the Chinese Communists, 1927–1945*. Cornell University Press, 1971.

Spence, Jonathan. *To Change China: Western Advisers in China, 1620–1960*. Little, Brown, 1969.

Suettinger, Robert. *Beyond Tiananmen: The Politics of U.S.-China Relations, 1989–2000.* Brookings Institution Press, 2003.

Sutter, Robert G. *U.S.-China Relations: Perilous Past, Uncertain Present*. Rowman & Littlefield, 2018.

Thurston, Anne F., ed. *Engaging China: Fifty Years of Sino-American* Relations. Columbia University Press, 2021.

Tucker, Nancy Bernkopf, ed. *China Confidential: American Diplomats and Sino-American Relations, 1945–1996*. Columbia University Press, 2001.

Tucker, Nancy Bernkopf. *Patterns in the Dust: Chinese-American Relations and the Recognition Controversy, 1949–1950*. Columbia University Press, 1983.

Tyler, Patrick. *A Great Wall: Six Presidents and China: An Investigative History*. Public Affairs, 1999.

Wang, Dong. *The United States and China: A History from the Eighteenth Century to the Present*. Asia Pacific Perspectives. 2nd ed. Rowman & Littlefield Publishers, 2021.

Young, Kenneth T. *Negotiating with the Chinese Communists: The United States Experience, 1953–1967*. Council on Foreign Relations, 1968.

2. Images and Perceptions

Arkush, David, and Leo O. Lee, eds. *Land Without Ghosts: Chinese Impressions of America from the Mid-Nineteenth Century to the Present*. University of California Press, 1989.

Goldstein, Jonathan, Jerry Israel, and Hilary Conroy, eds. *America Views China: American Images of China Then and Now*. Lehigh University Press, 1991.

Isaacs, Harold R. *Scratches on Our Minds: American Views of China and India*. New York: John Day Co., 1958.

Jespersen, T. Christopher. *American Images of China: 1931–1949*. Stanford University Press, 1996.

Li, Jing. *China's America: The Chinese View the United States, 1900–2000*. State University of New York Press, 2011.

McGiffert, Carola, ed. China *in the American Political Imagination*. CSIS Press, 2003.

McGiffert, Carola, ed. *Chinese Images of the United States*. CSIS Press, 2006.

Prasso, Sheridan. *The Asian Mystique: Dragon Ladies, Geisha Girls, & Our Fantasies of the Exotic Orient*. Public Affairs, 2005.

Schell, Orville. *Virtual Tibet: Searching for Shangri-La from the Himalayas to Hollywood.* Henry Holt and Company, 2000.

Shambaugh, David. *Beautiful Imperialist: China Perceives America, 1972–1980.* Princeton University Press, 1991.

Spelman, Douglas, ed. *The United States and China: Mutual Public Perceptions.* Woodrow Wilson International Center for Scholars, 2011.

3. Missionaries and Christianity

Bays, Daniel. *A New History of Christianity in China.* Wiley-Blackwell, 2011.

Bays, Daniel, and Ellen Widmer, eds. *China's Christian Colleges: Cross-Cultural Connections, 1900–1950.* Stanford University Press, 2009.

Bullock, Mary Brown. *American Transplant: The Rockefeller Foundation and Peking Union Medical College.* University of California Press, 1980.

Hersey, John. *The Call.* Alfred A. Knopf, 1985.

Hollinger, David A. *Protestants Abroad: How Missionaries Tried to Change the World but Changed America.* Princeton University Press, 2017.

Inboden, William. *Religion and American Foreign Policy, 1945–1960.* Cambridge University Press, 2008.

Fairbank, John K., ed. *The Missionary Enterprise in China and America.* Harvard University Press, 1974.

Fairbank, John K., and Suzanne W. Barnett, eds. *Christianity in China.* Harvard University Press, 1985.

Lin, Jennifer. *Shanghai Faithful. Betrayal and Forgiveness in a Chinese Christian Family.* Rowman & Littlefield, 2017.

Lutz, Jessie Gregory. *China and the Christian Colleges.* Cornell University Press, 1971.

Neils, Patricia. *United States Attitudes toward China: The Impact of American Missionaries.* M. E. Sharpe, 1990.

West, Philip. *Yenching University and Sino-Western Relations, 1916–1952.* Harvard East Asian Series. Harvard University Press, 2013.

Wiest, Jean-Paul. *Maryknoll in China: A History, 1918–1955.* Orbis Books, 1997.

Xi, Lian. *The Conversion of Missionaries: Liberalism in American Protestant Missions in China, 1907–1932.* Pennsylvania State University Press, 1997.

4. Chinese in the United States

Brooks, Charlotte. *American Exodus: Second-Generation Chinese Americans in China, 1901–1949.* University of California Press, 2019.

Hodges, Graham. *Anna May Wong: From Laundryman's Daughter to Hollywood Legend.* Palgrave MacMillan, 2004.

Hsu, Madeline Y. *The Good Immigrants: How the Yellow Peril Became the Model Minority.* Princeton University Press, 2015.

Huang, Yunte. *Charlie Chan: The Untold Story of the Honorable Detective and His Rendezvous with American History.* W. W. Norton, 2010.

Kingston, Maxine Hong. *China Men.* Alfred A. Knopf, 1977.

Kingston, Maxine Hong. *Woman Warrior: Memoirs of a Childhood among Ghosts*. Alfred A. Knopf, 1976.

Koehn, Peter H., and Xiao-huang Yin, eds. *The Expanding Roles of Chinese Americans in U.S.-China Relations*. M. E. Sharpe, 2002.

Lee, Erika. *At America's Gates: Chinese Immigration During the Exclusion Era, 1882–1943*. University of North Carolina Press, 2003.

Lee, Erika. *The Making of Asian America: A History*. Simon & Schuster, 2015.

Lee, Robert G. *Orientals: Asian Americans in Popular Culture*. Temple University Press, 1999.

Oyen, Meredith. *The Diplomacy of Migration: Transnational Lives and the Making of U.S.-Chinese Relations in the Cold War*. Cornell University Press, 2015.

Wu, Ellen. *The Color of Success: Asian Americans and the Origins of the Model Minority*. Princeton University Press, 2013.

Yung, Judy, Gordon H. Chang, and Him Mark Lai, eds. *Chinese American Voices: From the Gold Rush to the Present*. University of California Press, 2006.

Zia, Helen. *Last Boat Out of Shanghai: The Epic Story of the Chinese Who Fled Mao's Revolution*. Ballantine Books, 2019.

5. The Korean War

Carlson, Lewis H. *Remembered Prisoners of a Forgotten War: An Oral History of the Korean War POWs*. St. Martin's Press, 2002.

Chang, David C. *Hijacked War: The Story of Chinese POWs in the Korean War*. Stanford University Press, 2019.

Chen, Jian. *China's Road to the Korean War: The Making of the Sino-American Confrontation*. Columbia University Press, 1994.

Cumings, Bruce. *The Origins of the Korean War*. 2 vols. Princeton University Press, 1981, 1990.

Foot, Rosemary. *The Wrong War: American Policy and the Dimensions of the Korean Conflict, 1950–1953*. Cornell University Press, 1985.

Halberstam, David. *The Coldest Winter: America and the Korean War*. Hyperion, 2007.

Hastings, Max. *The Korean War*. Simon & Schuster, 1987.

Jin, Ha. *War Trash*. Vintage, 2004.

Lifton, Robert Jay. *Thought Reform and the Psychology of Totalism: A Study of "Brainwashing" in China*. University of North Carolina Press, 1989. First published 1961.

Merrill, John. *Korea: The Peninsular Origins of the War*. University of Delaware Press, 1989.

Young, Charles S. *Name, Rank, and Serial Number: Exploiting Korean War POWs at Home and Abroad*. Oxford University Press, 2014.

6. The Cold War

Brazinsky, Gregg A. *Winning the Third World: Sino-American Rivalry during the Cold War*. University of North Carolina Press, 2017.

Brooks, Charlotte. *Between Mao and McCarthy: Chinese American Politics in the Cold War Years*. University of Chicago Press, 2015.

Chen, Jian. *Mao's China and the Cold War*. University of North Carolina Press, 2001.

Fried, Richard M. *Nightmare in Red: The McCarthy Era in Perspective*. Oxford University Press, 1991.

Gaddis, John Lewis. *Strategies of Containment: A Critical Appraisal of Postwar American National Security*. Oxford University Press, 1982.

Gaddis, John Lewis. *The Cold War: A New History*. Penguin Press, 2005.

Hooper, Beverley. *China Stands Up: Ending the Western Presence, 1948–1950*. Allen and Unwin, 1986.

Hooper, Beverley. *Foreigners under Mao: Western Lives in China, 1949–1976*. Hong Kong University Press, 2016.

Klein, Christina. *Cold War Orientalism: Asia in the Middlebrow Imagination, 1945–1961*. University of California Press, 2003.

Mao, Joyce. *Asia First: China and the Making of Modern American Conservatism*. University of Chicago Press, 2015.

Rickett, Allyn, and Adele Rickett. *Prisoners of Liberation: Four Years in a Chinese Communist Prison*. Anchor Books, 1973. First published 1957 by Cameron Associates, Inc.

Tucker, Nancy Bernkopf. *The China Threat: Memories, Myths, and Realities in the 1950s*. Columbia University Press, 2012.

Westad, Odd Arne. *The Cold War*. Basic Books, 2017.

7. Business, Trade, and Economics

Bergsten, C. Fred, Gary Clyde Hufbauer, and Sean Miner. *Bridging the Pacific: Toward Free Trade and Investment between China and the United States*. Peterson Institute for International Economics, 2014.

Garnaut, Ross, Ligang Song, and Fang Cai. *China's 40 Years of Reform and Development: 1978–2018*. Australian National University Press, 2018.

Guo, Baogang, and Sujian Guo. *Greater China in an Era of Globalization: Challenges Facing Chinese Political Development*. Rowman & Littlefield Publishers, 2010.

Heilmann, Sebastian, and Dirk H. Schmidt. *China's Foreign Political and Economic Relations: An Unconventional Global Power*. Rowman & Littlefield Publishers, 2014.

Huang, Yasheng. *Capitalism with Chinese Characteristics: Entrepreneurship and the State*. Cambridge University Press, 2008.

Karabell, Zachary. *Superfusion: How China and America Became One Economy and Why the World's Prosperity Depends on It*. Simon & Schuster, 2009.

Kroeber, Arthur R. *China's Economy: What Everyone Needs to Know*. Oxford University Press, 2016.

Lardy, Nicholas. *China's Unfinished Economic Revolution*. Brookings Institution, 1998.

Lardy, Nicholas. *The State Strikes Back: The End of Economic Reform in China?* Peterson Institute for International Economics, 2019.

McGregor, James. *One Billion Customers: Lessons from the Front Lines of Doing Business in China*. Free Press, 2005.

Naughton, Barry. *The Chinese Economy: Adaptation and Growth*. MIT Press, 2007.

Pei, Minxin. *China's Crony Capitalism*. Harvard University Press, 2016.

Purvew, Bill. *Barefoot in the Boardroom: Venture and Misadventure in the People's Republic of China*. Allen & Unwin, 1991.

Roach, Stephen S. *Unbalanced: The Codependency of America and China*. Yale University Press, 2014.

Studwell, Joe. *China Dream: The Quest for the Last Great Untapped Market on Earth*. Grove Press, 2003.

Talley, Christian. *Forgotten Vanguard: Informal Diplomacy and the Rise of United States-China Trade*. University of Notre Dame Press, 2018.

Walter, Carl, and Fraser Howie. *Red Capitalism: The Fragile Financial Foundation of China's Extraordinary Rise*. 2nd ed. Wiley, 2012.

Zhang, Shuguang. *Economic Cold War: America's Embargo against China and the Sino-Soviet Alliance, 1949–1963*. Stanford University Press, 2001.

8. Law and Human Rights

Bell, Lynda, Andrew Nathan, and Ilan Peleg. *Negotiating Culture and Human Rights: Beyond Universalism and Relativism*. Columbia University Press, 2001.

Bovington, Gardner. *The Uyghurs: Strangers in Their Own Land*. Columbia University Press, 2010.

Calhoun, Craig. *Neither Gods nor Emperors: Students and the Struggle for Democracy in China*. University of California Press, 1997.

Clarke, Donald. *China's Legal System: New Developments, New Challenges*. Cambridge University Press, 2010.

Edwards, Randle, Louis Henkin, and Andrew Nathan. *Human Rights in Contemporary China*. Columbia University Press, 1986.

Gallagher, Mary Elizabeth. *Authoritarian Legality in China: Law, Workers, and the State*. Cambridge University Press, 2017.

Hom, Sharon, and Stacy Mosher, eds. *Challenging China: Struggle and Hope in an Era of Change*. Human Rights in China, 2007.

Lim, Louisa. *The People's Republic of Amnesia: Tiananmen Revisited*. Oxford University Press, 2014.

Lubman, Stanley. *Bird in a Cage: Legal Reform in China after Mao*. Stanford University Press, 2000.

Roberts, Sean R. *The War on the Uyghurs: China's Internal Campaign against a Muslim Minority*. Princeton University Press, 2020.

Turner, Karen, James V. Feinerman, and R. Kent Guy, *The Limits of the Rule of Law in China*. University of Washington Press, 2000.

Zhang, Liang. *The Tiananmen Papers*. Public Affairs, 2001.

9. Art

Andrews, Julia F. *Painters and Politics in the People's Republic of China*. University of California Press, 1994.

Andrews, Julia F., and Kuiyi Shen. *The Art of Modern China*. University of California Press, 2012.

Cohen, Warren I. *East Asian Art and American Culture, 1784–1900*. Columbia University Press, 1992.

Debevoise, Jane. *Between State and Market: Chinese Contemporary Art and the Post-Mao Era*. Brill, 2014.

Kao, Mayching, ed. *Twentieth Century Chinese Painting*. Oxford University Press, 1988.

Kraus, Richard C. *The Party and the Arty in China: The New Politics of Culture*. Rowman & Littlefield, 2004.

Lü, Peng. *A History of Art in 20th-Century China*. Charta, 2010.

O'Dea, Madeleine. *The Phoenix Years: Art, Resistance, and the Making of Modern China*. Pegasus Books, 2017.

Sullivan, Michael. *Art and Artists of Twentieth-Century China*. University of California Press, 1996.

Vine, Richard. *New China, New Art*. Prestel, 2008.

Vosper, Michelle, ed. *Creating Across Cultures: Women in the Arts from China, Hong Kong, Macau, and Taiwan*. East Slope Publishing Limited, 2017.

Wu, Hung. *Contemporary Chinese Art: A History, 1970s–2000s*. Thames & Hudson, 2014.

10. Education and Scholarly Exchange

Hayhoe, Ruth. *China's Universities and the Open Door*. M. E. Sharpe, 1989.

Kallgren, Joyce, and Denis Simon, eds. *Educational Exchanges: Essays on the Sino-American Experience*. Institute of East Asian Studies, University of California, Berkeley, 1987.

Lampton, David M. *A Relationship Restored: Trends in U.S.-China Educational Exchanges, 1978–1984*. National Academy Press, 1986.

Li, Cheng, ed. *Bridging Minds across the Pacific: U.S.-China Educational Exchanges, 1978–2003*. Lexington Books, 2005.

Ma, Yingyi. *Ambitious and Anxious: How Chinese College Students Succeed and Struggle in American Higher Education*. Columbia University Press, 2020.

Qian, Ning. Translated by T. K. Chu. *Chinese Students Encounter America*. University of Washington Press, 2002.

Renouf, Alice, and Mary Beth Ryan-Maher. *Yin-Yang: American Perspectives on Living in China*. Rowman & Littlefield, 2012.

Salzman, Mark. *Iron & Silk*. Vintage Books, 1987.

Ye, Weili. *Seeking Modernity in China's Name: Chinese Students in the United States, 1900–1927*. Stanford University Press, 2001.

11. Journalism and Media

Bernstein, Richard. *From the Center of the Earth: The Search for the Truth About China*. Little, Brown, 1982.

Butterfield, Fox. *China: Alive in the Bitter Sea*. Times Books, 1982.

French, Paul. *Through the Looking Glass: China's Foreign Journalists from Opium Wars to Mao*. Hong Kong University Press, 2009.

He, Qinglian. *The Fog of Censorship: Media Control in China*. Human Rights in China, 2008.

MacKinnon, Stephen, and Oris Friesen. *China Reporting: An Oral History of American Journalism in the 1930s & 1940s*. University of California Press, 1987.

Meng, Bingchun. *The Politics of Chinese Media: Consensus and Contestation*. Palgrave Macmillan, 2018.

Osnos, Evan. *Age of Ambition: Chasing Fortune, Truth, and Faith in the New China*. Farrar, Straus and Giroux, 2014.

Polumbaum, Judy. *China Ink: The Changing Face of Chinese Journalism*. Rowman & Littlefield, 2008.

Repnikova, Maria. *Media Politics in China: Improvising Power under Authoritarianism*. Cambridge University Press, 2017.

Shirk, Susan. *Changing Media, Changing China*. Oxford University Press, 2011.

Snow, Edgar. *Red Star over China*. Gollancz, 1937.

Snow, Edgar. *The Other Side of the River, Red China Today*. Random House, 1962.

Wong, Jan. *Jan Wong's China: Reports From a Not-So-Foreign Correspondent*. Doubleday Canada, 1999.

Yang, Guobin. *The Power of the Internet in China: Citizen Activism Online*. Columbia University Press, 2011.

12. Taiwan

Bush, Richard C. *At Cross Purposes: U.S.-Taiwan Relations since 1942*. M. E. Sharpe, 2004.

Bush, Richard C. *Untying the Knot: Making Peace in the Taiwan Strait*. Brookings Institution, 2005.

Dunch, Ryan, and Ashley Esarey, eds. *Taiwan in Dynamic Transition: Nation-building and Democratization*. University of Washington Press, 2020.

Goldstein, Steven M. *China and Taiwan*. Polity Press, 2015.

Kerr, George. *Formosa Betrayed*. Houghton Mifflin, 1965.

Rigger, Shelly. *Why Taiwan Matters: Small Island, Global Powerhouse*. Rowman & Littlefield, 2011.

Romberg, Alan. *Rein In at the Brink of the Precipice: American Policy toward Taiwan and US-PRC Relations*. Henry L. Stimson Center, 2003.

Shambaugh, David, ed. *Contemporary Taiwan*. Oxford University Press, 1998.

Taylor, Jay. *The Generalissimo: Chiang Kai-shek and the Struggle for Modern China*. Harvard University Press, 2009.

Tucker, Nancy Bernkopf. *Dangerous Strait: The U.S.-Taiwan-China Crisis*. Columbia University Press, 2005.

Tucker, Nancy Bernkopf. *Uncertain Friendships: Taiwan, Hong Kong and the United States, 1945–1992*. Twayne, 1994.

13. Hong Kong

Brown, Judith M., and Rosemary Foot. *Hong Kong's Transitions, 1842–1997*. Palgrave Macmillan, 1997.

Bush, Richard C. *Hong Kong in the Shadow of China: Living with the Leviathan*. Brookings Institution, 2016.

Chan, Holmes, ed. *Aftershock: Essays from Hong Kong*. 2nd ed. Small Tune Press, 2020.

Faure, David. *Colonialism and the Hong Kong Mentality*. Centre for Asian Studies, Hong Kong University, 2003.

Goodstadt, Leo F. *Uneasy Partners: The Conflict between Public Interest and Private Profit in Hong Kong*. 2nd ed. Hong Kong University Press, 2009.

Loh, Christine. *Underground Front: The Chinese Communist Party in Hong Kong*. 2nd ed. Hong Kong University Press, 2019.

Roberti, Mark. *The Fall of Hong Kong: China's Triumph and Britain's Betrayal*. 2nd ed. John Wiley, 1996.

Tsang, Steve. *A Modern History of Hong Kong*. I. B. Tauris, 2004.

Wasserstrom, Jeffrey. *Vigil: Hong Kong on the Brink*. Columbia Global Reports, 2020.

14. Chinese History, Politics, and Society

Chen, Te-ping. *Land of Big Numbers*. Houghton Mifflin Harcourt, 2021.

Cheng, Nian. *Life and Death in Shanghai*. Grove Press, 1987.

Economy, Elizabeth C. *The Third Revolution: Xi Jinping and the New Chinese State*. Oxford University Press, 2018.

Davis, Deborah. *The Consumer Revolution in Urban China*. University of California Press, 2000.

Dickson, Bruce J. *The Dictator's Dilemma: The Chinese Communist Party's Strategy for Survival*. Oxford University Press, 2016.

Dikötter, Frank. *The Cultural Revolution: A People's History, 1962–1976*. Bloomsbury Press, 2016.

Goldstein, Melvyn. *The Snow Lion and the Dragon: China, Tibet, and the Dalai Lama*. University of California Press, 1999.

Harding, Harry. *China's Second Revolution: Reform After Mao*. Brookings Institution, 1987.

Hessler, Peter. *Rivertown: Two Years on the Yangtze*. Harper Collins, 2001.

Hinton, William. *Fanshen: A Documentary of Revolution in a Chinese Village*. Vintage Books, 1966.

Joseph, William, ed. *Politics in China: An Introduction*. 2nd ed. Oxford University Press, 2014.

Lampton, David M. *Following the Leader: Ruling China from Deng Xiaoping to Xi Jinping*. University of California Press, 2014.

Lampton, David M. *The Three Faces of Chinese Power: Might, Money, and Minds*. University of California Press, 2008.

Lei, Ya-Wen. *The Contentious Public Sphere: Law, Media, and Authoritarian Rule in China*. Princeton University Press, 2018.

Leys, Simon. *Chinese Shadows*. Viking Press, 1977.

Li, Cheng. *Middle Class Shanghai: Reshaping U.S.-China Engagement*. Brookings Institution, 2021.

Li, Cheng. *Rediscovering China: Dynamics and Dilemmas of Reform*. Rowman & Littlefield, 1997.

Lieberthal, Kenneth. *Governing China: From Revolution Through Reform*. W. W. Norton, 1995.

MacFarquhar, Roderick, ed. *The Politics of China: Sixty Years of the People's Republic of China*. Cambridge University Press, 2011.

Minzner, Carl. *End of an Era: How China's Authoritarian Revival Is Undermining Its Rise*. Oxford University Press, 2018.

Pan, Philip P. *Out of Mao's Shadow: The Struggle for the Soul of a New China*. Simon & Schuster, 2008.

Pomfret, John. *Chinese Lessons: Five Classmates and the Story of the New China*. Henry Holt, 2006.

Schell, Orville. *Discos and Democracy: China in the Throes of Reform*. Pantheon Books, 1988.

Schell, Orvillle, and John DeLury. *Wealth and Power: China's Long March to the Twenty-first Century*. Random House, 2013.

Segal, Adam. *The Hacked World Order: How Nations Fight, Trade, Maneuver, and Manipulate in the Digital Age*. Public Affairs, 2016.

Shambaugh, David. *China's Leaders: From Mao to Now*. Polity Press, 2021.

Shirk, Susan. *China: Fragile Superpower*. Oxford University Press, 2007.

Simon, Denis Fred, and Merle Goldman, eds. *Science and Technology in Post-Mao China*. Council on East Asian Studies, Harvard University 1989.

Spence, Jonathan D. *The Search for Modern China*. 3rd ed. W. W. Norton & Co., 2013.

Teets, Jessica C. *Civil Society under Authoritarianism: The China Model*. Cambridge University Press, 2014.

Tsai, Kellee. *Capitalism without Democracy*. Cornell University Press, 2007.

Vogel, Ezra F. *Deng Xiaoping and the Transformation of China*. Harvard University Press, 2011.

Wong, Jan. *Red China Blues: My Long March from Mao to Now*. Doubleday/Anchor Books, 1996.

Index

For the benefit of digital users, indexed terms that span two pages (e.g., 52–53) may, on occasion, appear on only one of those pages.